(top row from Left)
Horio
Konomi (Author)
Eiji
Kabaji

(middle row from Left)
Umpire
Oishi
Tachibana

(bottom row from Left)
Saori
Kachiro
Ryoma
Sakuno

Sushi Tennis Team

I invited all the voice actors who work hard every week on the anime to my office for a tennis tournament! Let's definitely do it again!!

– Takeshi Konomi, 2002

About Takeshi Konomi

Takeshi Konomi exploded onto the manga scene with the incredible **THE PRINCE OF TENNIS**. His refined art style and sleek character designs proved popular with **Weekly Shonen Jump** readers, and **THE PRINCE OF TENNIS** became the No. 1 sports manga in Japan almost overnight. Its cast of fascinating male tennis players attracted legions of female readers even though it was originally intended to be a boys' comic. The manga continues to be a success in Japan. A hit anime series was created, as well as several video games and mountains of merchandise.

THE PRINCE OF TENNIS
VOL. 14
The SHONEN JUMP Manga

**STORY AND ART BY
TAKESHI KONOMI**

English Adaptation/Michelle Pangilinan
Translation/Joe Yamazaki
Touch-up Art & Lettering/Andy Ristaino
Graphics and Cover Design/Sam Elzway & Izumi Hirayama
Editor/Michelle Pangilinan

Editor in Chief, Books/Alvin Lu
Editor in Chief, Magazines/Marc Weidenbaum
VP of Publishing Licensing/Rika Inouye
VP of Sales/Gonzalo Ferreyra
Sr. VP of Marketing/Liza Coppola
Publisher/Hyoe Narita

Printed in the U.S.A.

Published by VIZ Media, LLC
P.O. Box 77010
San Francisco, CA 94107

SHONEN JUMP Manga Edition
10 9 8 7 6 5 4 3 2
First printing, July 2006
Second printing, November 2007

PARENTAL ADVISORY
THE PRINCE OF TENNIS
is rated A and is suitable
for readers of all ages.
ratings.viz.com

THE WORLD'S
MOST POPULAR MANGA

www.viz.com

www.shonenjump.com

Shonen Jump Manga

VOL. 14
Seishun's Ultimate Man

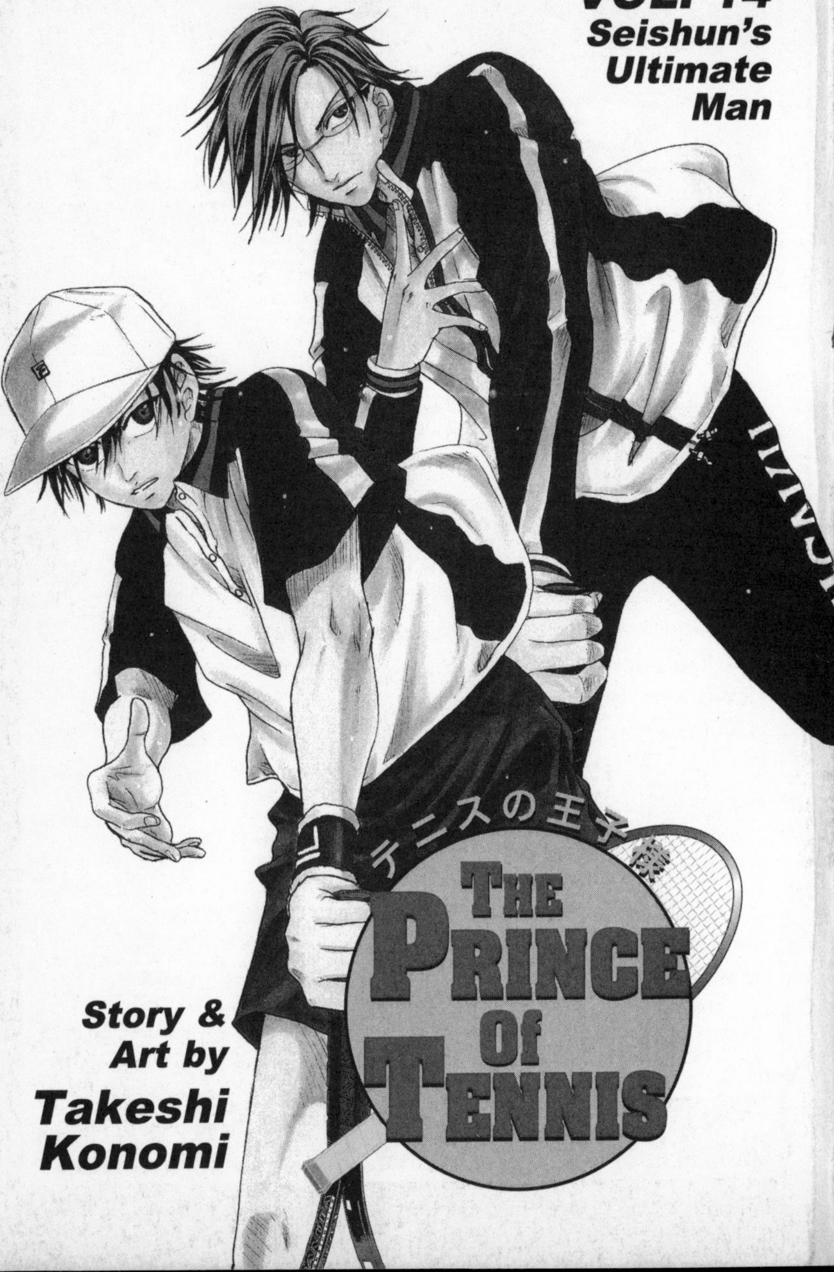
テニスの王子様

THE PRINCE OF TENNIS

Story & Art by
Takeshi Konomi

ENNIS CLUB

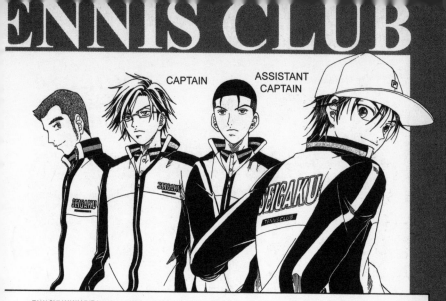

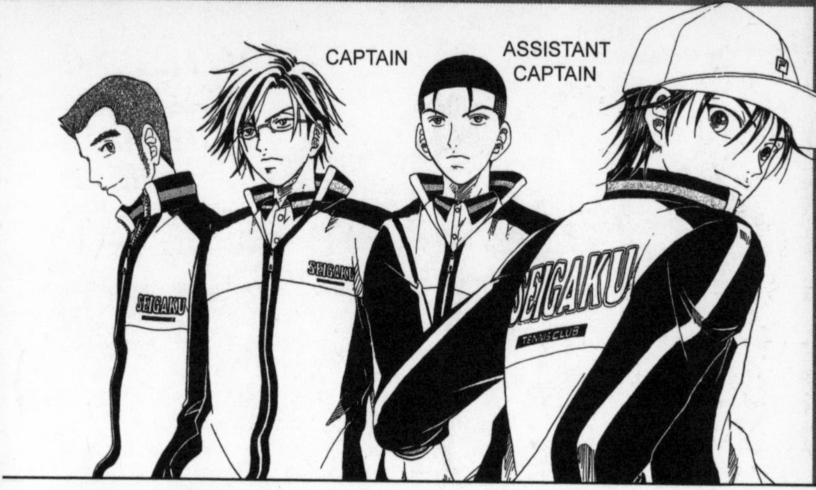
CAPTAIN
ASSISTANT CAPTAIN
SEIGAKU
SEIGAKU
SEIGAKU
SEIGAKU
TENNIS CLUB

●TAKASHI KAWAMURA●KUNIMITSU TEZUKA●SHUICHIRO OISHI● RYOMA ECHIZEN ●

Ryoma Echizen, a student at Seishun Academy, is a tennis prodigy who won four consecutive US Junior tournaments. He is the first 7th-grade starter to see action in the District Preliminaries! Despite a few mishaps, Seishun advances to the finals of the City Tournament. Their opponent in the finals is the powerhouse Yamabuki Junior High School. Ryoma plays in the championship match against Jin, another tennis prodigy, and struggles to stay in the match. But in the end, Ryoma's courage tops Jin's pride. Seishun wins the championship and finally earns a ticket to the Kanto Tournament.

The intra-squad ranking matches that will decide the starters for the Kanto Tournament is underway! While the current starters steadily win, Sadaharu, who lost his starter position, faces Seishun's ultimate man—team captain Kunimitsu!

STORY &

HARACTERS

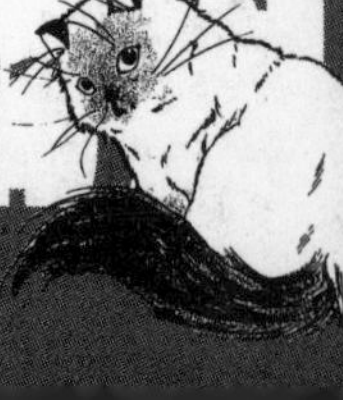

SEIGAKU T

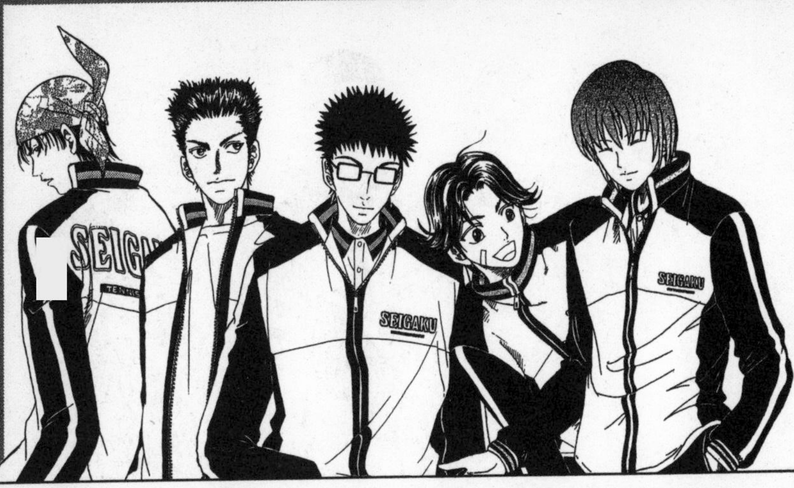

● KAORU KAIDO ● TAKESHI MOMOSHIRO ● SADAHARU INUI ● EIJI KIKUMARU ● SHUSUKE FUJI ●

THE PRINCE OF TENNIS

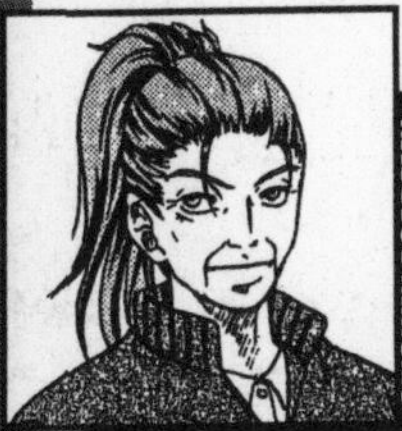

SEISHUN ACADEMY TENNIS TEAM COACH

SUMIRE RYUZAKI

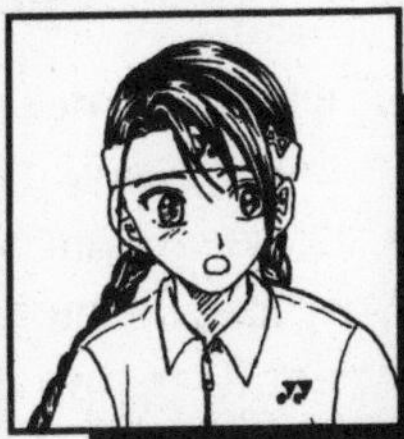

SEISHUN TENNIS TEAM

SAKUNO RYUZAKI

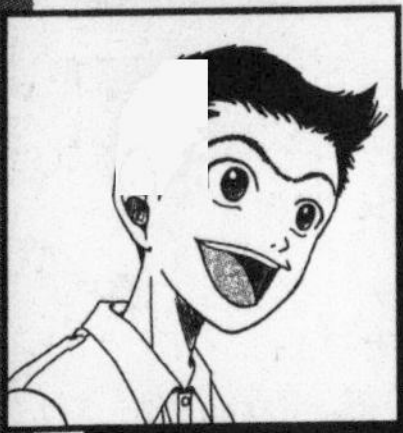

SEISHUN TENNIS TEAM

SATOSHI HORIO

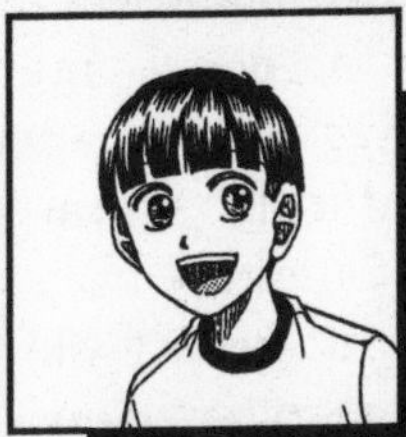

SEISHUN TENNIS TEAM

KACHIRO KATO

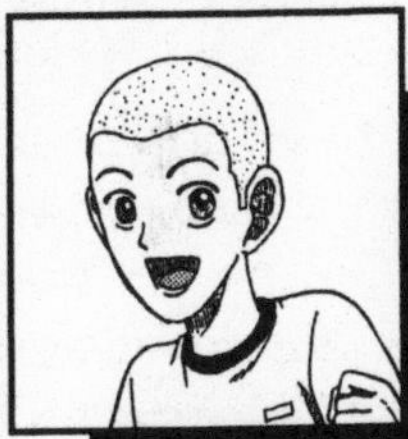

SEISHUN TENNIS TEAM

KATSUO MIZUNO

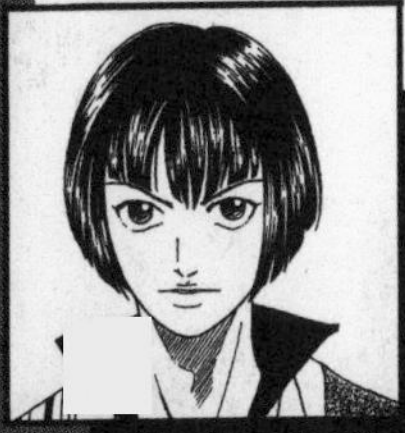

HYOTEI ACADEMY

GAKUTO MUKAHI

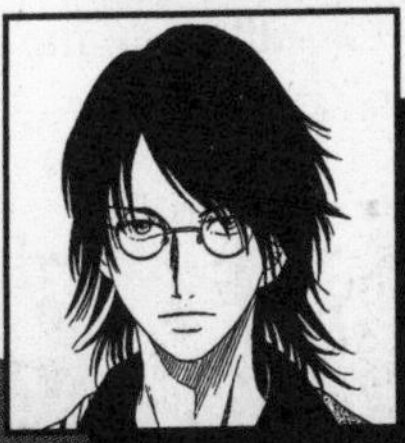

HYOTEI ACADEMY

YUSHI OSHITARI

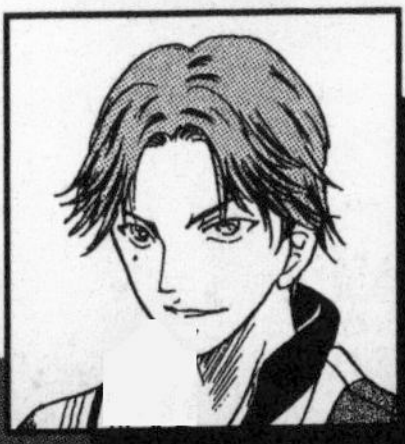

HYOTEI ACADEMY

KEIGO ATOBE

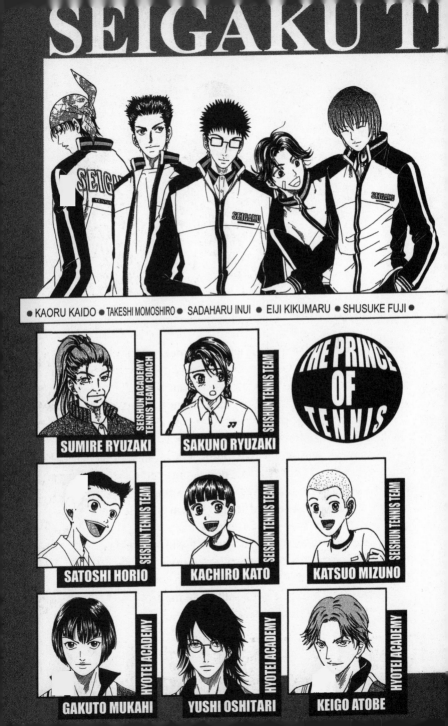

CONTENTS

Vol. 14
Seishun's Ultimate Man

Genius 115: Seishun's Ultimate Man	7
Genius 116: Dark Clouds	27
Genius 117: Challenging Spirit	47
Genius 118: Birth of the New Ultimate Seishun Squad	67
Genius 119: Rivals Assemble	87
Genius 120: Birth of a New Pair?!	107
Genius 121: Ryo Once Again	125
Genius 122: Clash! Hyotei vs. Seishun!	145
Genius 123: Where is Ryoma...?!	165

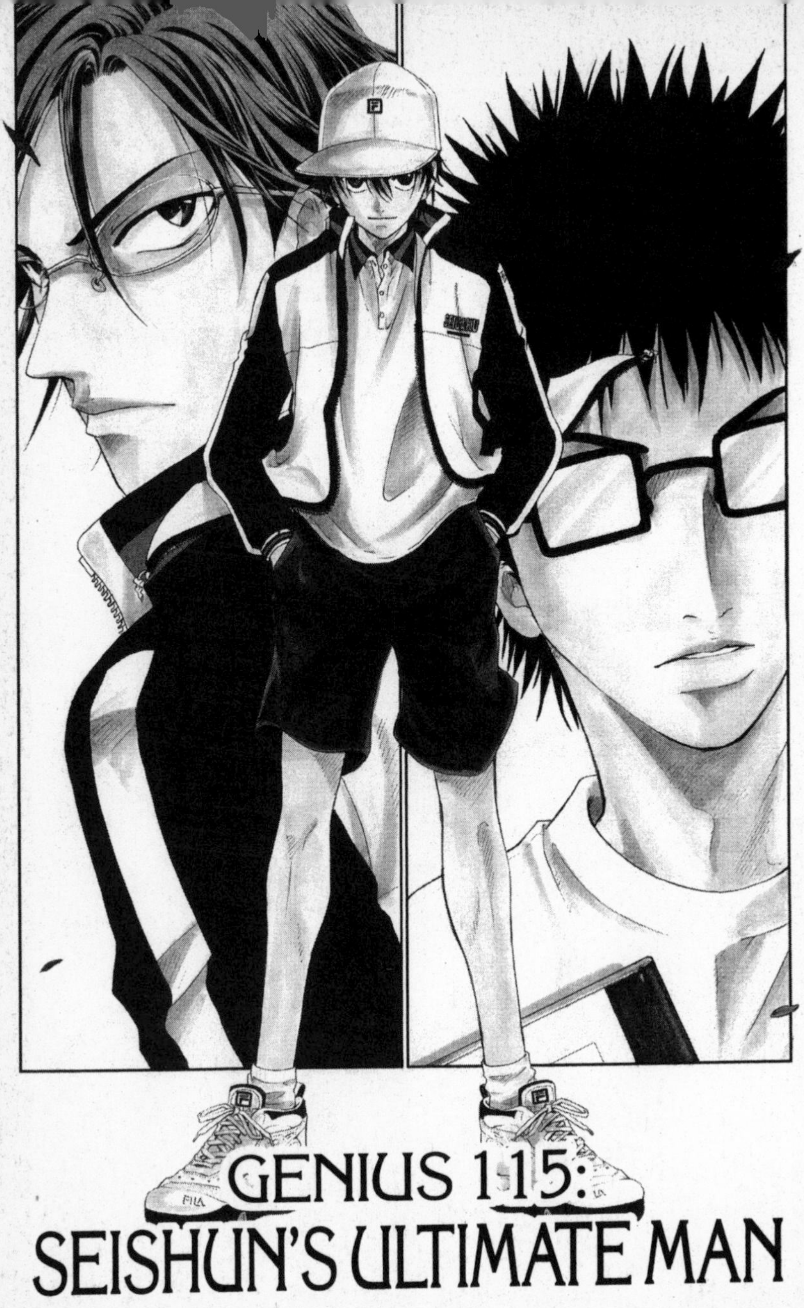

GENIUS 115: SEISHUN'S ULTIMATE MAN

テニスの王子様

THE PRINCE OF TENNIS

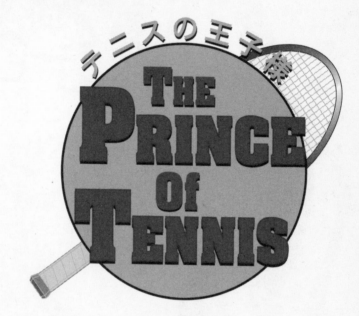

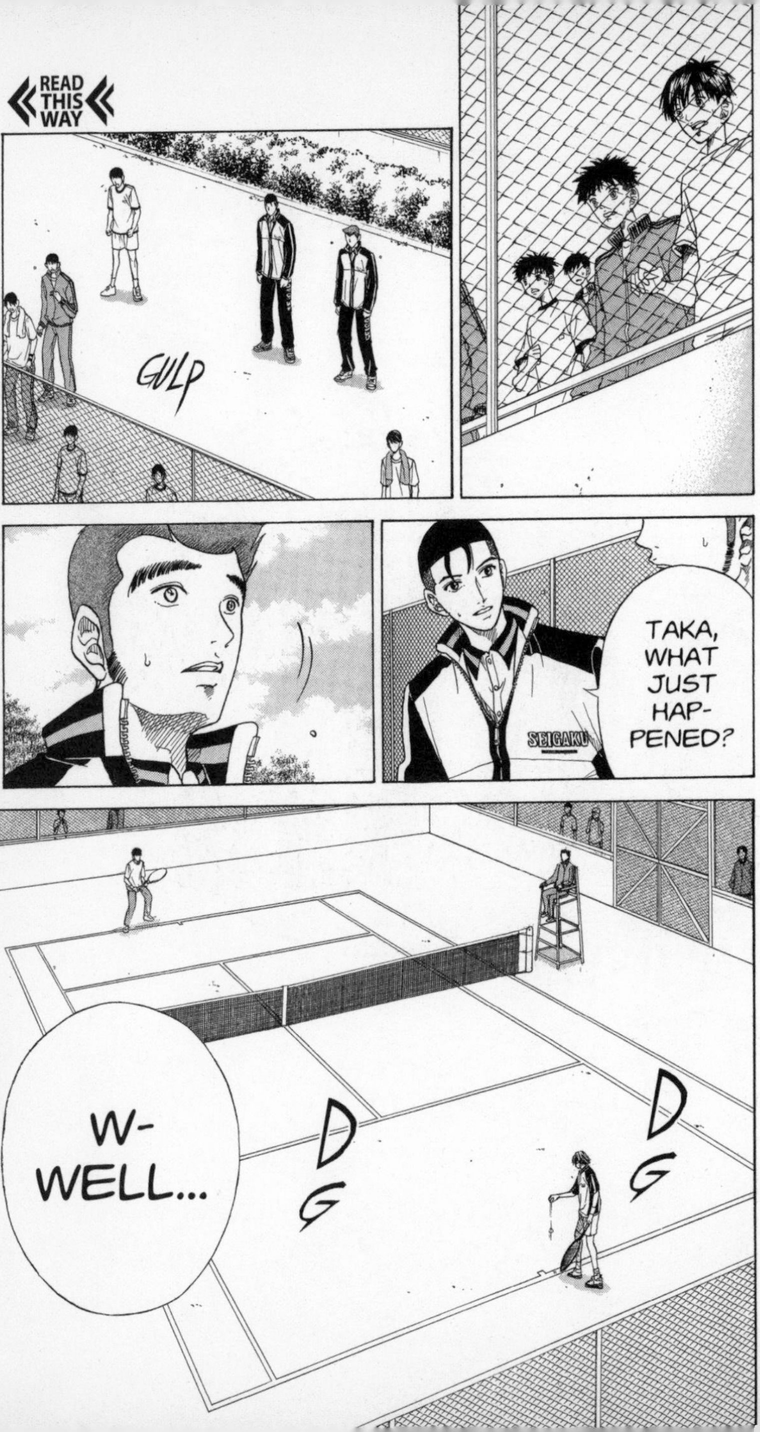
READ THIS WAY
GULP
TAKA, WHAT JUST HAP-PENED?
SEIGAKU
W-WELL...
DG
DG

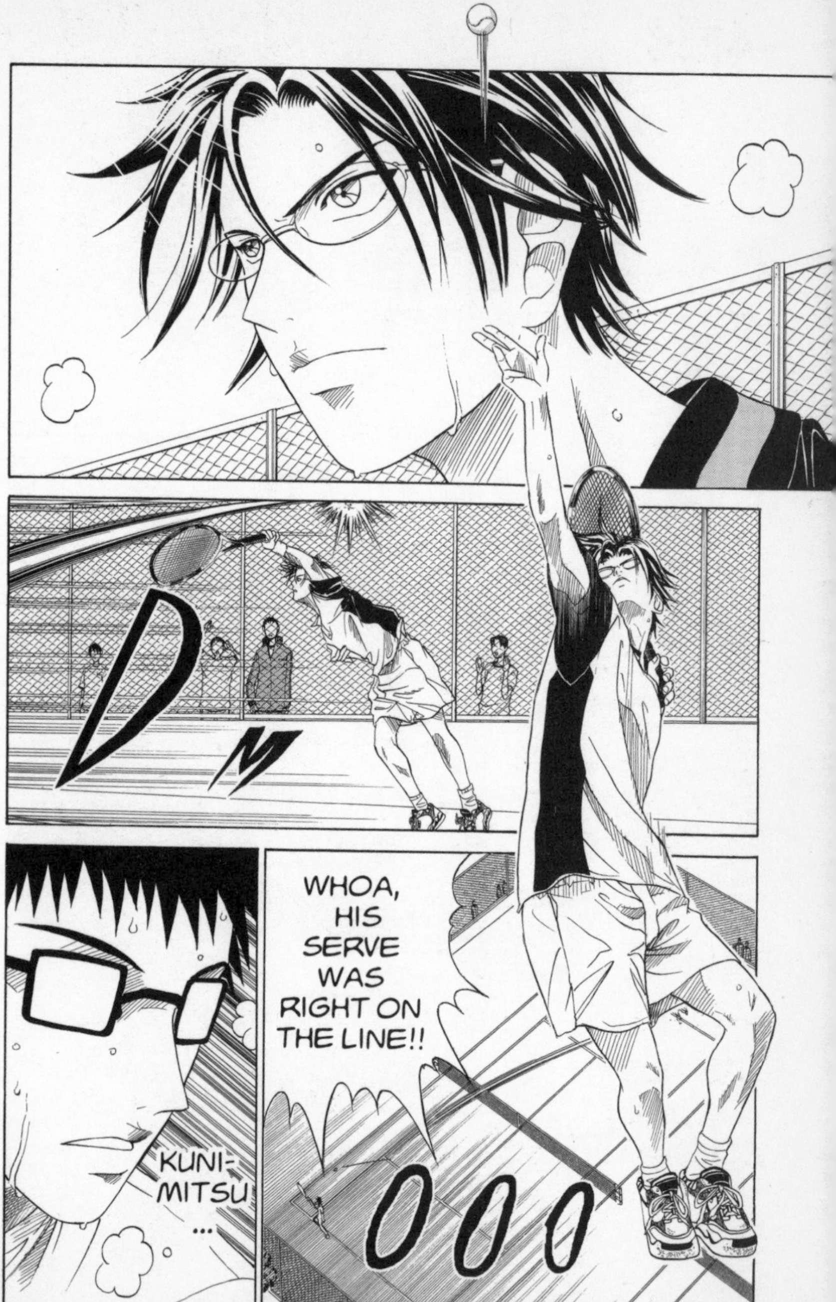
DM
WHOA, HIS SERVE WAS RIGHT ON THE LINE!!
OOO
KUNIMITSU...

READ THIS WAY

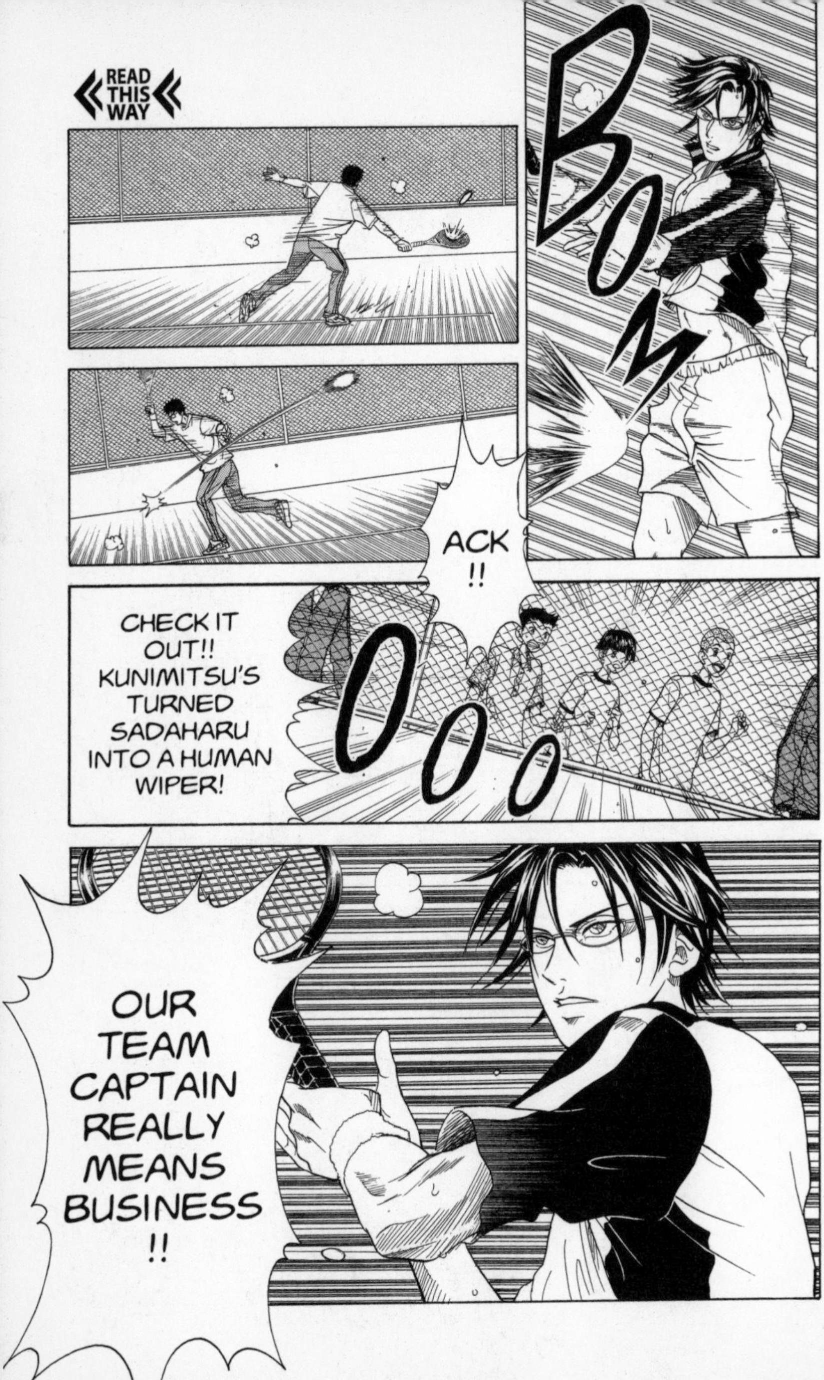
BOOM
ACK !!
CHECK IT OUT!! KUNIMITSU'S TURNED SADAHARU INTO A HUMAN WIPER!
OOO
OUR TEAM CAPTAIN REALLY MEANS BUSINESS !!

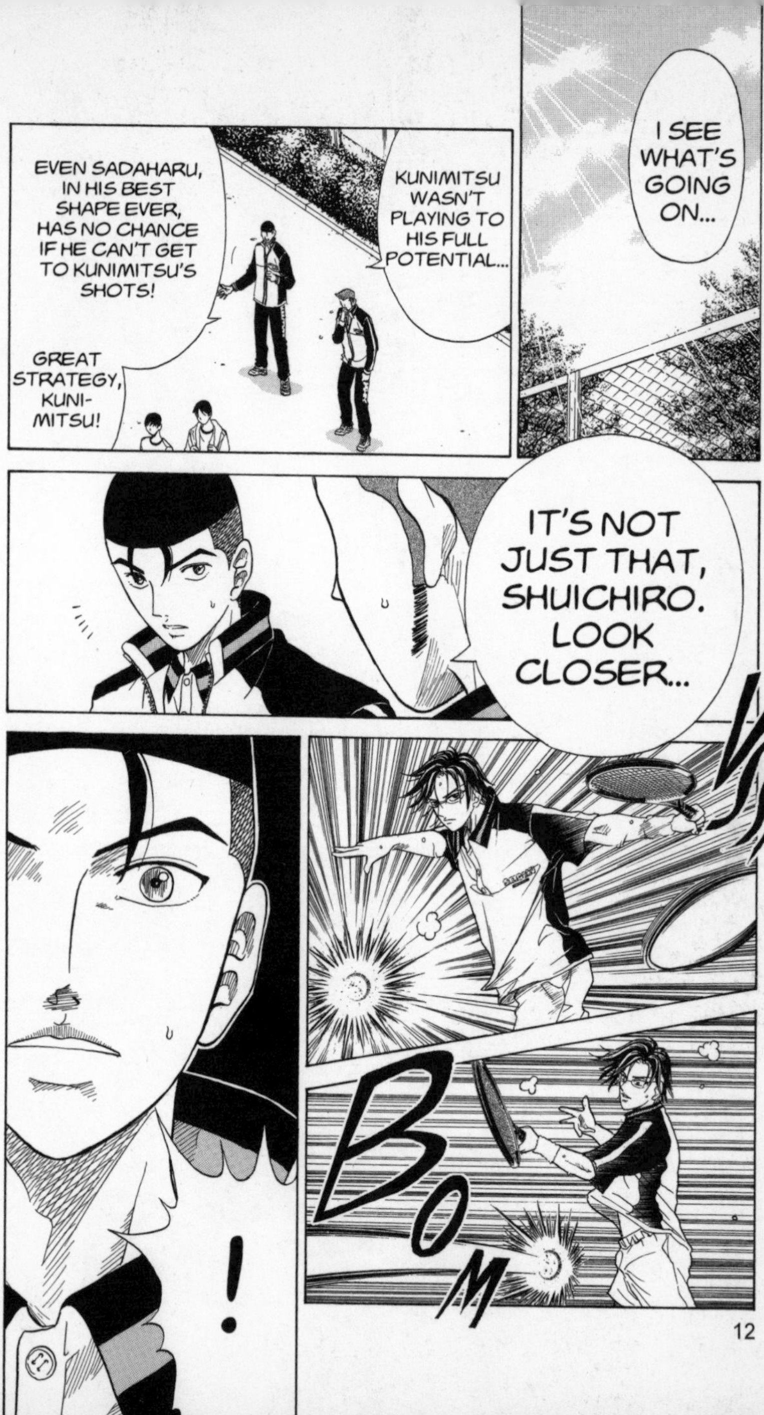
I SEE WHAT'S GOING ON...
KUNIMITSU WASN'T PLAYING TO HIS FULL POTENTIAL...
EVEN SADAHARU, IN HIS BEST SHAPE EVER, HAS NO CHANCE IF HE CAN'T GET TO KUNIMITSU'S SHOTS!
GREAT STRATEGY, KUNI-MITSU!
IT'S NOT JUST THAT, SHUICHIRO. LOOK CLOSER...
VSSH
BOOM
!

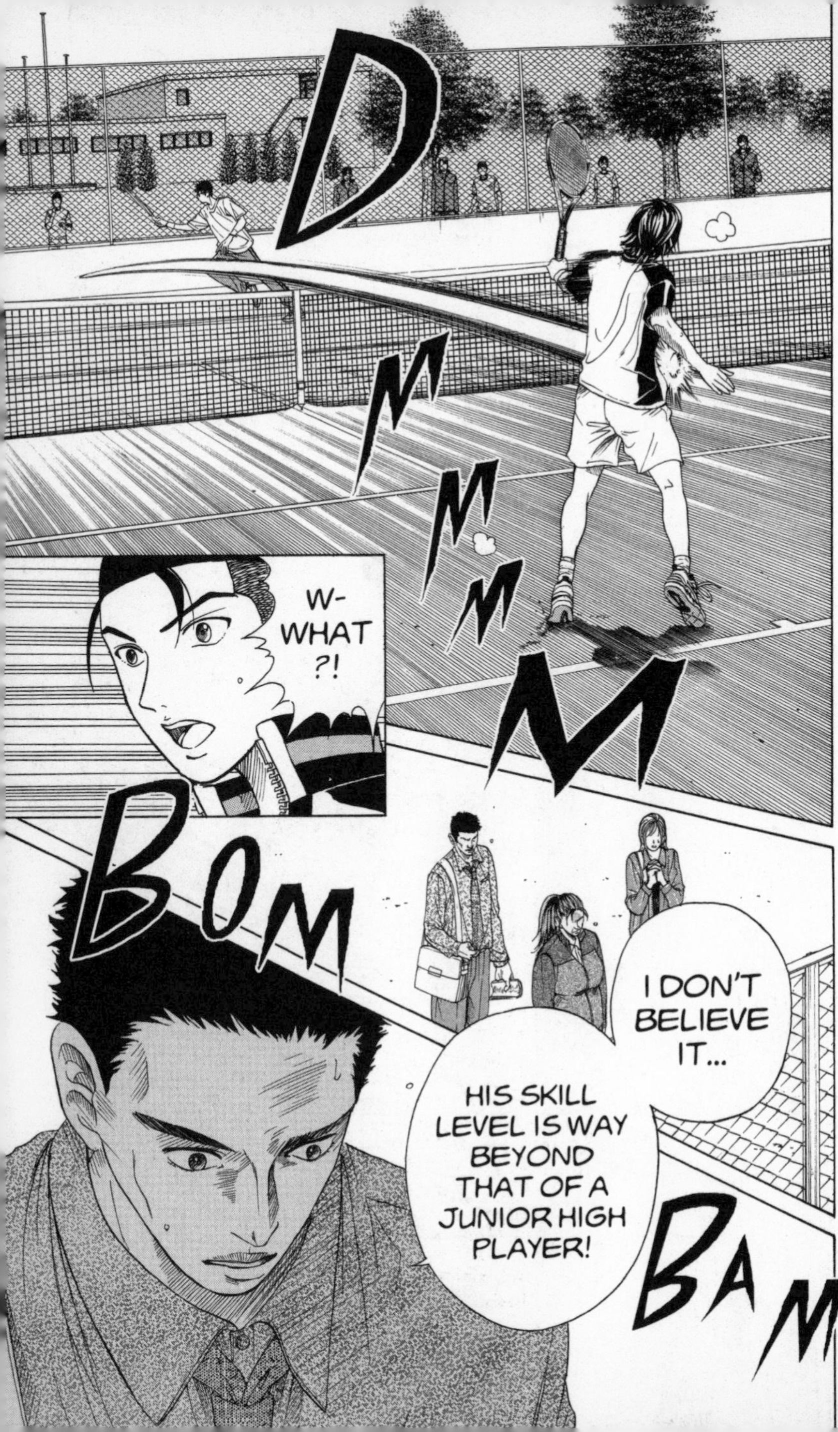
DMMMM
W-WHAT?!
BOM
I DON'T BELIEVE IT...
HIS SKILL LEVEL IS WAY BEYOND THAT OF A JUNIOR HIGH PLAYER!
BAM

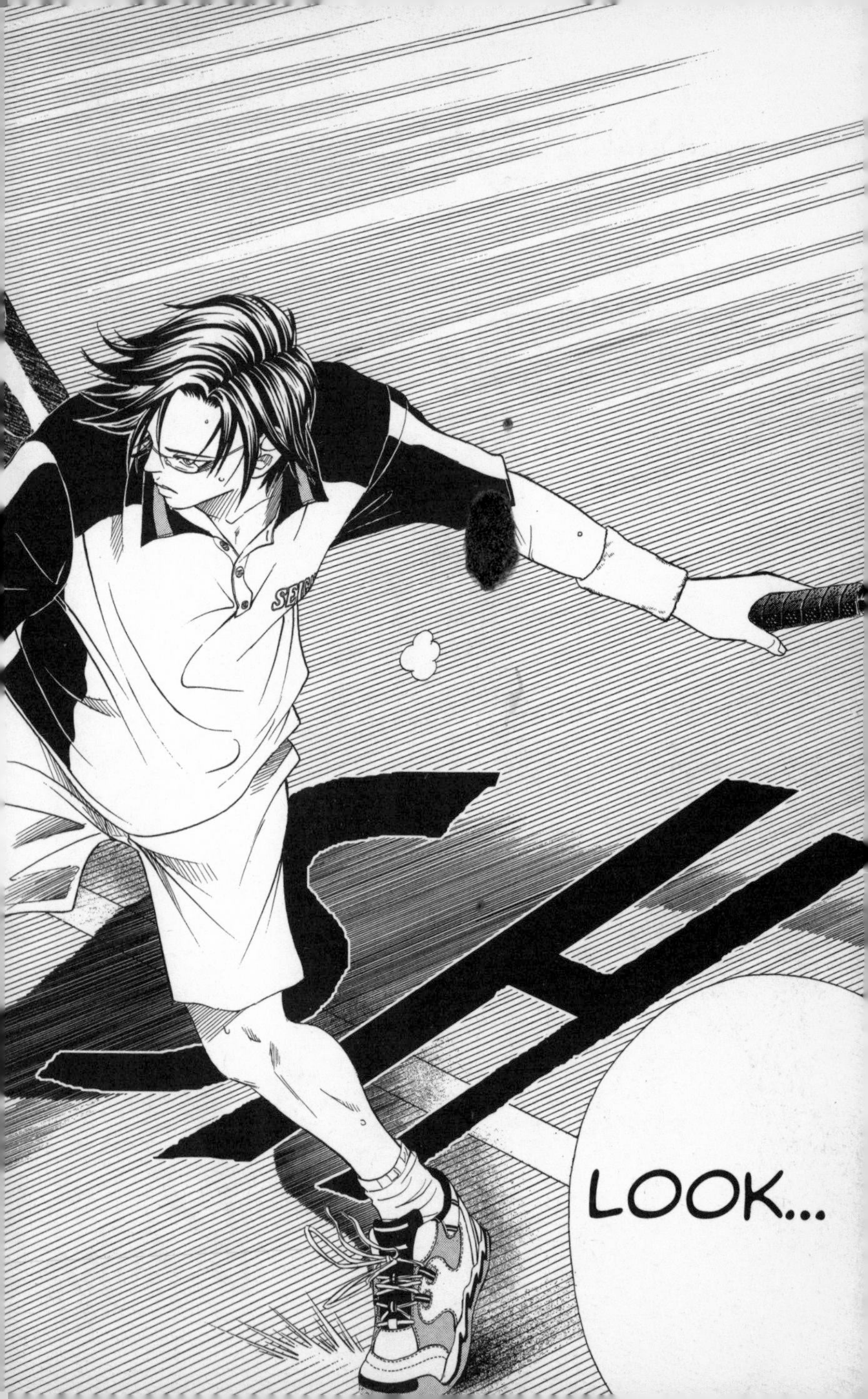
LOOK...

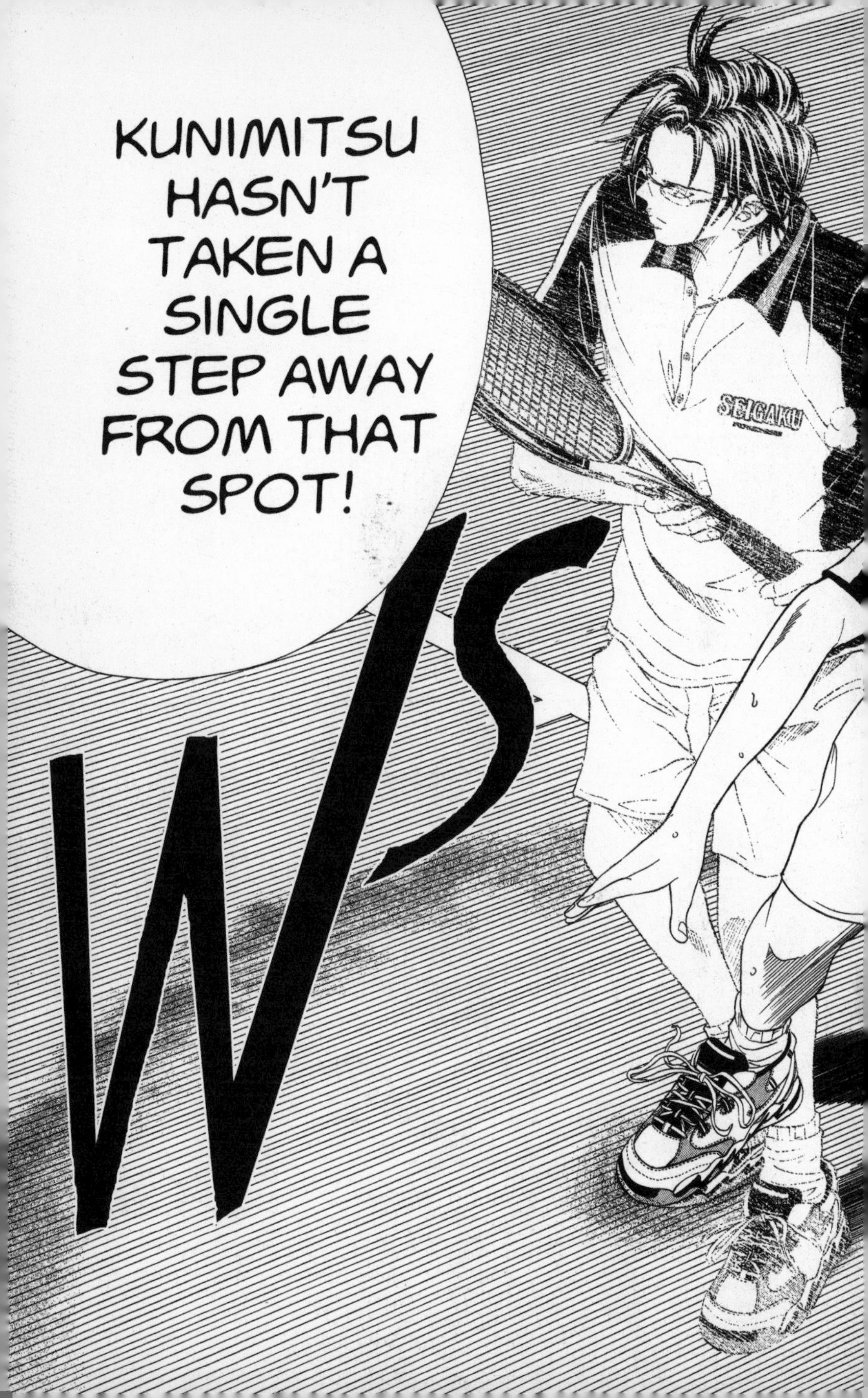
KUNIMITSU HASN'T TAKEN A SINGLE STEP AWAY FROM THAT SPOT!
WS
SEIGAKU

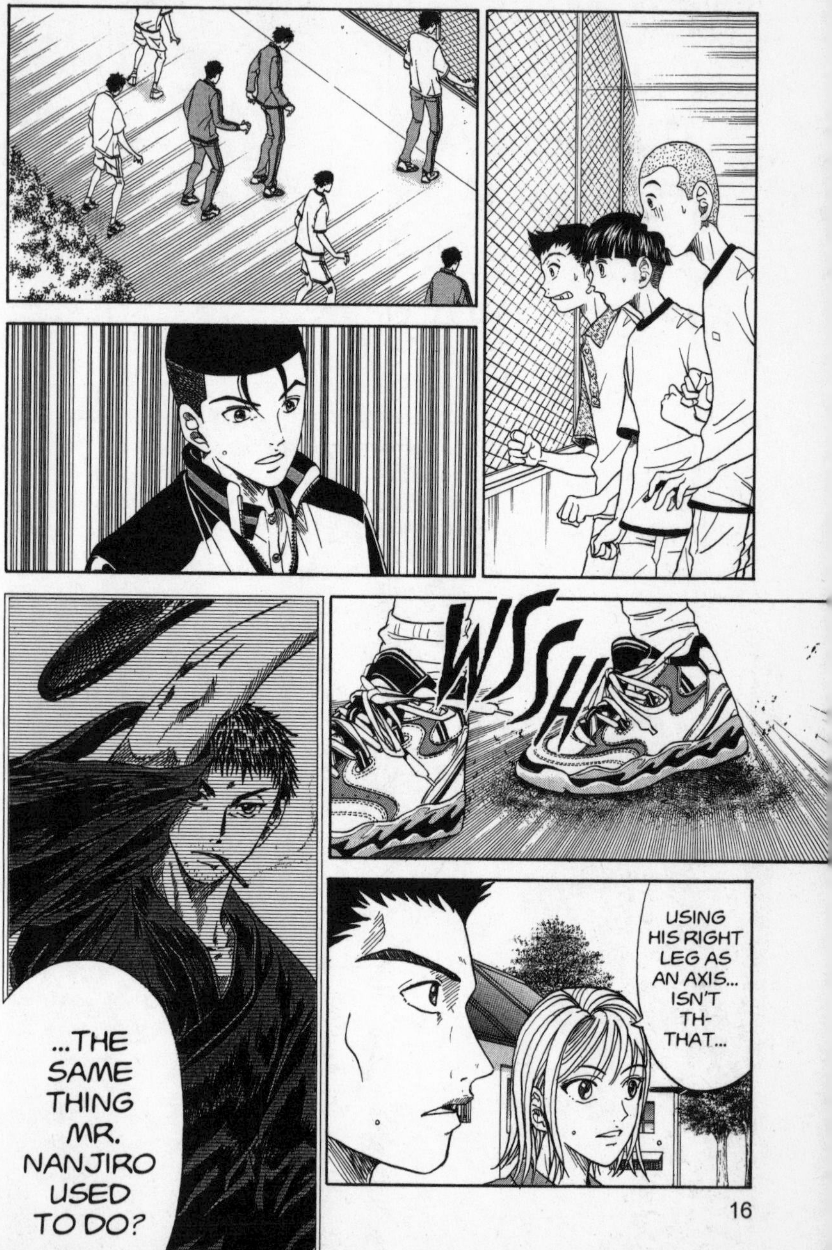
WSSH
USING HIS RIGHT LEG AS AN AXIS... ISN'T TH- THAT...
...THE SAME THING MR. NANJIRO USED TO DO?

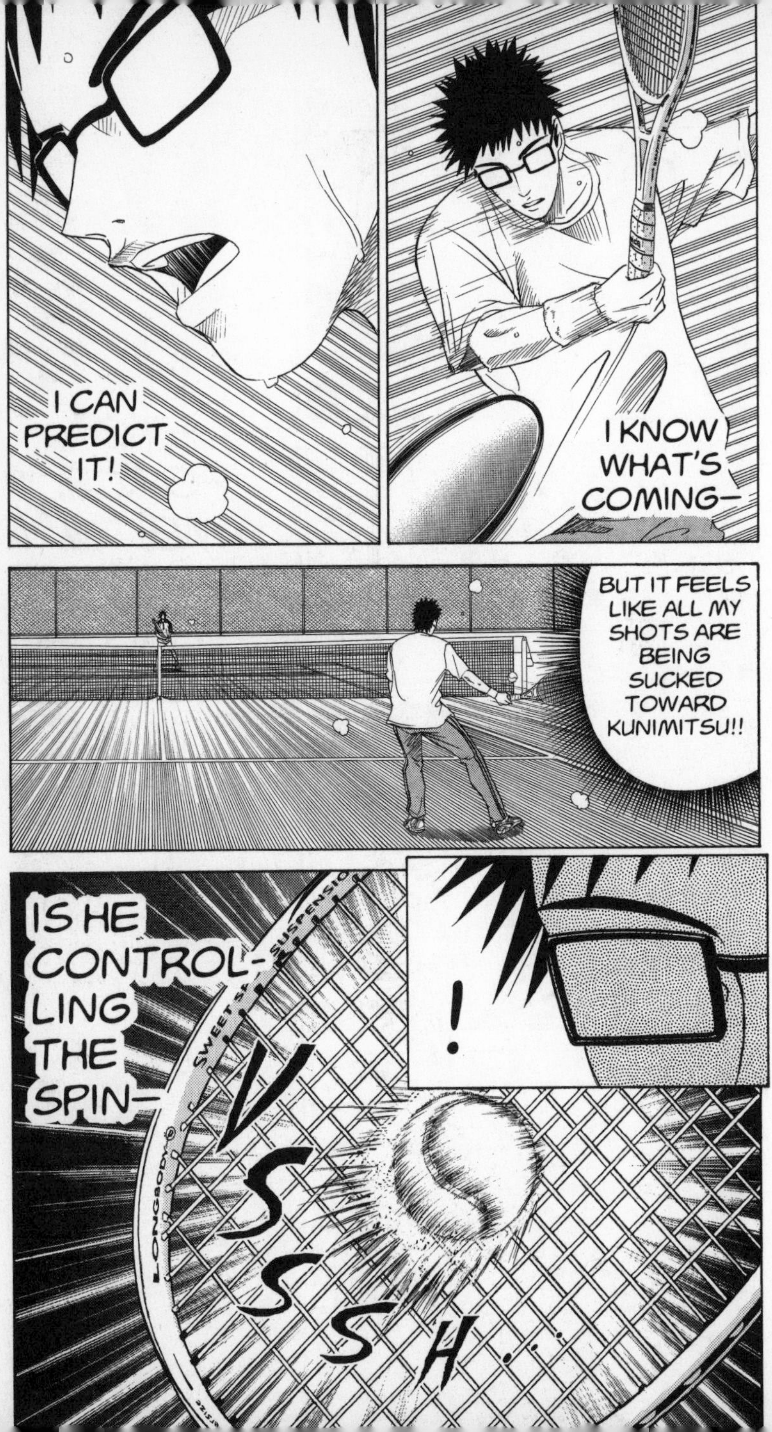
I KNOW WHAT'S COMING—
I CAN PREDICT IT!
BUT IT FEELS LIKE ALL MY SHOTS ARE BEING SUCKED TOWARD KUNIMITSU!!
!
IS HE CONTROL-LING THE SPIN—
VSSSH...

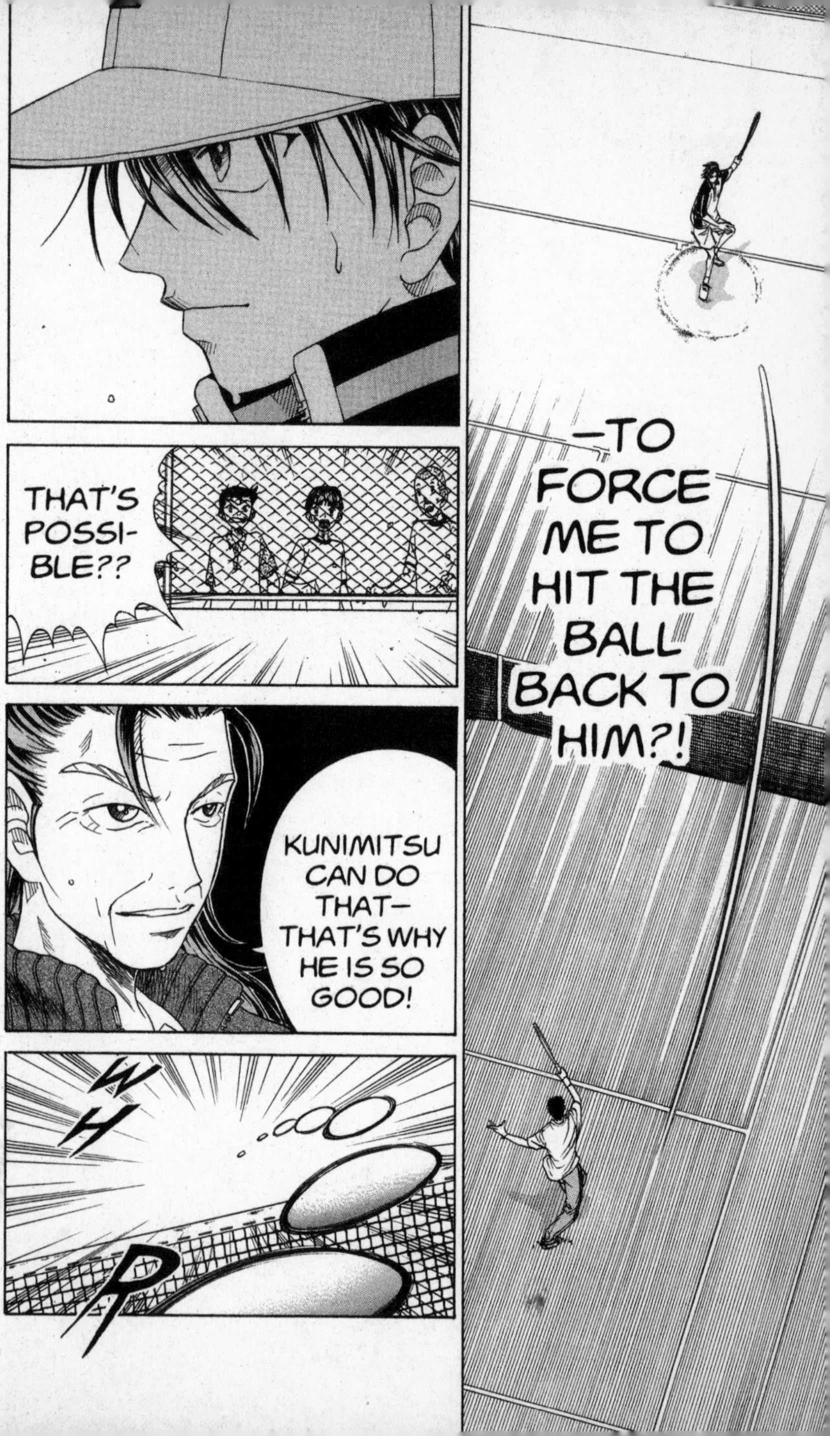
—TO FORCE ME TO HIT THE BALL BACK TO HIM?!
THAT'S POSSI-BLE??
KUNIMITSU CAN DO THAT—THAT'S WHY HE IS SO GOOD!
WHR

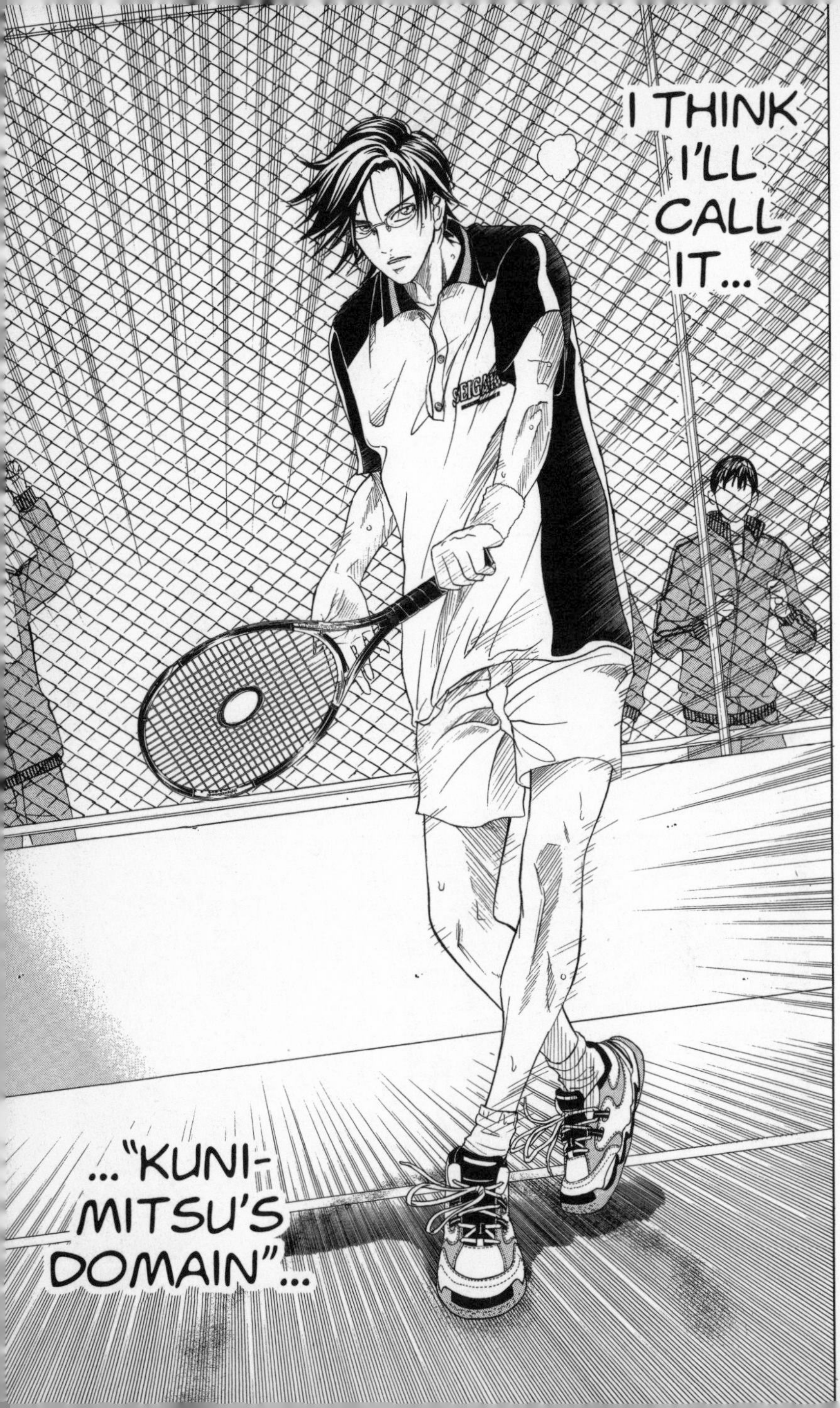
I THINK I'LL CALL IT...
..."KUNI-MITSU'S DOMAIN"...

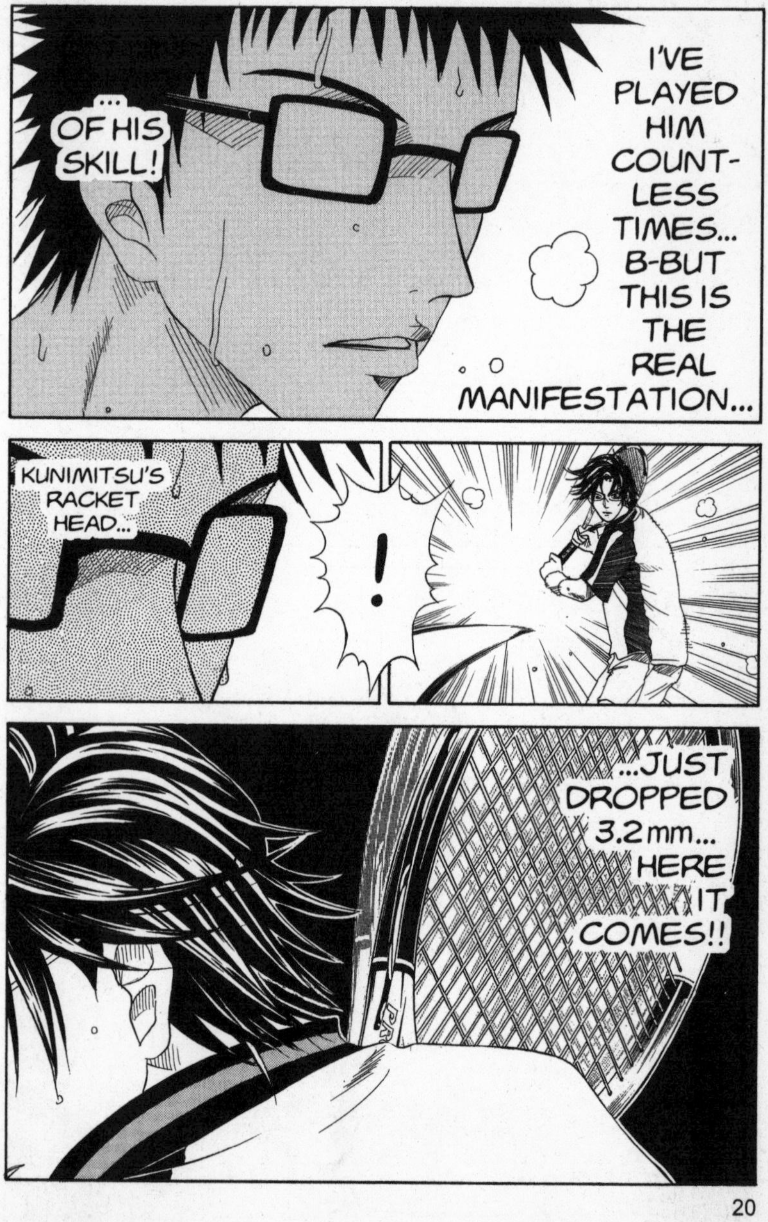
I'VE PLAYED HIM COUNT-LESS TIMES... B-BUT THIS IS THE REAL MANIFESTATION...
...OF HIS SKILL!
!
KUNIMITSU'S RACKET HEAD...
...JUST DROPPED 3.2mm... HERE IT COMES!!

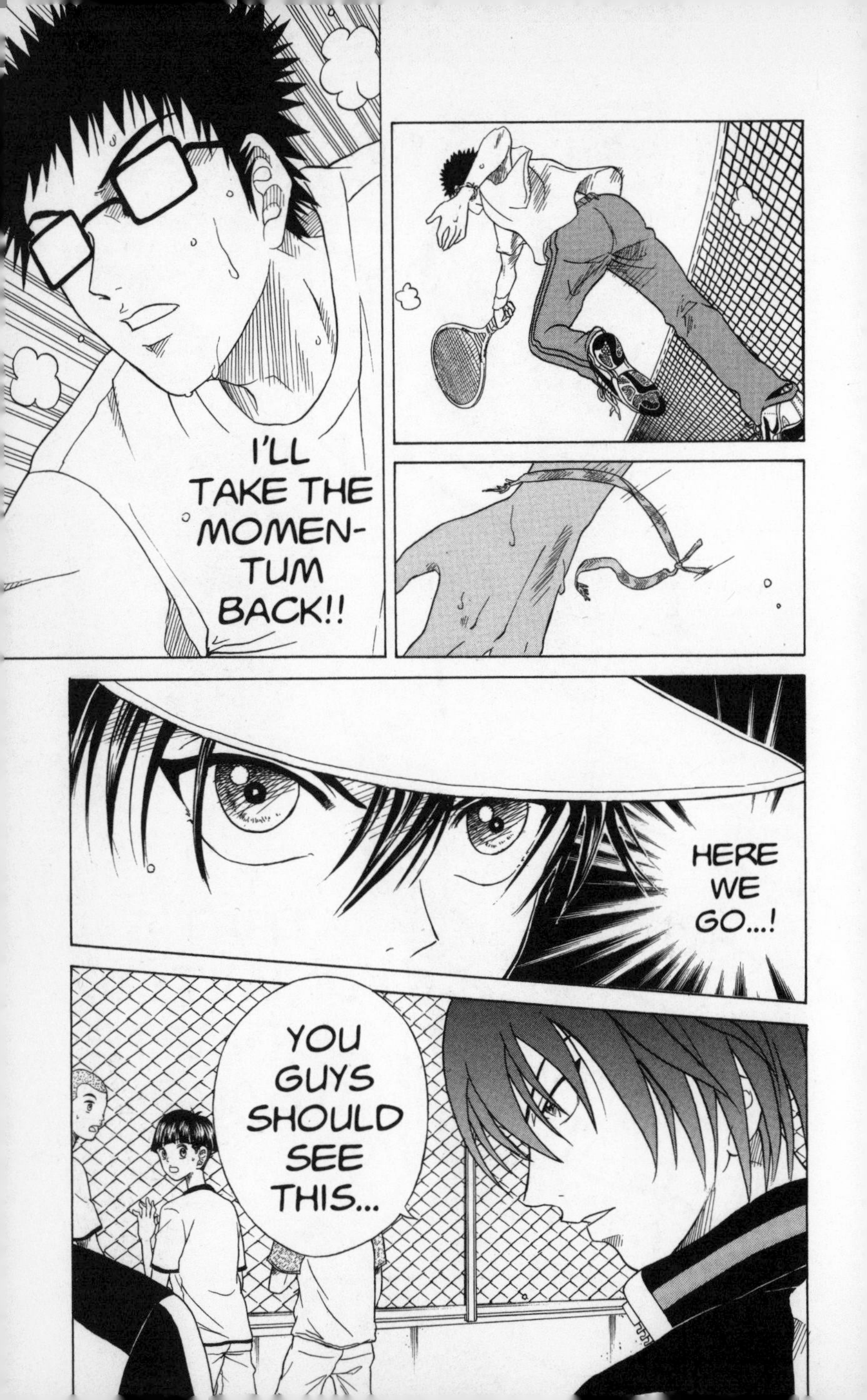
I'LL TAKE THE MOMEN-TUM BACK!!
HERE WE GO...!
YOU GUYS SHOULD SEE THIS...

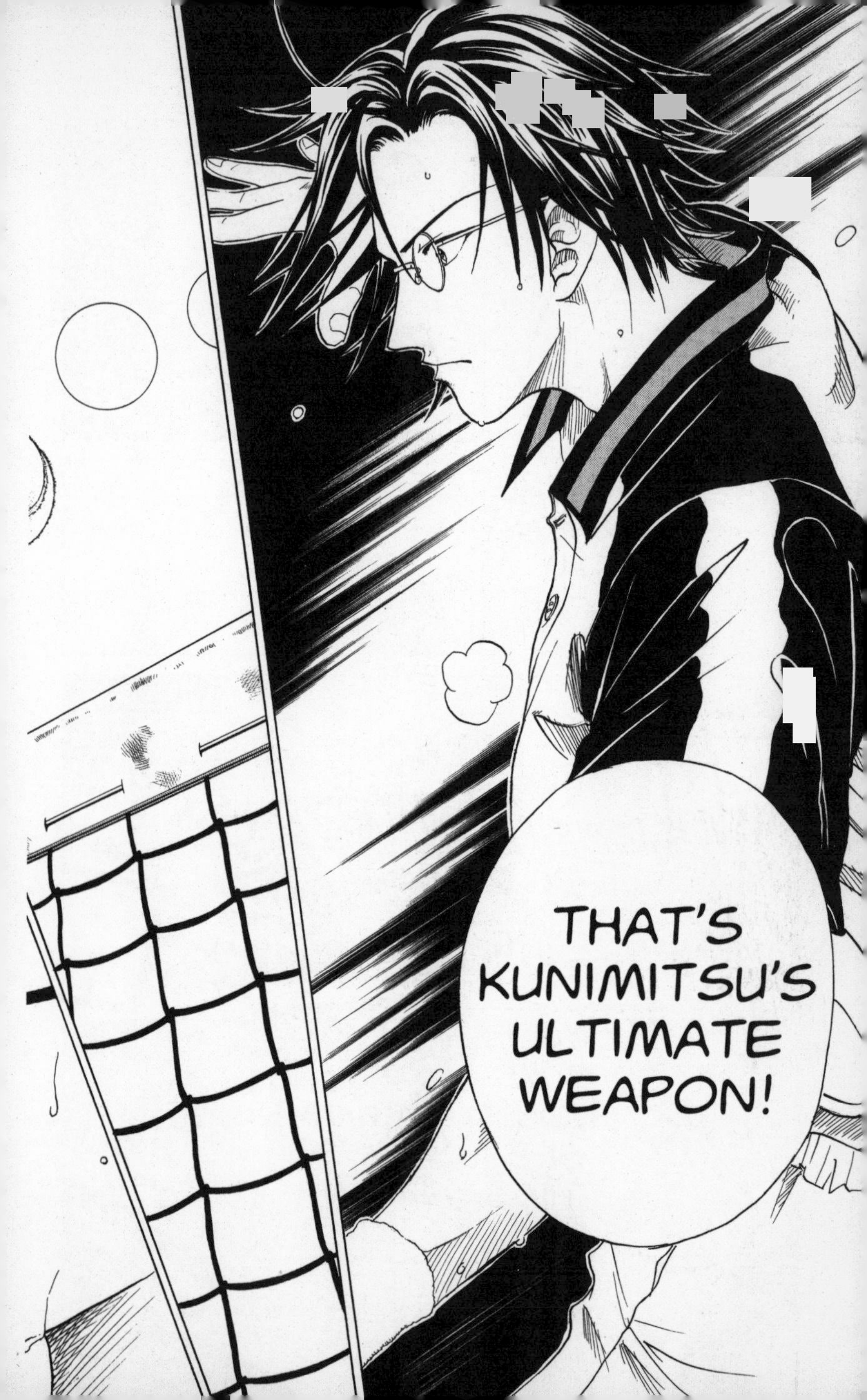
THAT'S KUNIMITSU'S ULTIMATE WEAPON!

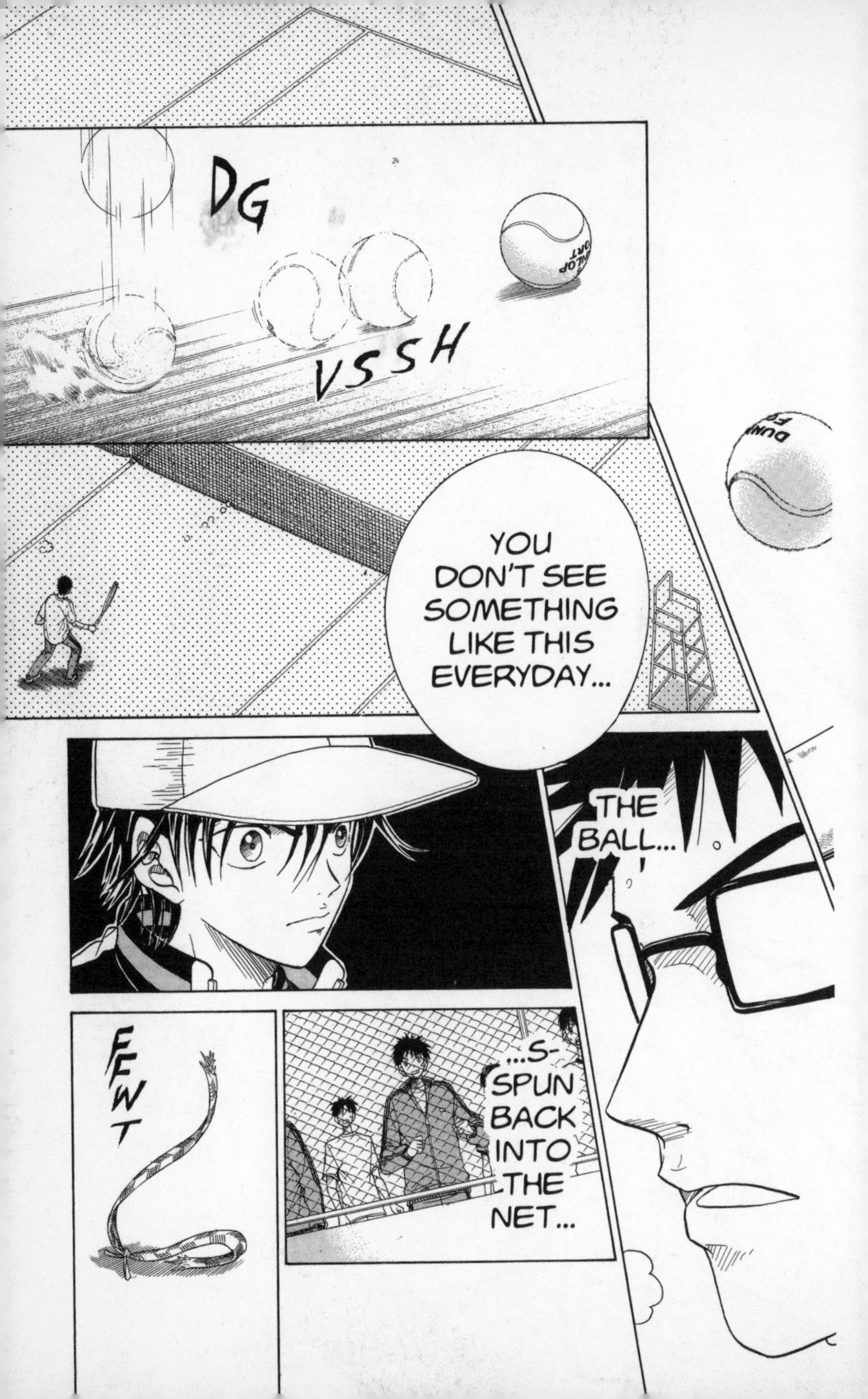
DG
VSSH
YOU DON'T SEE SOMETHING LIKE THIS EVERYDAY...
THE BALL...
...S-SPUN BACK INTO THE NET...
FFWT

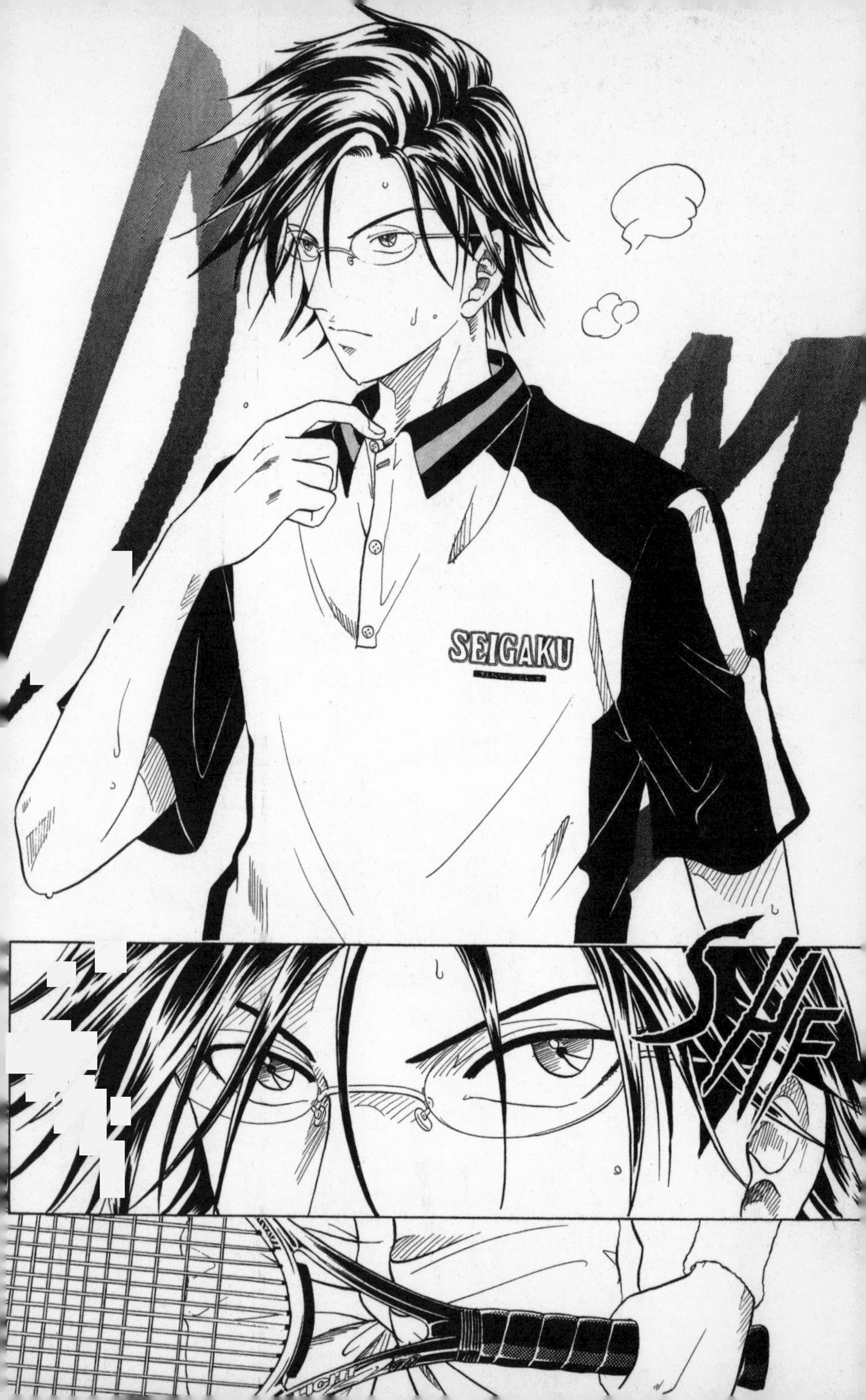
SEIGAKU

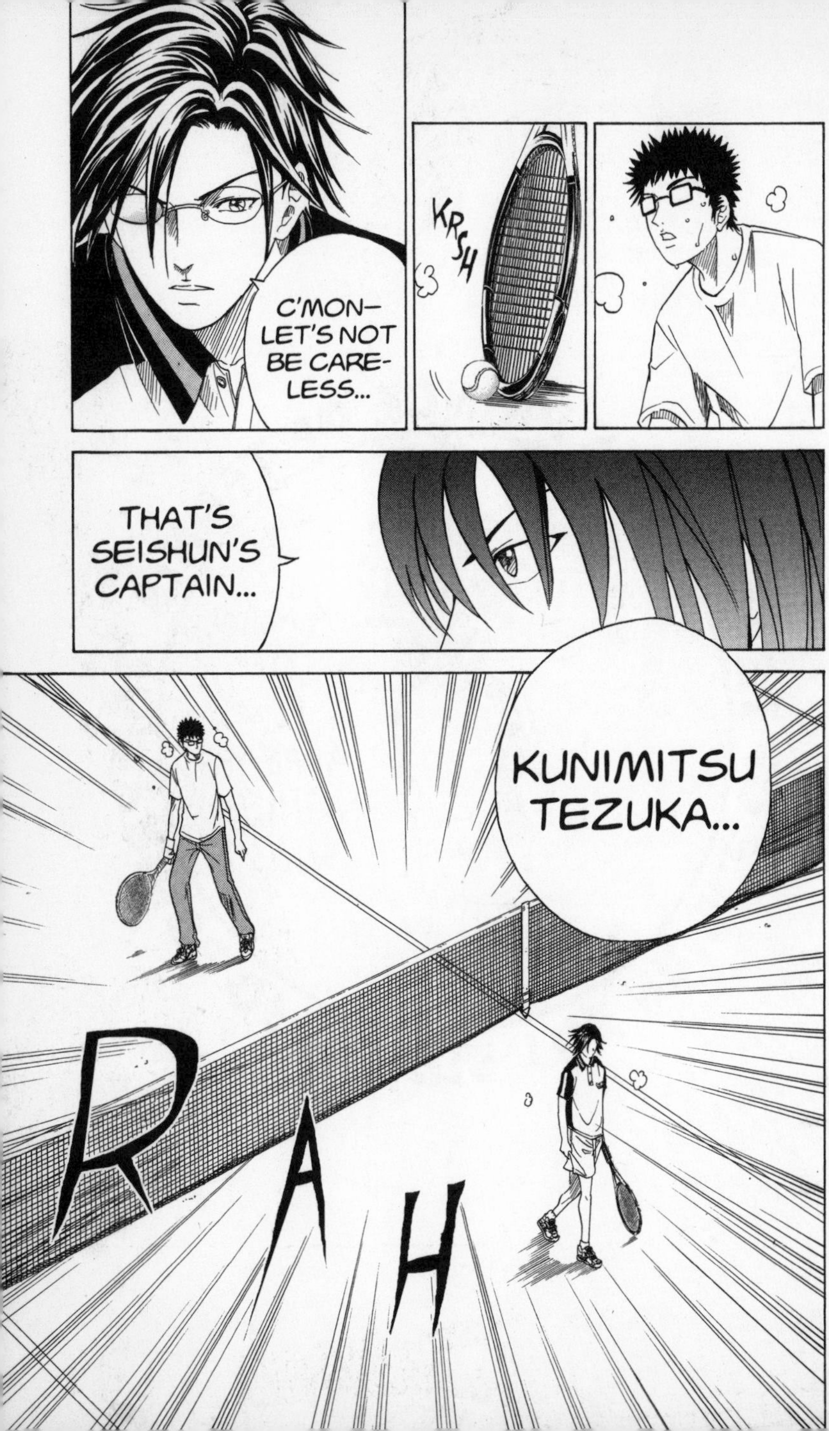
KRSH
C'MON—LET'S NOT BE CARE-LESS...
THAT'S SEISHUN'S CAPTAIN...
KUNIMITSU TEZUKA...
RAH

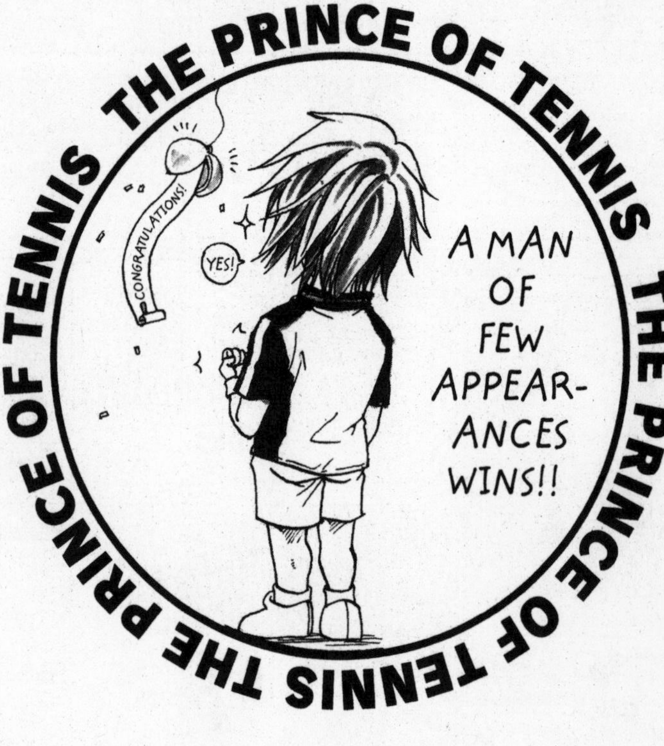
THE PRINCE OF TENNIS THE PRINCE OF TENNIS THE PRINCE OF TENNIS
CONGRATULATIONS!
YES!
A MAN OF FEW APPEAR-ANCES WINS!!

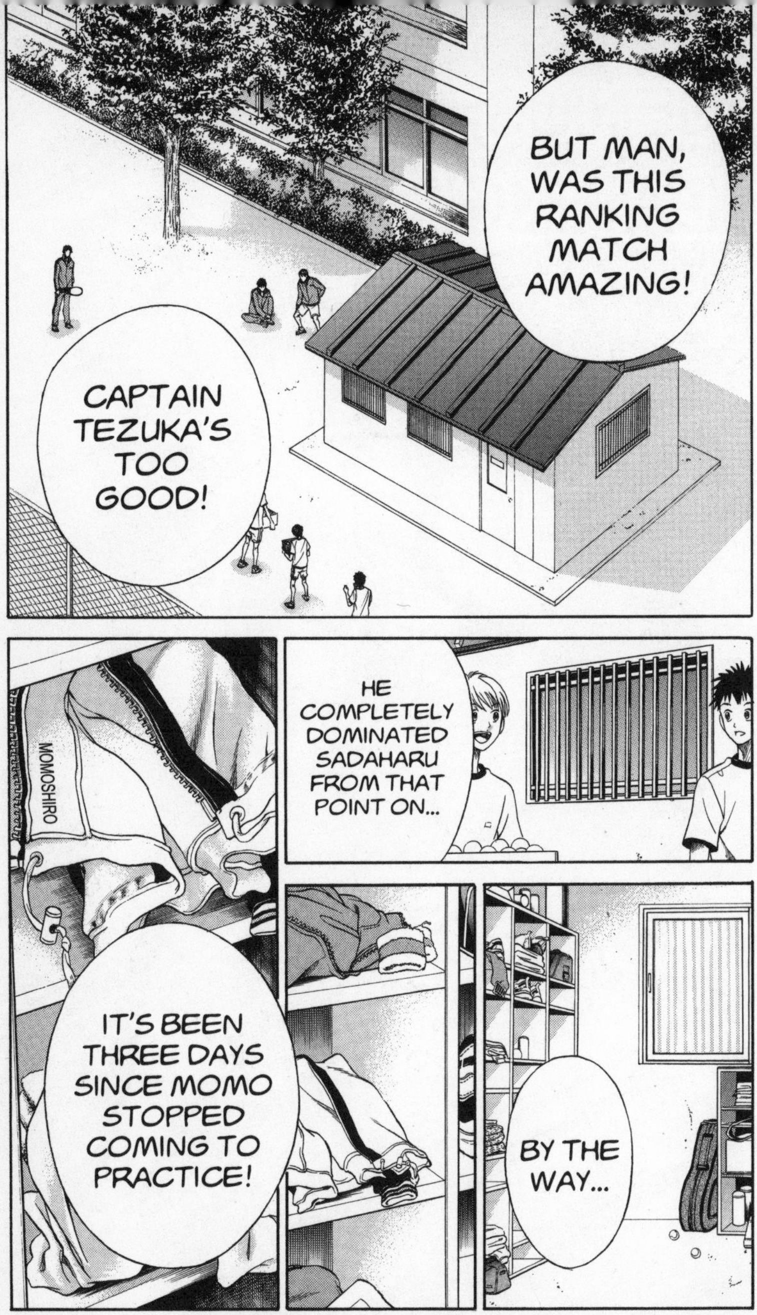
BUT MAN, WAS THIS RANKING MATCH AMAZING!
CAPTAIN TEZUKA'S TOO GOOD!
HE COMPLETELY DOMINATED SADAHARU FROM THAT POINT ON...
BY THE WAY...
MOMOSHIRO
IT'S BEEN THREE DAYS SINCE MOMO STOPPED COMING TO PRACTICE!

GENIUS 116: DARK CLOUDS

GENIUS 116: DARK CLOUDS

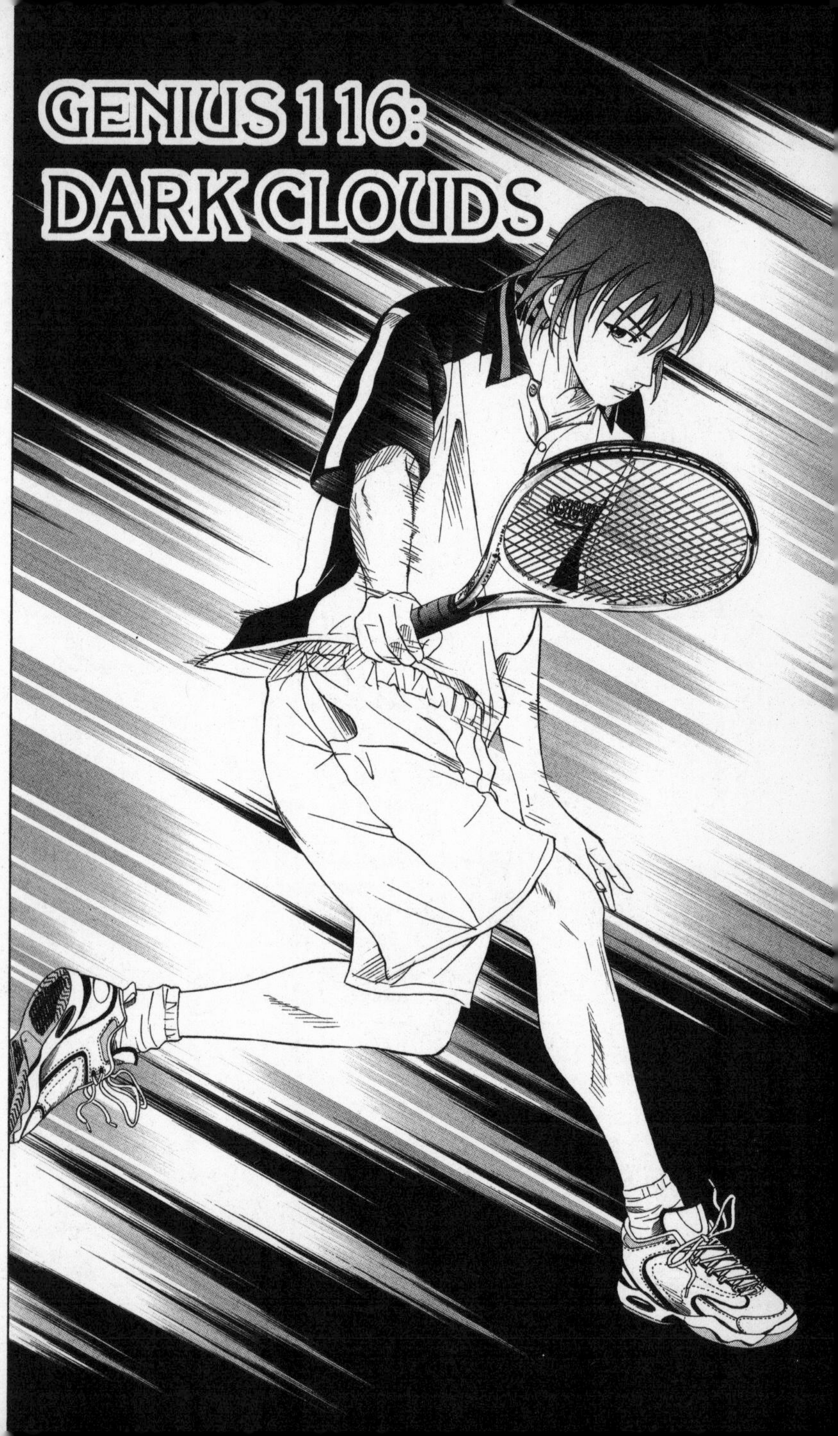

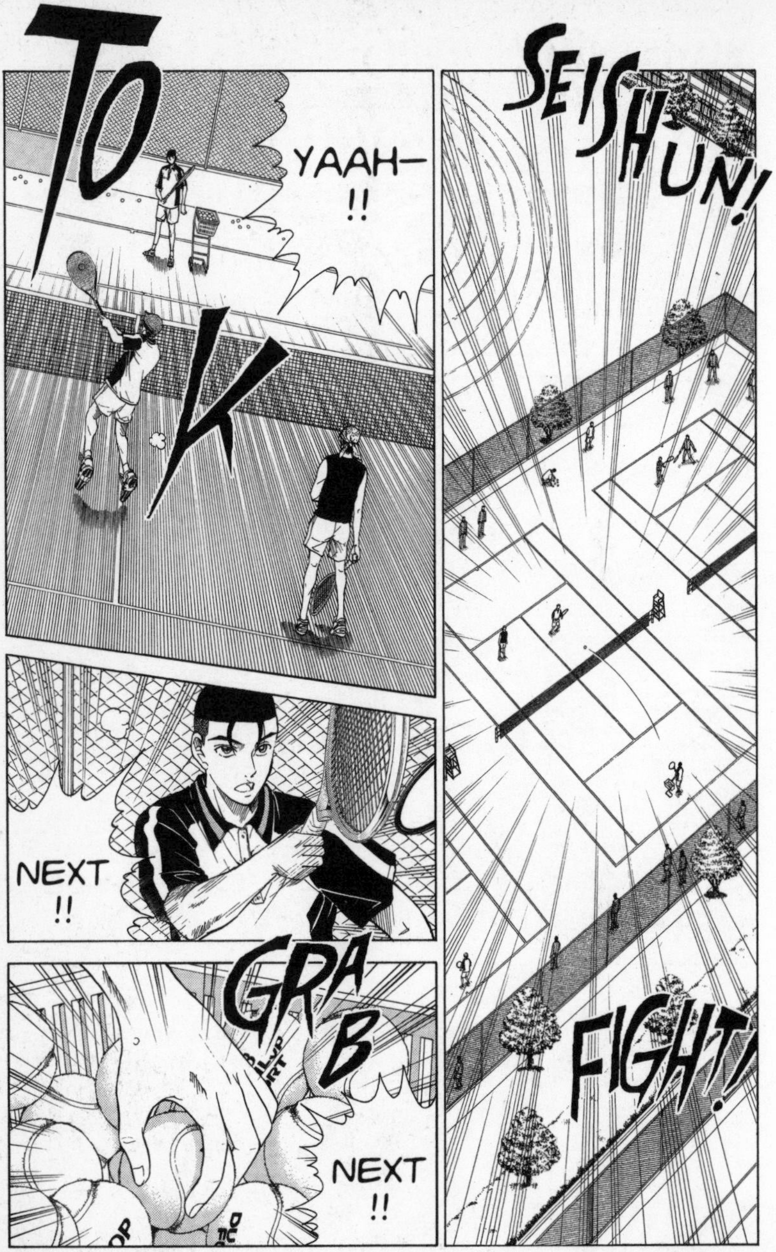
SEISHUN!
FIGHT!
TOK
YAAH— !!
NEXT !!
GRAB
NEXT !!

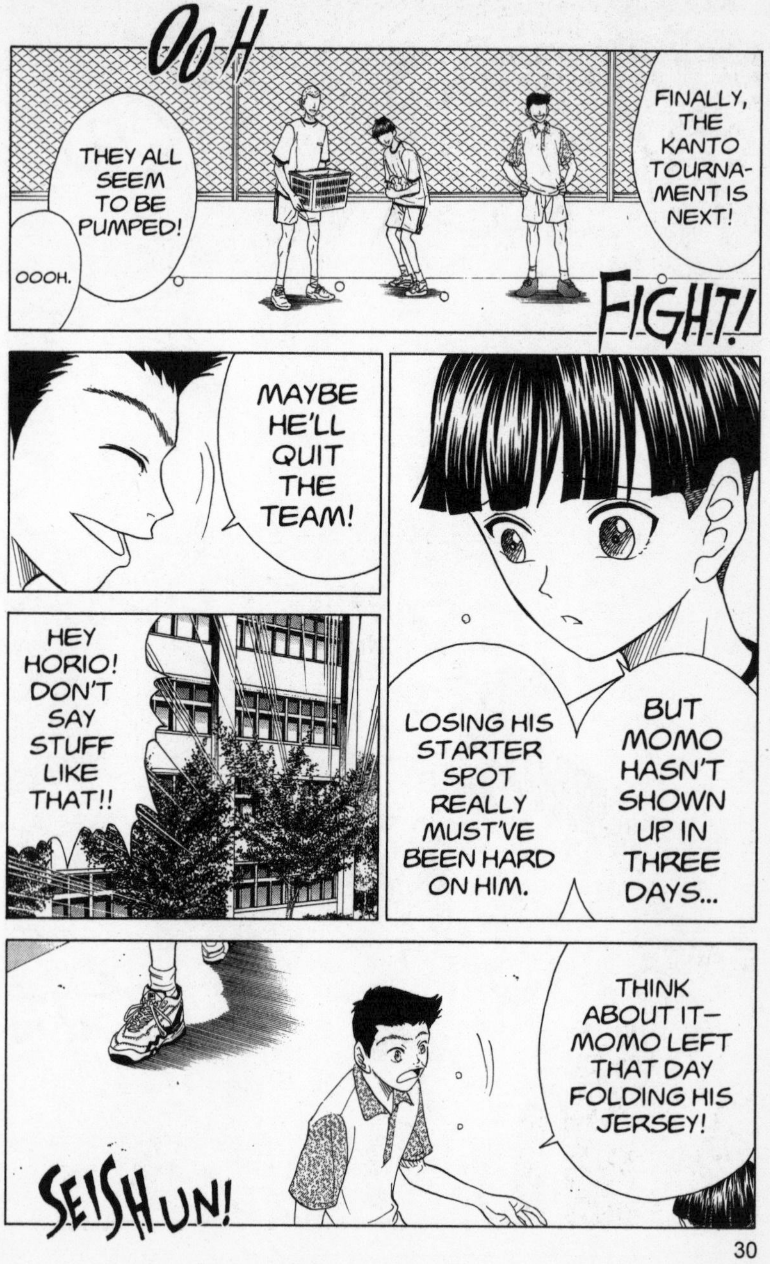
FINALLY, THE KANTO TOURNAMENT IS NEXT!
FIGHT!
OOH
THEY ALL SEEM TO BE PUMPED!
OOOH.
BUT MOMO HASN'T SHOWN UP IN THREE DAYS...
LOSING HIS STARTER SPOT REALLY MUST'VE BEEN HARD ON HIM.
MAYBE HE'LL QUIT THE TEAM!
HEY HORIO! DON'T SAY STUFF LIKE THAT!!
THINK ABOUT IT—MOMO LEFT THAT DAY FOLDING HIS JERSEY!
SEISHUN!

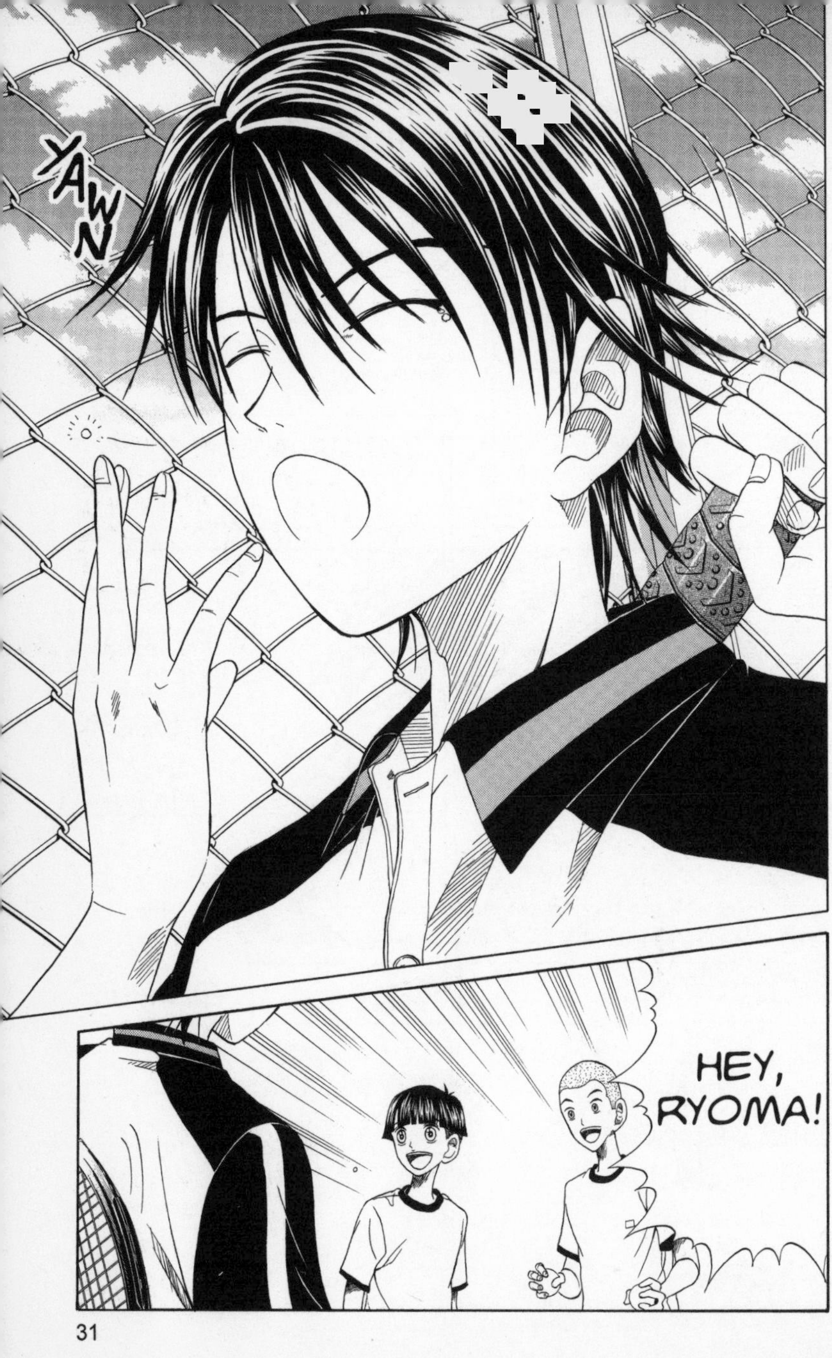
YAWN
HEY, RYOMA!

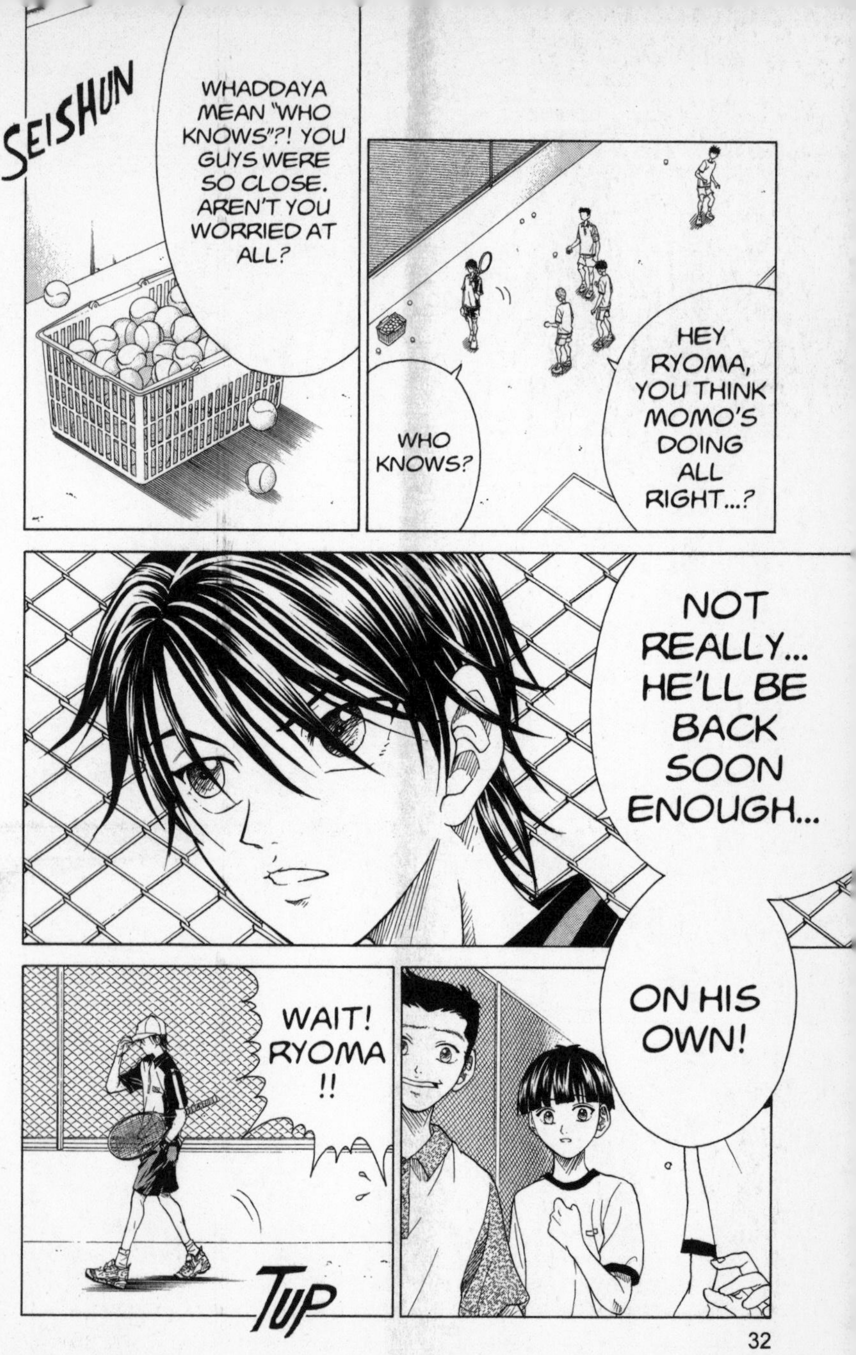
HEY RYOMA, YOU THINK MOMO'S DOING ALL RIGHT...?
WHO KNOWS?
SEISHUN
WHADDAYA MEAN "WHO KNOWS"?! YOU GUYS WERE SO CLOSE. AREN'T YOU WORRIED AT ALL?
NOT REALLY... HE'LL BE BACK SOON ENOUGH...
ON HIS OWN!
WAIT! RYOMA !!
TUP

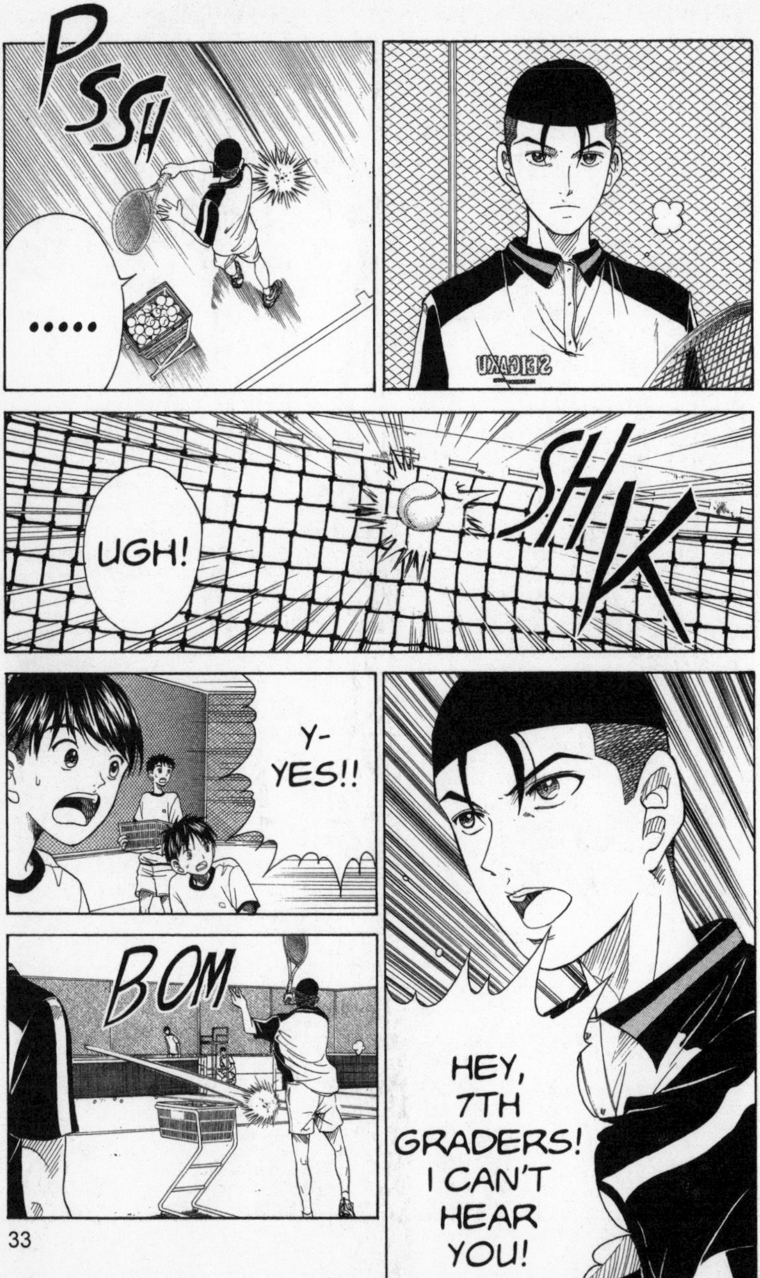
PSSH
.....
SHK
UGH!
HEY, 7TH GRADERS! I CAN'T HEAR YOU!
Y-YES!!
BOM

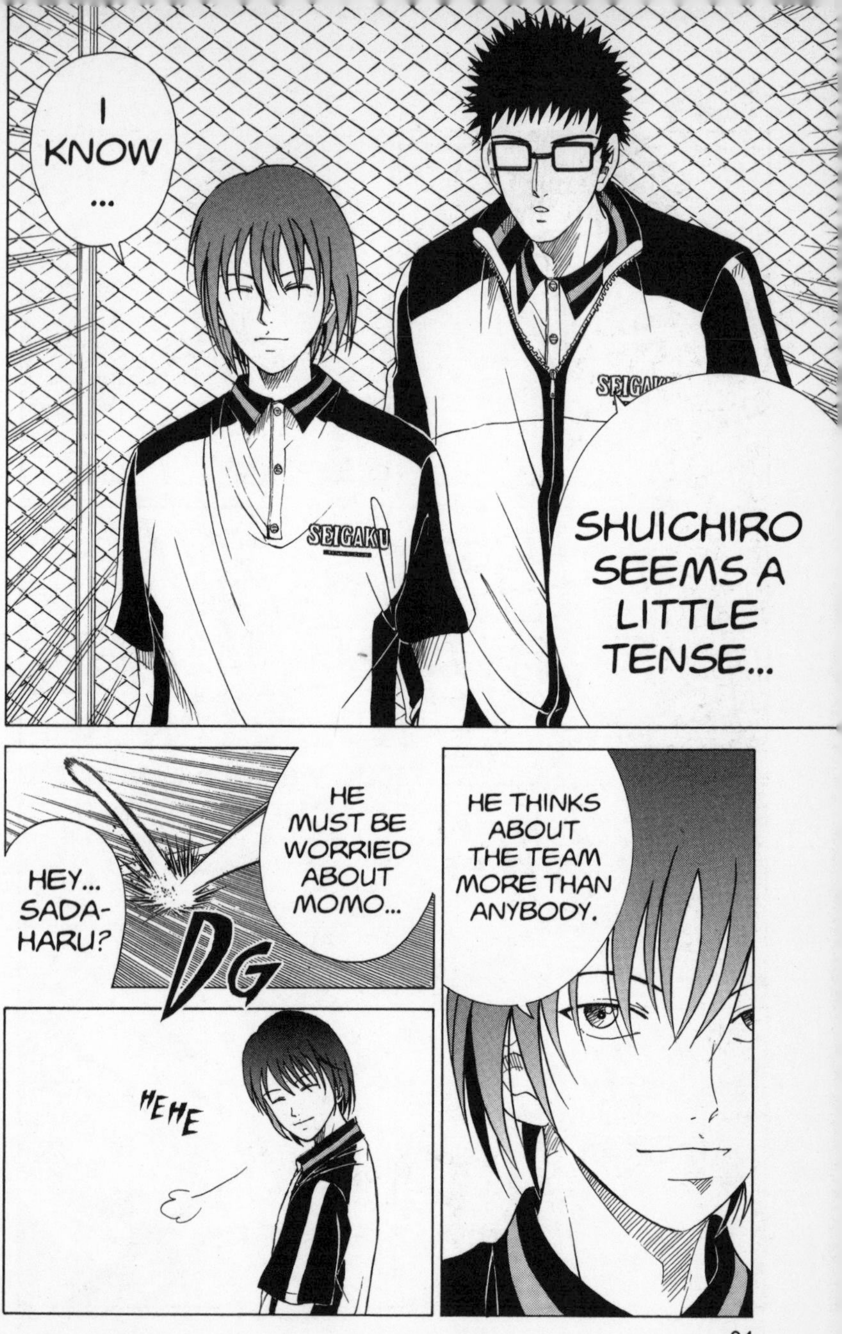
SHUICHIRO SEEMS A LITTLE TENSE...
I KNOW ...
HE THINKS ABOUT THE TEAM MORE THAN ANYBODY.
HE MUST BE WORRIED ABOUT MOMO...
HEY... SADA-HARU?
DG
HEHE

READ THIS WAY

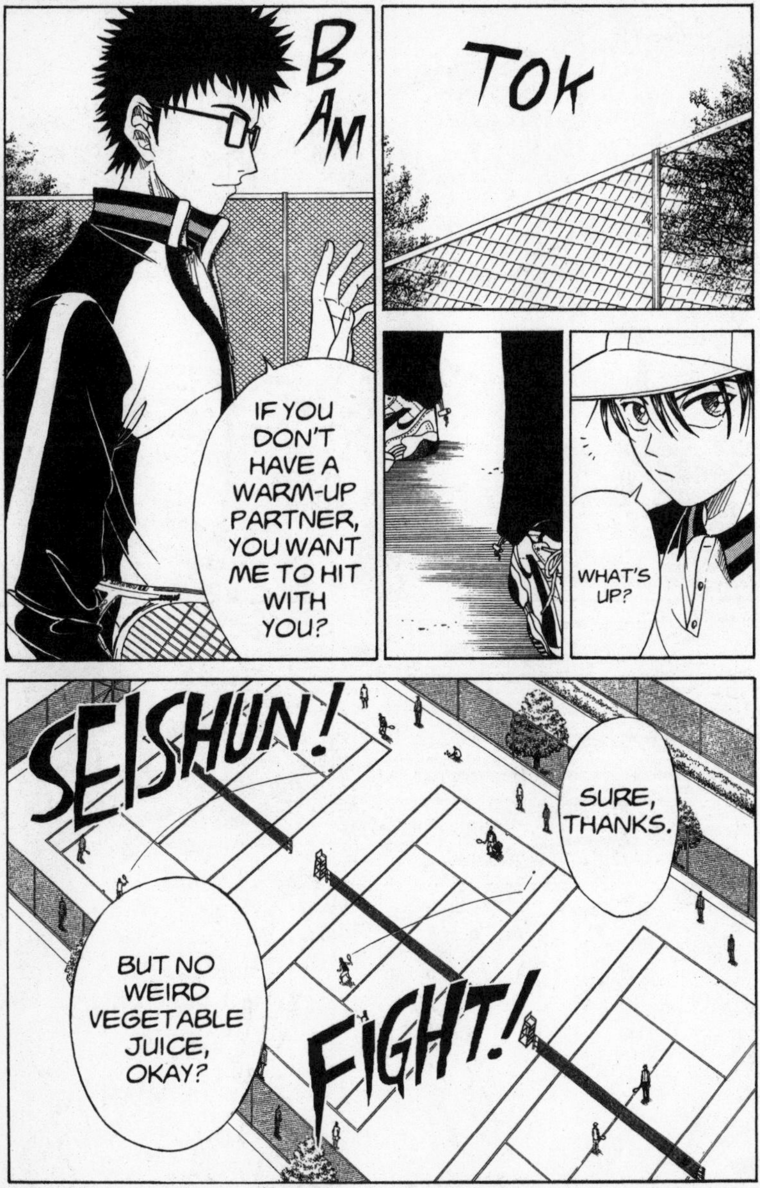
TOK
WHAT'S UP?
BAM
IF YOU DON'T HAVE A WARM-UP PARTNER, YOU WANT ME TO HIT WITH YOU?
SURE, THANKS.
SEISHUN!
BUT NO WEIRD VEGETABLE JUICE, OKAY?
FIGHT!

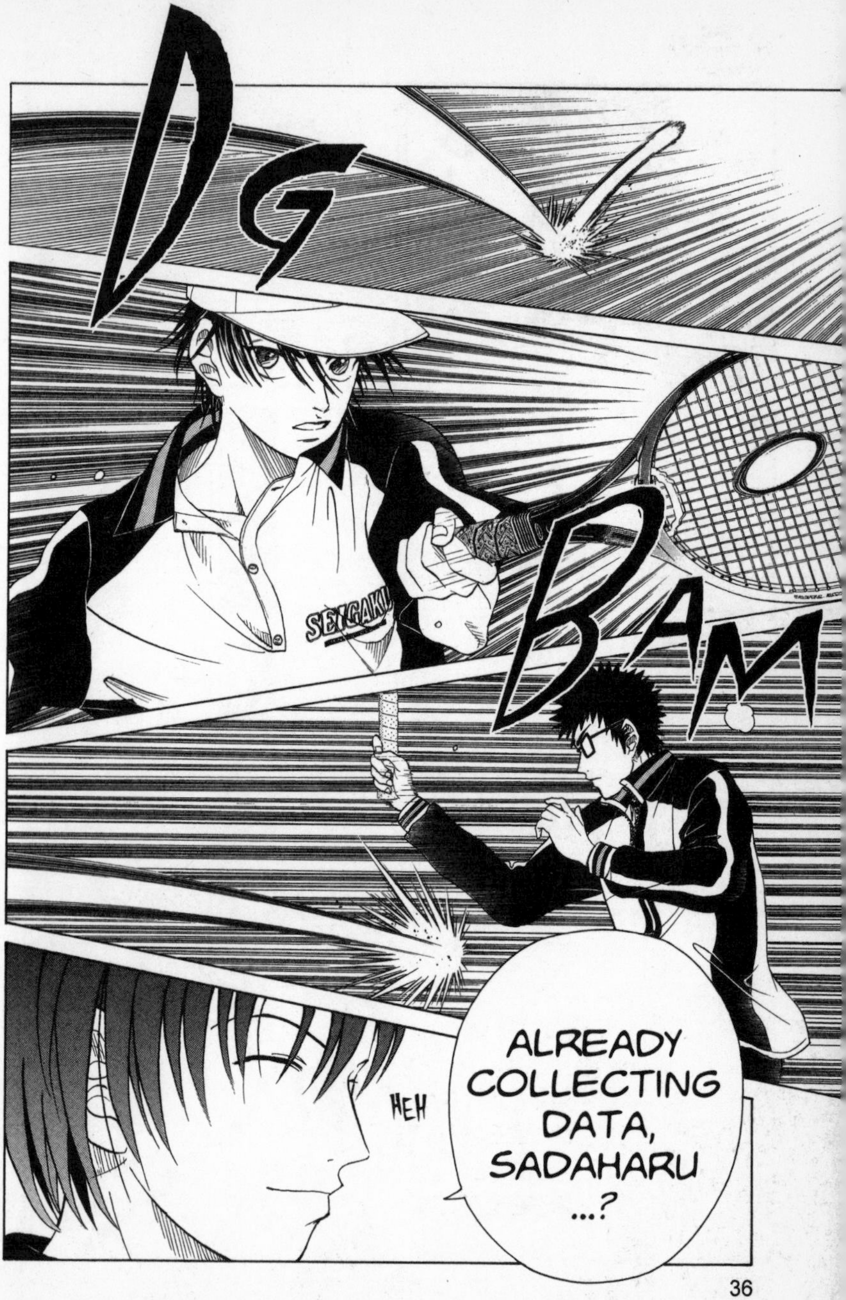
DG
BAM
HEH
ALREADY COLLECTING DATA, SADAHARU ...?

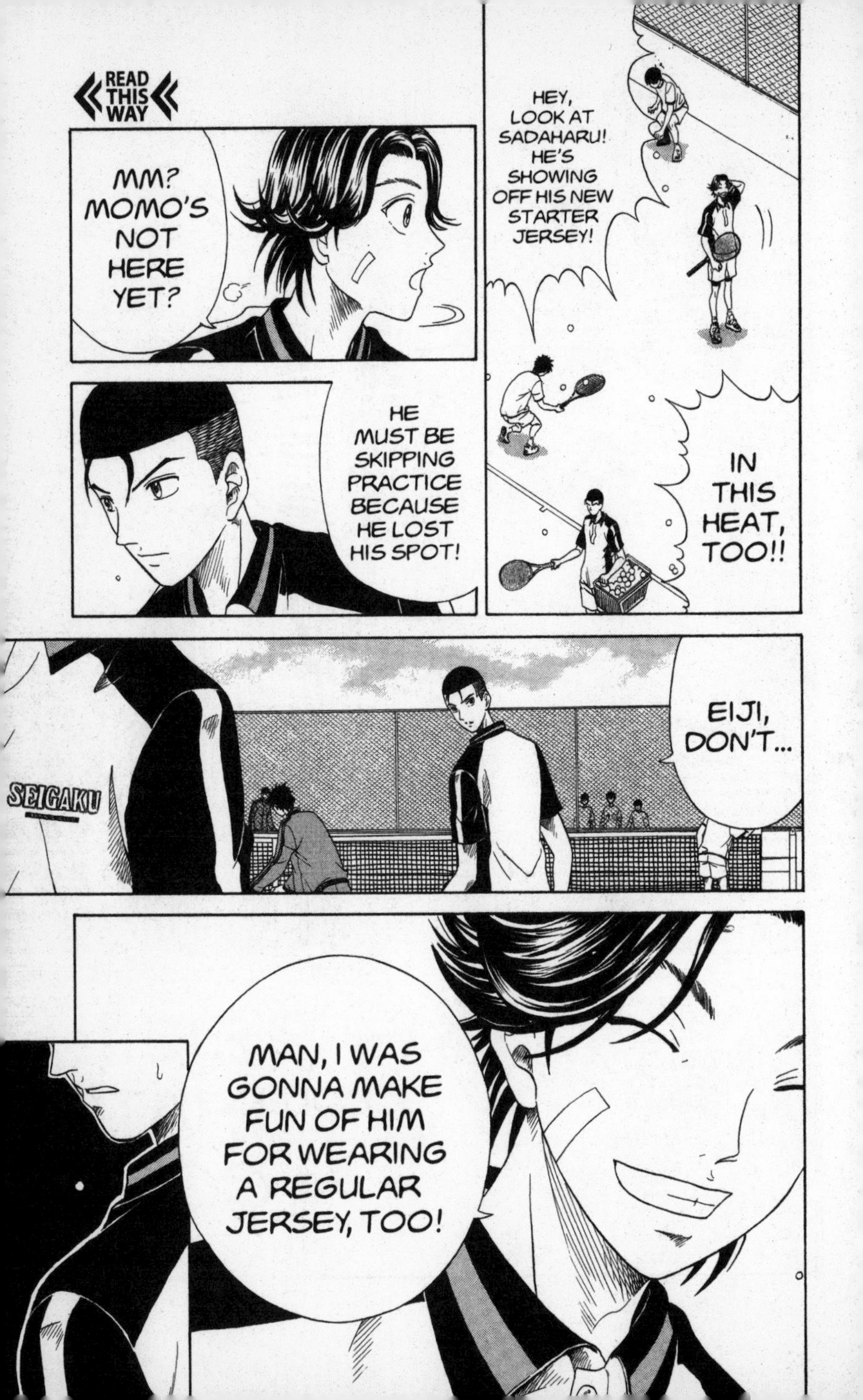

READ THIS WAY
HEY, LOOK AT SADAHARU! HE'S SHOWING OFF HIS NEW STARTER JERSEY!
IN THIS HEAT, TOO!!
MM? MOMO'S NOT HERE YET?
HE MUST BE SKIPPING PRACTICE BECAUSE HE LOST HIS SPOT!
EIJI, DON'T...
SEIGAKU
MAN, I WAS GONNA MAKE FUN OF HIM FOR WEARING A REGULAR JERSEY, TOO!

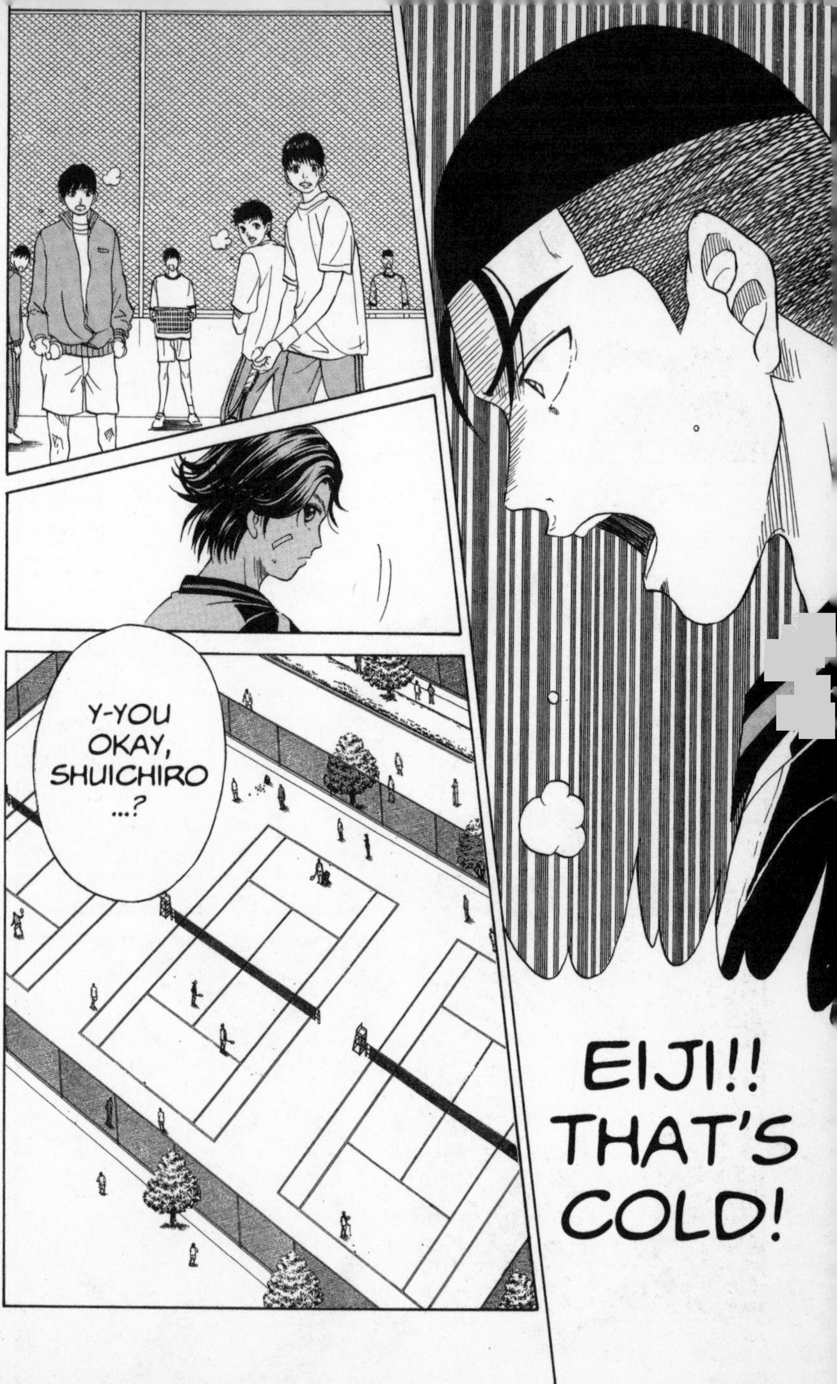
EIJI!! THAT'S COLD!
Y-YOU OKAY, SHUICHIRO ...?

READ THIS WAY

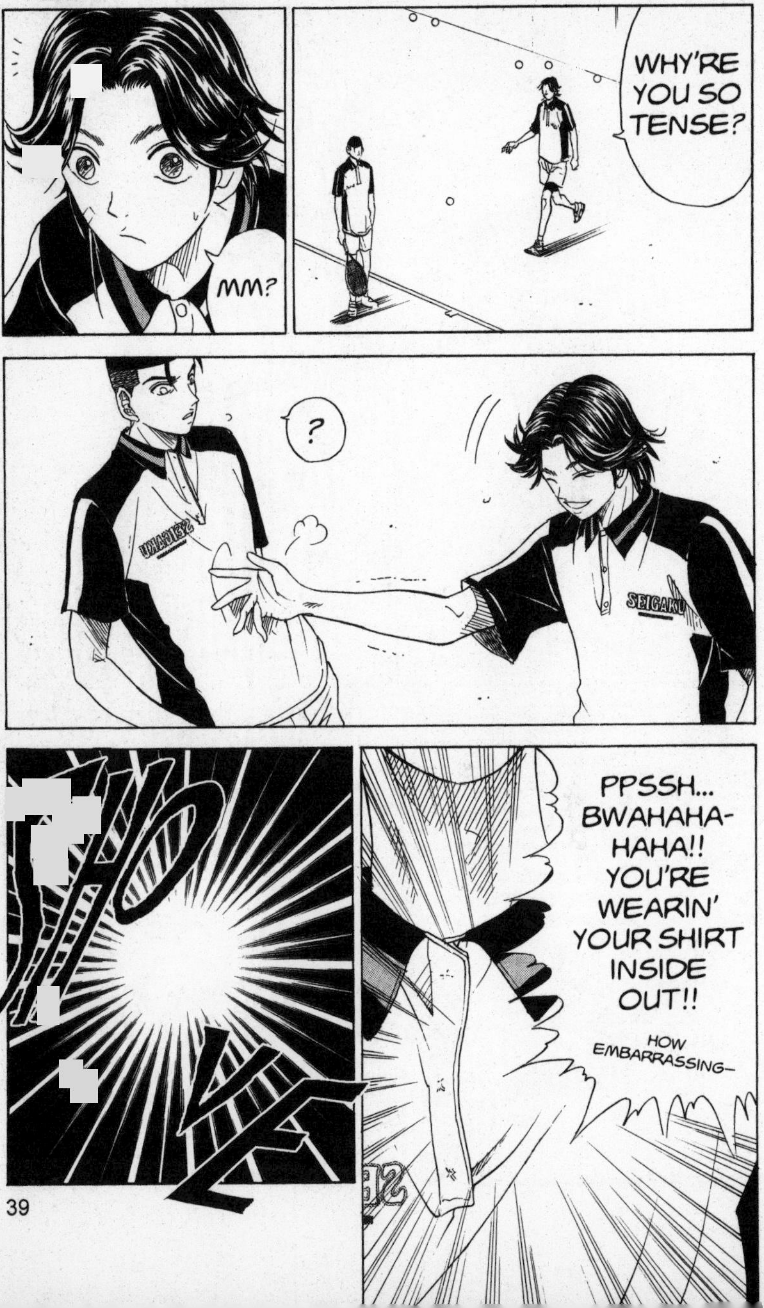
WHY'RE YOU SO TENSE?
MM?
?
PPSSH... BWAHAHA-HAHA!! YOU'RE WEARIN' YOUR SHIRT INSIDE OUT!!
HOW EMBARRASSING—

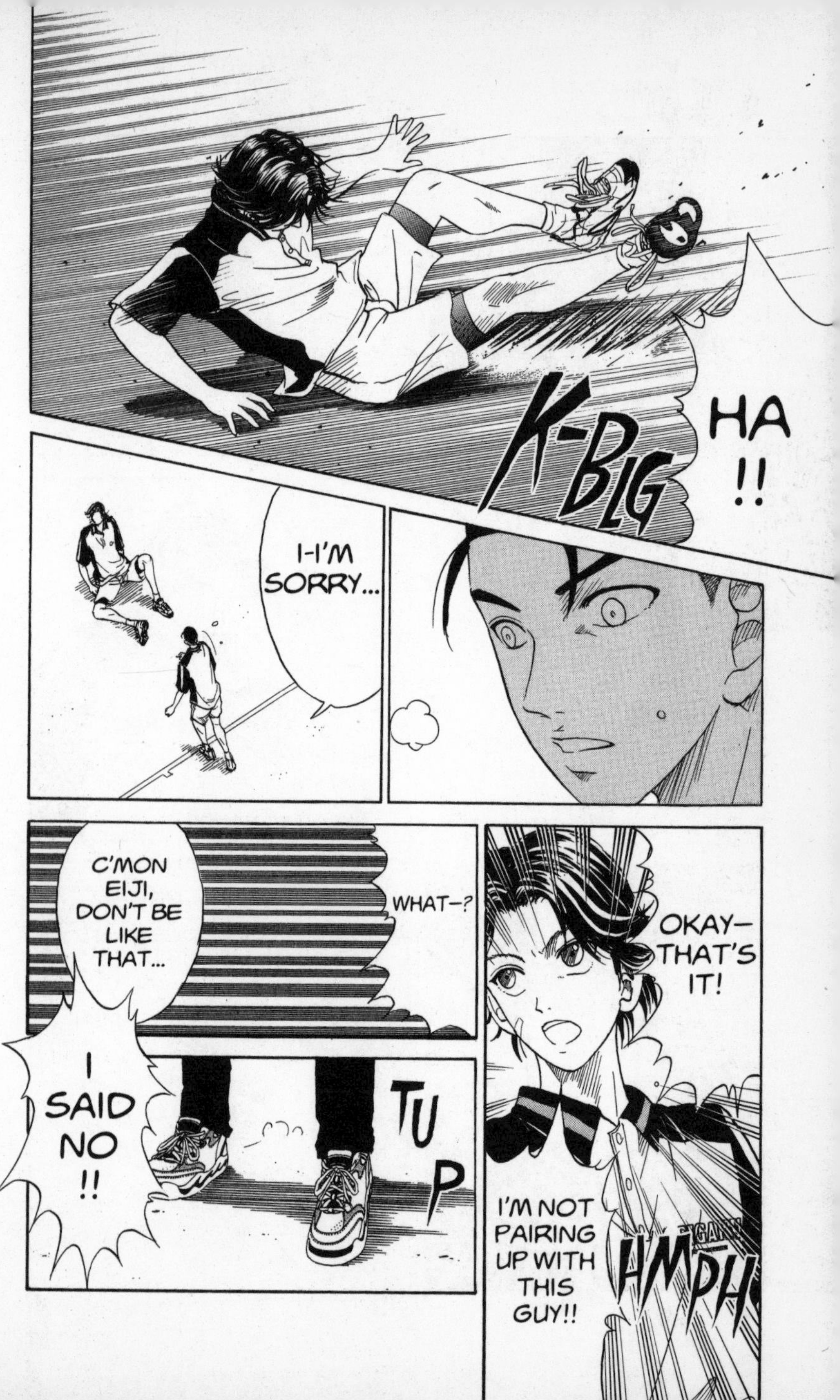
HA !!
K-BLG
I-I'M SORRY...
OKAY— THAT'S IT!
I'M NOT PAIRING UP WITH THIS GUY!!
HMPH
WHAT—?
C'MON EIJI, DON'T BE LIKE THAT...
I SAID NO !!
TU P

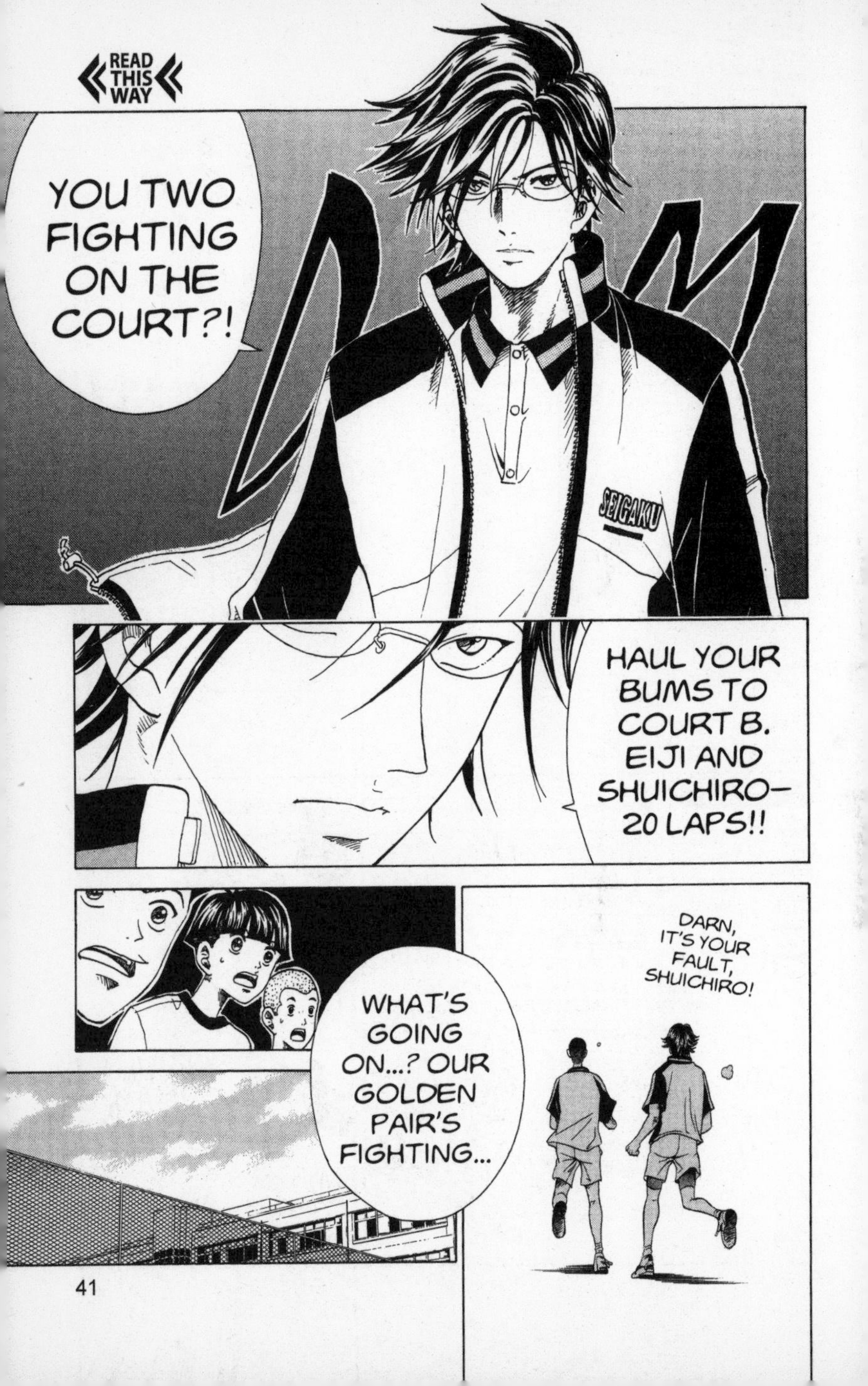
READ THIS WAY
YOU TWO FIGHTING ON THE COURT?!
HAUL YOUR BUMS TO COURT B. EIJI AND SHUICHIRO— 20 LAPS!!
DARN, IT'S YOUR FAULT, SHUICHIRO!
WHAT'S GOING ON...? OUR GOLDEN PAIR'S FIGHTING...
SEIGAKU

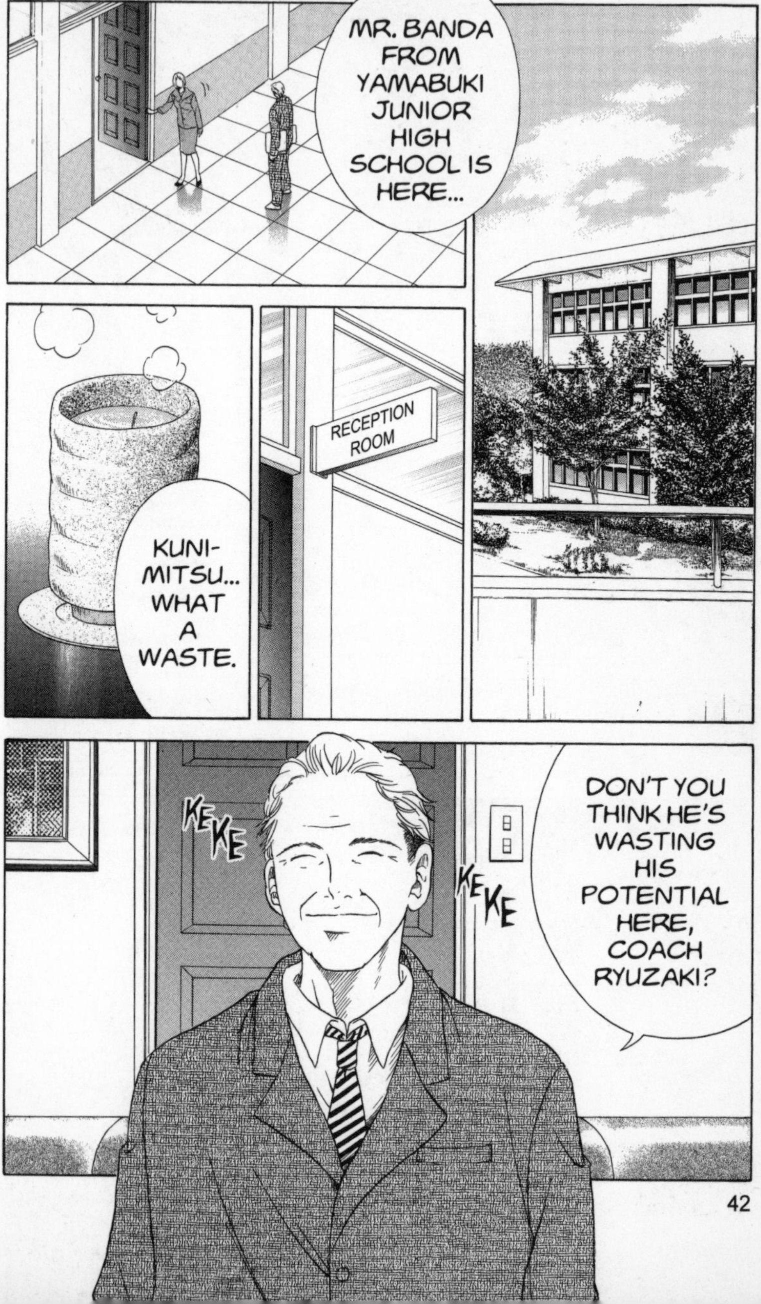
MR. BANDA FROM YAMABUKI JUNIOR HIGH SCHOOL IS HERE...
RECEPTION ROOM
KUNI-MITSU... WHAT A WASTE.
DON'T YOU THINK HE'S WASTING HIS POTENTIAL HERE, COACH RYUZAKI?
KEKE
KEKE

READ THIS WAY

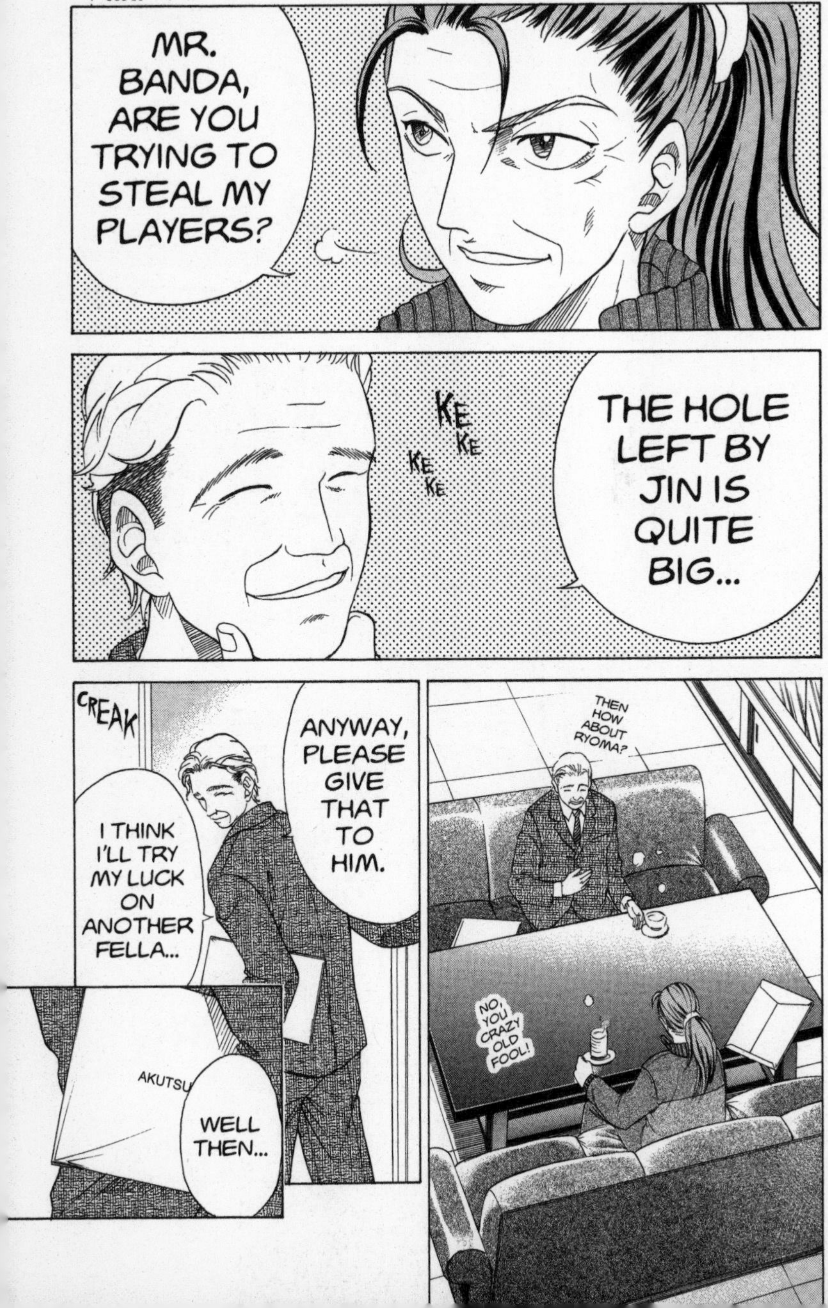
MR. BANDA, ARE YOU TRYING TO STEAL MY PLAYERS?
THE HOLE LEFT BY JIN IS QUITE BIG...
KE KE
KE KE
THEN HOW ABOUT RYOMA?
NO, YOU CRAZY OLD FOOL!
CREAK
ANYWAY, PLEASE GIVE THAT TO HIM.
I THINK I'LL TRY MY LUCK ON ANOTHER FELLA...
AKUTSU
WELL THEN...

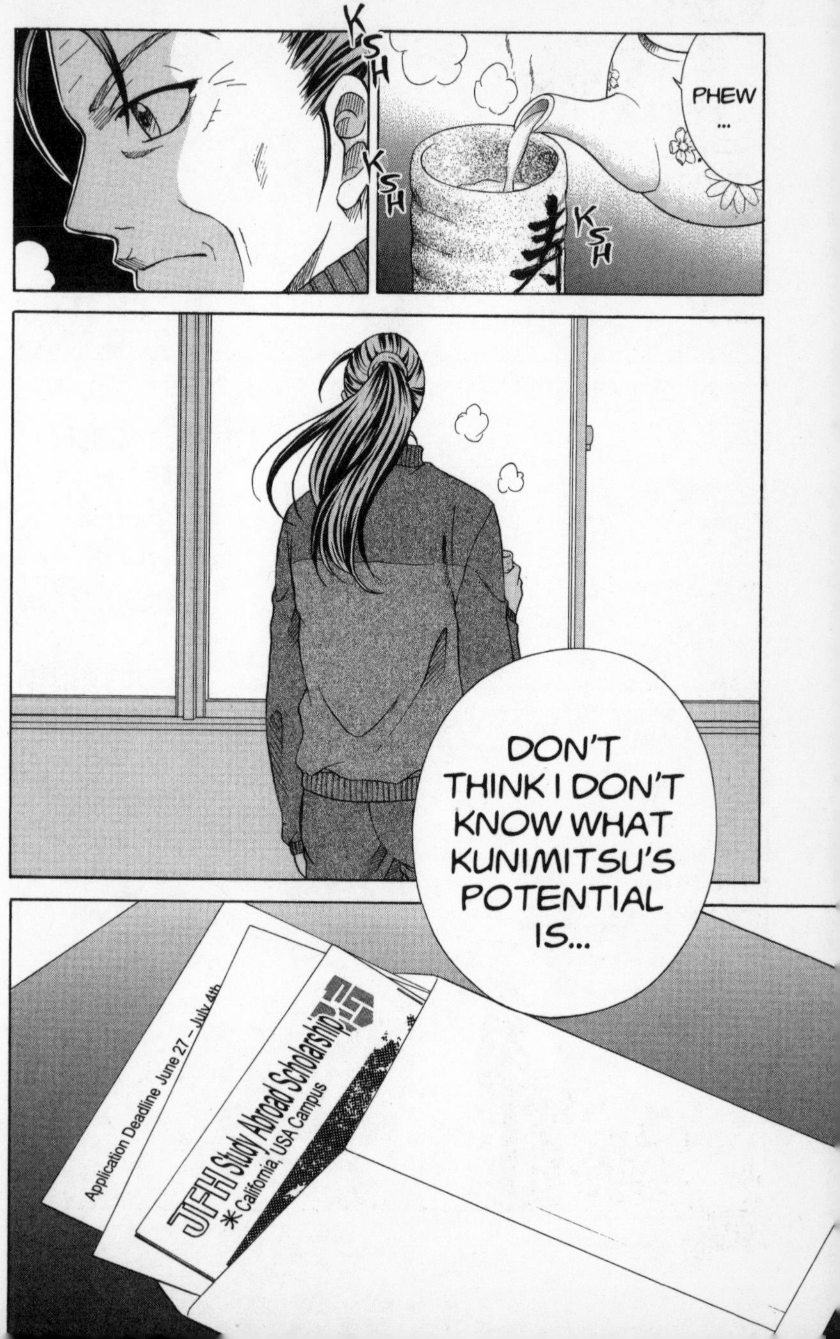
PHEW ...
KSH
KSH
KSH
DON'T THINK I DON'T KNOW WHAT KUNIMITSU'S POTENTIAL IS...
Application Deadline June 27 – July 4th
JFH Study Abroad Scholarship
* California, USA Campus

READ THIS WAY

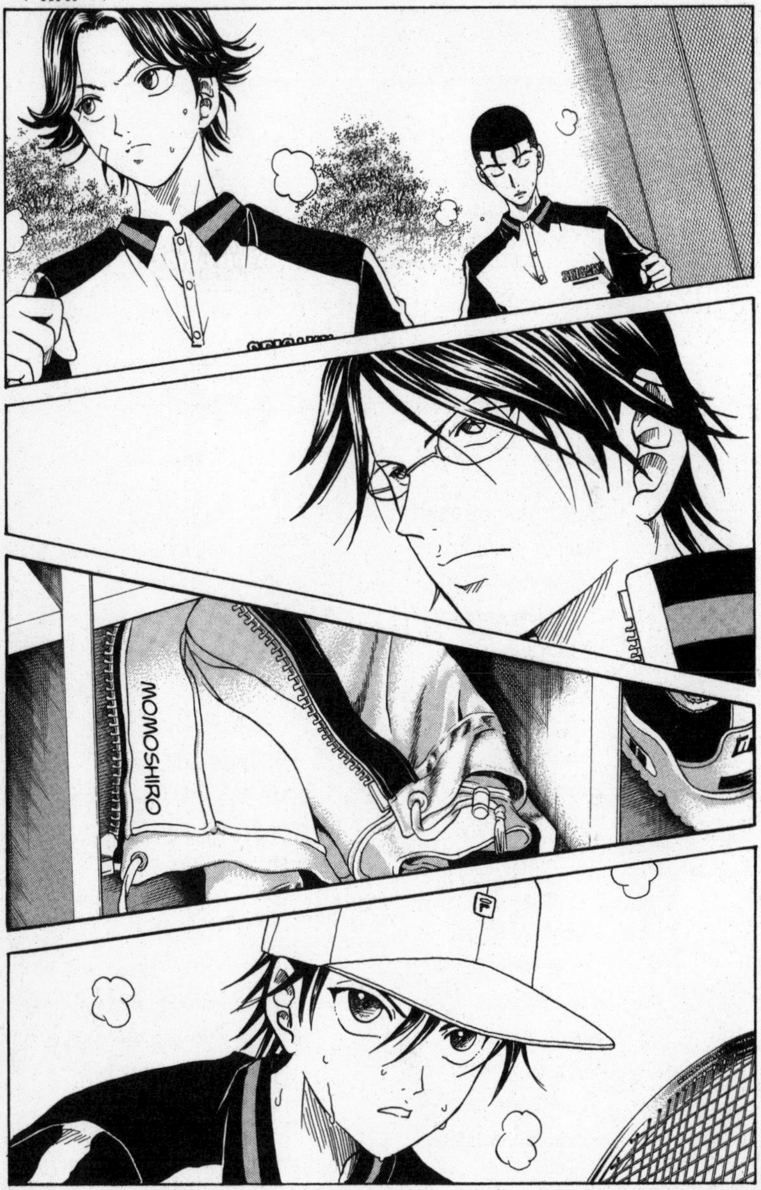
MOMOSHIRO

Attend Class with Captain Tezuka!

9th Grade Class 1 Classmates!!

Thank you for waiting! Once again we received an unbelievable amount of submissions. Those of you who entered must've been waiting eagerly for this announcement... We had to carefully screen all the submissions. Thank you for all the messages and support for Kunimitsu! So these are the people who'll be running 100 laps around the court with Kunimitsu (laugh)!

9th Grade Class 1 Attendance Roster

	(Boys)		(Girls)
1	Atushi Wagatsuma	1	Kayo Aoki
2	Kazuto Iwamuro	2	Madoka Inosaka
3	Kenshiro Kato	3	Mai Ishihara
4	Jun Kanazawa	4	Miyuki Kawamura
5	Akio Kawamura	5	Ryoko Kikuchi
6	Toshihumi Kikuchi	6	Kahori Kishimoto
7	Shu Uetsuki	7	Haruka Uetsuki
8	Jun Sakurai	8	Hazuki Shida
9	Kazuhiro Sugiyama	9	Yuuki Shinomiya
10	Takeshi Takeda	10	Megumi Tani
11	Kaoru Tatsumi	11	Humi Tamura
12	Kunimitsu Tezuka	12	Hitomi Nakajima
13	Wataru Megumi	13	Yumi Hirano
14	Shinji Yamaguchi	14	Sachi Fujita
15	Koji Yoshioka	15	Hatsumi Matsuura
16	Noaya Yoshida	16	Kyoko Matsushima
17	Yuya Yoshida	17	Satomi Yakuwa
18	Yuuki Watanabe	18	Takako Yoshino
19	Yukimoto Watabe		

Total: 37 (Titles omitted from name)

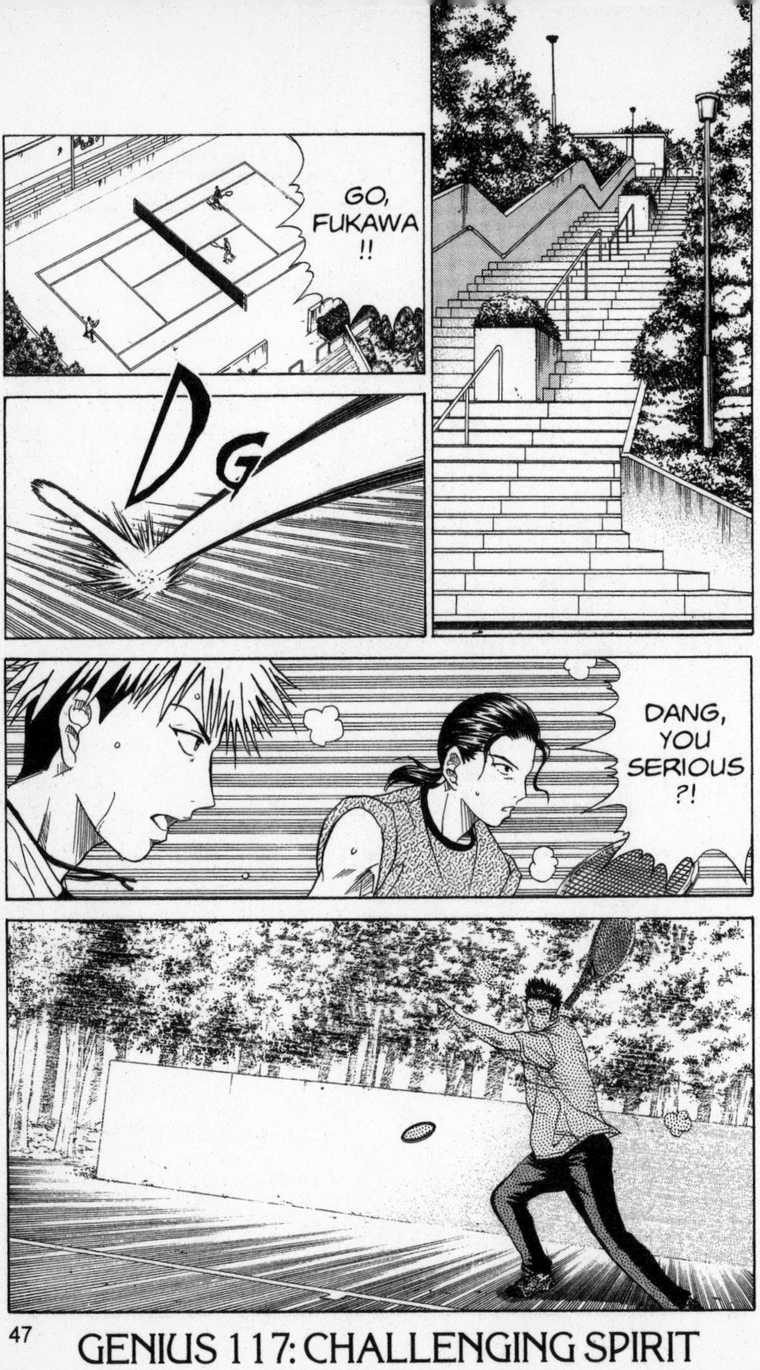
GO, FUKAWA!!
DG
DANG, YOU SERIOUS?!

GENIUS 117: CHALLENGING SPIRIT

GENIUS 117: CHALLENGING SPIRIT

READ THIS WAY

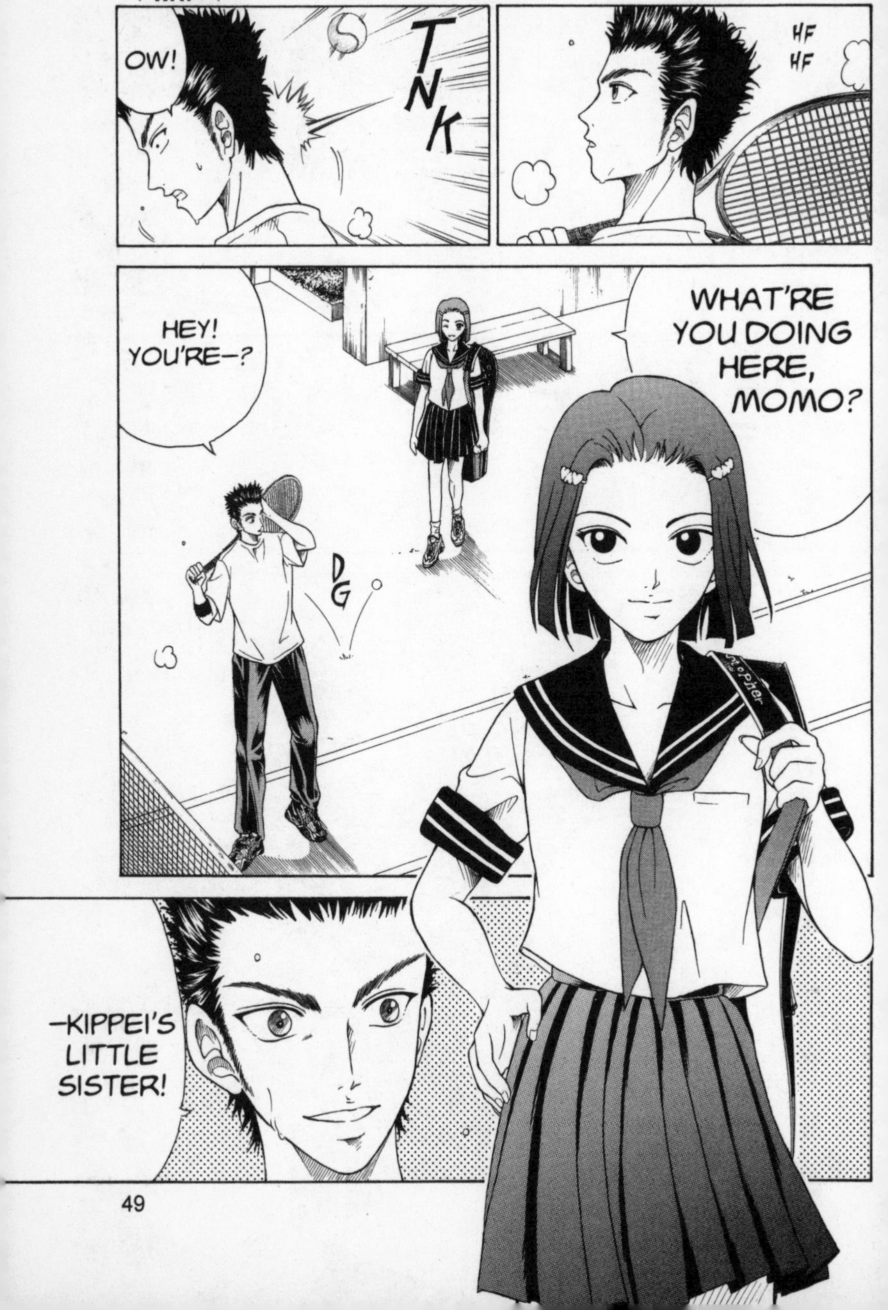
HF
HF
TNK
OW!
WHAT'RE YOU DOING HERE, MOMO?
HEY! YOU'RE--?
DG
-KIPPEI'S LITTLE SISTER!

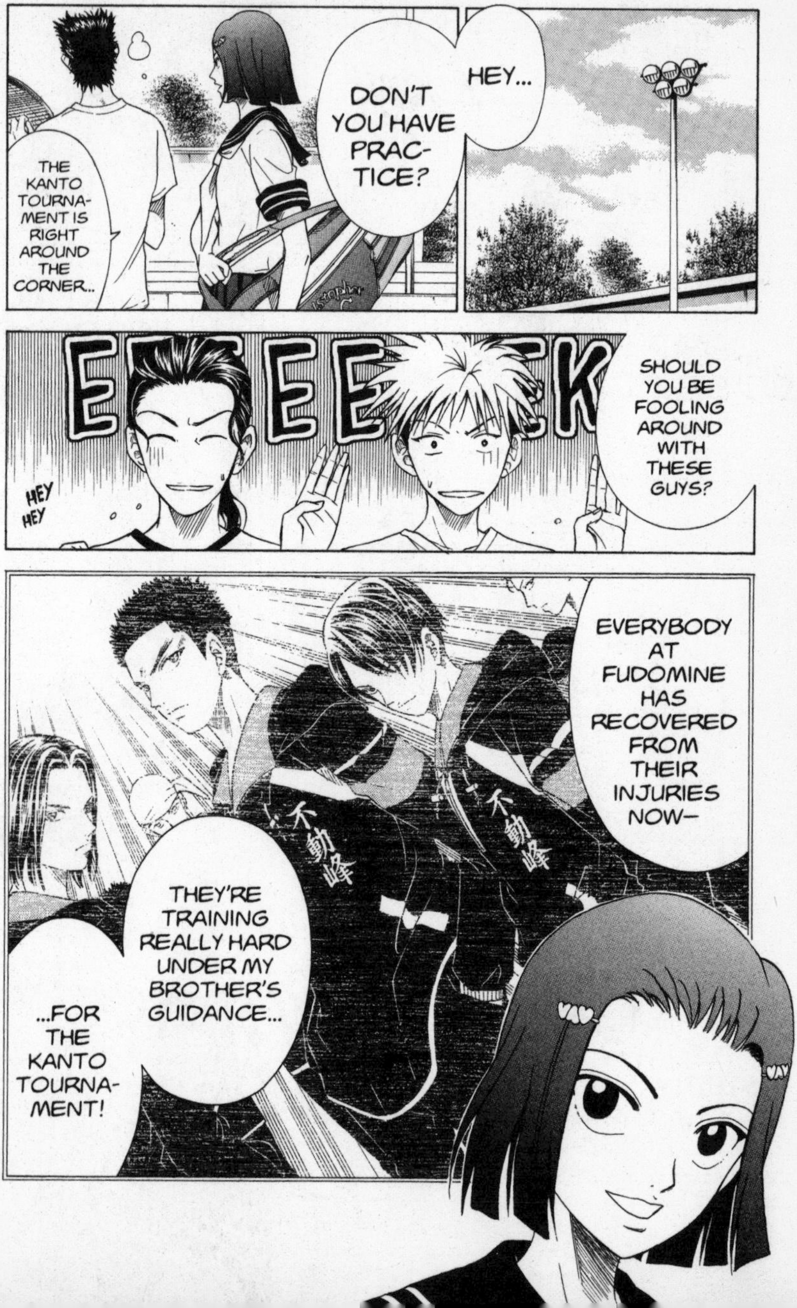
HEY...
DON'T YOU HAVE PRAC-TICE?
THE KANTO TOURNA-MENT IS RIGHT AROUND THE CORNER...
SHOULD YOU BE FOOLING AROUND WITH THESE GUYS?
HEY HEY
EVERYBODY AT FUDOMINE HAS RECOVERED FROM THEIR INJURIES NOW—
不動峰
不動峰
THEY'RE TRAINING REALLY HARD UNDER MY BROTHER'S GUIDANCE...
...FOR THE KANTO TOURNA-MENT!

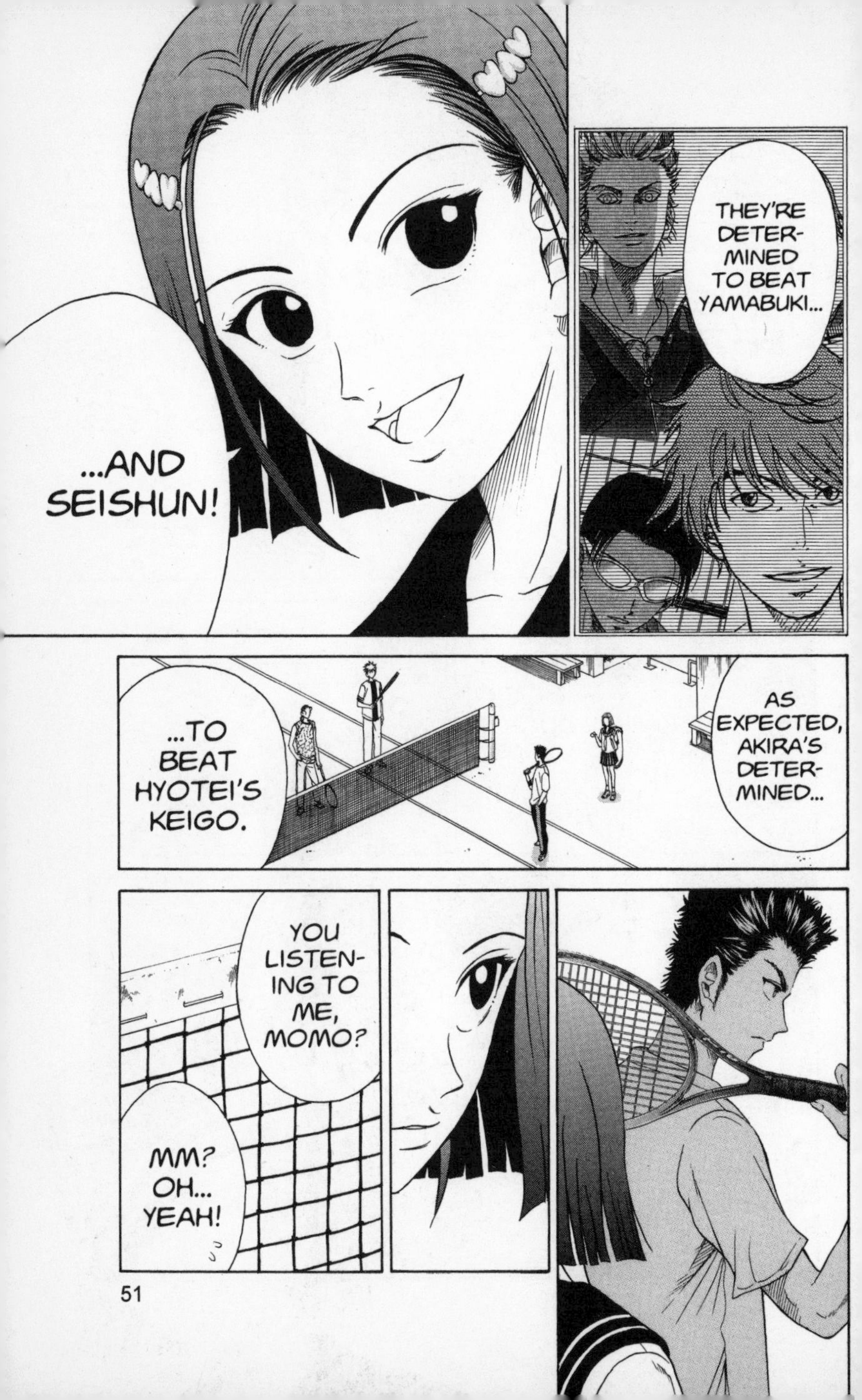
THEY'RE DETERMINED TO BEAT YAMABUKI...
...AND SEISHUN!
AS EXPECTED, AKIRA'S DETERMINED...
...TO BEAT HYOTEI'S KEIGO.
YOU LISTENING TO ME, MOMO?
MM? OH... YEAH!

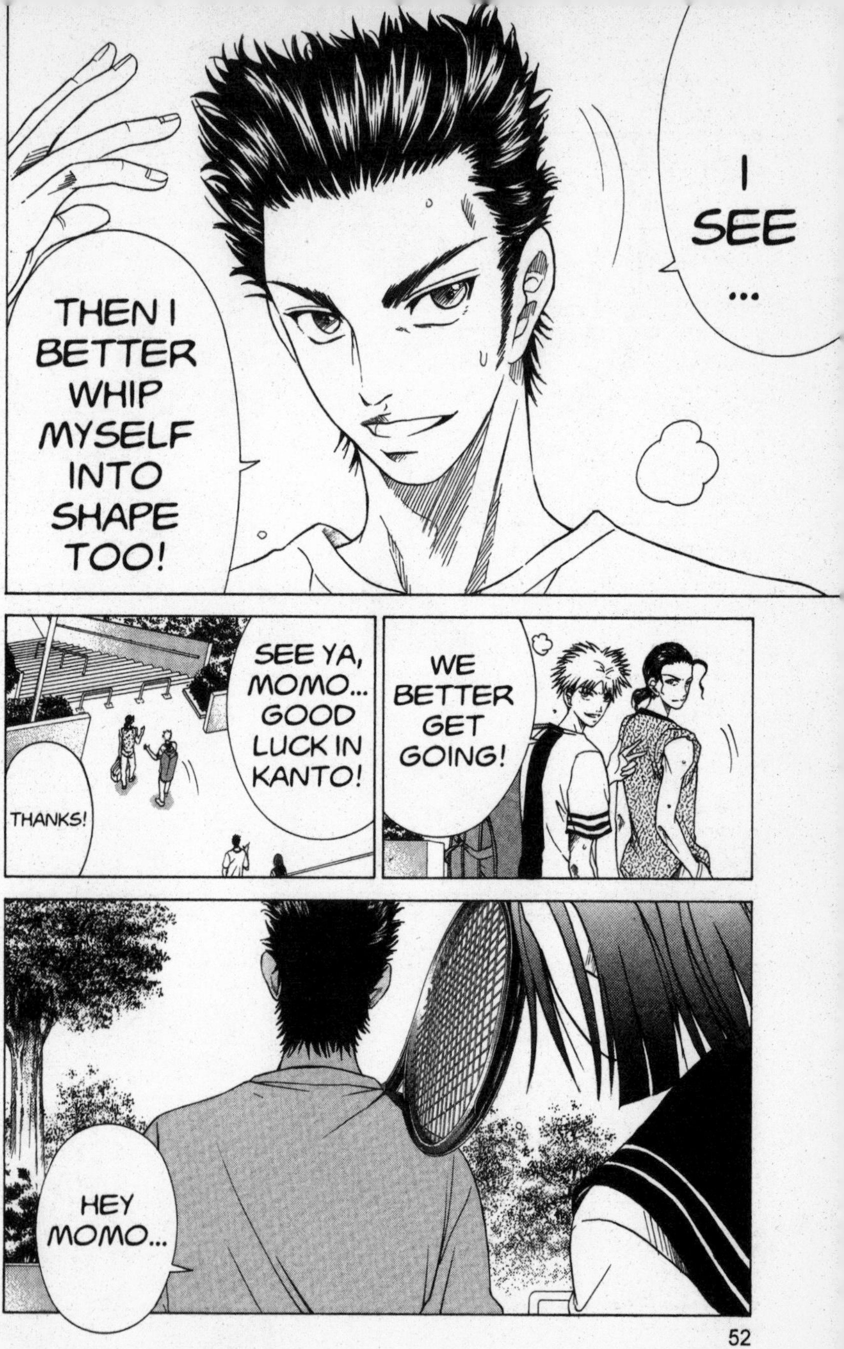
I SEE ...
THEN I BETTER WHIP MYSELF INTO SHAPE TOO!
WE BETTER GET GOING!
SEE YA, MOMO... GOOD LUCK IN KANTO!
THANKS!
HEY MOMO...

READ THIS WAY

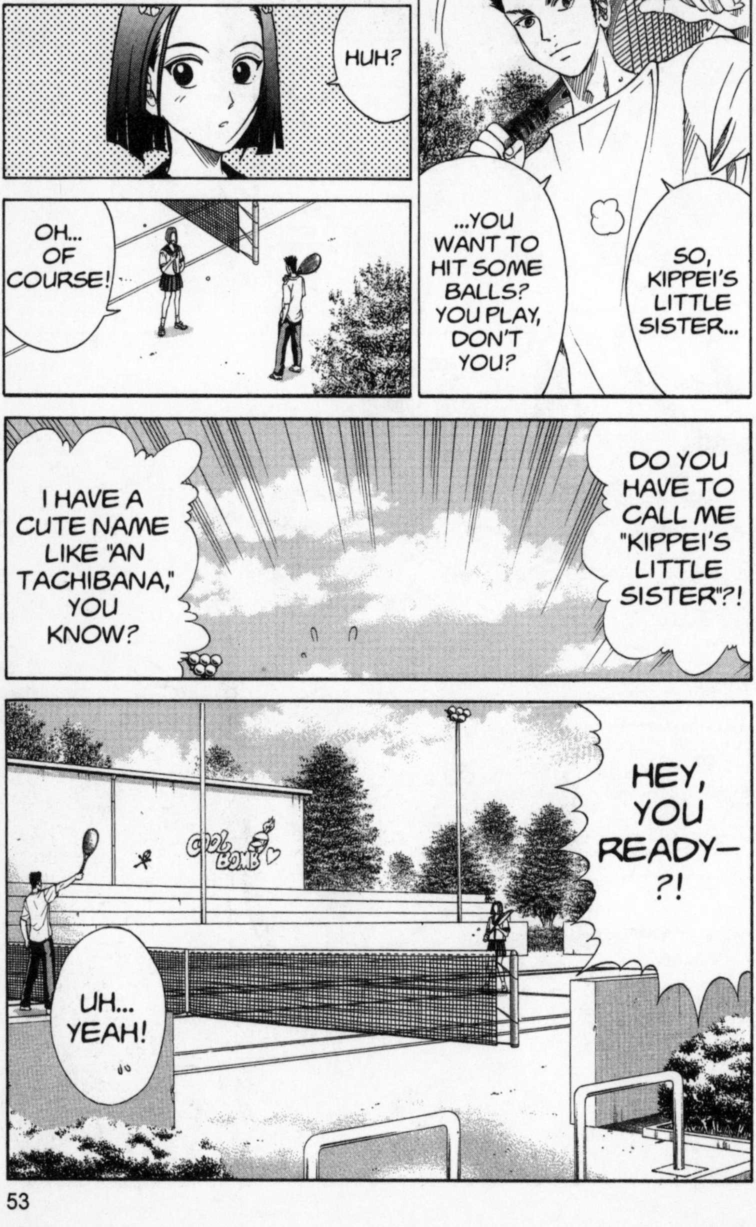
SO, KIPPEI'S LITTLE SISTER...
...YOU WANT TO HIT SOME BALLS? YOU PLAY, DON'T YOU?
HUH?
OH... OF COURSE!
DO YOU HAVE TO CALL ME "KIPPEI'S LITTLE SISTER"?!
I HAVE A CUTE NAME LIKE "AN TACHIBANA," YOU KNOW?
HEY, YOU READY—?!
COOL BOMB
UH... YEAH!

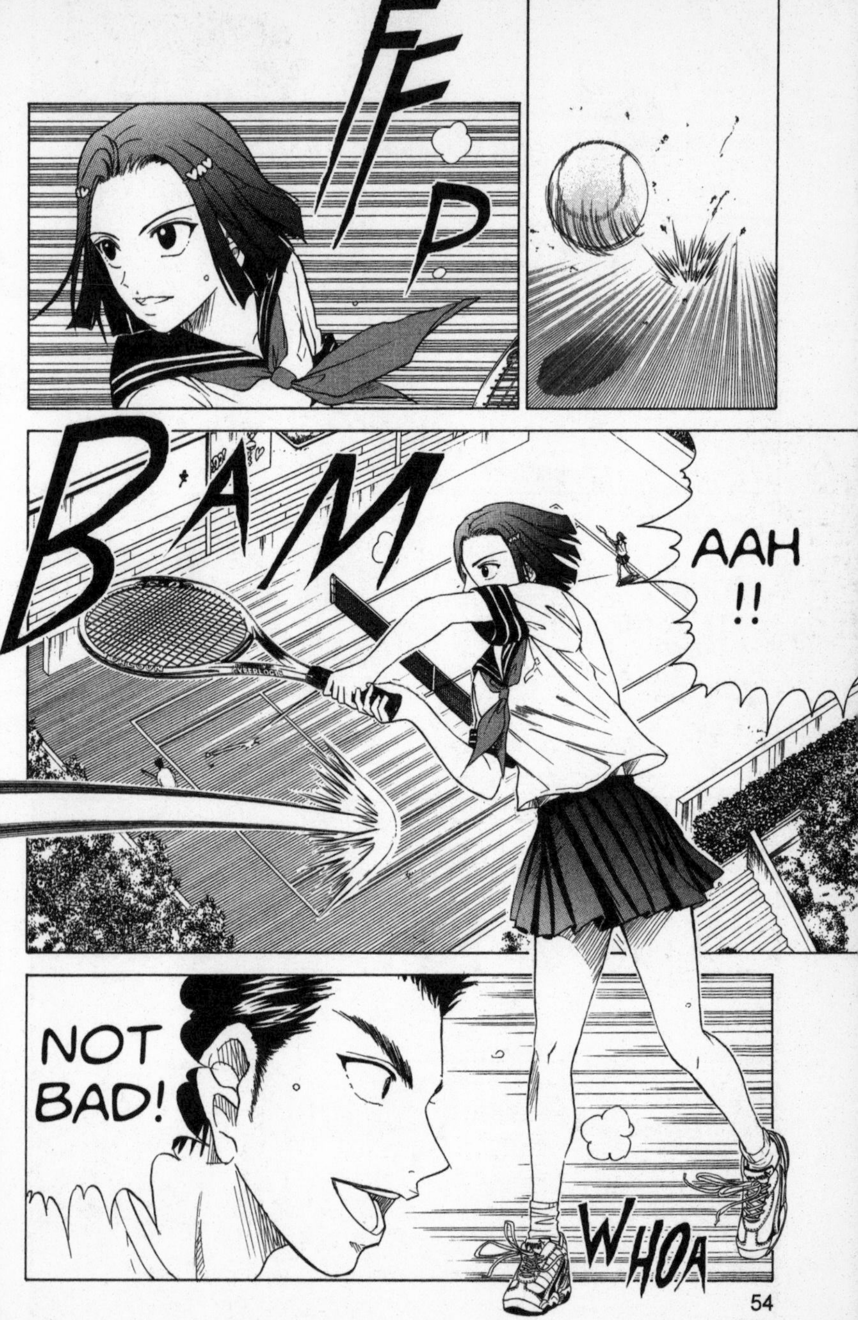
FFP
BAM
AAH !!
NOT BAD!
WHOA

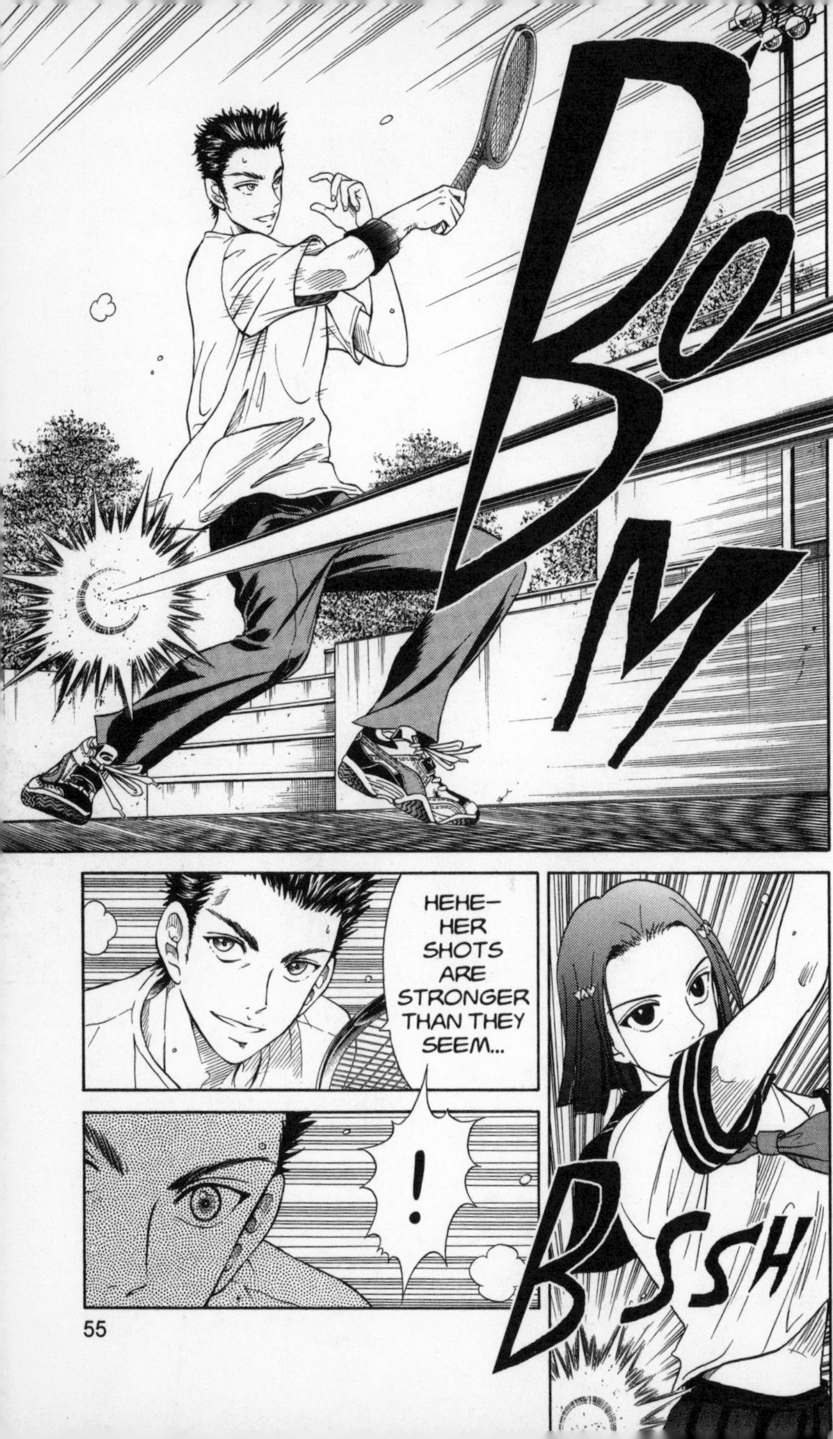
BSSH
HEHE-HER SHOTS ARE STRONGER THAN THEY SEEM...
!

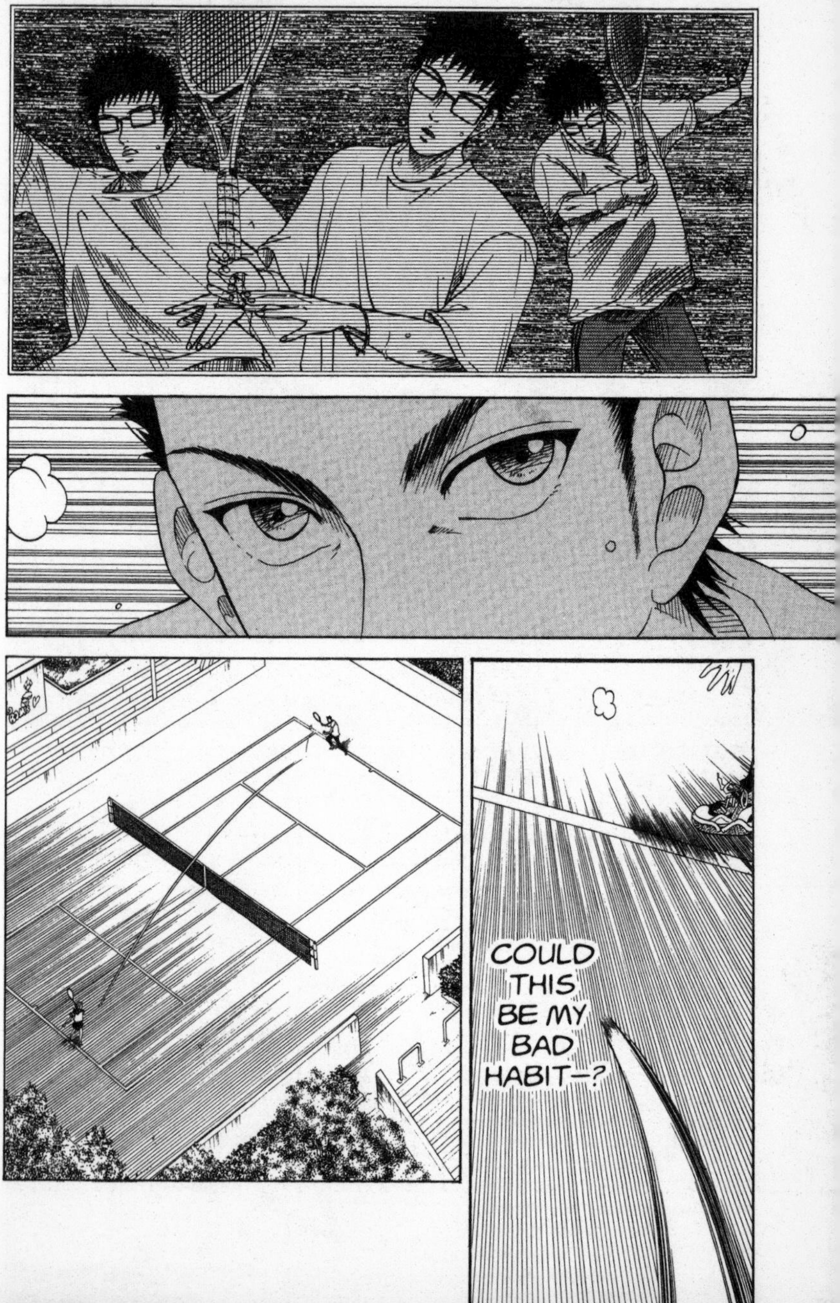
COULD THIS BE MY BAD HABIT--?

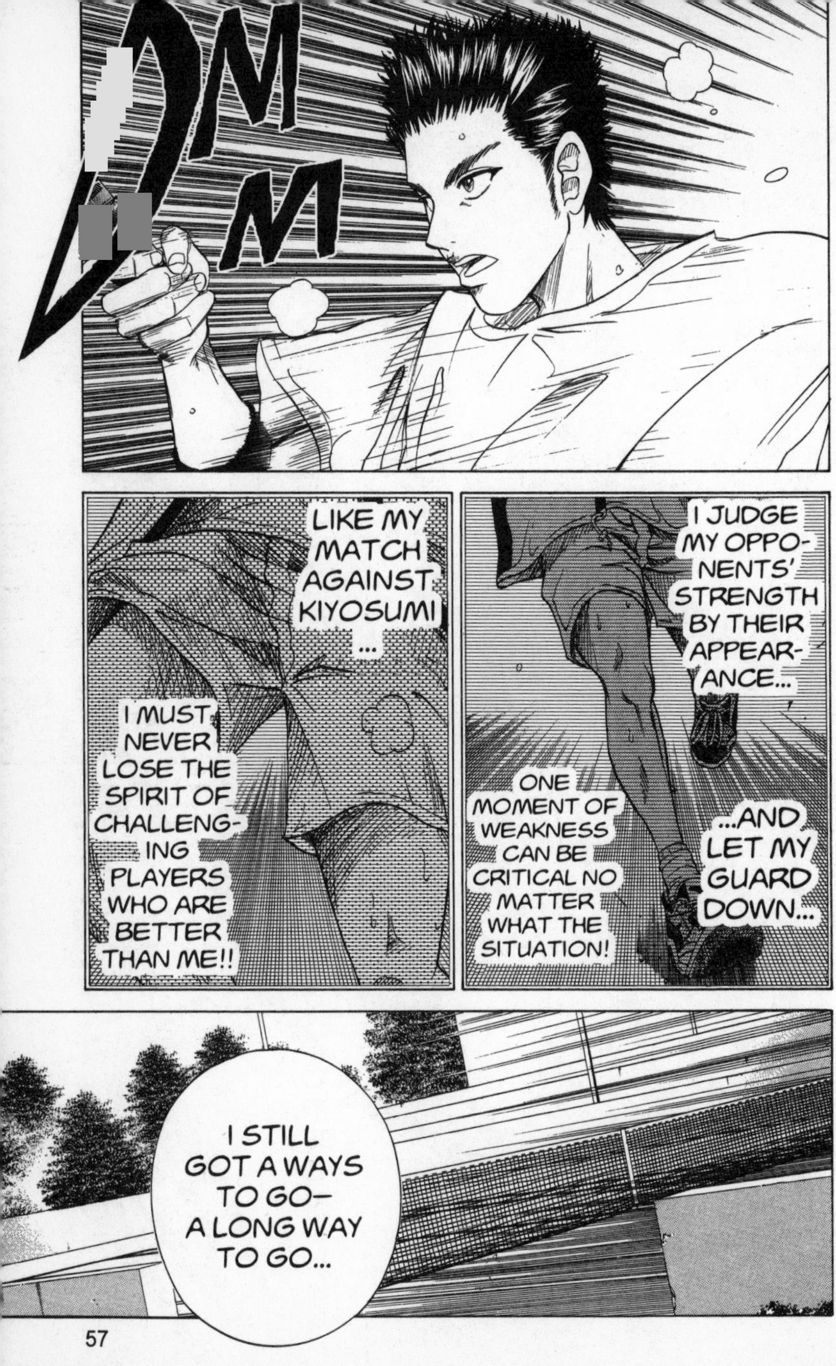
I JUDGE MY OPPONENTS' STRENGTH BY THEIR APPEARANCE...
...AND LET MY GUARD DOWN...
ONE MOMENT OF WEAKNESS CAN BE CRITICAL NO MATTER WHAT THE SITUATION!
LIKE MY MATCH AGAINST KIYOSUMI...
I MUST NEVER LOSE THE SPIRIT OF CHALLENGING PLAYERS WHO ARE BETTER THAN ME!!
I STILL GOT A WAYS TO GO— A LONG WAY TO GO...

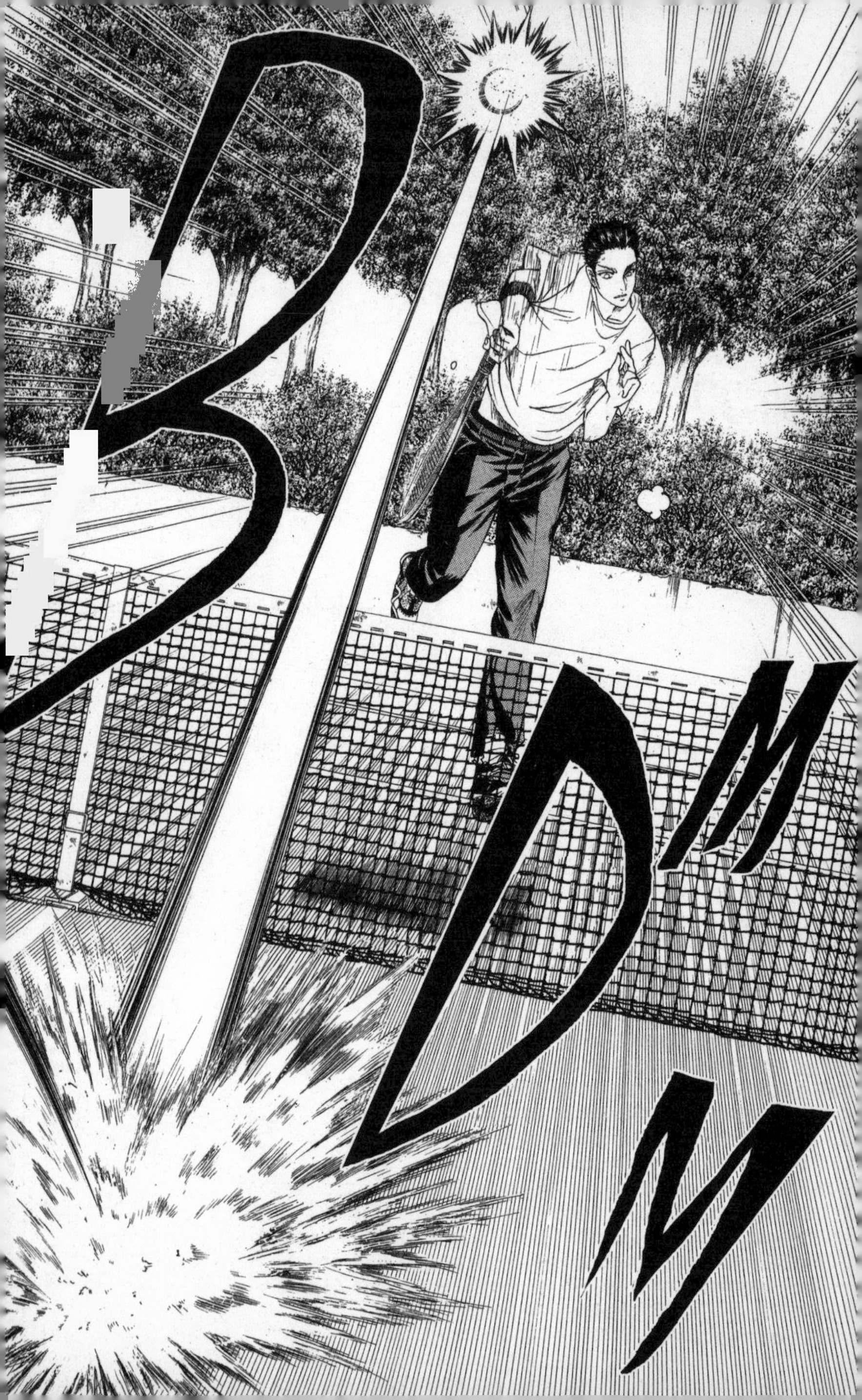

READ THIS WAY

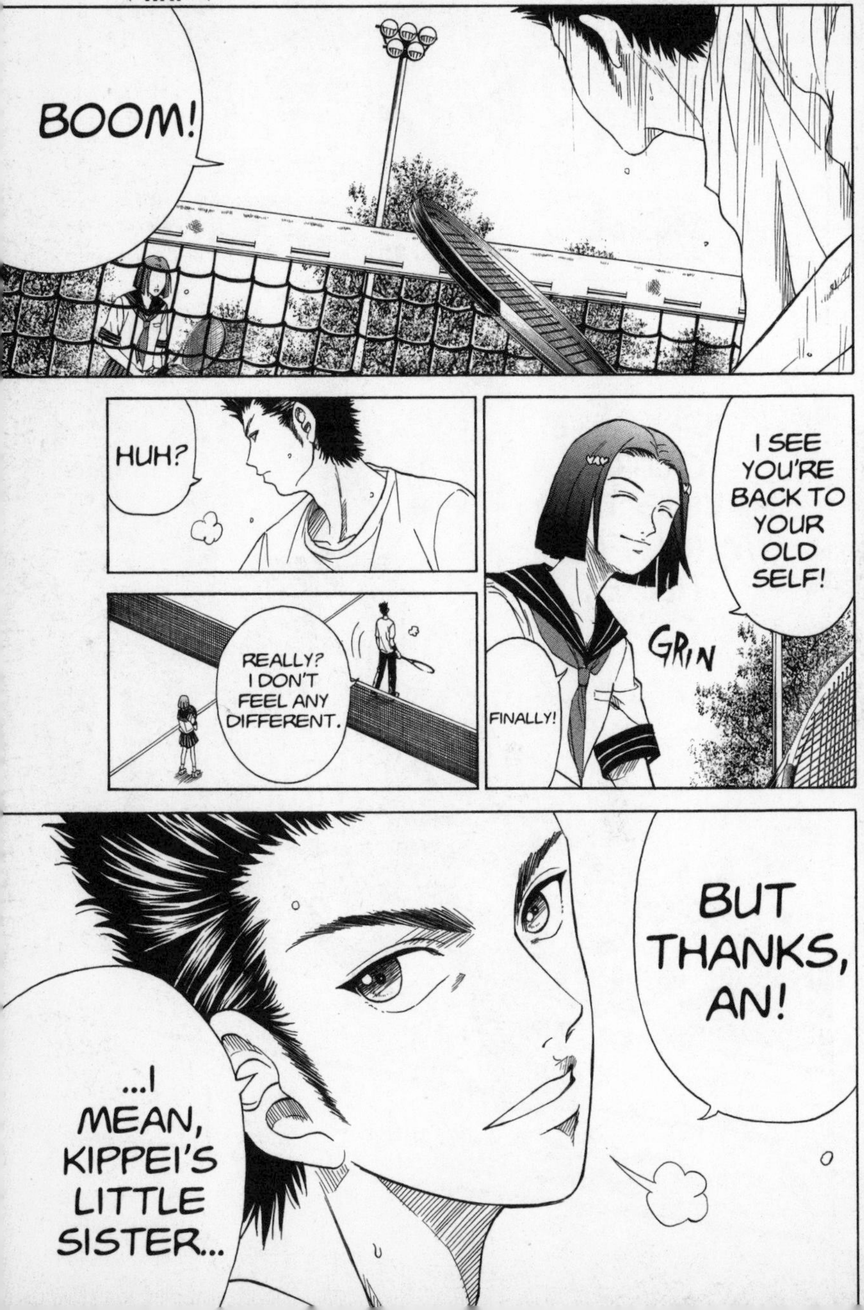
BOOM!
I SEE YOU'RE BACK TO YOUR OLD SELF!
GRIN
FINALLY!
HUH?
REALLY? I DON'T FEEL ANY DIFFERENT.
BUT THANKS, AN!
...I MEAN, KIPPEI'S LITTLE SISTER...

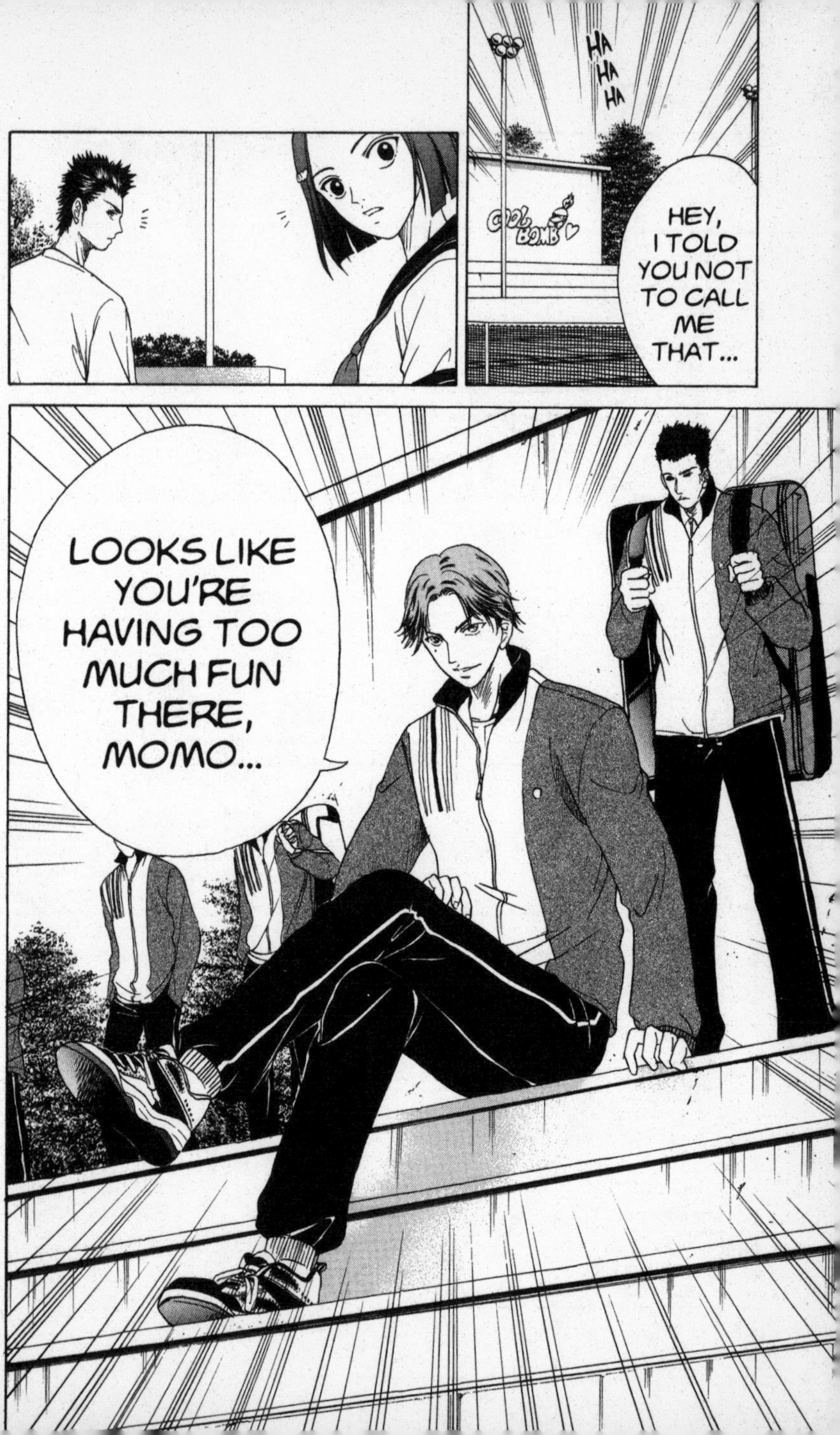
HA HA HA
HEY, I TOLD YOU NOT TO CALL ME THAT...
COOL BOMB
LOOKS LIKE YOU'RE HAVING TOO MUCH FUN THERE, MOMO...

READ THIS WAY

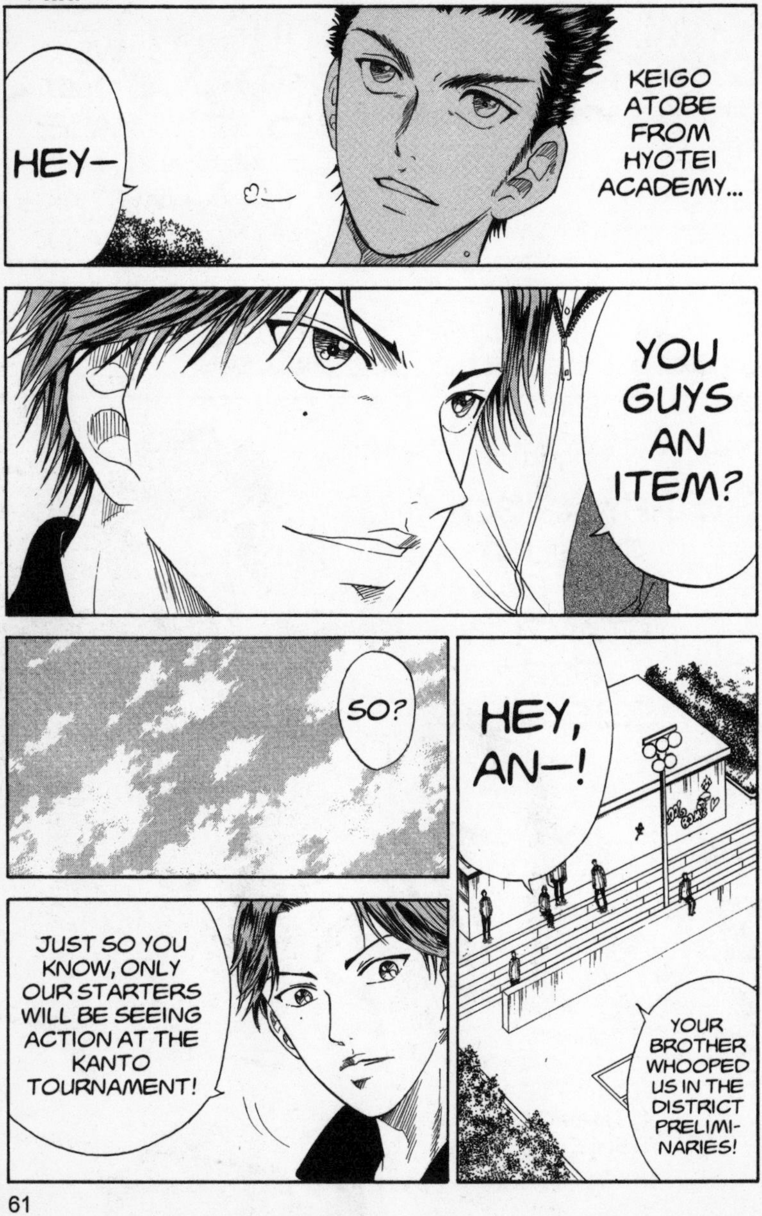
KEIGO ATOBE FROM HYOTEI ACADEMY...
HEY—
YOU GUYS AN ITEM?
HEY, AN—!
YOUR BROTHER WHOOPED US IN THE DISTRICT PRELIMI-NARIES!
SO?
JUST SO YOU KNOW, ONLY OUR STARTERS WILL BE SEEING ACTION AT THE KANTO TOURNAMENT!

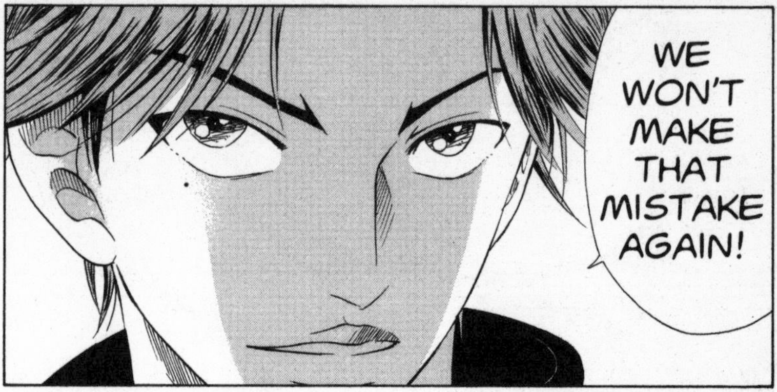
WE WON'T MAKE THAT MISTAKE AGAIN!

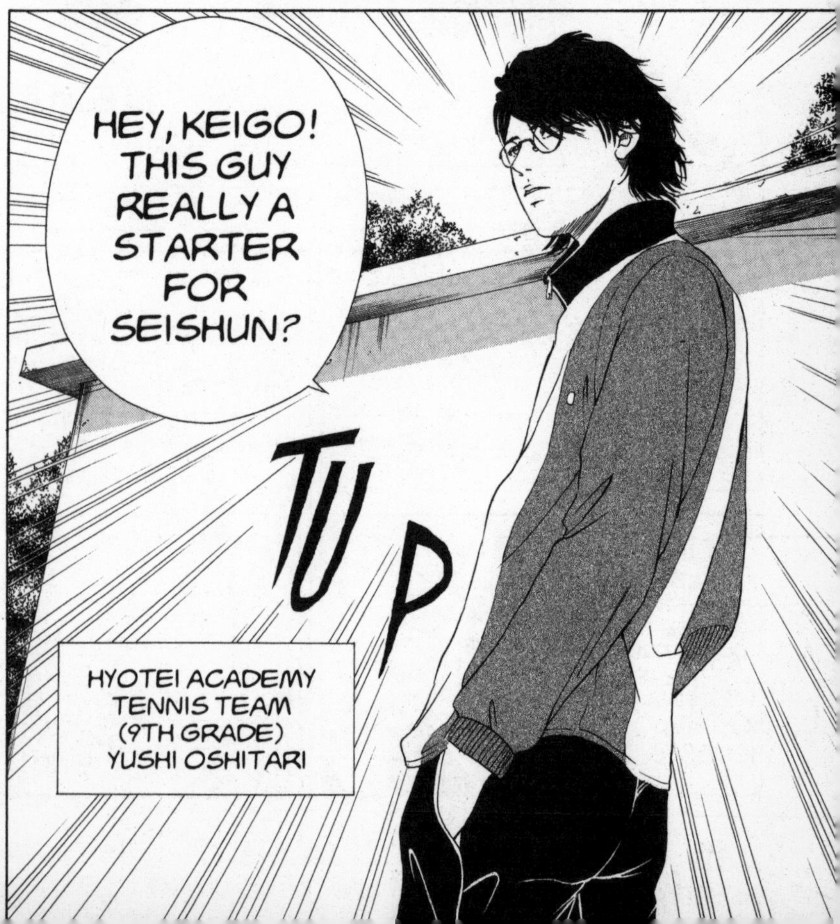
HEY, KEIGO! THIS GUY REALLY A STARTER FOR SEISHUN?
TUP
HYOTEI ACADEMY TENNIS TEAM (9TH GRADE) YUSHI OSHITARI

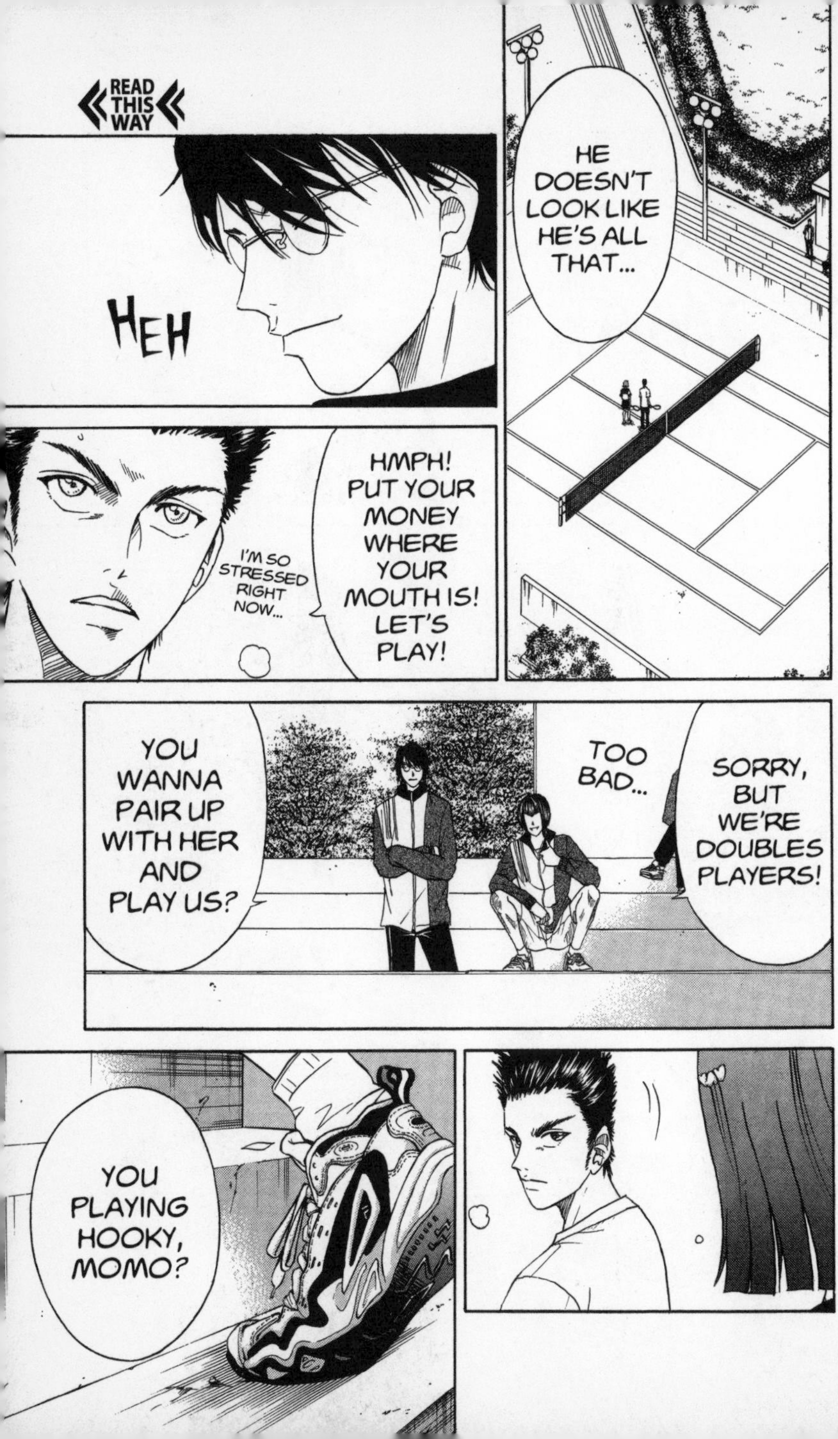
READ THIS WAY
HE DOESN'T LOOK LIKE HE'S ALL THAT...
HEH
HMPH! PUT YOUR MONEY WHERE YOUR MOUTH IS! LET'S PLAY!
I'M SO STRESSED RIGHT NOW...
SORRY, BUT WE'RE DOUBLES PLAYERS!
TOO BAD...
YOU WANNA PAIR UP WITH HER AND PLAY US?
YOU PLAYING HOOKY, MOMO?

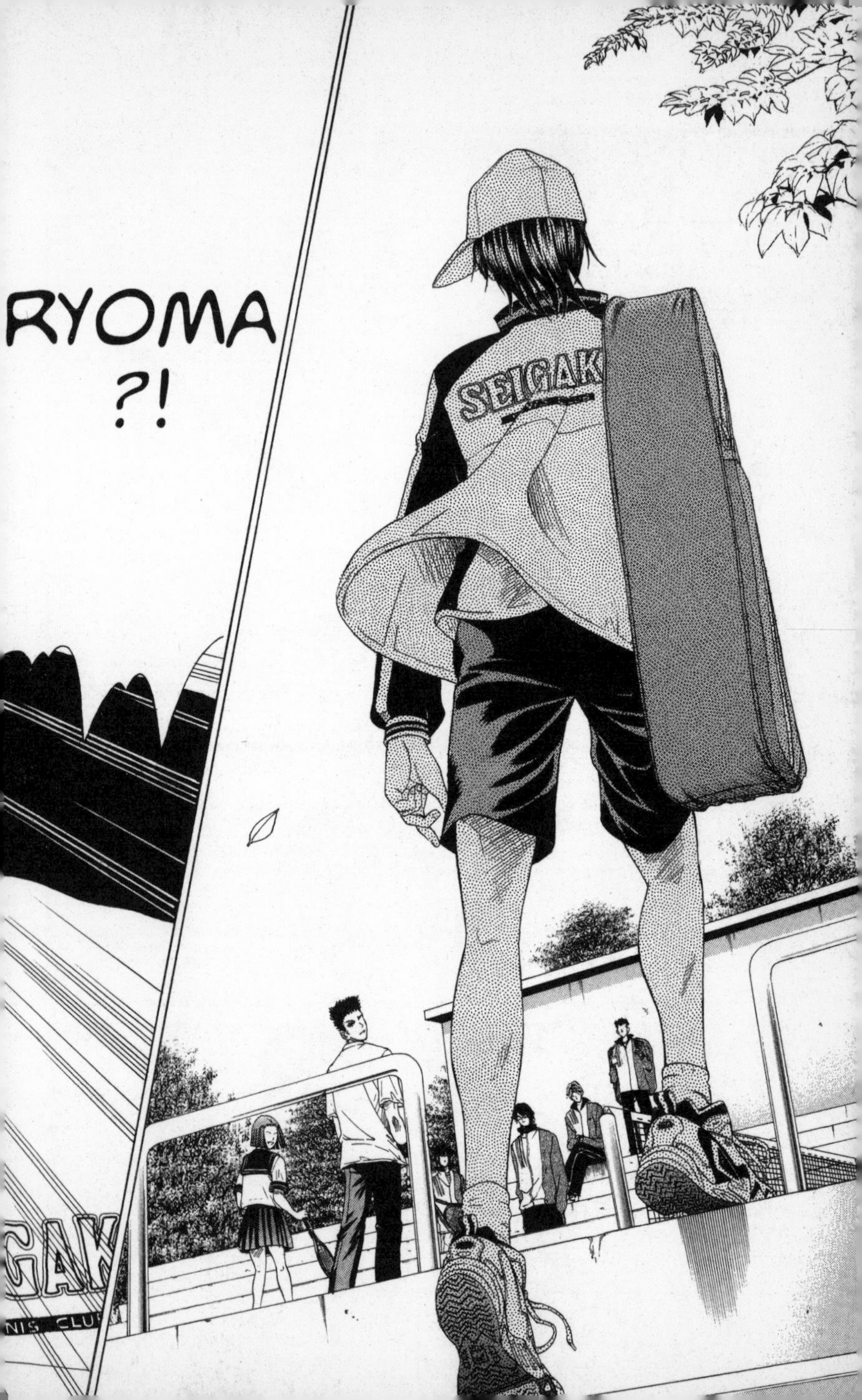
RYOMA ?!
SEIGAKU
GAK
NIS CLU

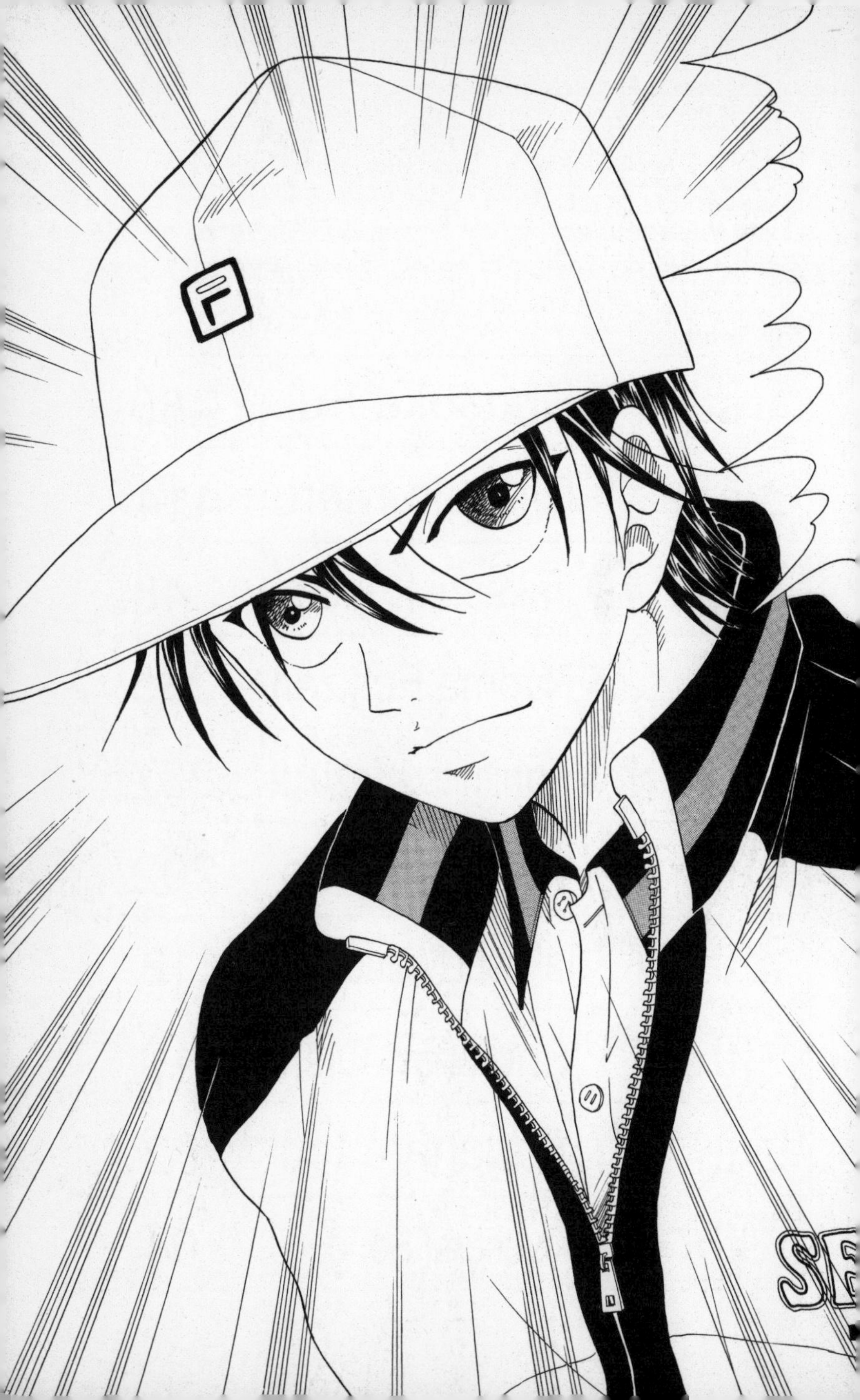

2002 Valentine's Day Chocolate Tally (1)

I was shocked!! For the first time in JUMP history, fans sent 68 boxes of chocolates to my workplace! Usually it's three to four boxes, tops. Thank you so much!

Top Ten!!			Total: 2827
1st		Shusuke Fuji	480
2nd		Eiji Kikumaru	414
3rd		Takeshi Konomi	348
4th		Ryoma Echizen	285
5th		Kunimitsu Tezuka	237
6th		Kaoru Kaido	202
7th		Takeshi Momoshiro	118
8th		Shuichiro Oishi	119
9th		Sadaharu Inui	82
10th		Kiyosumi Sengoku	64

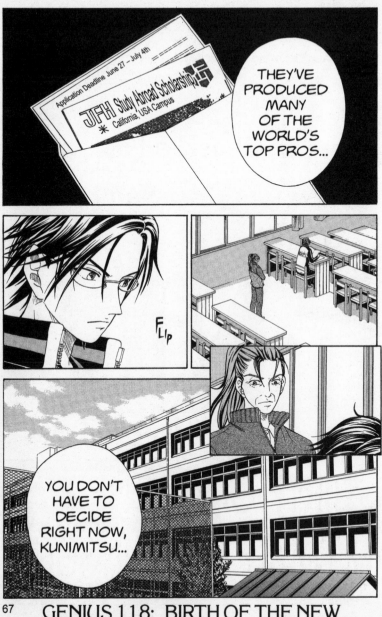

Application Deadline June 27 – July 4th
JFH Study Abroad Scholarship
California, USA Campus
THEY'VE PRODUCED MANY OF THE WORLD'S TOP PROS...
FLIP
YOU DON'T HAVE TO DECIDE RIGHT NOW, KUNIMITSU...

GENIUS 118: BIRTH OF THE NEW ULTIMATE SEISHUN SQUAD

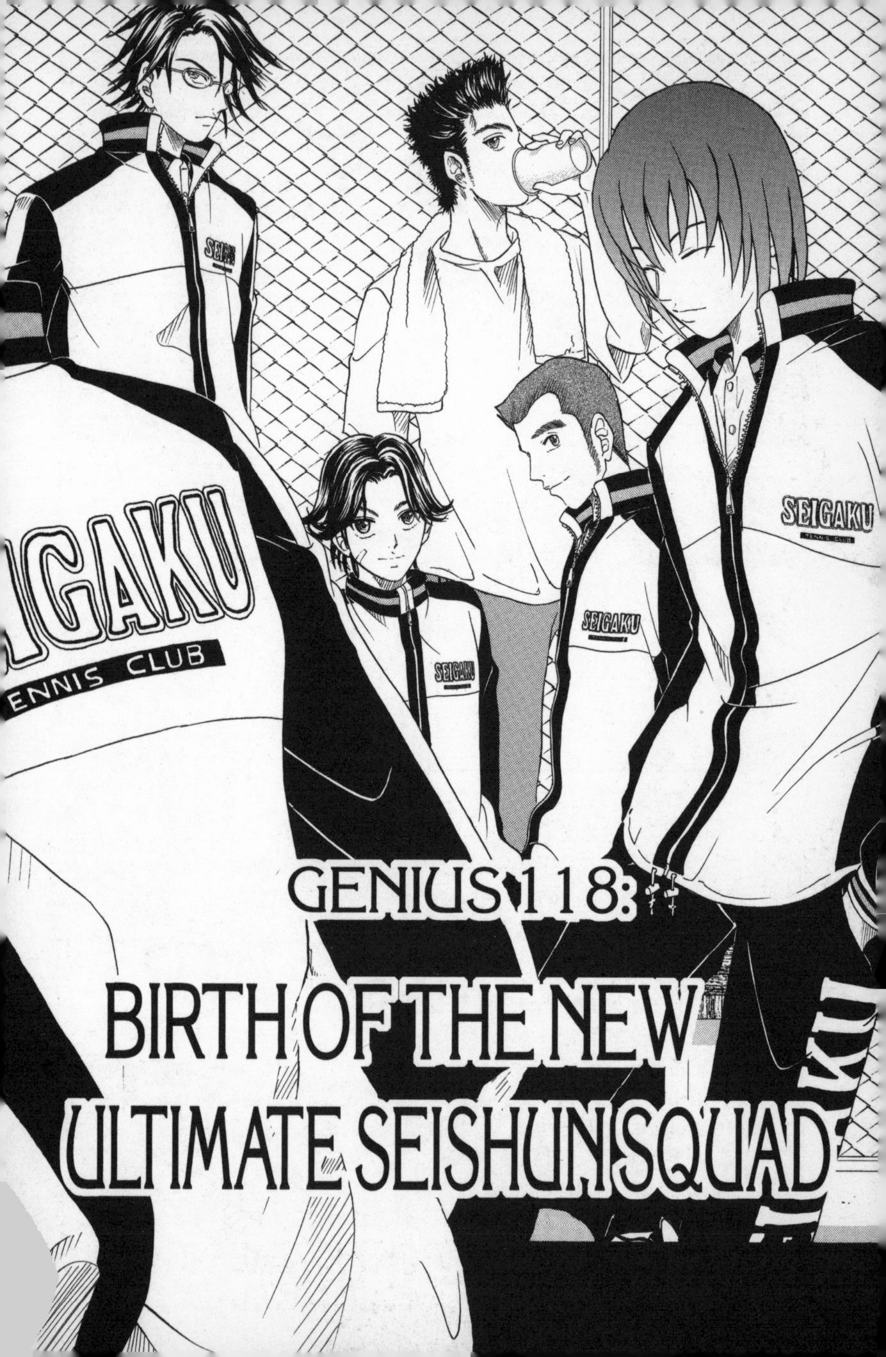
SEIGAKU
IGAKU
ENNIS CLUB
SEIGAKU
SEIGAKU
SEIGAKU
TENNIS CLUB

GENIUS 118: BIRTH OF THE NEW ULTIMATE SEISHUN SQUAD

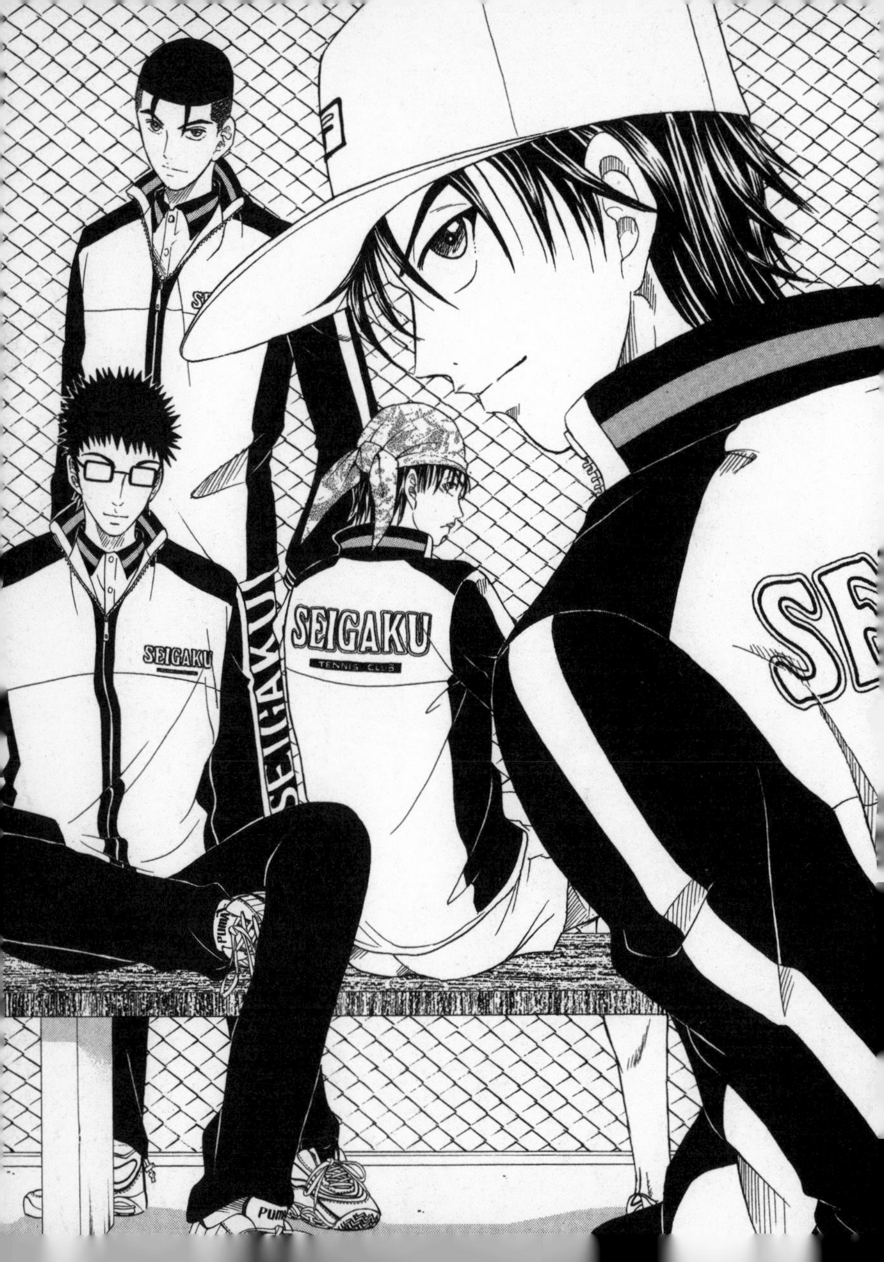
SEIGAKU
SEIGAKU
TENNIS CLUB
SEIGAKU
PUMA
PUMA

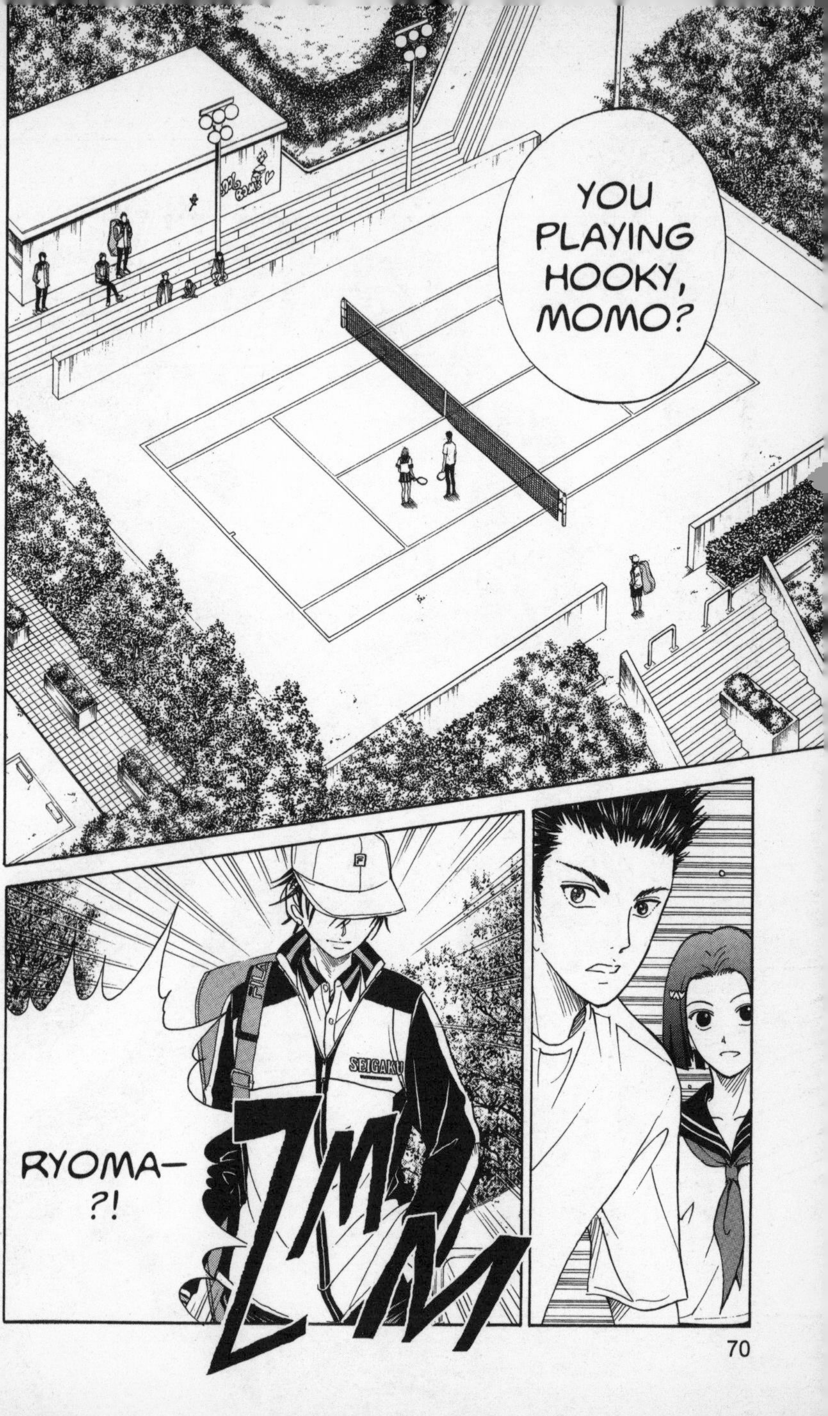
YOU PLAYING HOOKY, MOMO?
RYOMA-?!
ZM ZM

READ THIS WAY

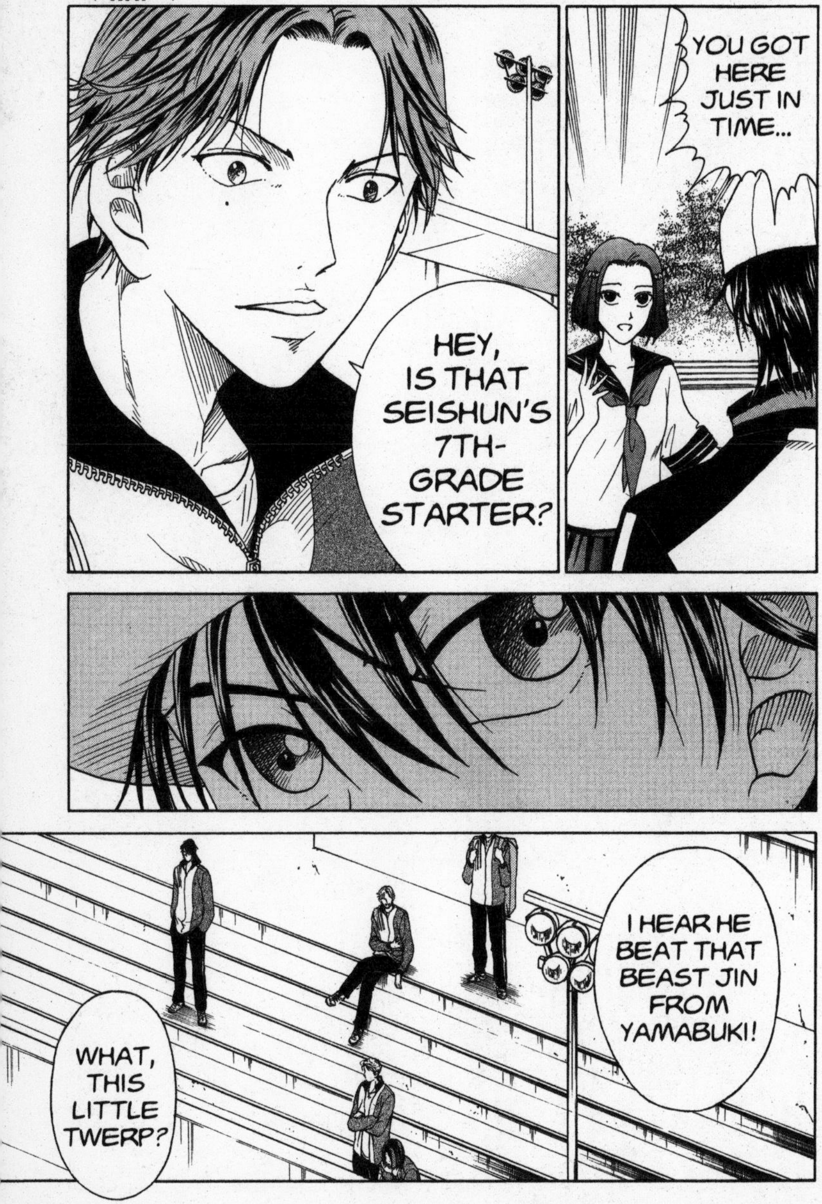
YOU GOT HERE JUST IN TIME...
HEY, IS THAT SEISHUN'S 7TH-GRADE STARTER?
I HEAR HE BEAT THAT BEAST JIN FROM YAMABUKI!
WHAT, THIS LITTLE TWERP?

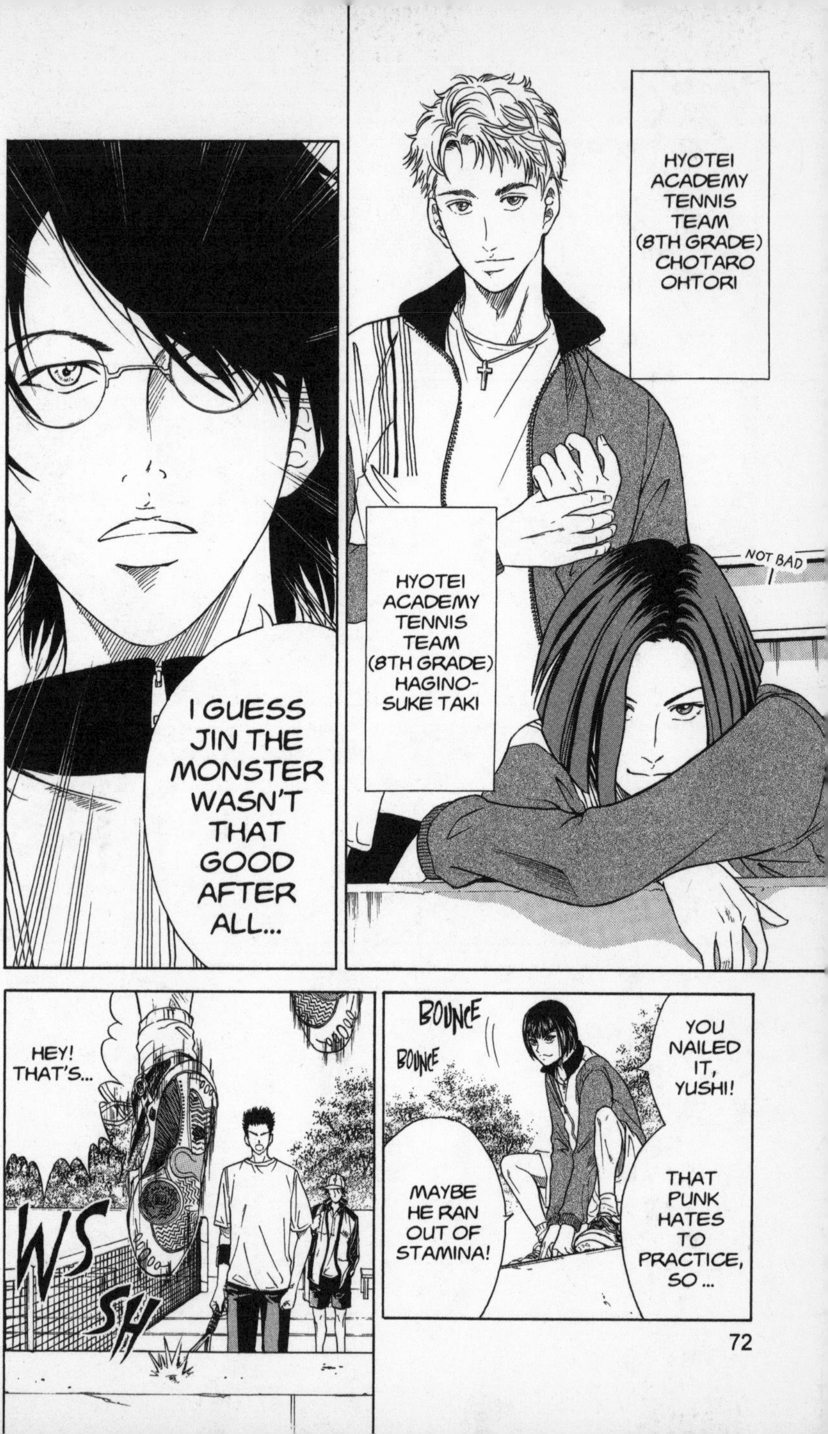
HYOTEI ACADEMY TENNIS TEAM (8TH GRADE) CHOTARO OHTORI
NOT BAD
HYOTEI ACADEMY TENNIS TEAM (8TH GRADE) HAGINO-SUKE TAKI
I GUESS JIN THE MONSTER WASN'T THAT GOOD AFTER ALL...
BOUNCE
BOUNCE
YOU NAILED IT, YUSHI!
THAT PUNK HATES TO PRACTICE, SO ...
MAYBE HE RAN OUT OF STAMINA!
HEY! THAT'S...
WSSH

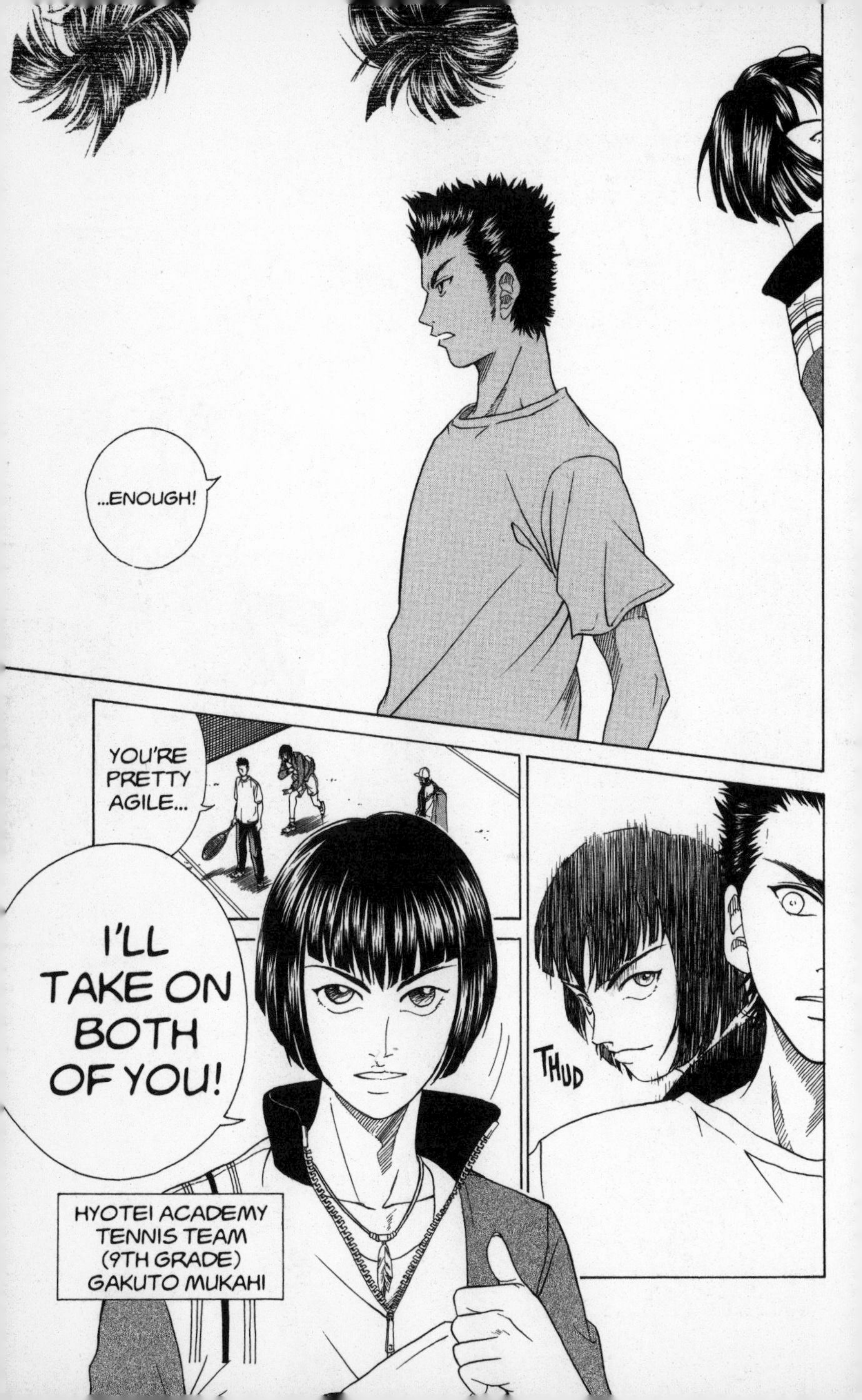
...ENOUGH!
THUD
YOU'RE PRETTY AGILE...
I'LL TAKE ON BOTH OF YOU!
HYOTEI ACADEMY TENNIS TEAM (9TH GRADE) GAKUTO MUKAHI

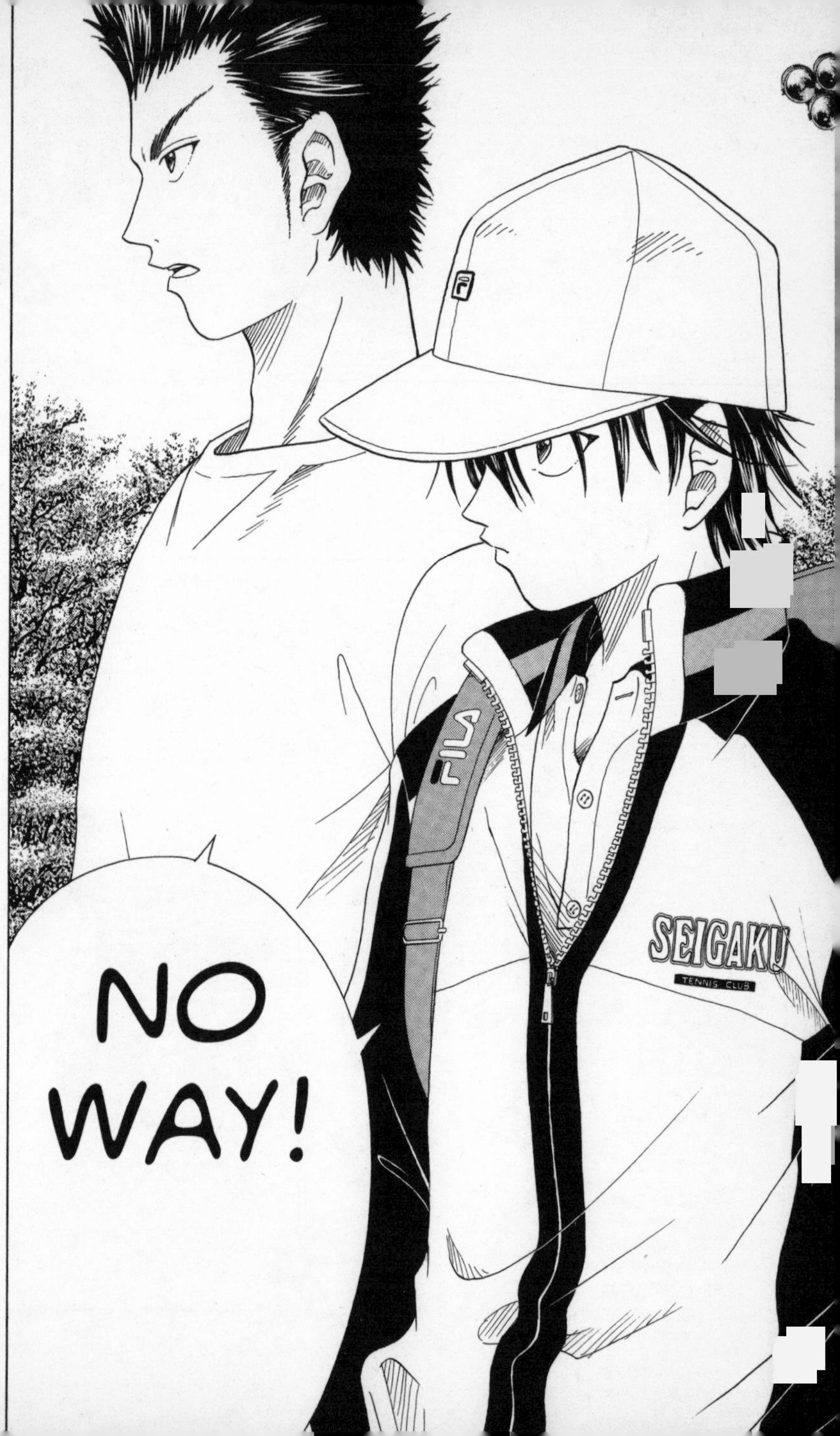
NO WAY!
SEIGAKU
TENNIS CLUB

READ THIS WAY

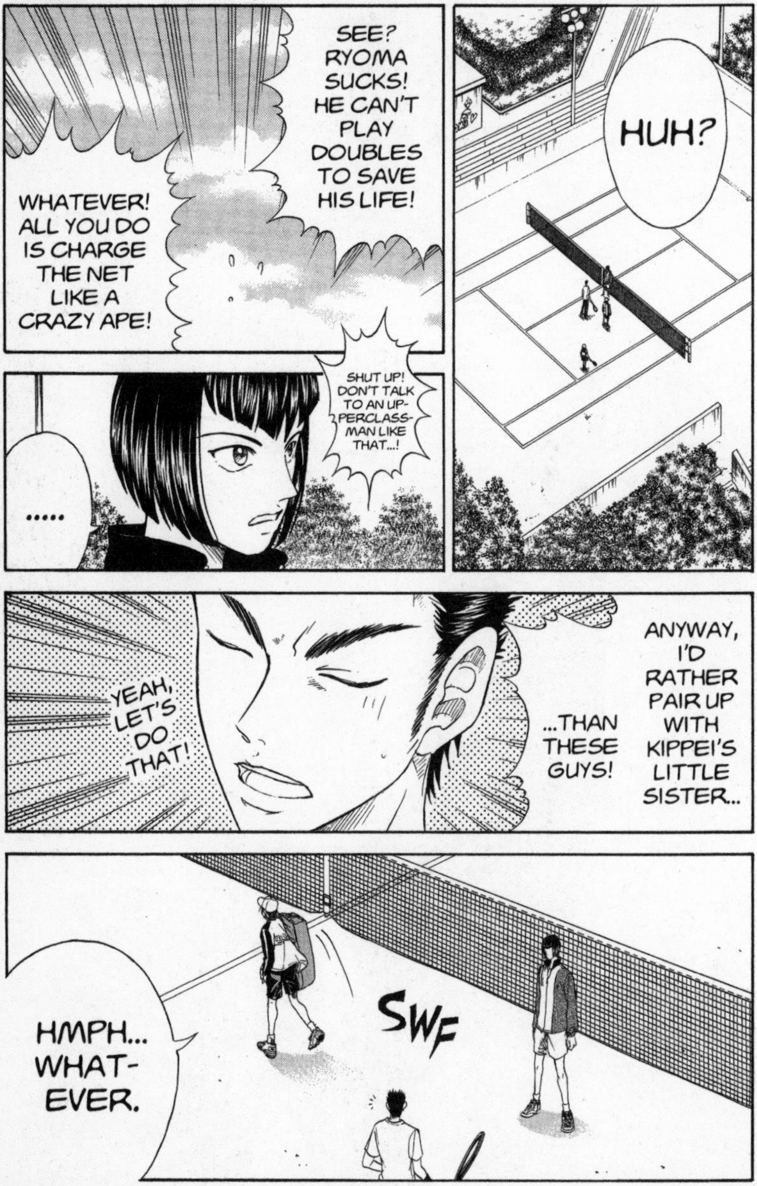
HUH?
SEE? RYOMA SUCKS! HE CAN'T PLAY DOUBLES TO SAVE HIS LIFE!
WHATEVER! ALL YOU DO IS CHARGE THE NET LIKE A CRAZY APE!
SHUT UP! DON'T TALK TO AN UPPERCLASSMAN LIKE THAT...!
.....
ANYWAY, I'D RATHER PAIR UP WITH KIPPEI'S LITTLE SISTER...
...THAN THESE GUYS!
YEAH, LET'S DO THAT!
SWF
HMPH... WHAT-EVER.

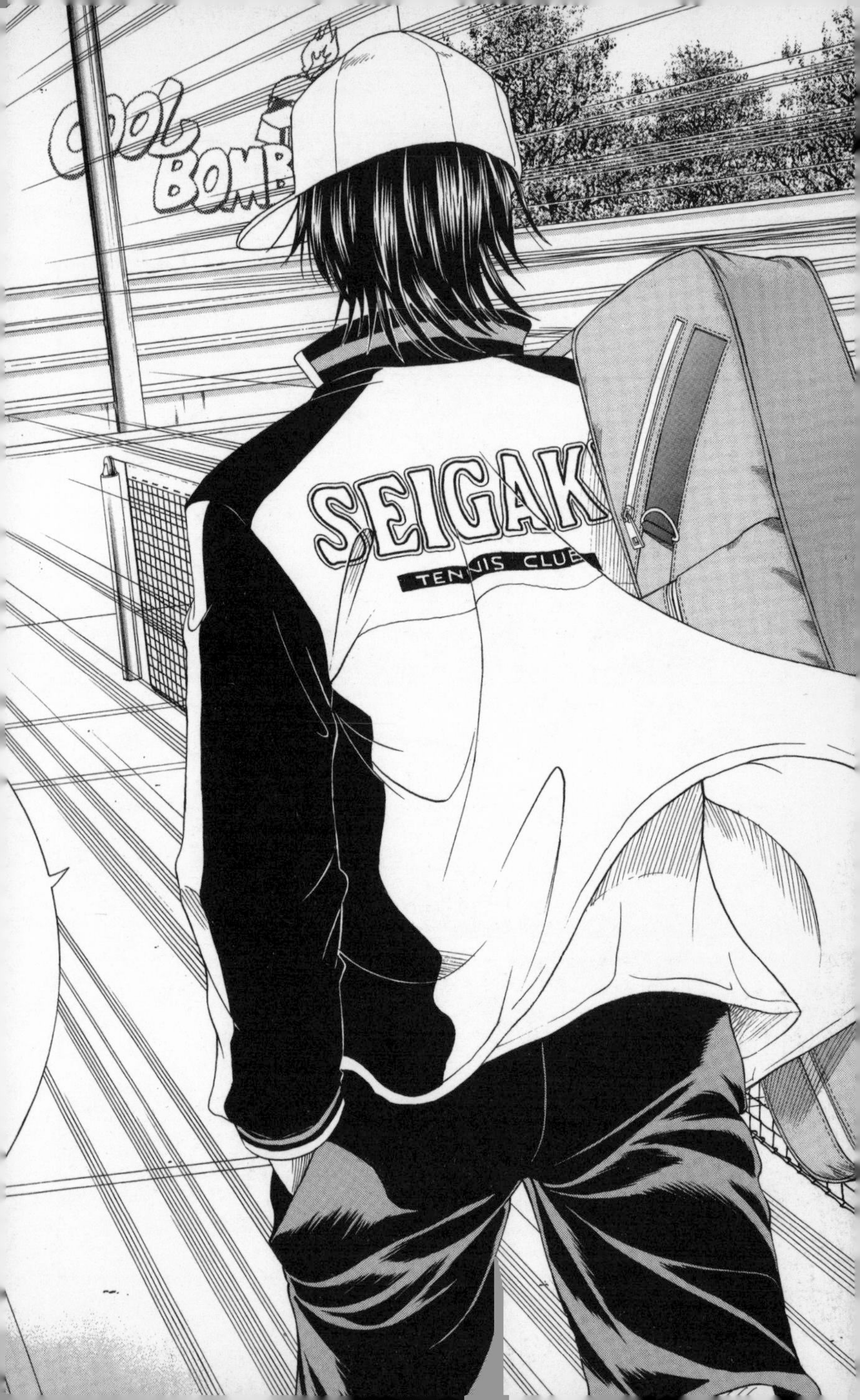
COOL BOMB
SEIGAKU
TENNIS CLUB

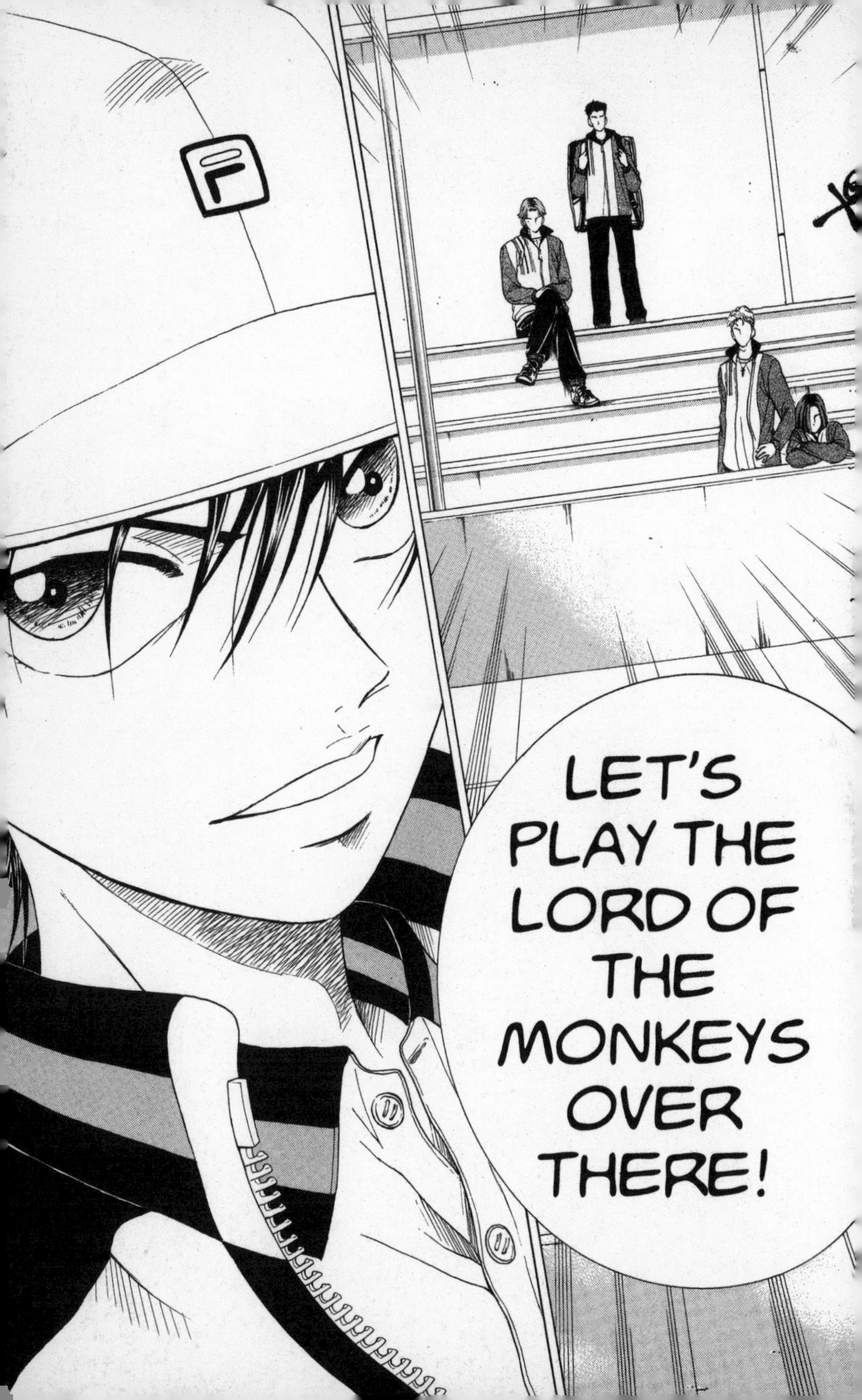
LET'S PLAY THE LORD OF THE MONKEYS OVER THERE!

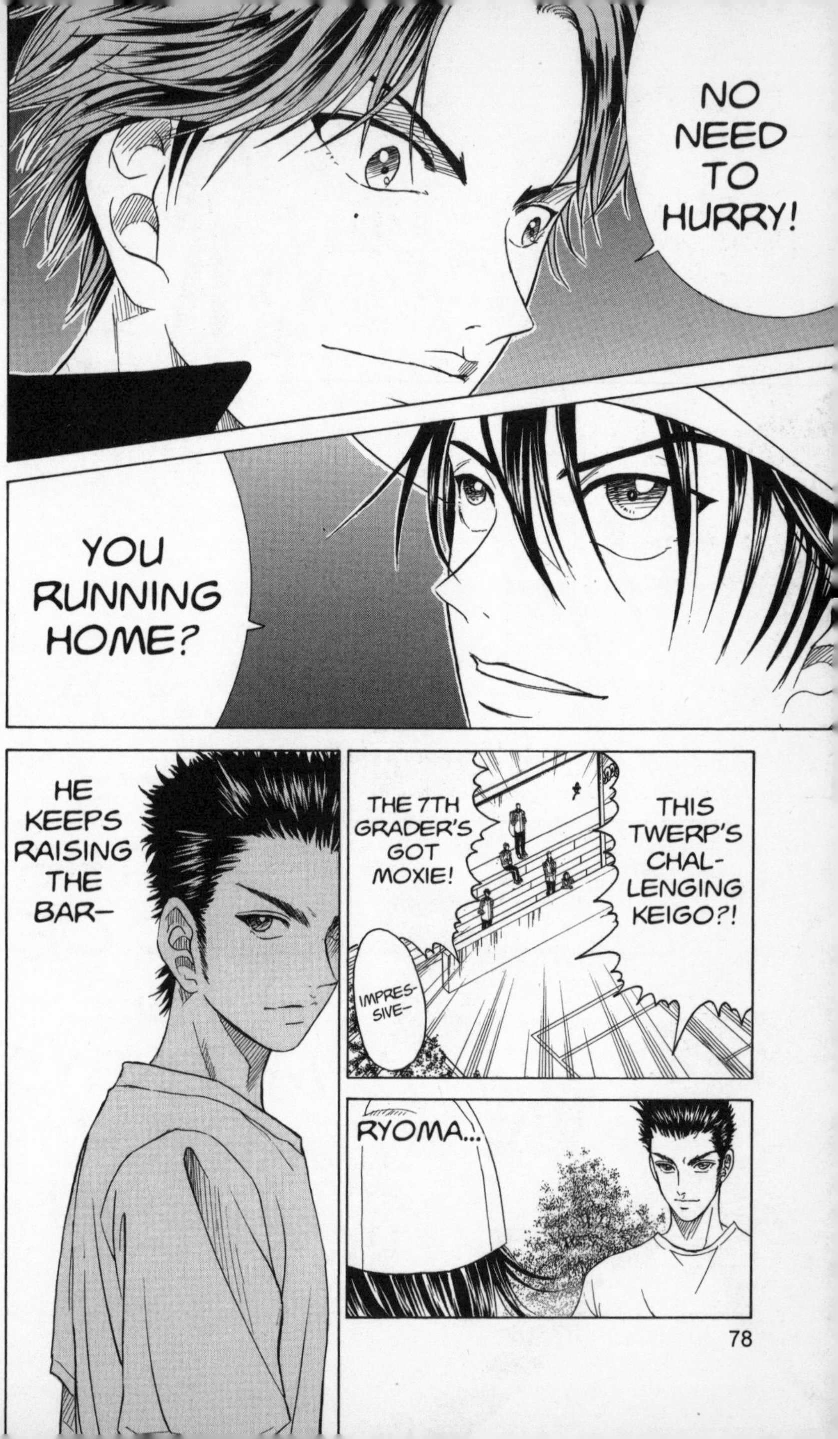
NO NEED TO HURRY!
YOU RUNNING HOME?
THIS TWERP'S CHAL-LENGING KEIGO?!
THE 7TH GRADER'S GOT MOXIE!
IMPRES-SIVE—
RYOMA...
HE KEEPS RAISING THE BAR—

READ THIS WAY

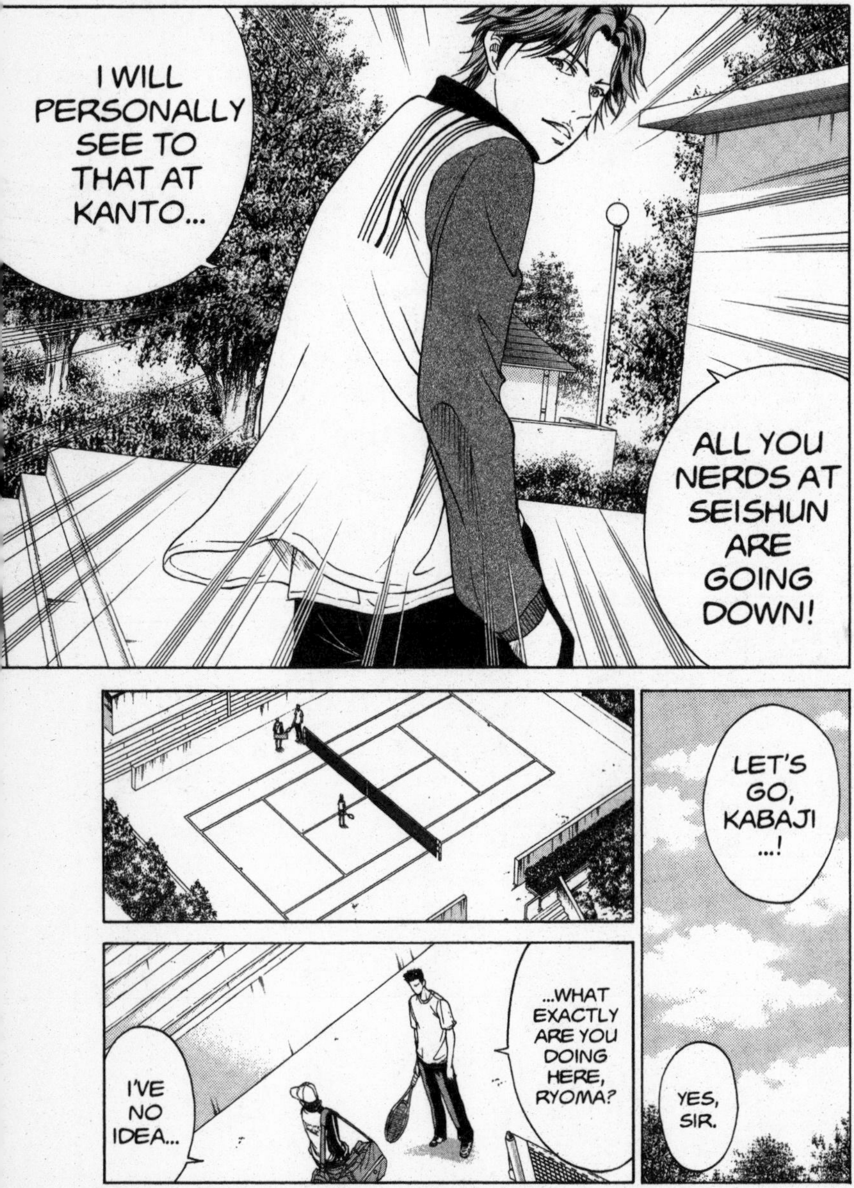
ALL YOU NERDS AT SEISHUN ARE GOING DOWN!
I WILL PERSONALLY SEE TO THAT AT KANTO...
LET'S GO, KABAJI ...!
YES, SIR.
...WHAT EXACTLY ARE YOU DOING HERE, RYOMA?
I'VE NO IDEA...

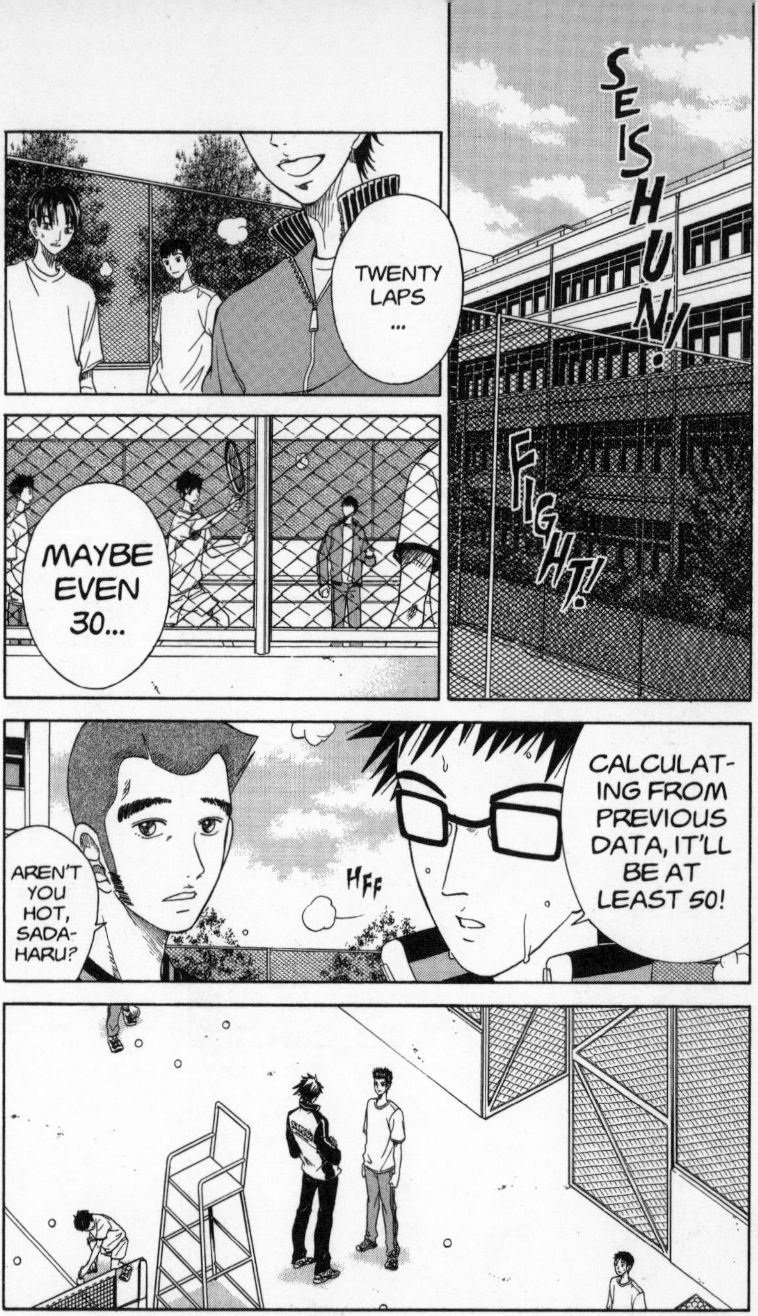
SEISHUN!
FIGHT!
TWENTY LAPS ...
MAYBE EVEN 30...
CALCULATING FROM PREVIOUS DATA, IT'LL BE AT LEAST 50!
HFF
AREN'T YOU HOT, SADAHARU?

READ THIS WAY

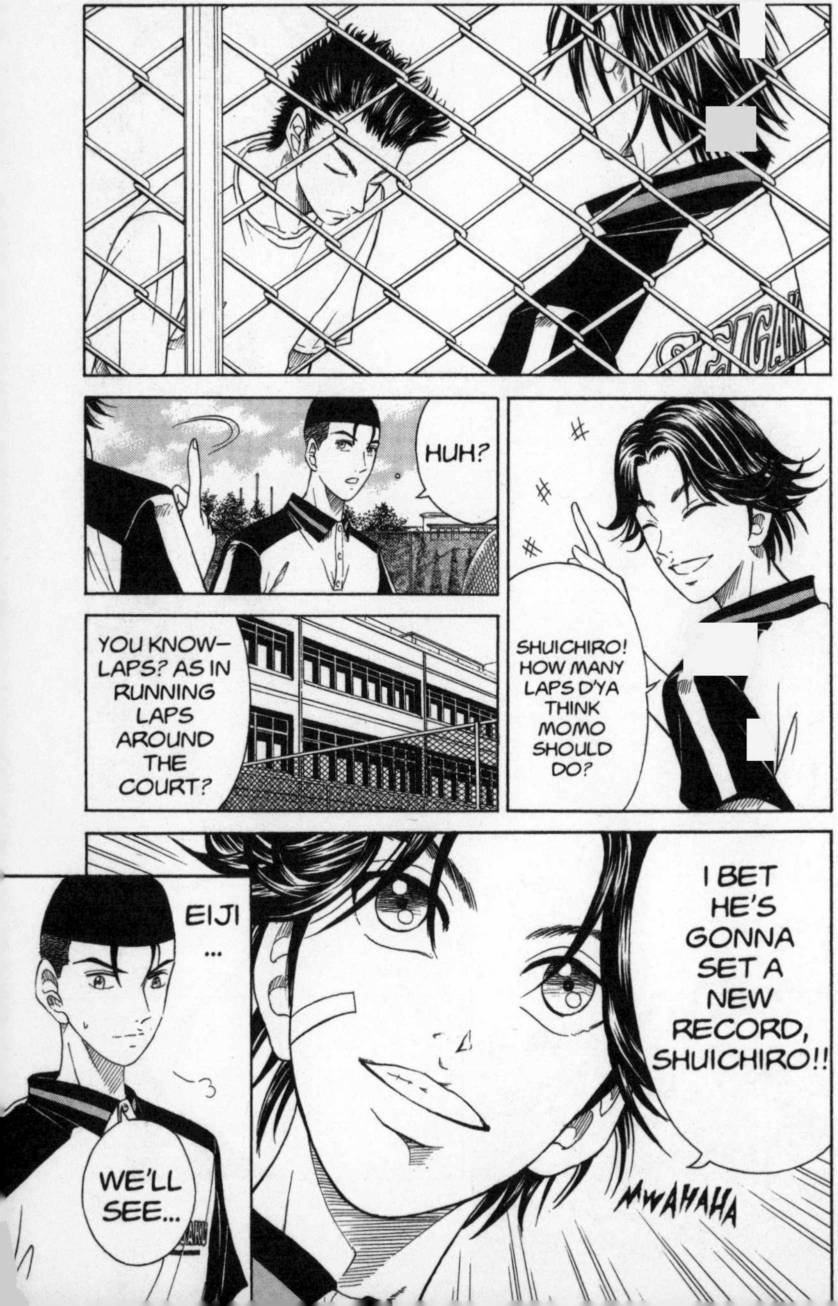
SHUICHIRO! HOW MANY LAPS D'YA THINK MOMO SHOULD DO?
HUH?
YOU KNOW— LAPS? AS IN RUNNING LAPS AROUND THE COURT?
I BET HE'S GONNA SET A NEW RECORD, SHUICHIRO!!
MWAHAHA
EIJI ...
WE'LL SEE...

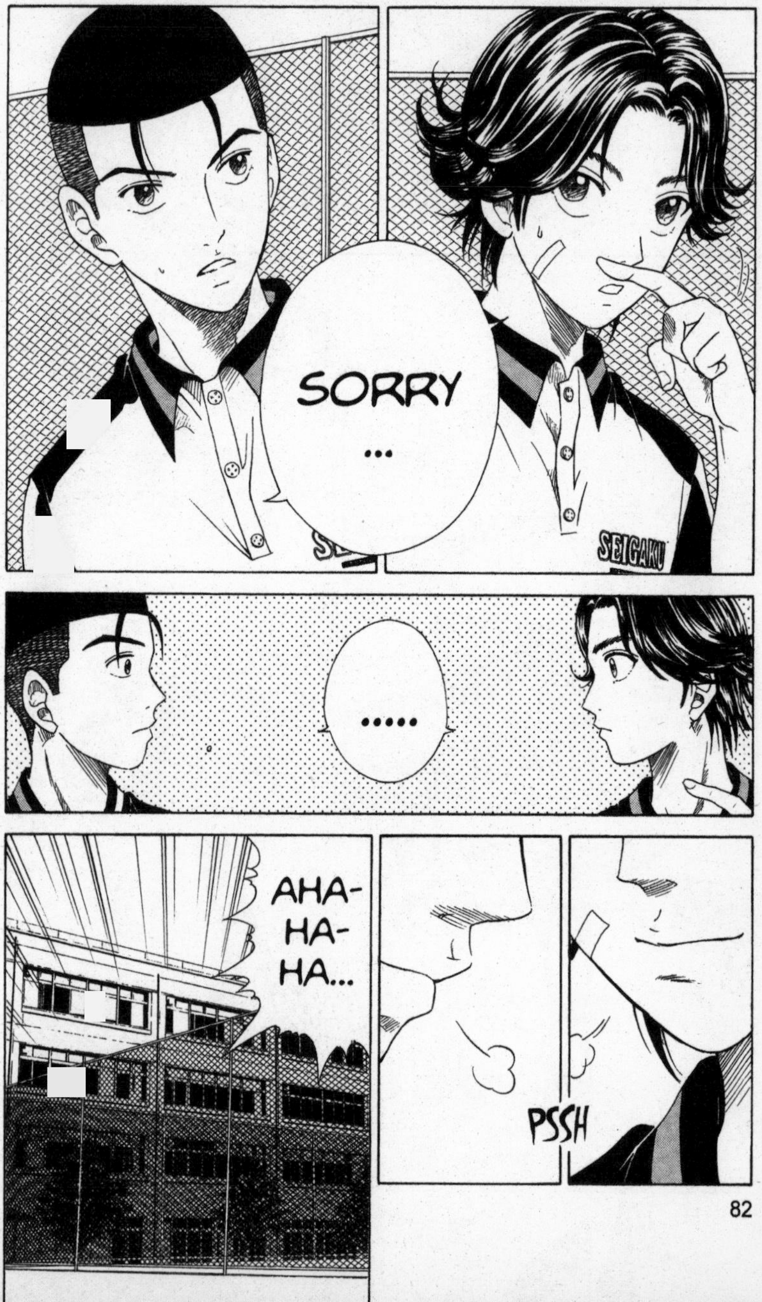
SORRY
...
.....
PSSH
AHA-HA-HA...

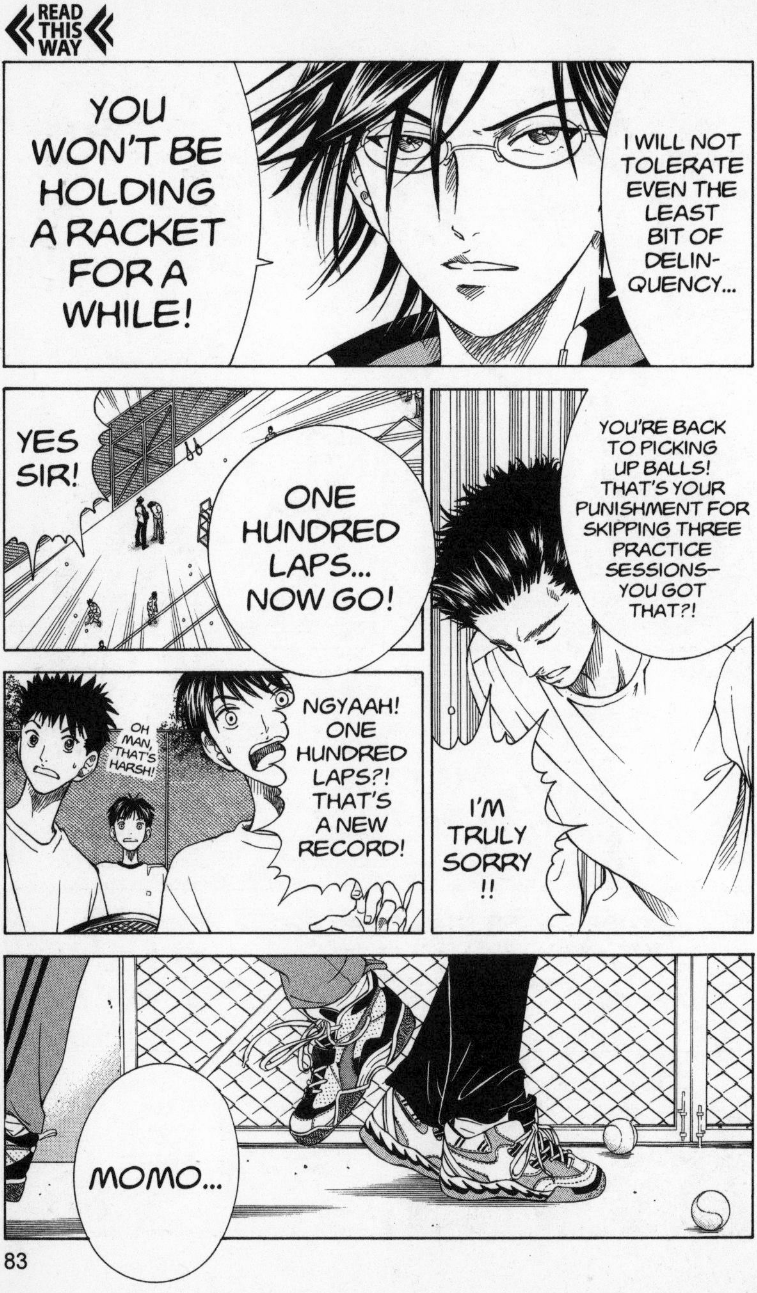
READ THIS WAY
I WILL NOT TOLERATE EVEN THE LEAST BIT OF DELIN-QUENCY...
YOU WON'T BE HOLDING A RACKET FOR A WHILE!
YOU'RE BACK TO PICKING UP BALLS! THAT'S YOUR PUNISHMENT FOR SKIPPING THREE PRACTICE SESSIONS— YOU GOT THAT?!
I'M TRULY SORRY !!
ONE HUNDRED LAPS... NOW GO!
YES SIR!
NGYAAH! ONE HUNDRED LAPS?! THAT'S A NEW RECORD!
OH MAN, THAT'S HARSH!
MOMO...

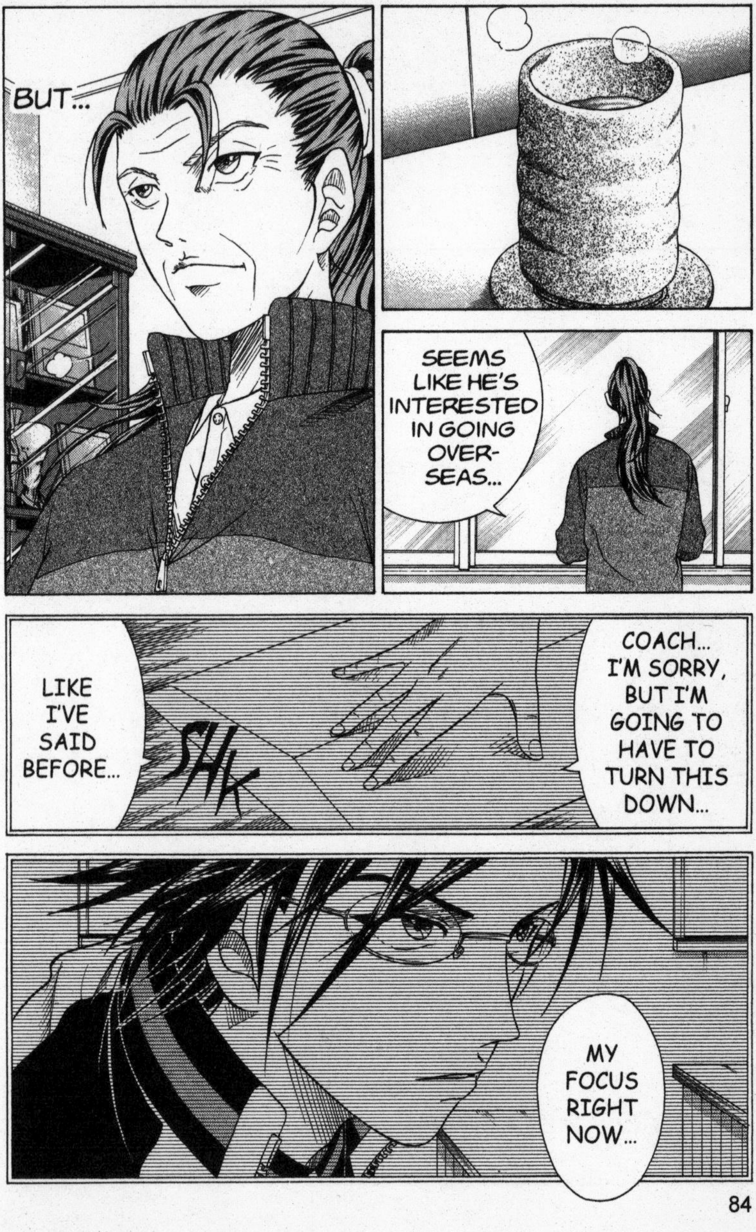
SEEMS LIKE HE'S INTERESTED IN GOING OVER-SEAS...
BUT...
COACH... I'M SORRY, BUT I'M GOING TO HAVE TO TURN THIS DOWN...
SHK
LIKE I'VE SAID BEFORE...
MY FOCUS RIGHT NOW...

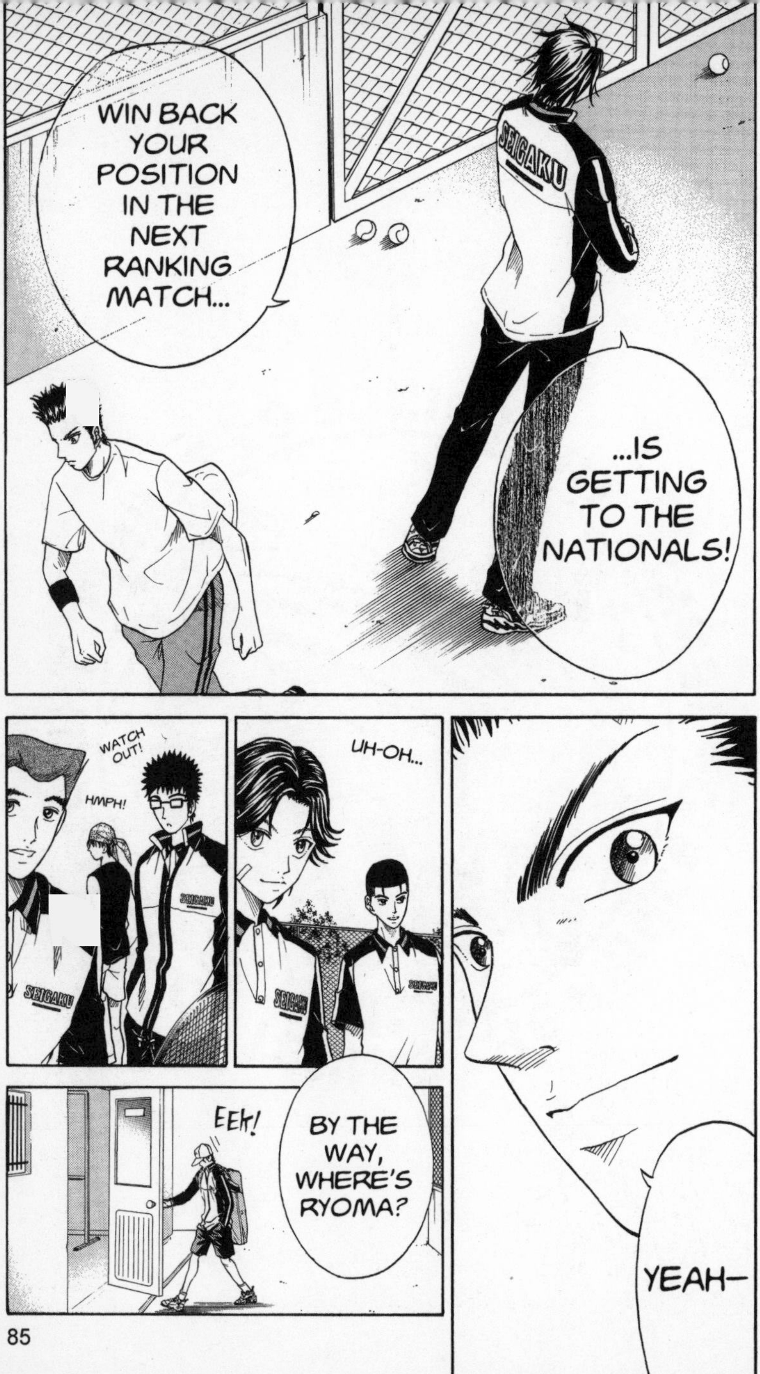
WIN BACK YOUR POSITION IN THE NEXT RANKING MATCH...
...IS GETTING TO THE NATIONALS!
YEAH—
UH-OH...
WATCH OUT!
HMPH!
BY THE WAY, WHERE'S RYOMA?
EEK!

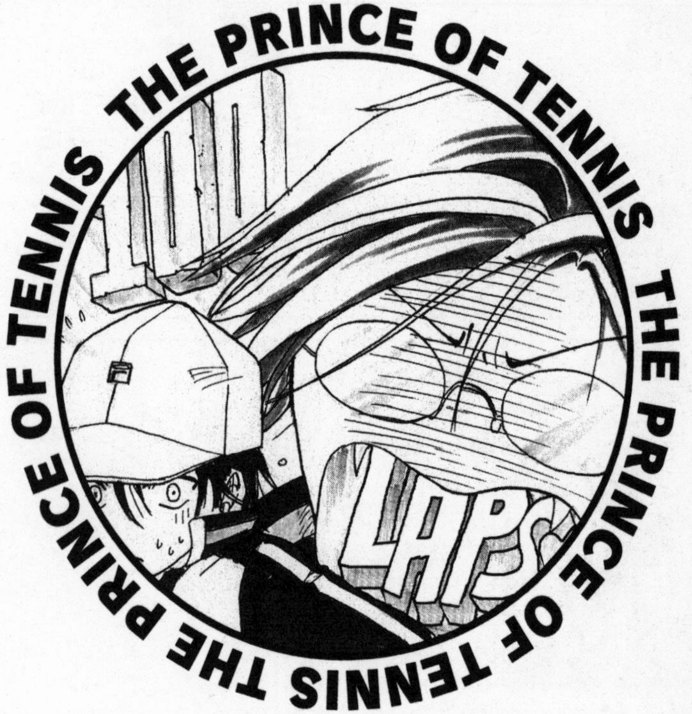
THE PRINCE OF TENNIS THE PRINCE OF TENNIS THE PRINCE OF TENNIS
LAPS

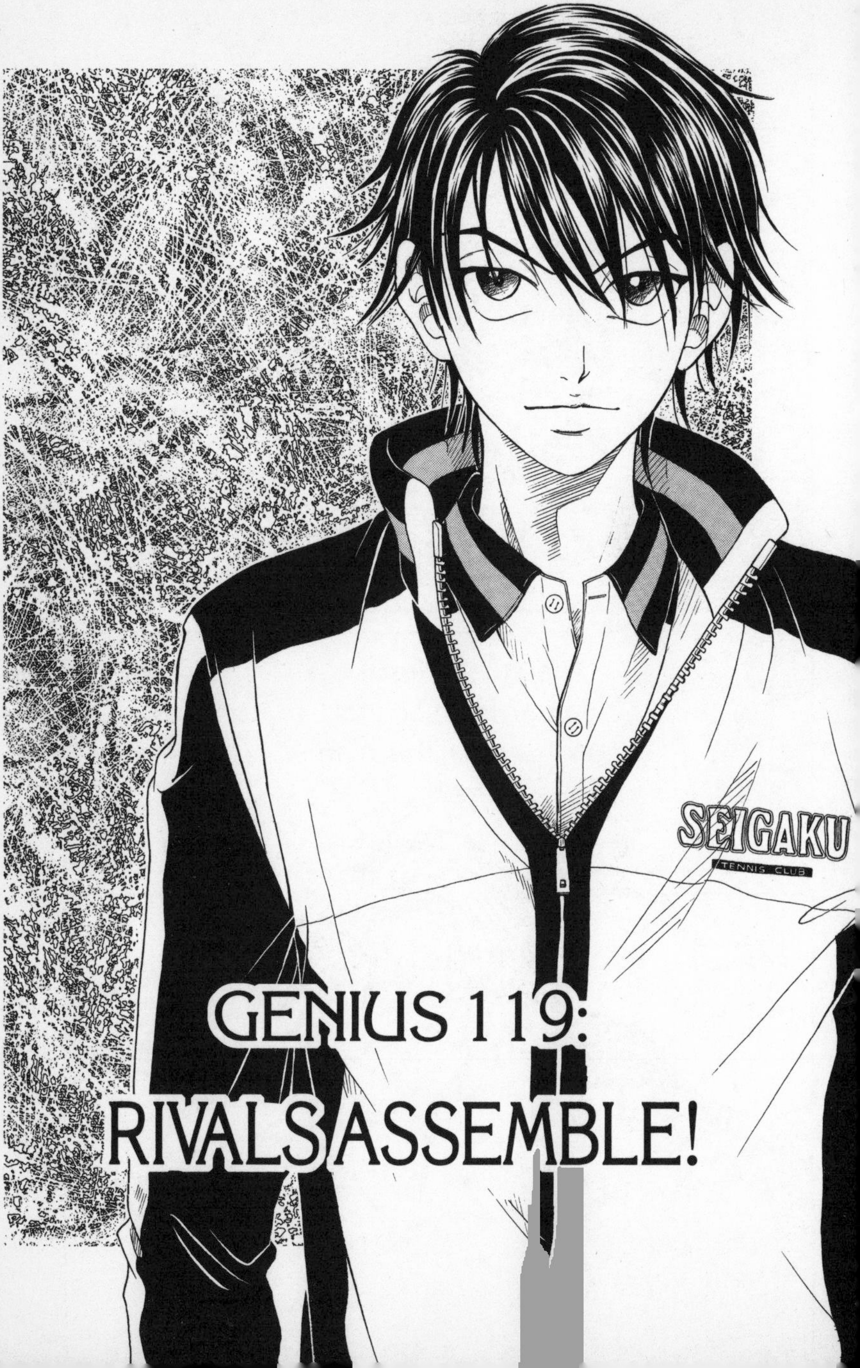
SEIGAKU
TENNIS CLUB
GENIUS 119:
RIVALS ASSEMBLE!

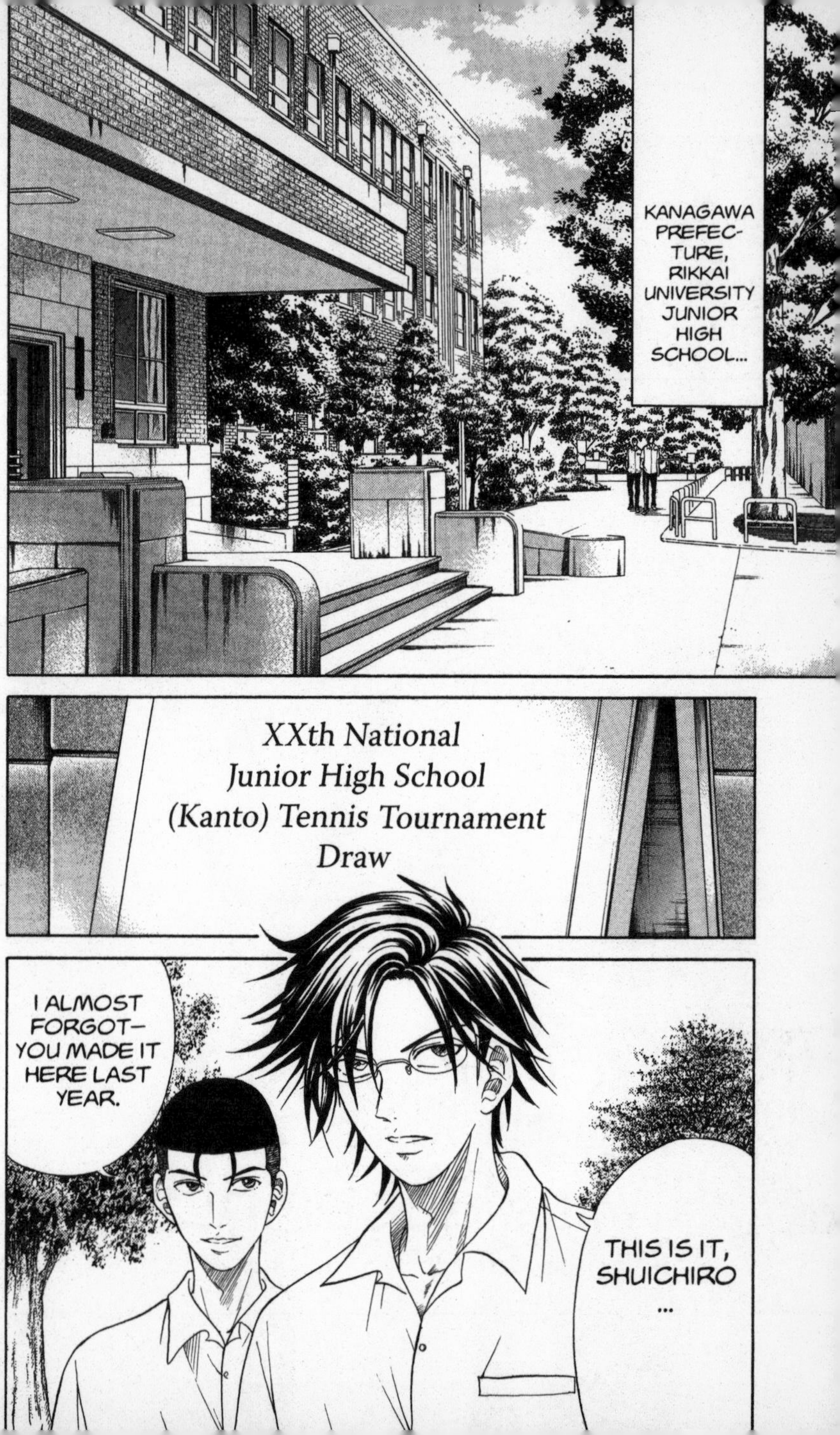
KANAGAWA PREFEC-TURE, RIKKAI UNIVERSITY JUNIOR HIGH SCHOOL...
XXth National Junior High School (Kanto) Tennis Tournament Draw
THIS IS IT, SHUICHIRO ...
I ALMOST FORGOT– YOU MADE IT HERE LAST YEAR.

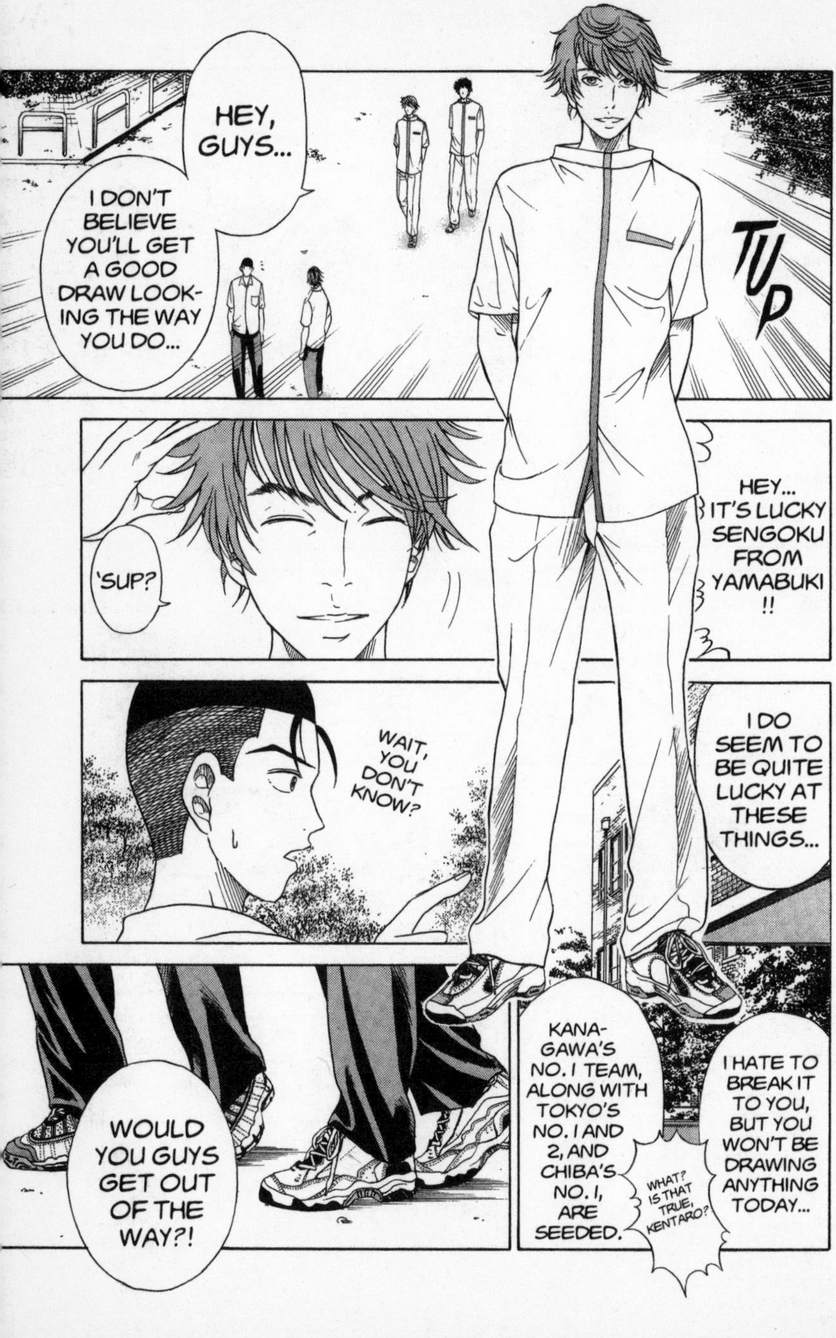
TUP
HEY, GUYS...
I DON'T BELIEVE YOU'LL GET A GOOD DRAW LOOKING THE WAY YOU DO...
HEY... IT'S LUCKY SENGOKU FROM YAMABUKI !!
'SUP?
I DO SEEM TO BE QUITE LUCKY AT THESE THINGS...
WAIT, YOU DON'T KNOW?
I HATE TO BREAK IT TO YOU, BUT YOU WON'T BE DRAWING ANYTHING TODAY...
KANAGAWA'S NO. 1 TEAM, ALONG WITH TOKYO'S NO. 1 AND 2, AND CHIBA'S NO. 1, ARE SEEDED.
WHAT? IS THAT TRUE, KENTARO?
WOULD YOU GUYS GET OUT OF THE WAY?!

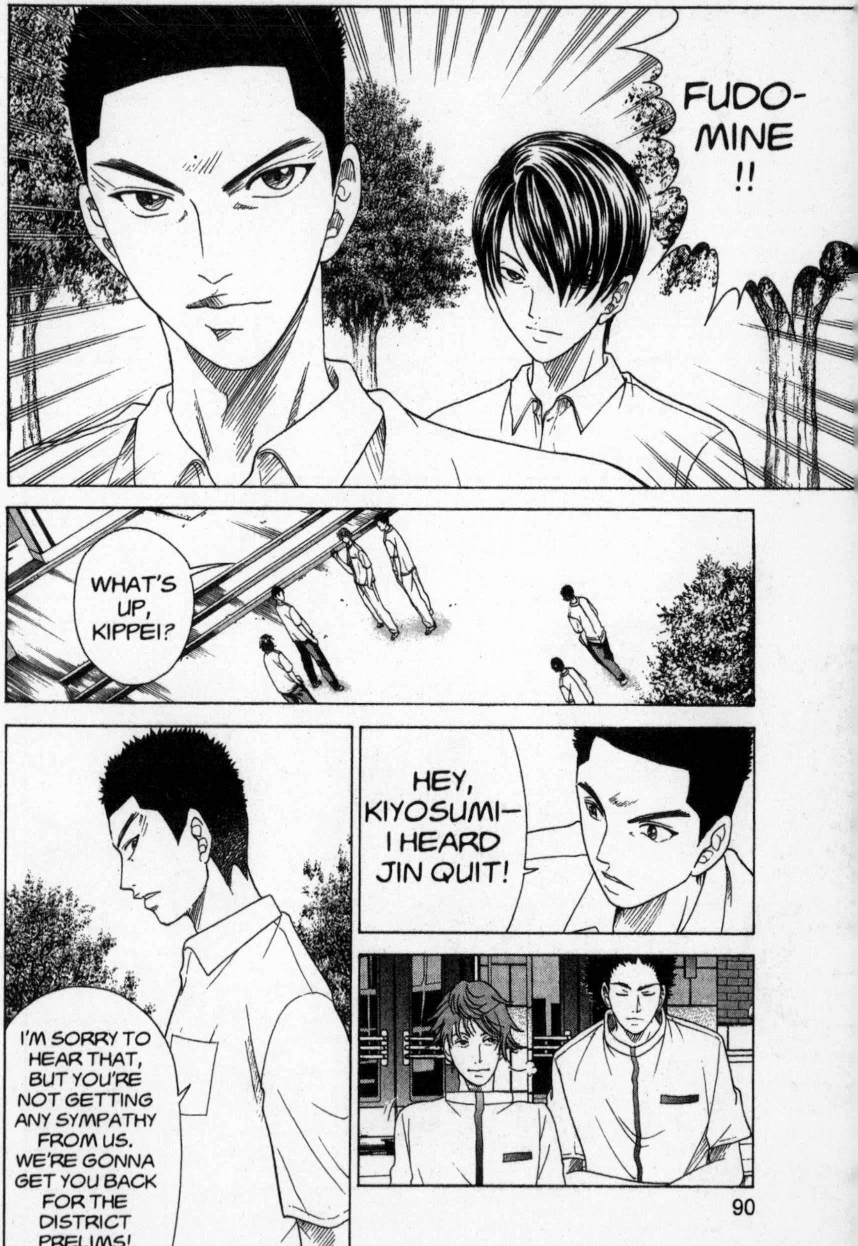
FUDO-MINE!!
WHAT'S UP, KIPPEI?
HEY, KIYOSUMI- I HEARD JIN QUIT!
I'M SORRY TO HEAR THAT, BUT YOU'RE NOT GETTING ANY SYMPATHY FROM US. WE'RE GONNA GET YOU BACK FOR THE DISTRICT PRELIMS!

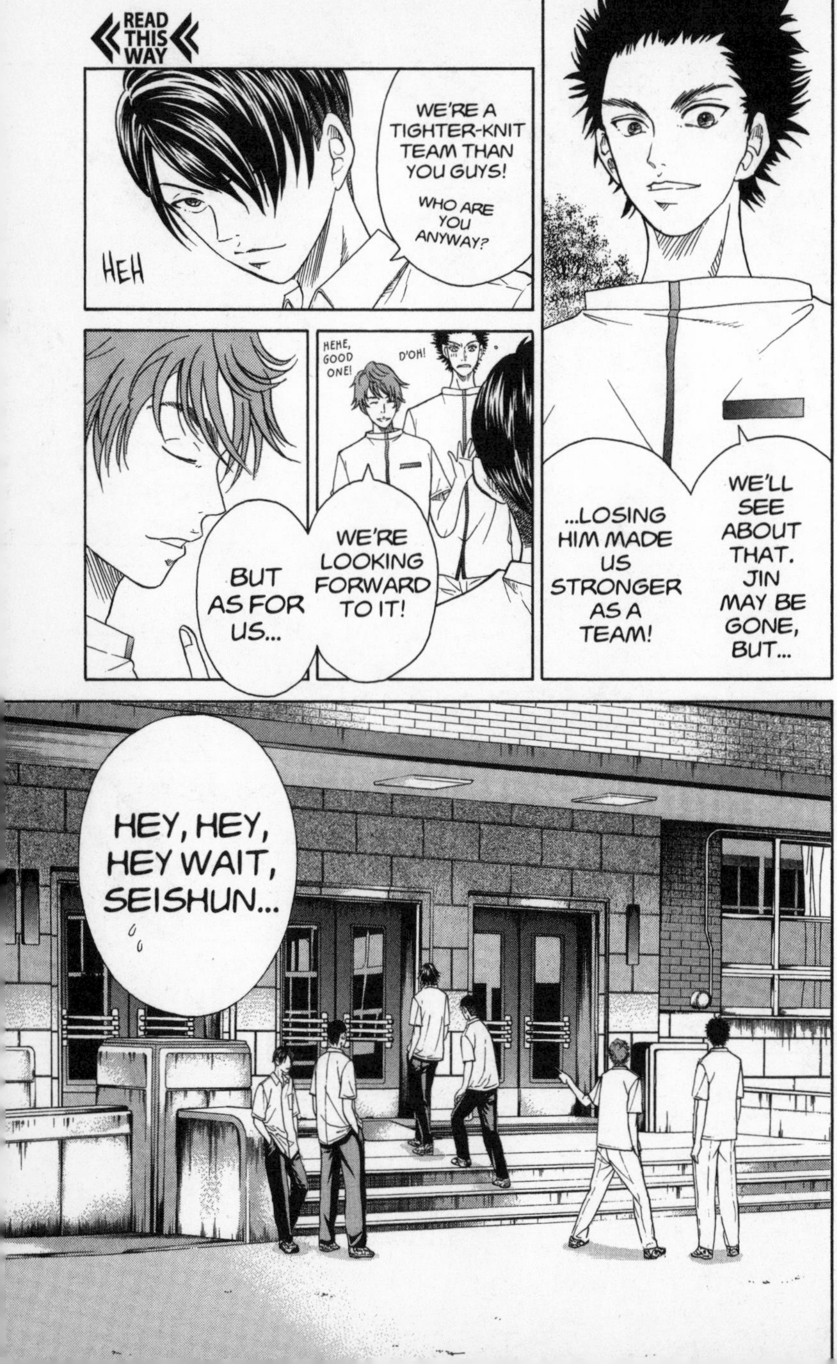
READ THIS WAY
WE'LL SEE ABOUT THAT. JIN MAY BE GONE, BUT...
...LOSING HIM MADE US STRONGER AS A TEAM!
WE'RE A TIGHTER-KNIT TEAM THAN YOU GUYS!
WHO ARE YOU ANYWAY?
HEH
D'OH!
HEHE, GOOD ONE!
WE'RE LOOKING FORWARD TO IT!
BUT AS FOR US...
HEY, HEY, HEY WAIT, SEISHUN...

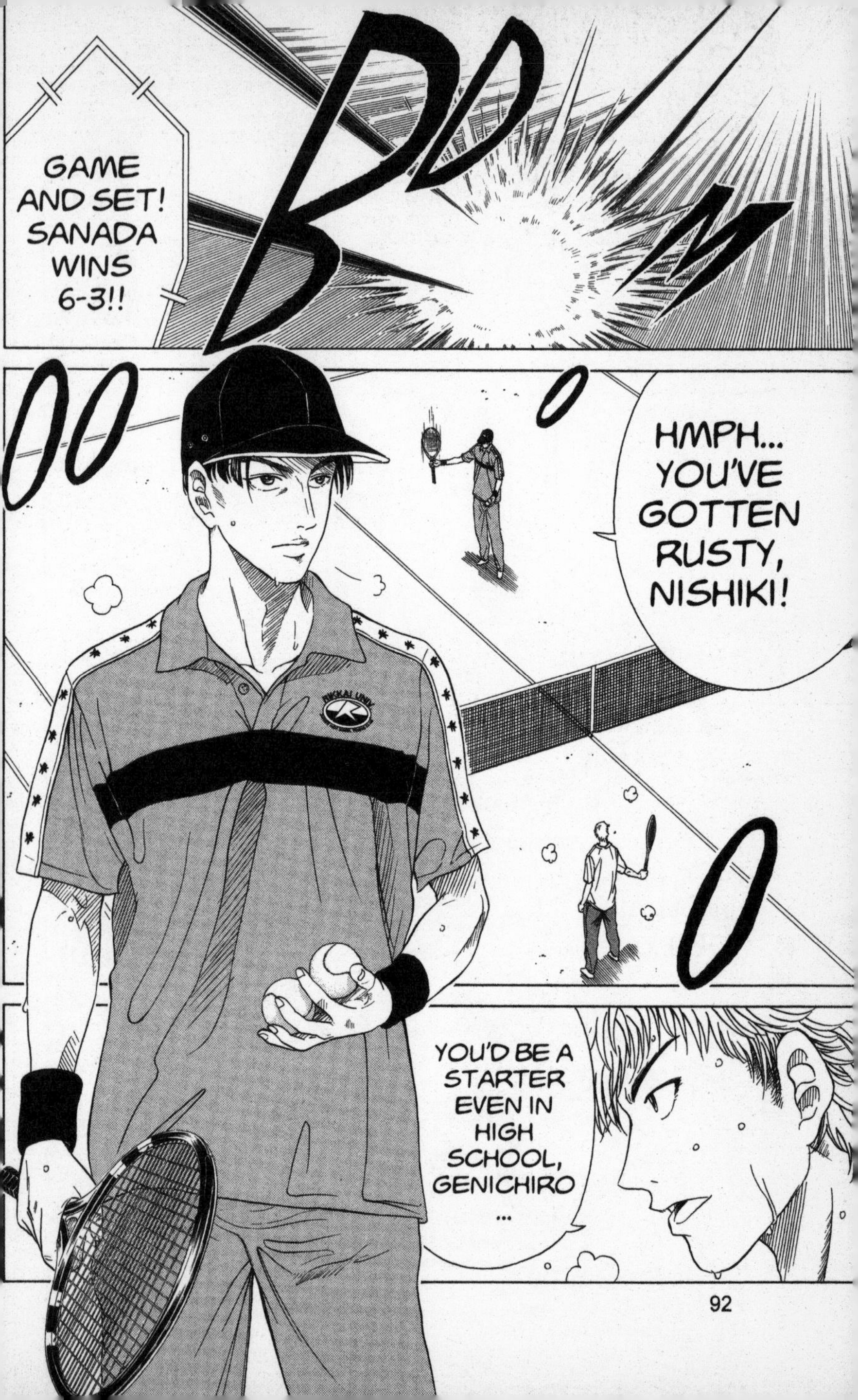
BOOOOM
GAME AND SET! SANADA WINS 6-3!!
HMPH... YOU'VE GOTTEN RUSTY, NISHIKI!
YOU'D BE A STARTER EVEN IN HIGH SCHOOL, GENICHIRO ...

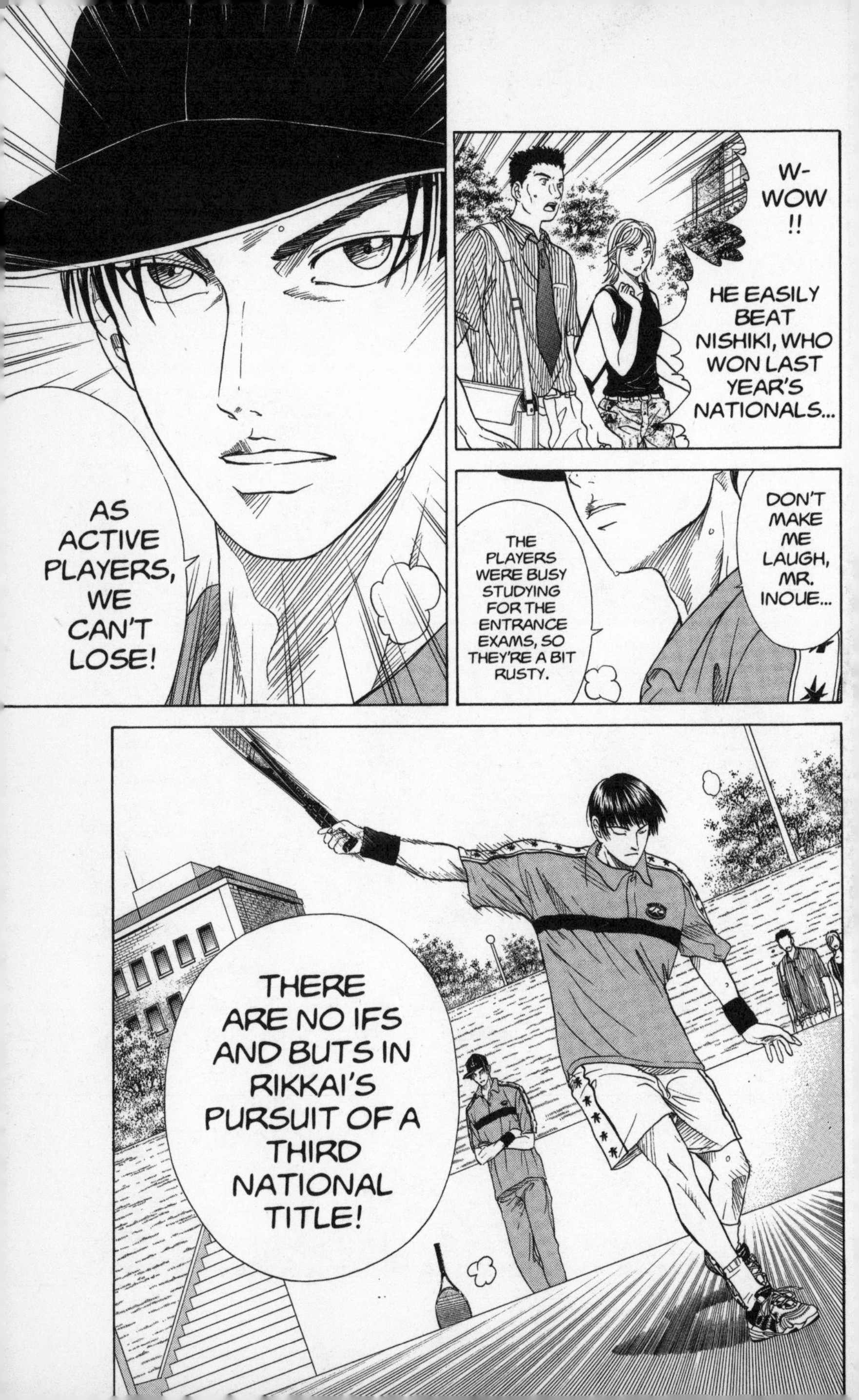
W-WOW !!
HE EASILY BEAT NISHIKI, WHO WON LAST YEAR'S NATIONALS...
DON'T MAKE ME LAUGH, MR. INOUE...
THE PLAYERS WERE BUSY STUDYING FOR THE ENTRANCE EXAMS, SO THEY'RE A BIT RUSTY.
AS ACTIVE PLAYERS, WE CAN'T LOSE!
THERE ARE NO IFS AND BUTS IN RIKKAI'S PURSUIT OF A THIRD NATIONAL TITLE!

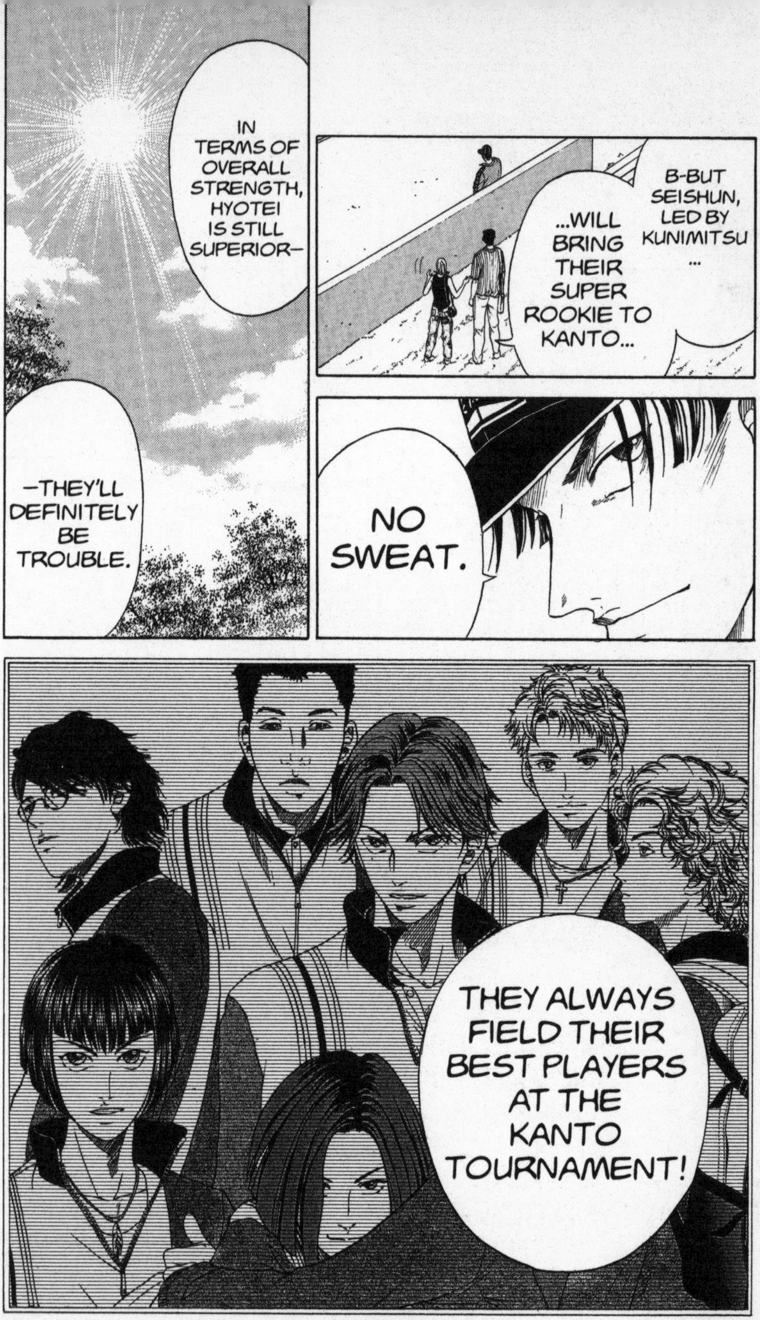
B-BUT SEISHUN, LED BY KUNIMITSU ...
...WILL BRING THEIR SUPER ROOKIE TO KANTO...
NO SWEAT.
IN TERMS OF OVERALL STRENGTH, HYOTEI IS STILL SUPERIOR—
—THEY'LL DEFINITELY BE TROUBLE.
THEY ALWAYS FIELD THEIR BEST PLAYERS AT THE KANTO TOURNAMENT!

READ THIS WAY

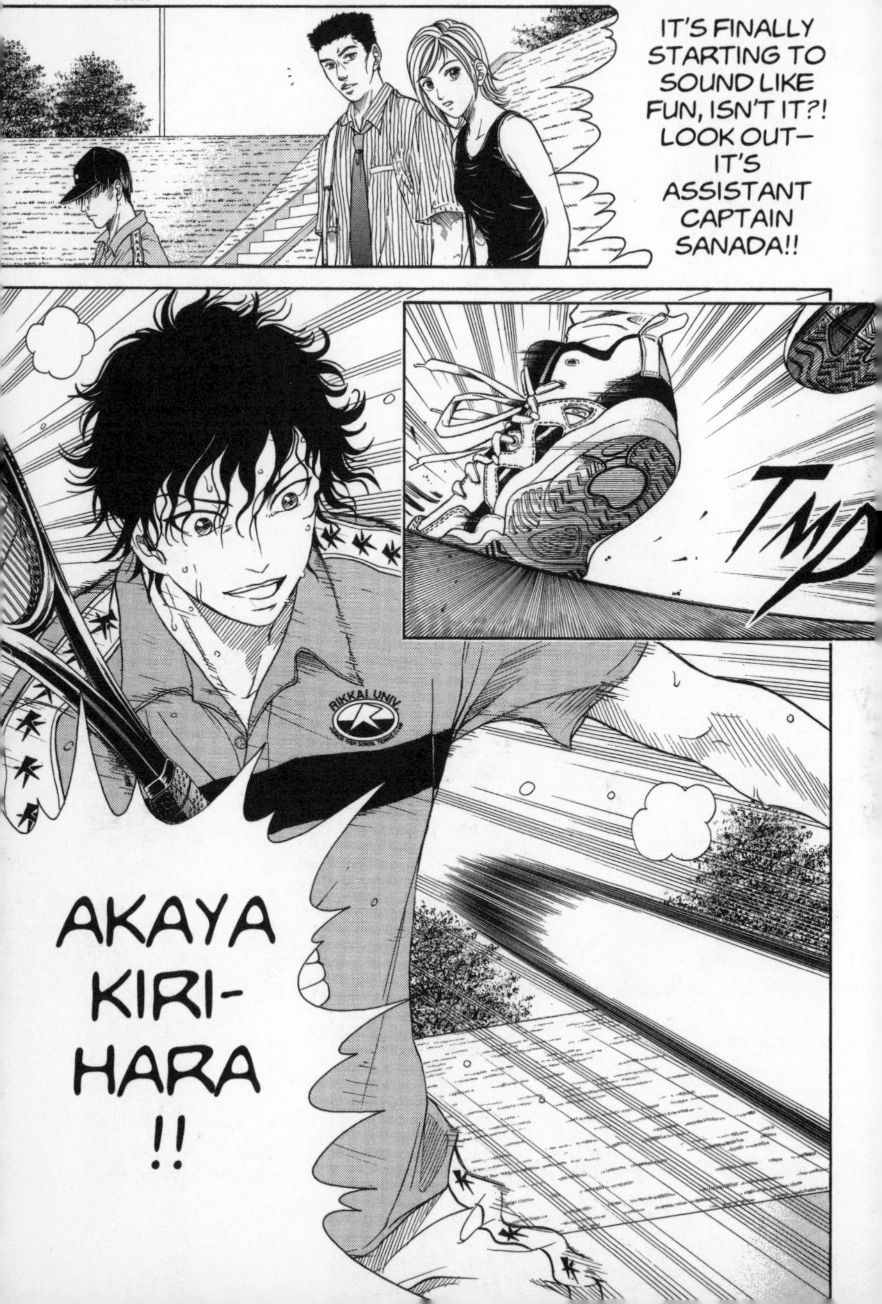
IT'S FINALLY STARTING TO SOUND LIKE FUN, ISN'T IT?! LOOK OUT—IT'S ASSISTANT CAPTAIN SANADA!!
TMP
AKAYA KIRI-HARA!!

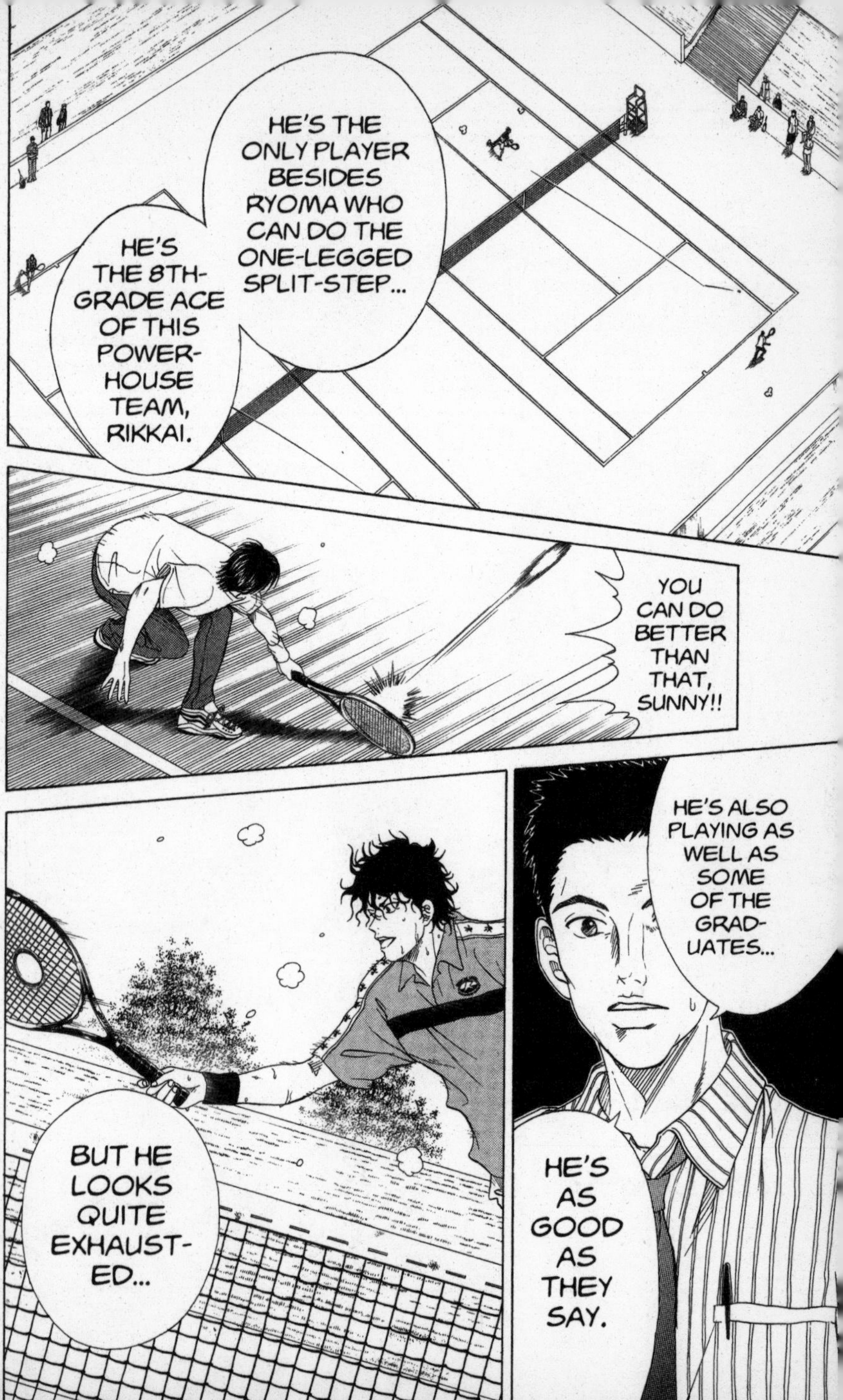
HE'S THE ONLY PLAYER BESIDES RYOMA WHO CAN DO THE ONE-LEGGED SPLIT-STEP...
HE'S THE 8TH-GRADE ACE OF THIS POWER-HOUSE TEAM, RIKKAI.
YOU CAN DO BETTER THAN THAT, SUNNY!!
HE'S ALSO PLAYING AS WELL AS SOME OF THE GRAD-UATES...
HE'S AS GOOD AS THEY SAY.
BUT HE LOOKS QUITE EXHAUST-ED...

READ THIS WAY

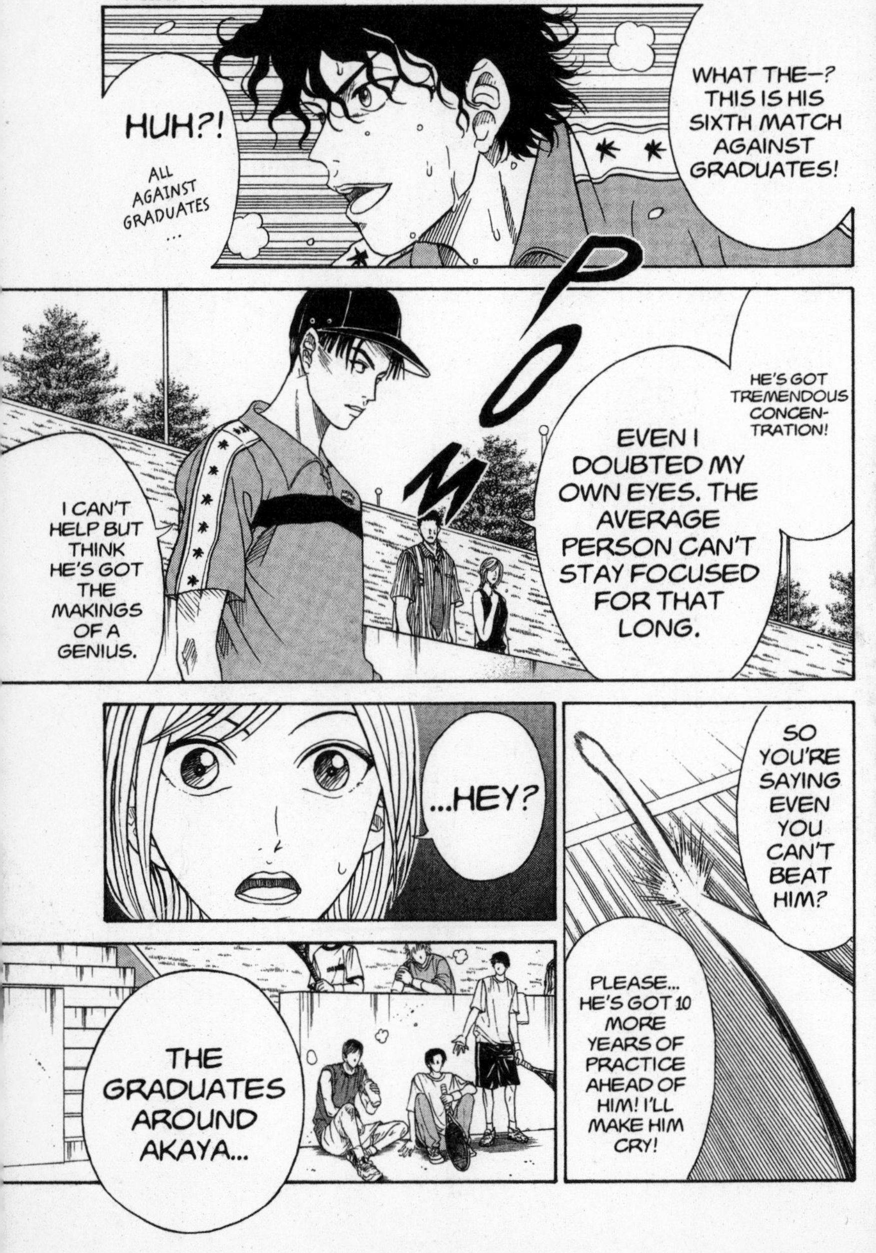
WHAT THE—? THIS IS HIS SIXTH MATCH AGAINST GRADUATES!
HUH?!
ALL AGAINST GRADUATES ...
HE'S GOT TREMENDOUS CONCENTRATION!
EVEN I DOUBTED MY OWN EYES. THE AVERAGE PERSON CAN'T STAY FOCUSED FOR THAT LONG.
POM
I CAN'T HELP BUT THINK HE'S GOT THE MAKINGS OF A GENIUS.
SO YOU'RE SAYING EVEN YOU CAN'T BEAT HIM?
PLEASE... HE'S GOT 10 MORE YEARS OF PRACTICE AHEAD OF HIM! I'LL MAKE HIM CRY!
...HEY?
THE GRADUATES AROUND AKAYA...

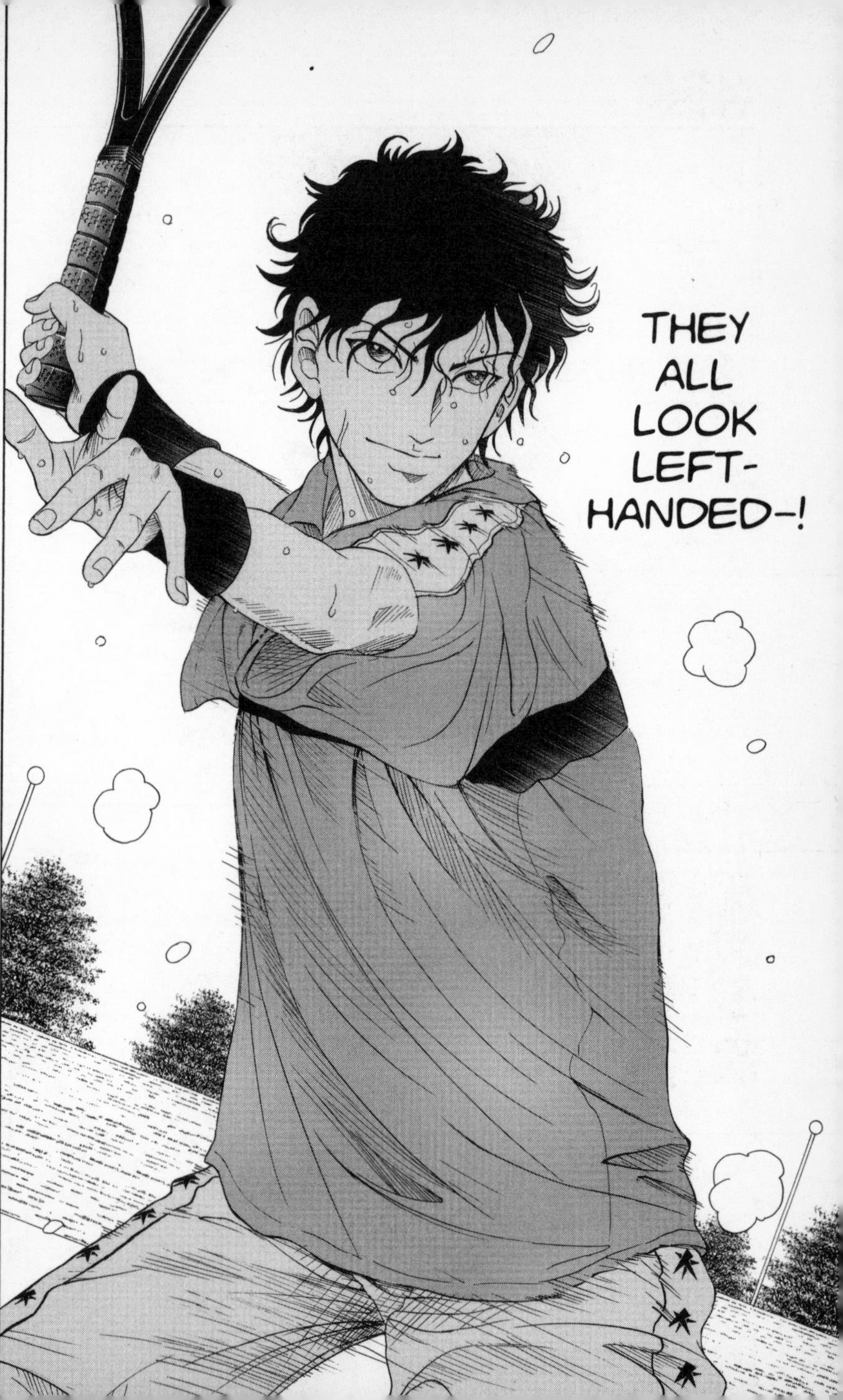
THEY ALL LOOK LEFT-HANDED--!

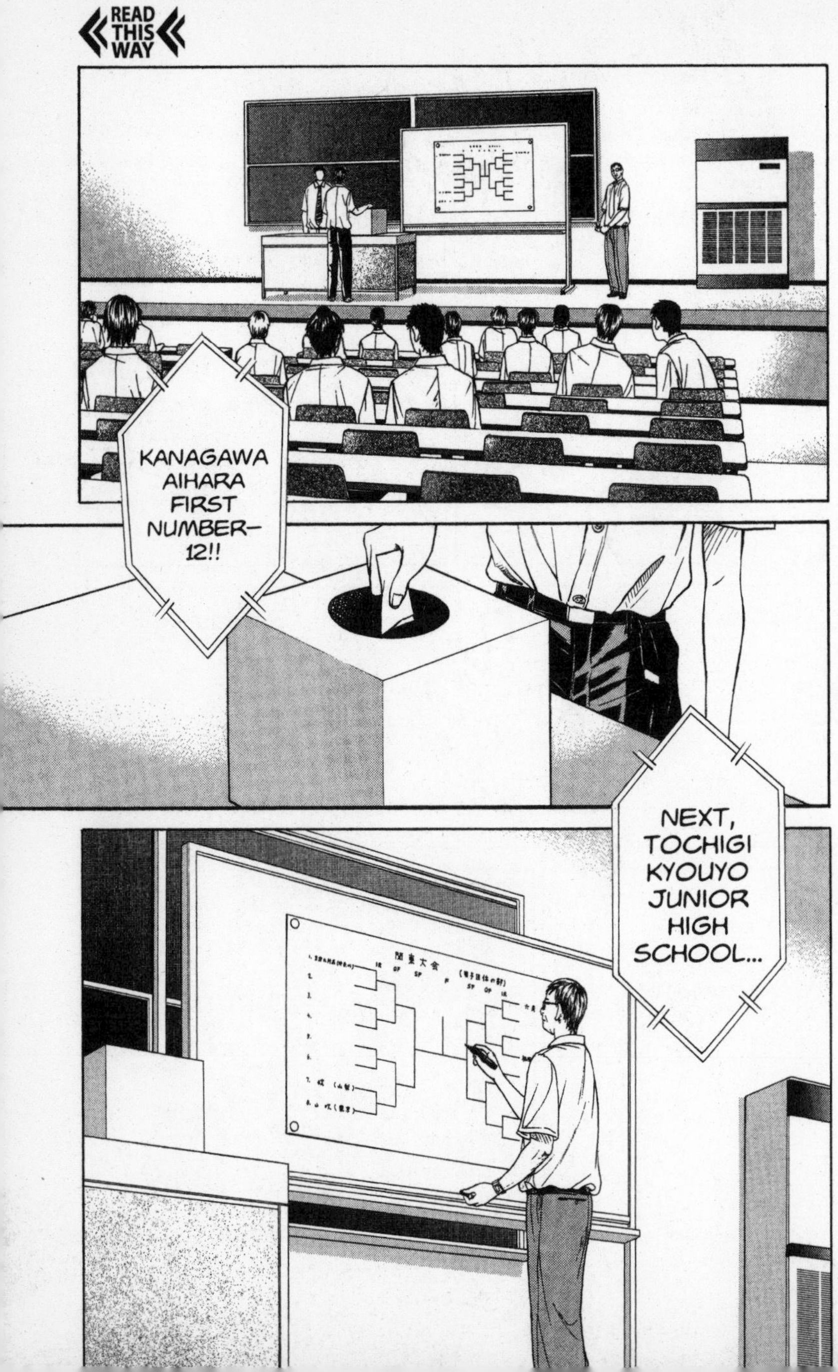
READ THIS WAY
KANAGAWA AIHARA FIRST NUMBER-12!!
NEXT, TOCHIGI KYOUYO JUNIOR HIGH SCHOOL...

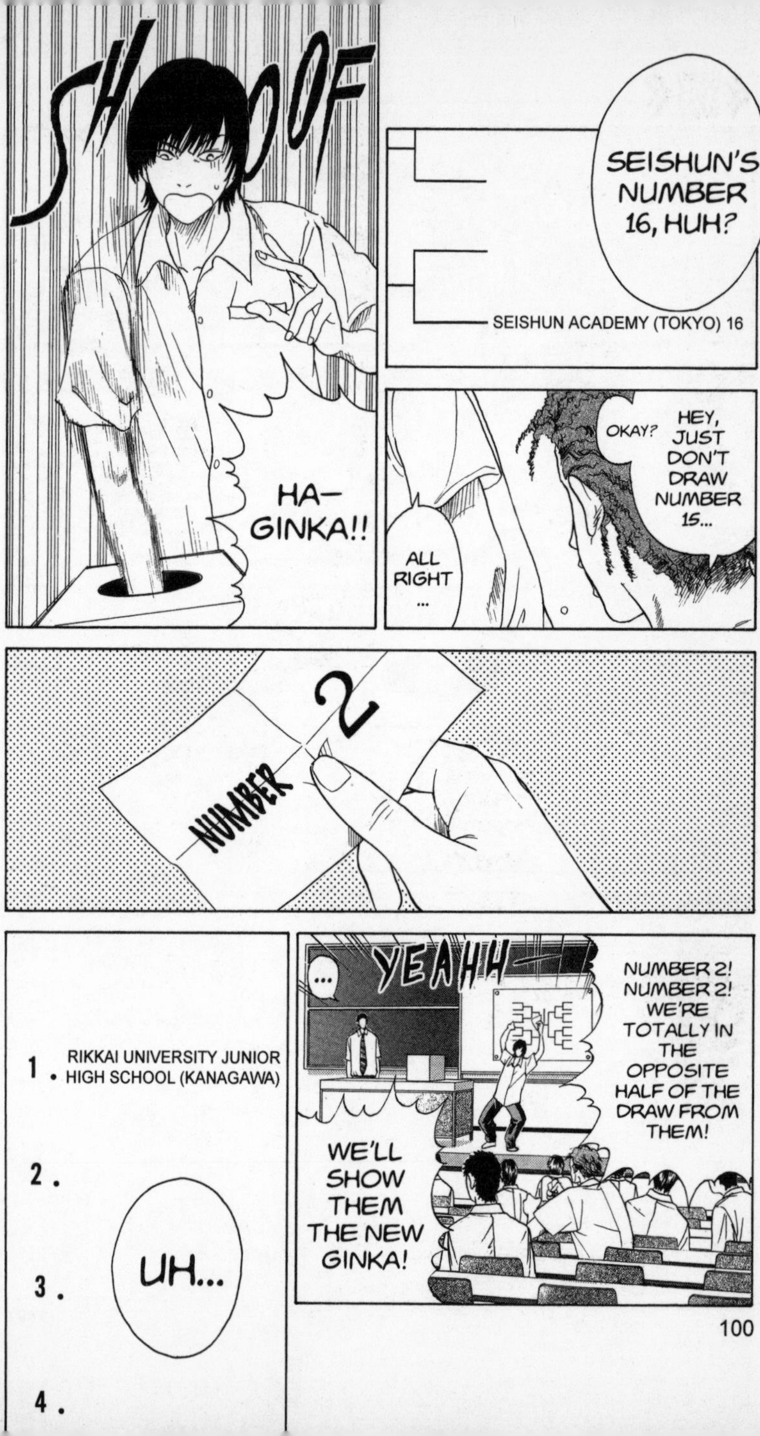
SEISHUN'S NUMBER 16, HUH?
SEISHUN ACADEMY (TOKYO) 16
HEY, JUST DON'T DRAW NUMBER 15...
OKAY?
ALL RIGHT ...
SHOOF
HA-GINKA!!
2
NUMBER
YEAHH
...
NUMBER 2! NUMBER 2! WE'RE TOTALLY IN THE OPPOSITE HALF OF THE DRAW FROM THEM!
WE'LL SHOW THEM THE NEW GINKA!
1. RIKKAI UNIVERSITY JUNIOR HIGH SCHOOL (KANAGAWA)
2.
3.
4.
UH...

READ THIS WAY

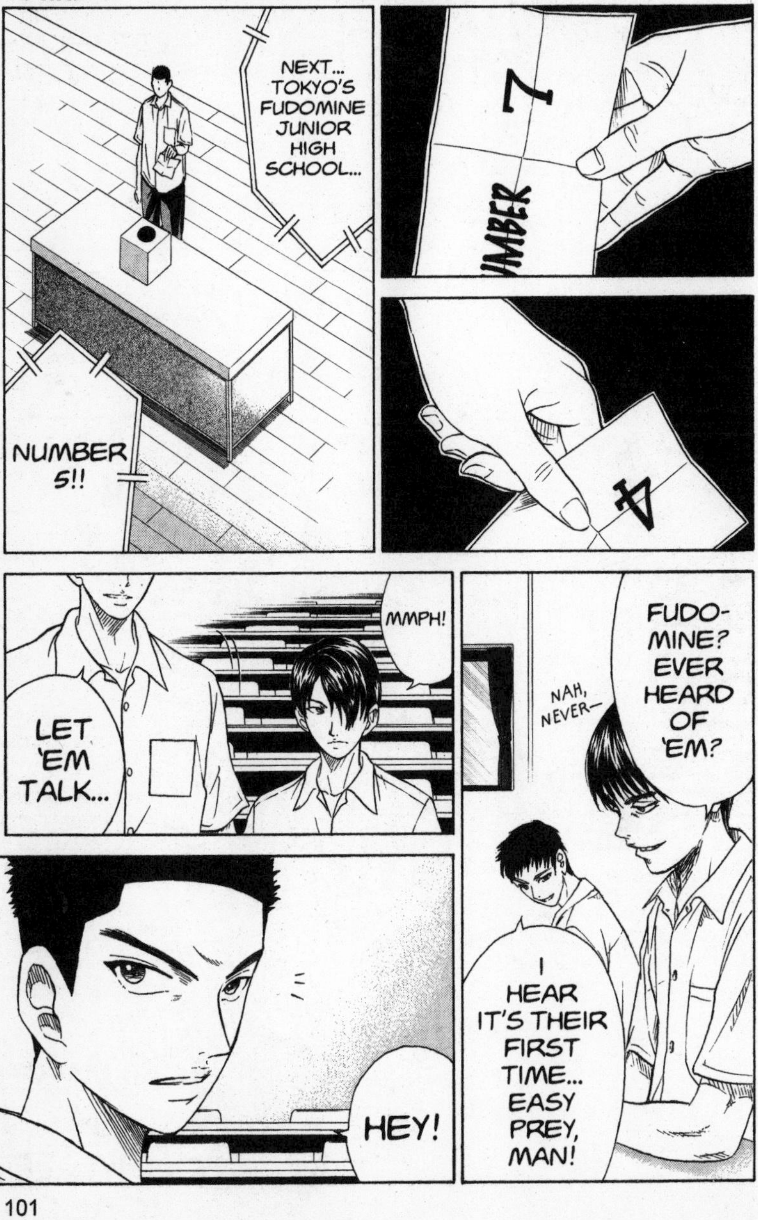
7
4
NEXT... TOKYO'S FUDOMINE JUNIOR HIGH SCHOOL...
NUMBER 5!!
FUDO-MINE? EVER HEARD OF 'EM?
NAH, NEVER—
I HEAR IT'S THEIR FIRST TIME... EASY PREY, MAN!
MMPH!
LET 'EM TALK...
HEY!

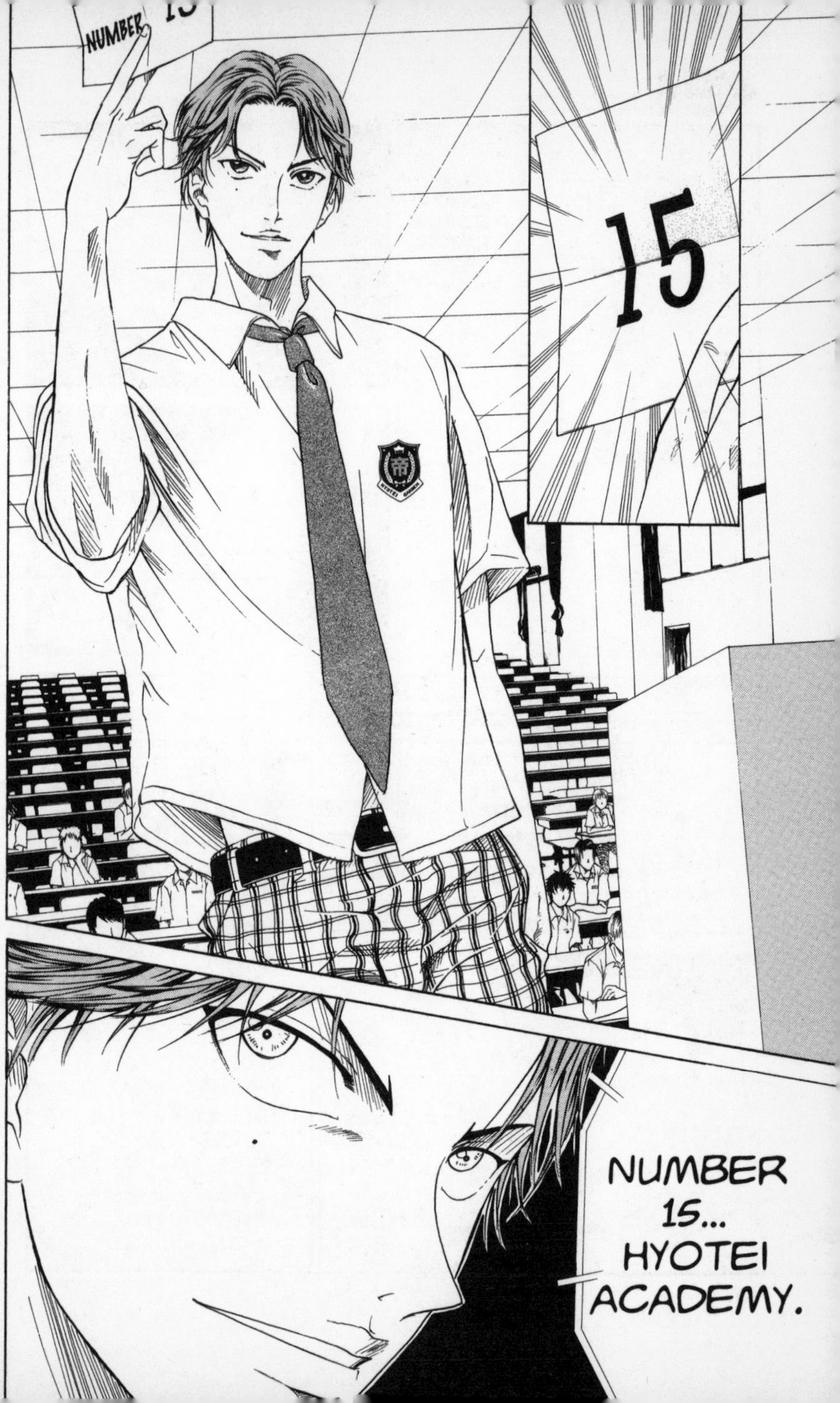
NUMBER
15
NUMBER 15... HYOTEI ACADEMY.

READ THIS WAY

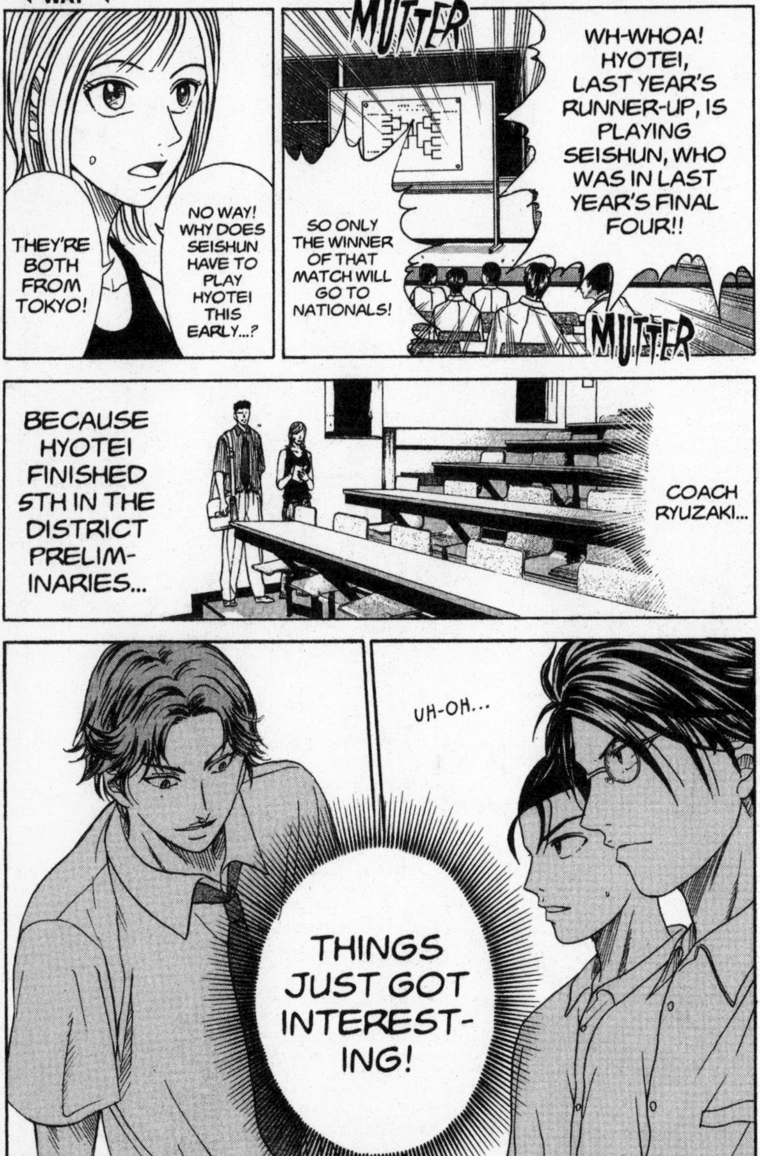
MUTTER
WH-WHOA! HYOTEI, LAST YEAR'S RUNNER-UP, IS PLAYING SEISHUN, WHO WAS IN LAST YEAR'S FINAL FOUR!!
SO ONLY THE WINNER OF THAT MATCH WILL GO TO NATIONALS!
MUTTER
NO WAY! WHY DOES SEISHUN HAVE TO PLAY HYOTEI THIS EARLY...?
THEY'RE BOTH FROM TOKYO!
COACH RYUZAKI...
BECAUSE HYOTEI FINISHED 5TH IN THE DISTRICT PRELIM-INARIES...
UH-OH...
THINGS JUST GOT INTEREST-ING!

(BOYS' TEAM DIVISION)

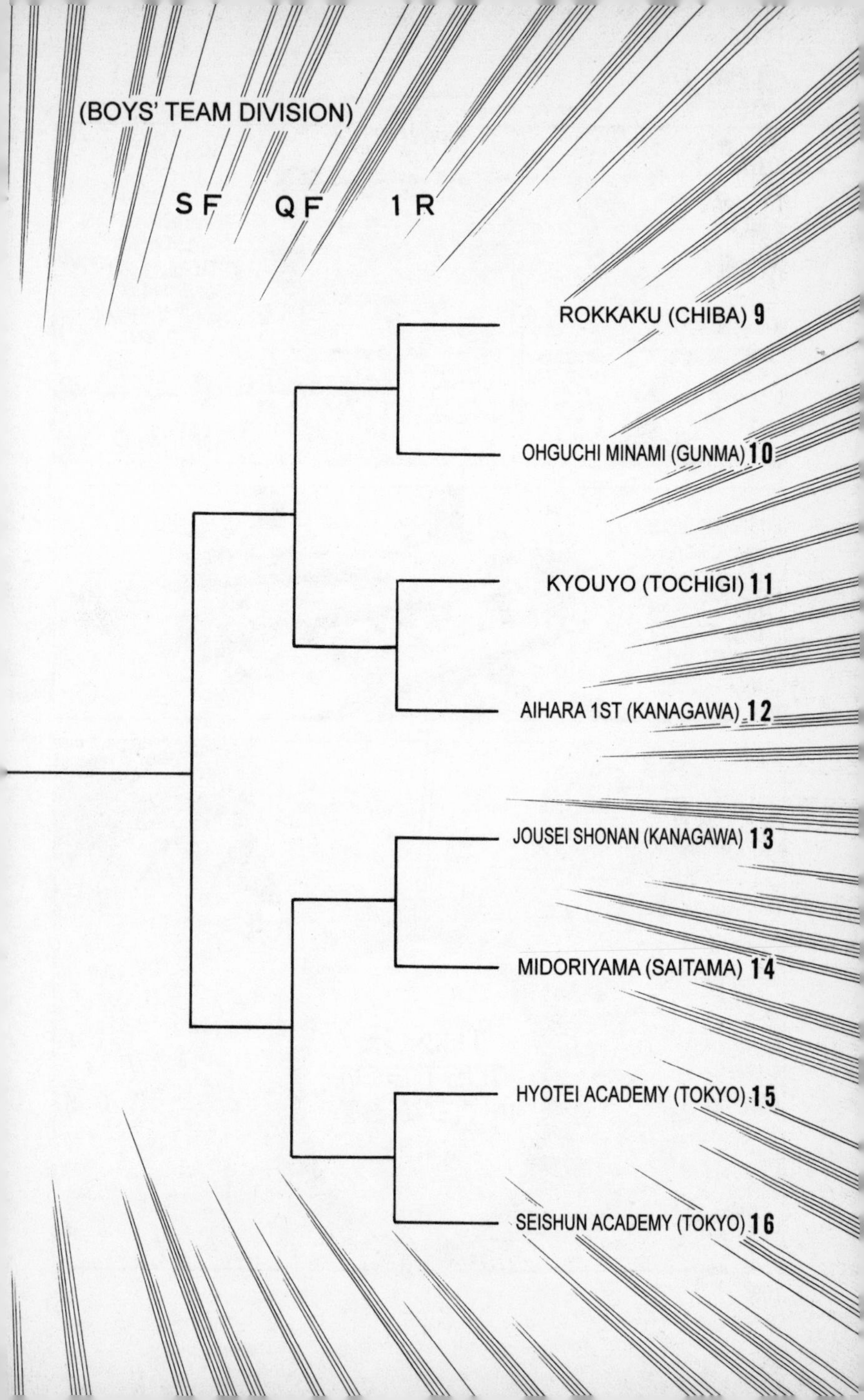
SF
QF
1R
ROKKAKU (CHIBA) 9
OHGUCHI MINAMI (GUNMA) 10
KYOUYO (TOCHIGI) 11
AIHARA 1ST (KANAGAWA) 12
JOUSEI SHONAN (KANAGAWA) 13
MIDORIYAMA (SAITAMA) 14
HYOTEI ACADEMY (TOKYO) 15
SEISHUN ACADEMY (TOKYO) 16

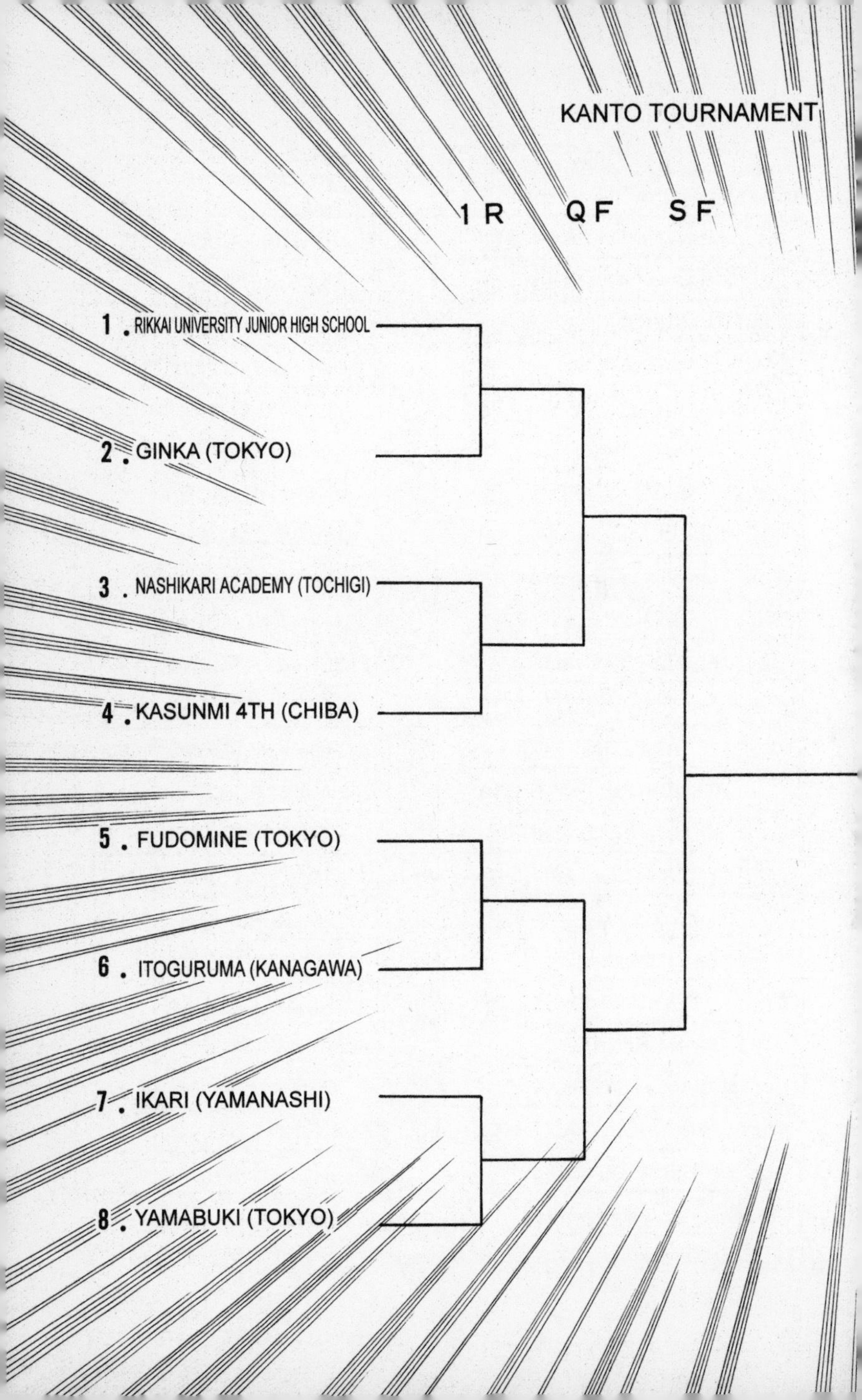
KANTO TOURNAMENT
1 R
Q F
S F
1. RIKKAI UNIVERSITY JUNIOR HIGH SCHOOL
2. GINKA (TOKYO)
3. NASHIKARI ACADEMY (TOCHIGI)
4. KASUNMI 4TH (CHIBA)
5. FUDOMINE (TOKYO)
6. ITOGURUMA (KANAGAWA)
7. IKARI (YAMANASHI)
8. YAMABUKI (TOKYO)

2002 VALENTINE'S DAY CHOCOLATE TALLY (1)

11TH AND BELOW!!

Rank	Name	Votes
11TH	MUNEHIRO KABAJI	60
12TH	TAKASHI KAWAMURA	45
13TH	SHINJI IBU	43
14TH	AKIRA KAMIO	39
15TH	JIN AKUTSU	24
	HAJIME MIZUKI	
17TH	KEIGO ATOBE	22
	KIPPEI TACHIBANA	
19TH	YOSHIRO AKAZAWA	15
	KALPIN	
	KENTARO MINAMI	
22ND	RYO SHISHIDO	13
	TAICHI DAN	
24TH	ATSUSHI KISARAZU	10
	TOUJI MUROMACHI	
26TH	YUSHI OSHITARI	9
	YUTA FUJI	
	TK WORKS	
29TH	TETSU ISHIDA	7
	INAKICHI NITOBE	
	MASAMI HIGASHIKATA	
32ND	MASASHI ARAI	6
	KYOUSUKE UCHIMURA	

Rank	Name	Votes
34TH	HAZUE KAIDO	5
	AKAYA KIRIHARA	
36TH	GAKUTO MUKAHI	4
	SHINYA YANAGISAWA	
38TH	CHOTARO OHTORI	3
	KACHIRO KATO	
	ICHIRO KANEDA	
	MASAYA SAKURAI	
	GENICHIRO SANADA	
	TAKUYA NOMURA	
	MICHIRU FUKUSHI	
	HIGASHI (EDITOR)	
46TH	JIRO AKUTAGAWA	2
	NANJIRO ECHIZEN	
	HAGINOSUKE TAKI	
49TH	TOMOYA IZUMI	1
	AN TACHIBANA	
	KUNIKAZU TEZUKA	
	KUNIHARU TEZUKA	
	KIMIYOSHI FUKAWA	
	RENJI YANAGI	
	SAKUNO RYUZAKI	

ASSESSMENT: KABAJI'S APPEARANCE WAS A SURPRISE. THANK YOU FOR THE CHOCOLATES AND OTHER GIFTS. I'M HAPPY I CREPT INTO 3RD. *(LAUGH)*

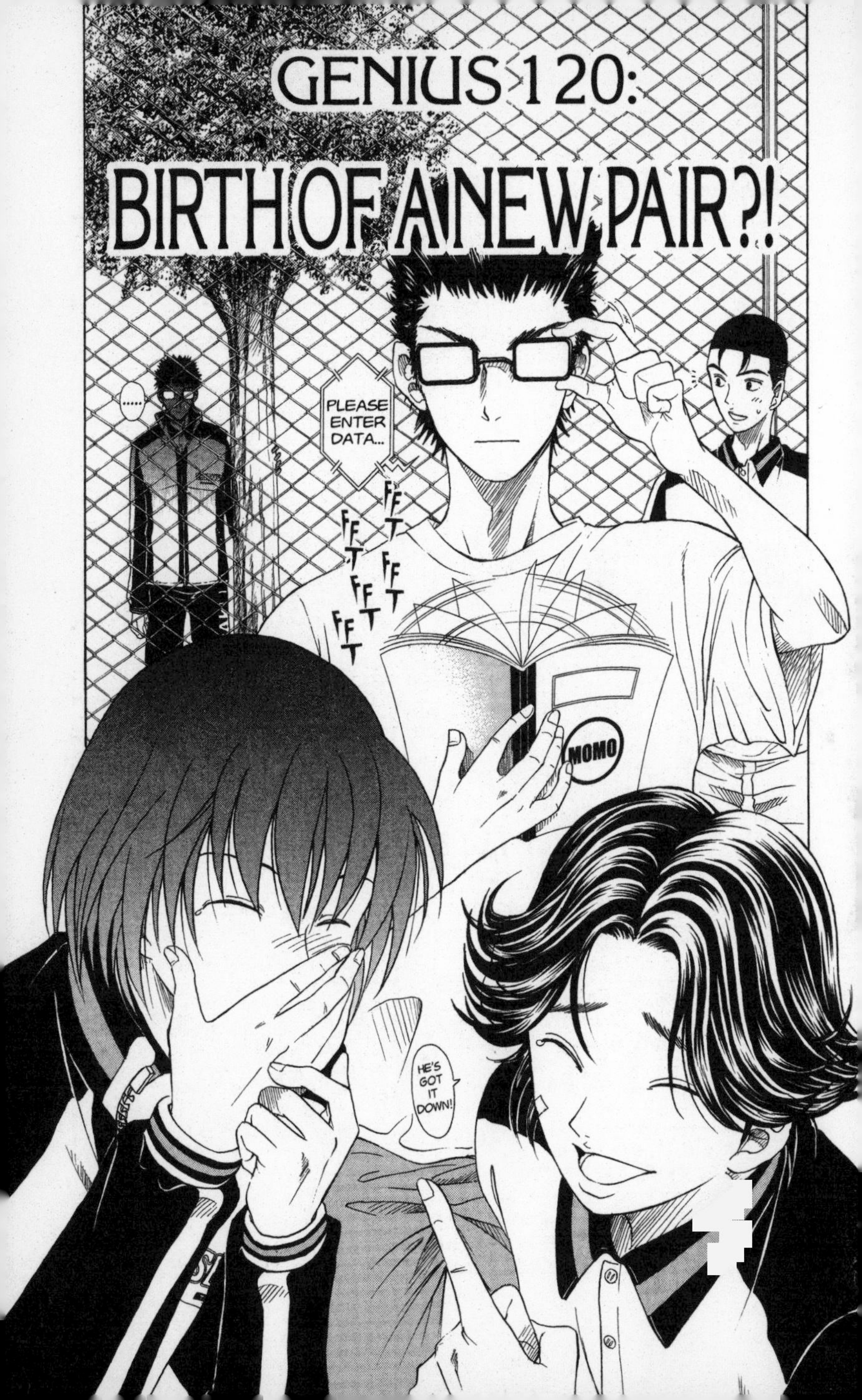
GENIUS 120:
BIRTH OF A NEW PAIR?!
......
PLEASE ENTER DATA...
FFT FFT FFT FFT FFT
MOMO
HE'S GOT IT DOWN!

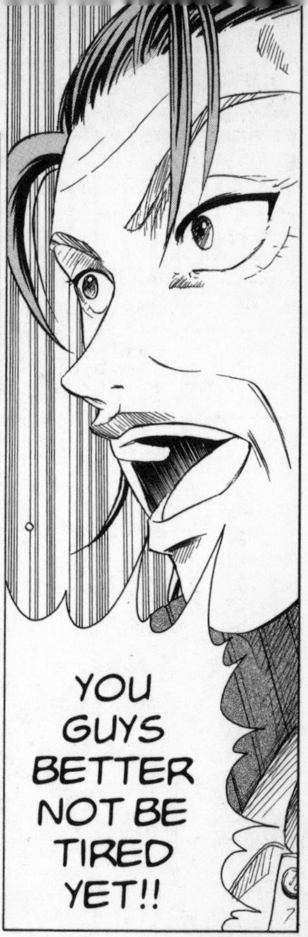
YOU GUYS BETTER NOT BE TIRED YET!!
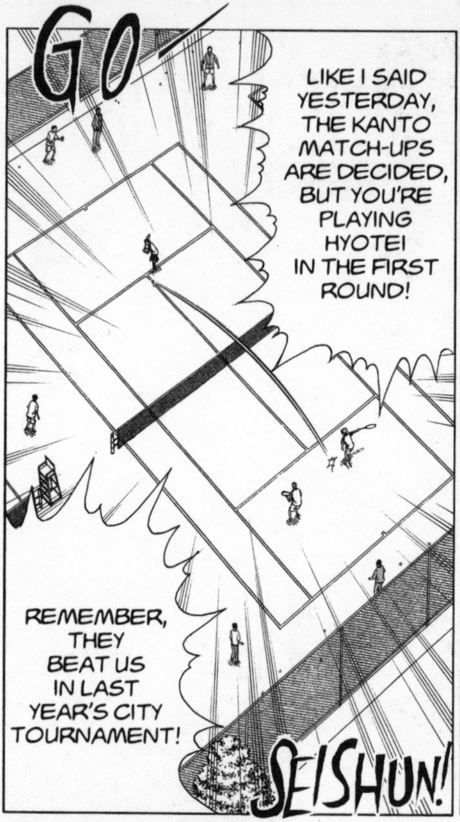
LIKE I SAID YESTERDAY, THE KANTO MATCH-UPS ARE DECIDED, BUT YOU'RE PLAYING HYOTEI IN THE FIRST ROUND!
REMEMBER, THEY BEAT US IN LAST YEAR'S CITY TOURNAMENT!
GO—
SEISHUN!
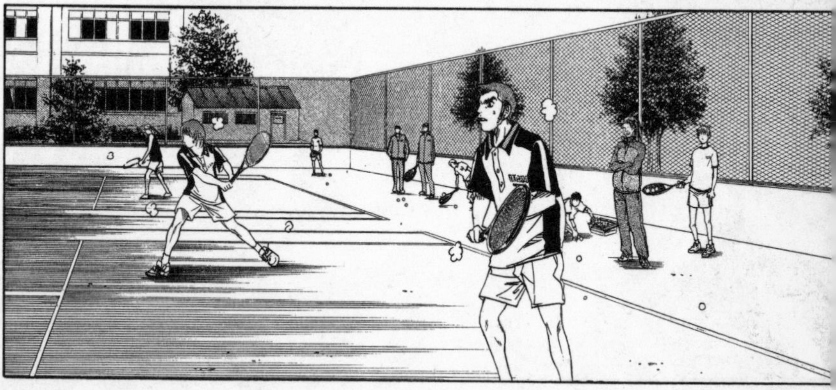

READ THIS WAY

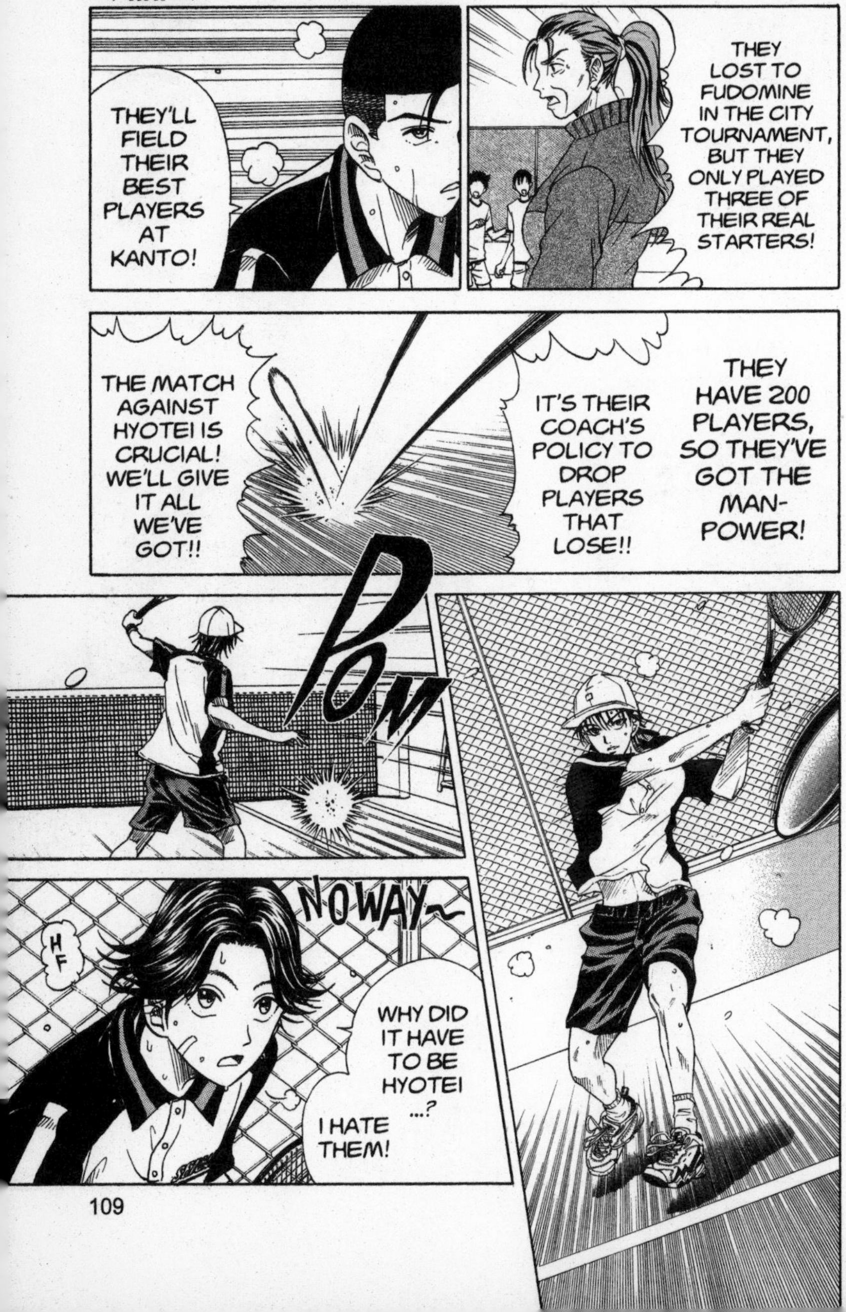
THEY LOST TO FUDOMINE IN THE CITY TOURNAMENT, BUT THEY ONLY PLAYED THREE OF THEIR REAL STARTERS!
THEY'LL FIELD THEIR BEST PLAYERS AT KANTO!
THEY HAVE 200 PLAYERS, SO THEY'VE GOT THE MAN-POWER!
IT'S THEIR COACH'S POLICY TO DROP PLAYERS THAT LOSE!!
THE MATCH AGAINST HYOTEI IS CRUCIAL! WE'LL GIVE IT ALL WE'VE GOT!!
POM
NO WAY~
HF
WHY DID IT HAVE TO BE HYOTEI ...?
I HATE THEM!

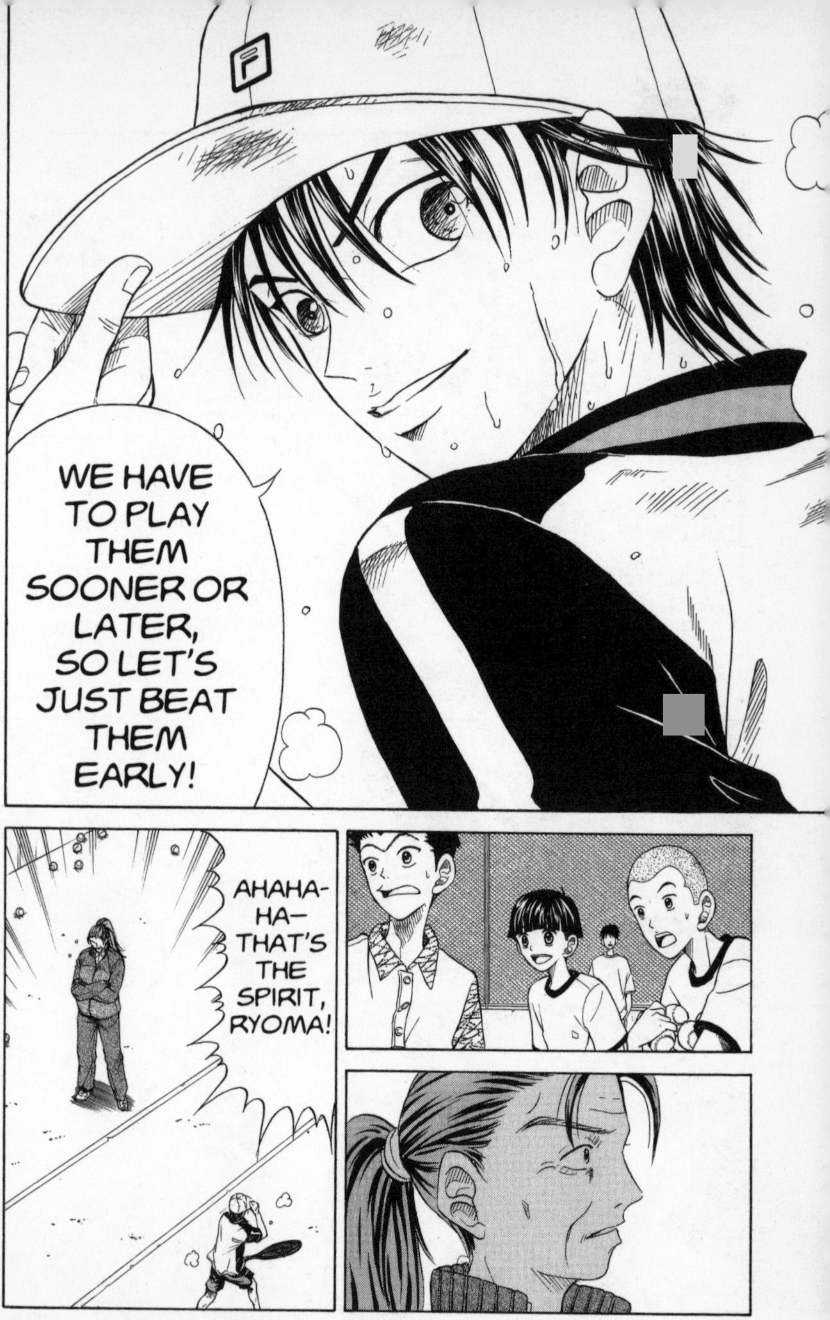
WE HAVE TO PLAY THEM SOONER OR LATER, SO LET'S JUST BEAT THEM EARLY!
AHAHA-HA— THAT'S THE SPIRIT, RYOMA!

READ THIS WAY

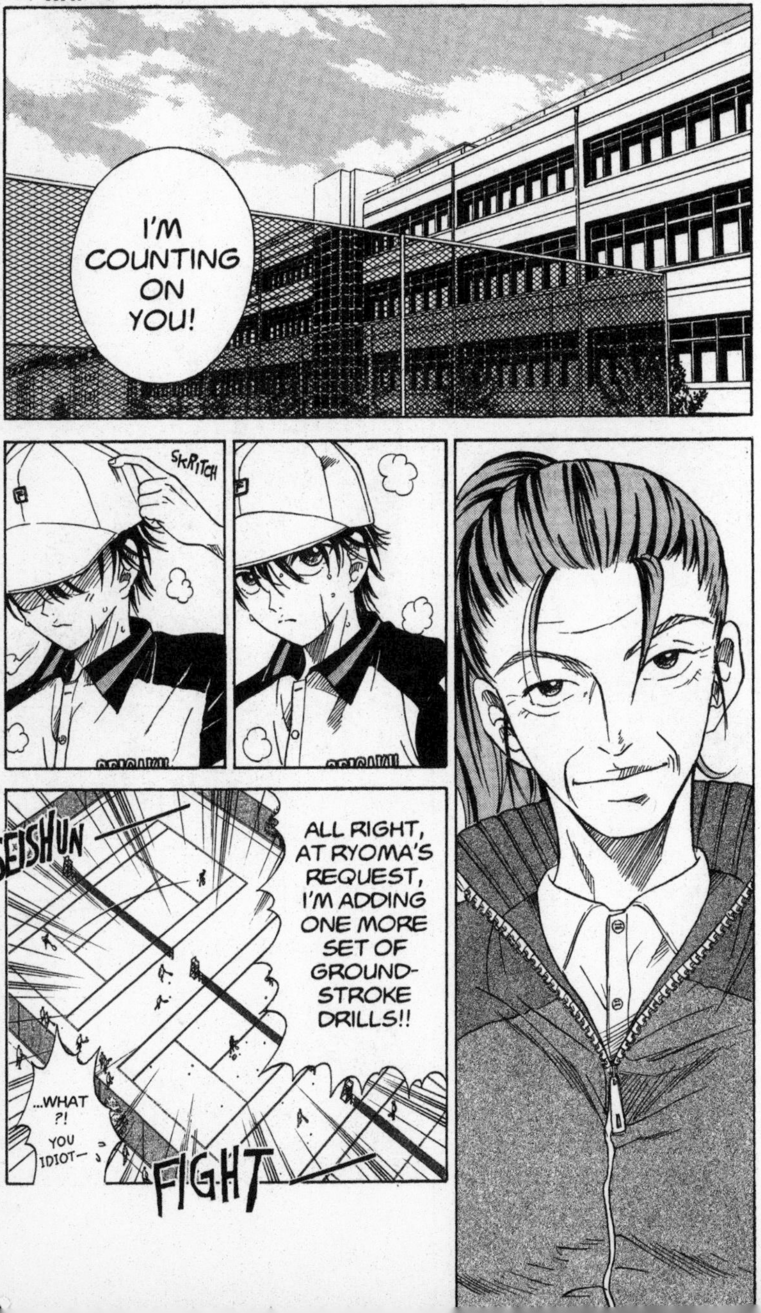
I'M COUNTING ON YOU!
SKRITCH
ALL RIGHT, AT RYOMA'S REQUEST, I'M ADDING ONE MORE SET OF GROUND-STROKE DRILLS!!
SEISHUN
...WHAT ?!
YOU IDIOT—
FIGHT

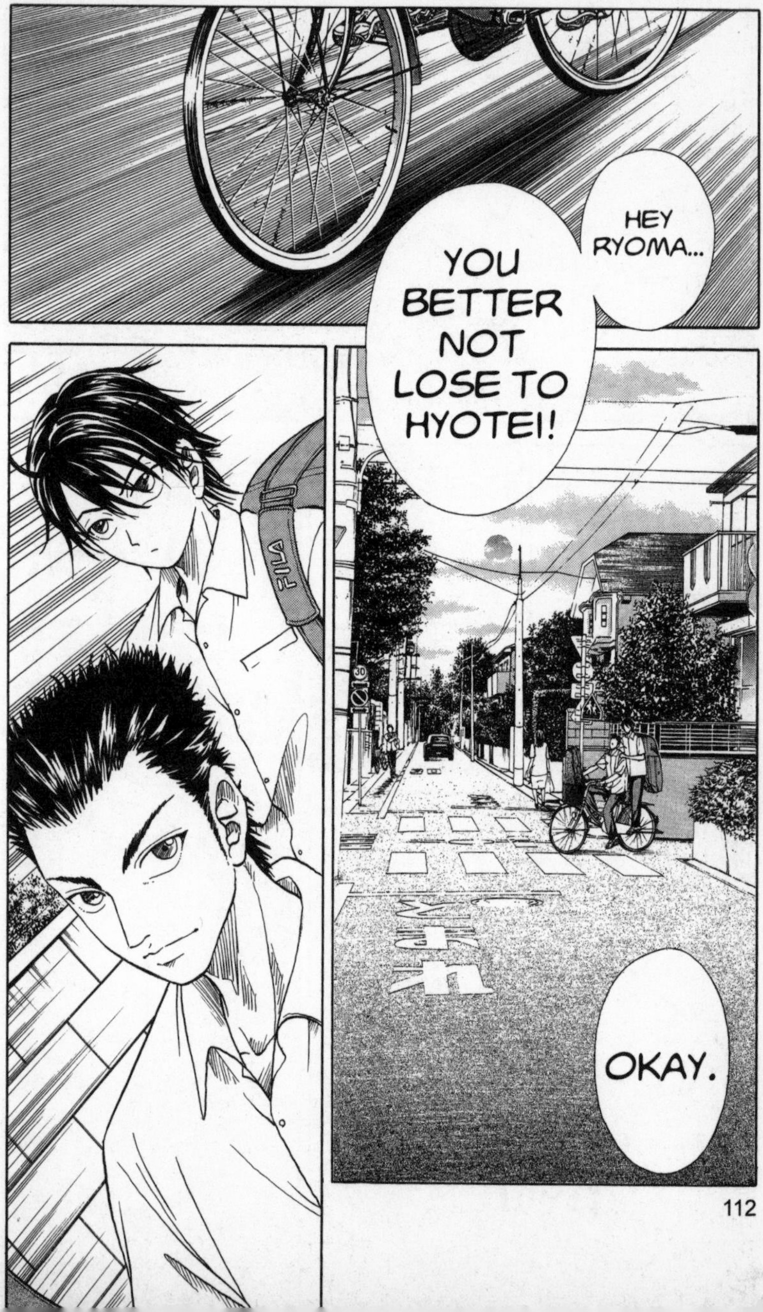
HEY RYOMA...
YOU BETTER NOT LOSE TO HYOTEI!
OKAY.

READ THIS WAY

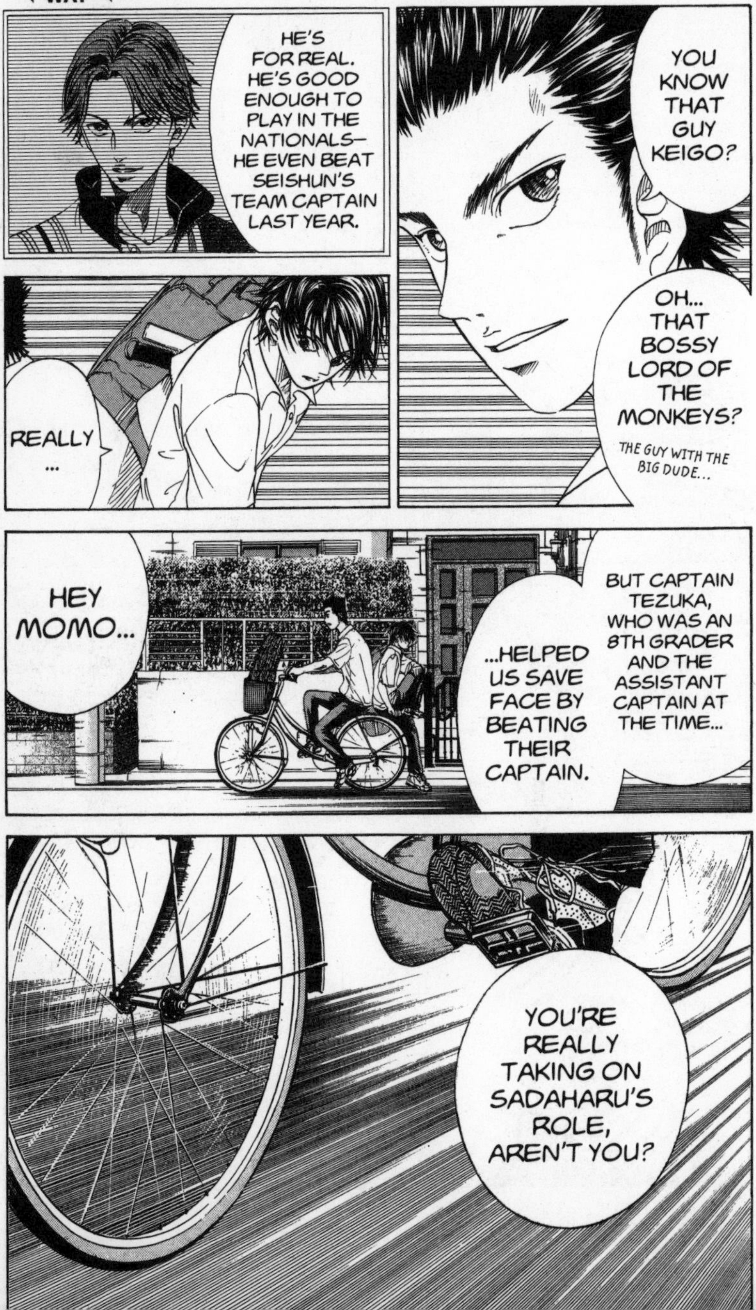

YOU KNOW THAT GUY KEIGO?
OH... THAT BOSSY LORD OF THE MONKEYS?
THE GUY WITH THE BIG DUDE...
HE'S FOR REAL. HE'S GOOD ENOUGH TO PLAY IN THE NATIONALS— HE EVEN BEAT SEISHUN'S TEAM CAPTAIN LAST YEAR.
REALLY ...
BUT CAPTAIN TEZUKA, WHO WAS AN 8TH GRADER AND THE ASSISTANT CAPTAIN AT THE TIME...
...HELPED US SAVE FACE BY BEATING THEIR CAPTAIN.
HEY MOMO...
YOU'RE REALLY TAKING ON SADAHARU'S ROLE, AREN'T YOU?

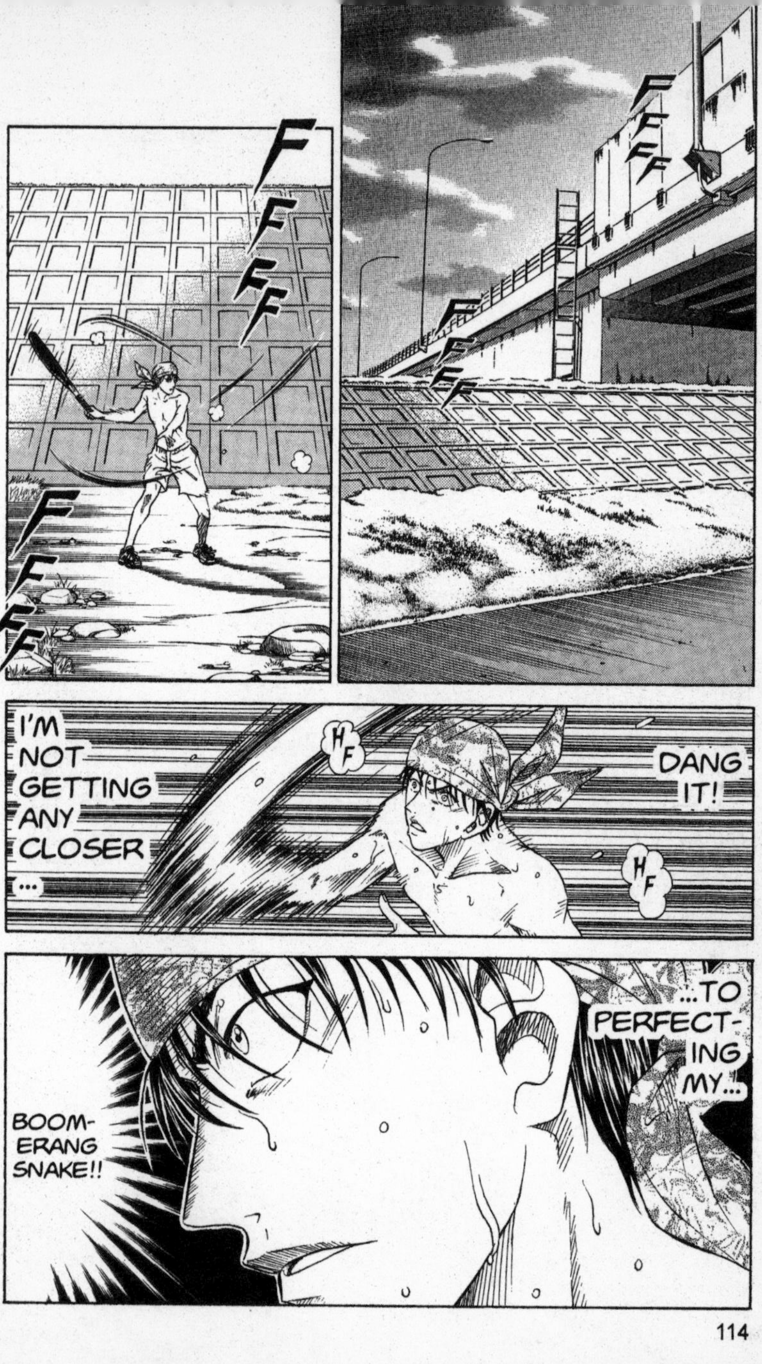
FFFF
FFFF
FFFF
FFFF
DANG IT!
HF
HF
I'M NOT GETTING ANY CLOSER...
...TO PERFECTING MY...
BOOMERANG SNAKE!!

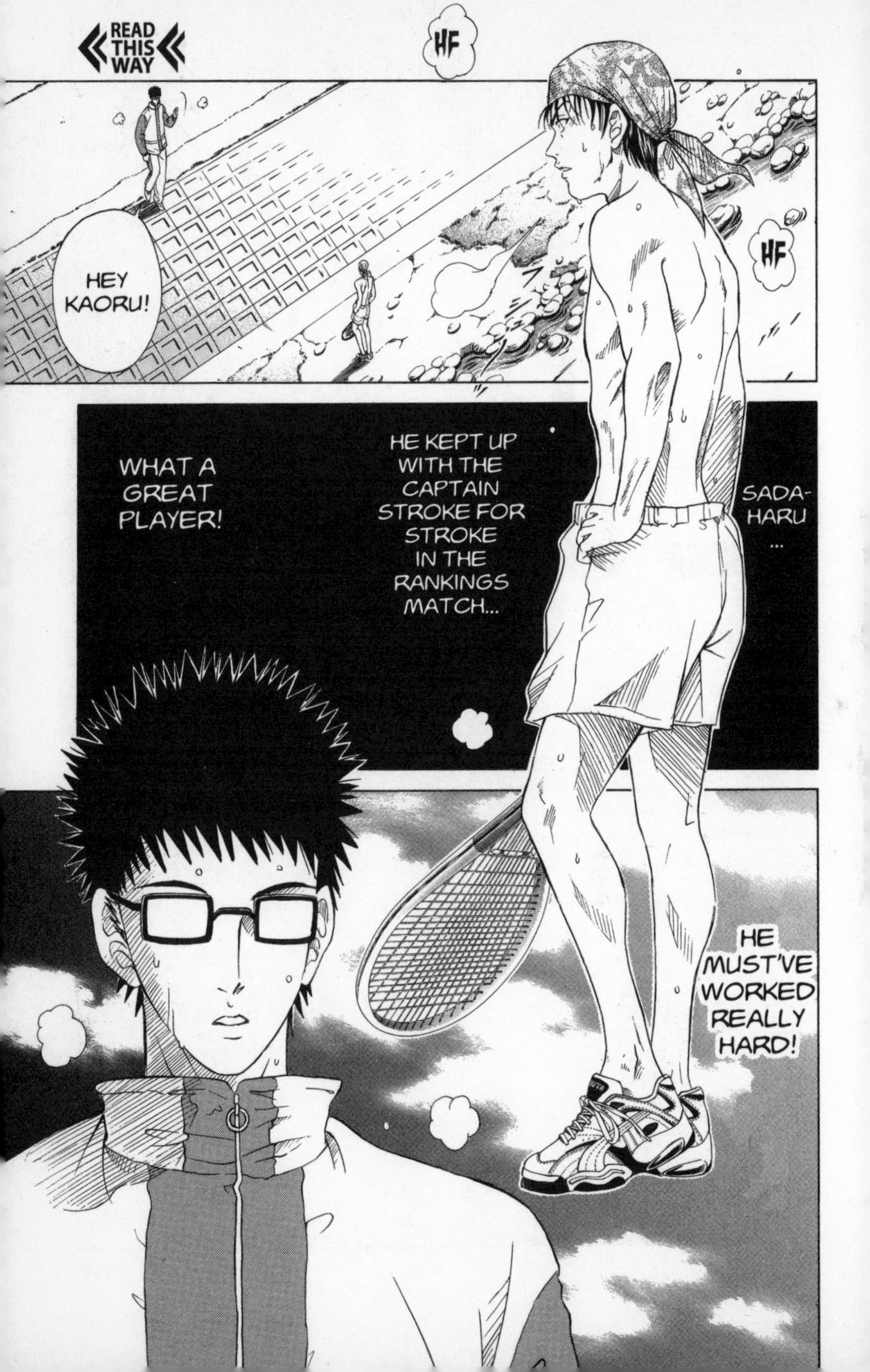
READ THIS WAY
HF
HF
HEY KAORU!
SADAHARU...
HE KEPT UP WITH THE CAPTAIN STROKE FOR STROKE IN THE RANKINGS MATCH...
WHAT A GREAT PLAYER!
HE MUST'VE WORKED REALLY HARD!

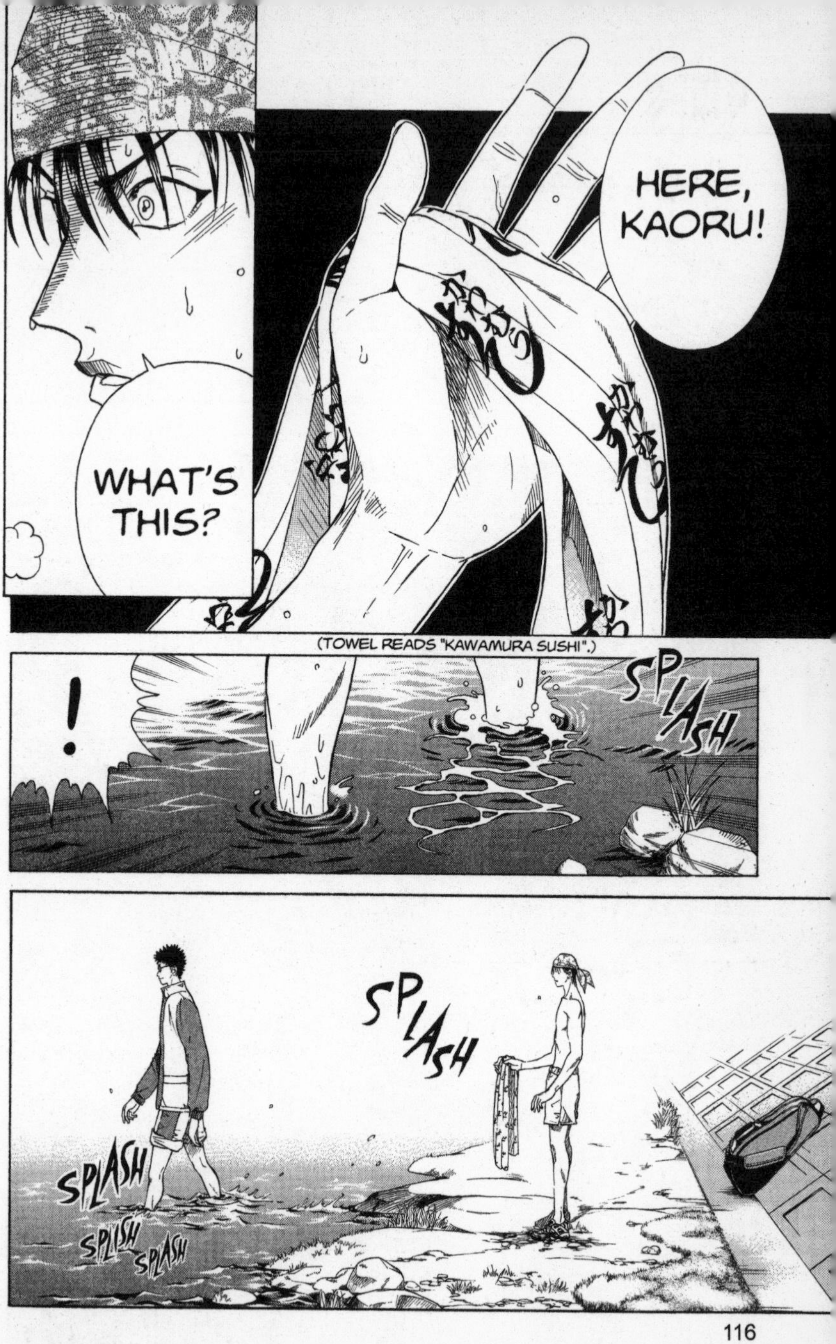
HERE, KAORU!
WHAT'S THIS?
(TOWEL READS "KAWAMURA SUSHI".)
SPLASH
!
SPLASH
SPLASH
SPLASH
SPLASH

READ THIS WAY

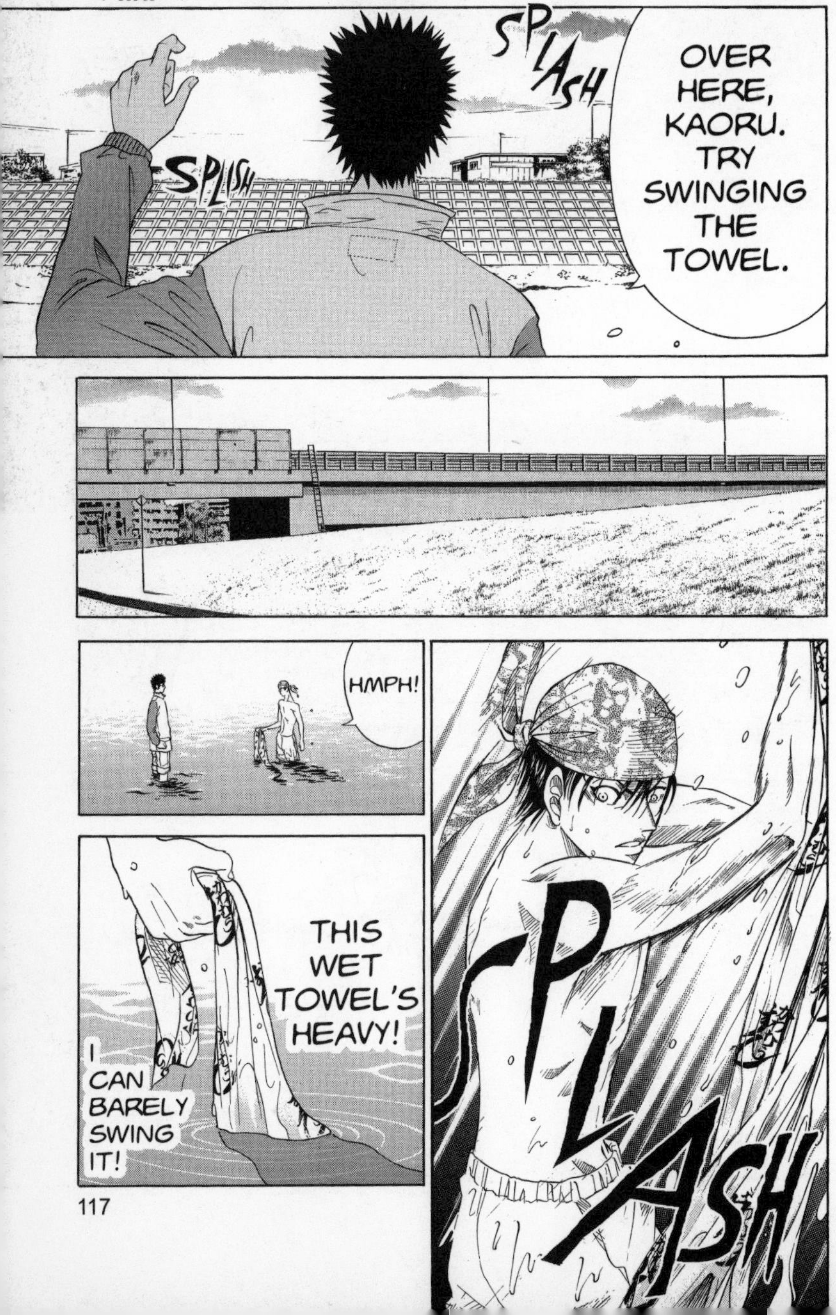
OVER HERE, KAORU. TRY SWINGING THE TOWEL.
SPLASH
SPLISH
SPLASH
HMPH!
THIS WET TOWEL'S HEAVY!
I CAN BARELY SWING IT!

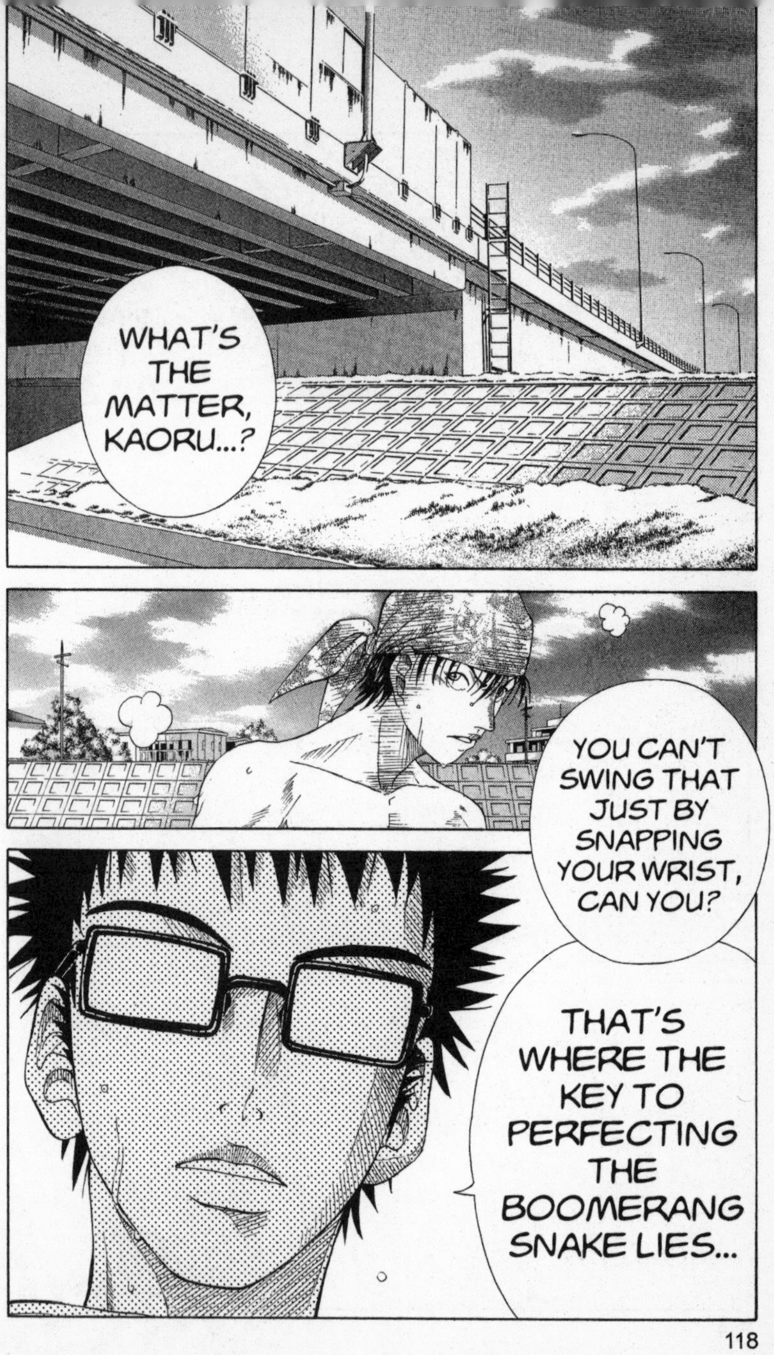
WHAT'S THE MATTER, KAORU...?
YOU CAN'T SWING THAT JUST BY SNAPPING YOUR WRIST, CAN YOU?
THAT'S WHERE THE KEY TO PERFECTING THE BOOMERANG SNAKE LIES...

READ THIS WAY

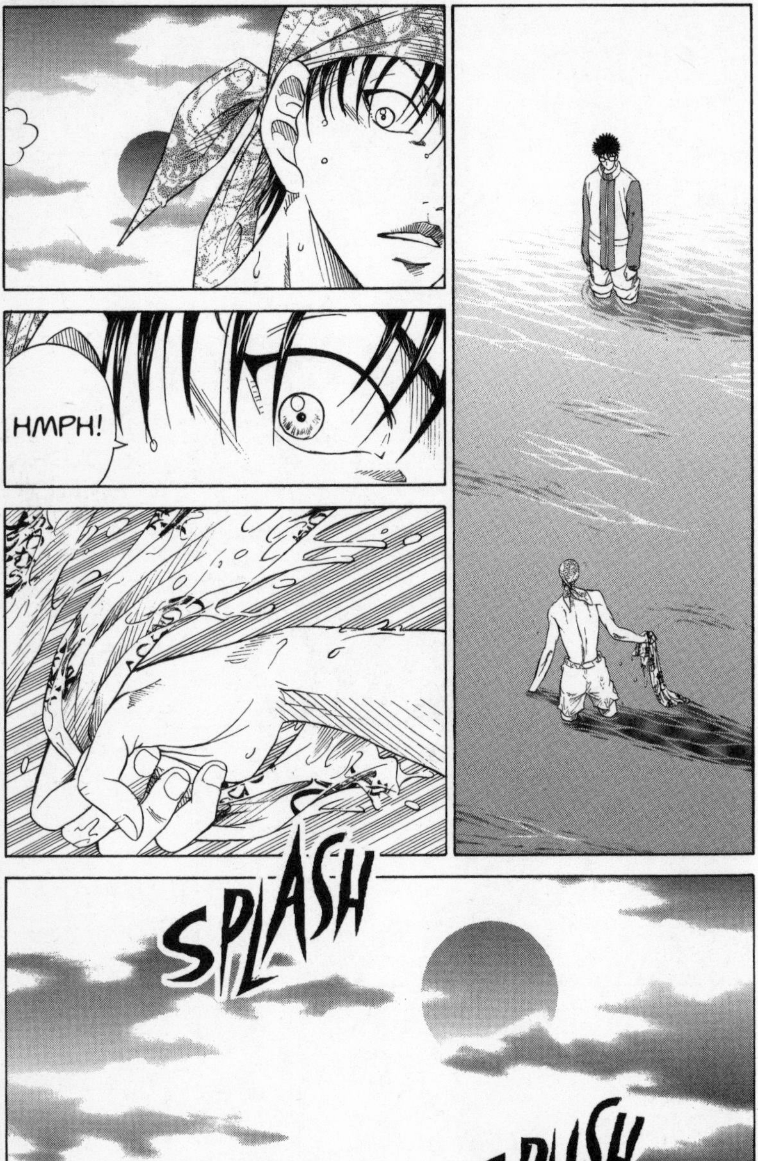
HMPH!
SPLASH
SPLISH

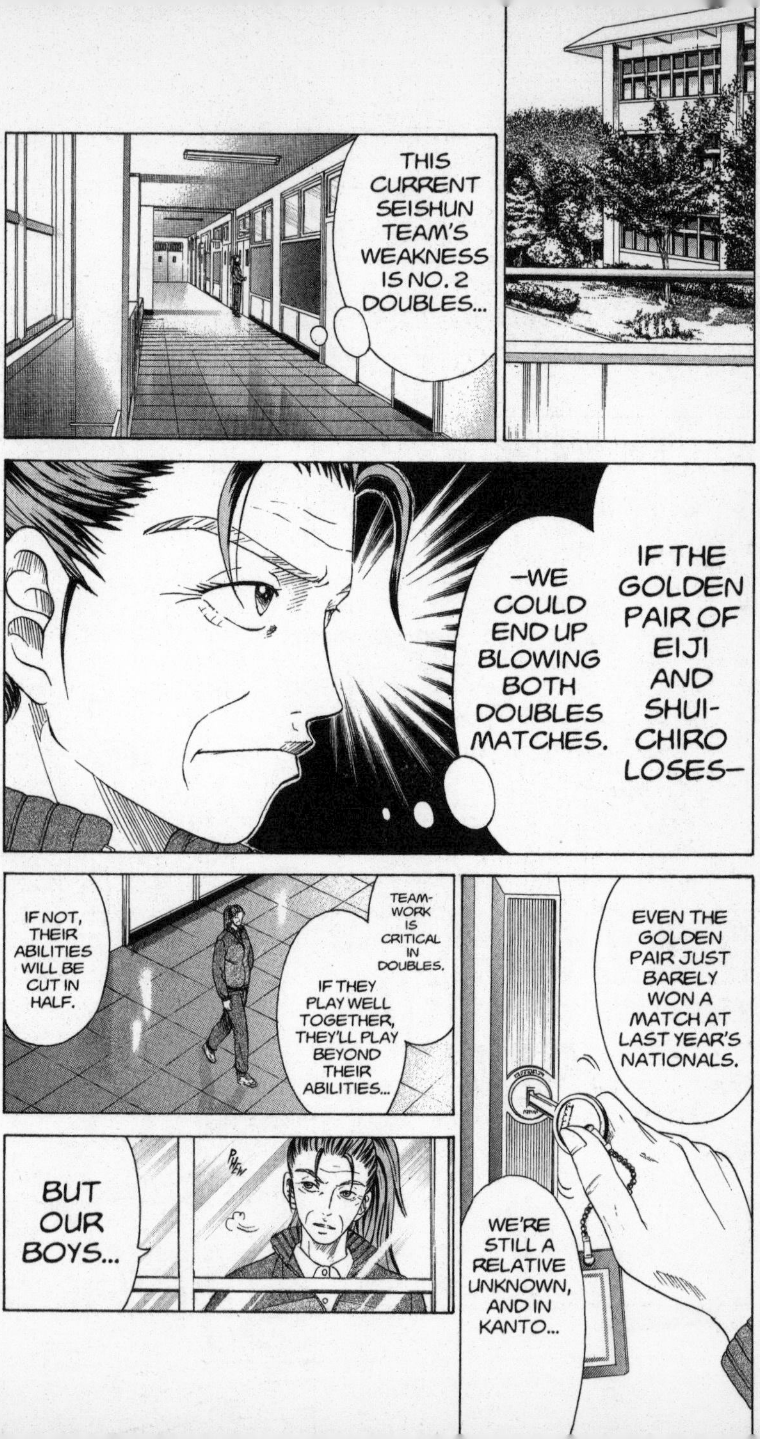
THIS CURRENT SEISHUN TEAM'S WEAKNESS IS NO. 2 DOUBLES...
IF THE GOLDEN PAIR OF EIJI AND SHUI-CHIRO LOSES—
—WE COULD END UP BLOWING BOTH DOUBLES MATCHES.
EVEN THE GOLDEN PAIR JUST BARELY WON A MATCH AT LAST YEAR'S NATIONALS.
WE'RE STILL A RELATIVE UNKNOWN, AND IN KANTO...
TEAM-WORK IS CRITICAL IN DOUBLES.
IF THEY PLAY WELL TOGETHER, THEY'LL PLAY BEYOND THEIR ABILITIES...
IF NOT, THEIR ABILITIES WILL BE CUT IN HALF.
PHEW
BUT OUR BOYS...

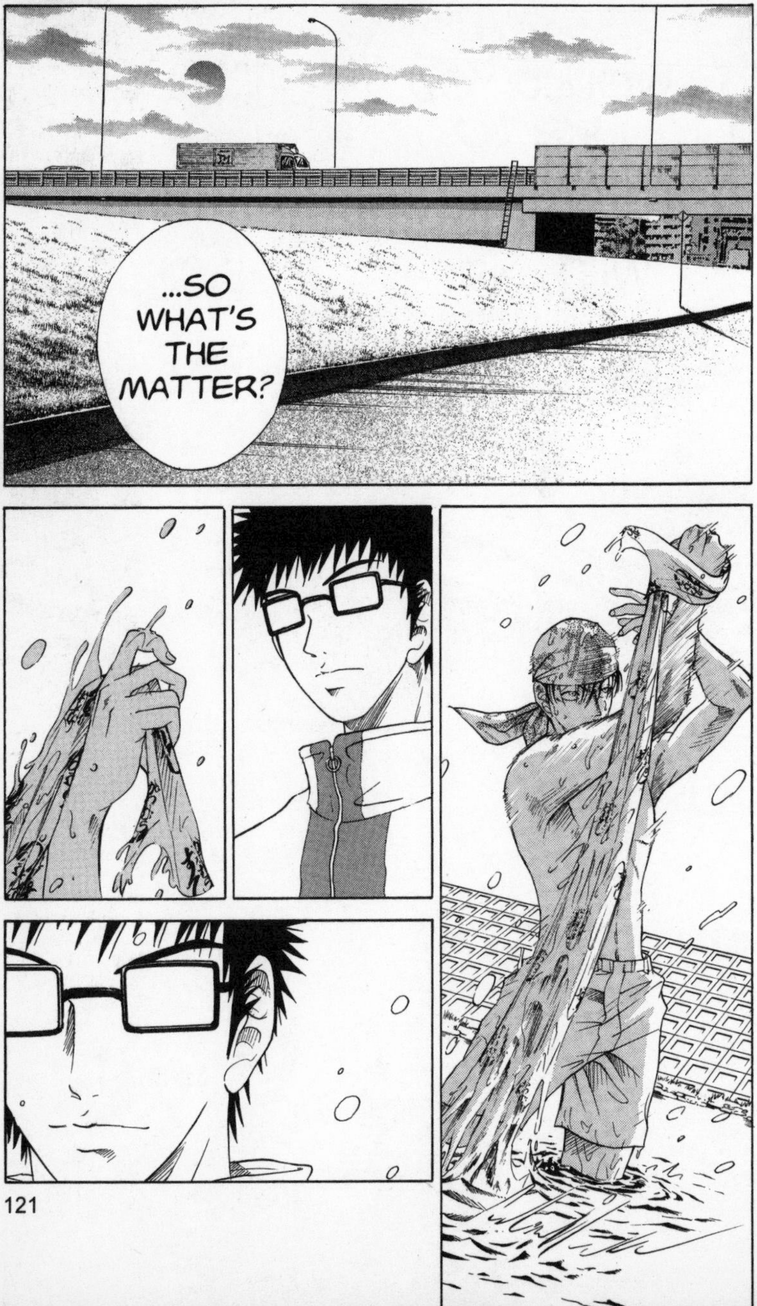
...SO WHAT'S THE MATTER?

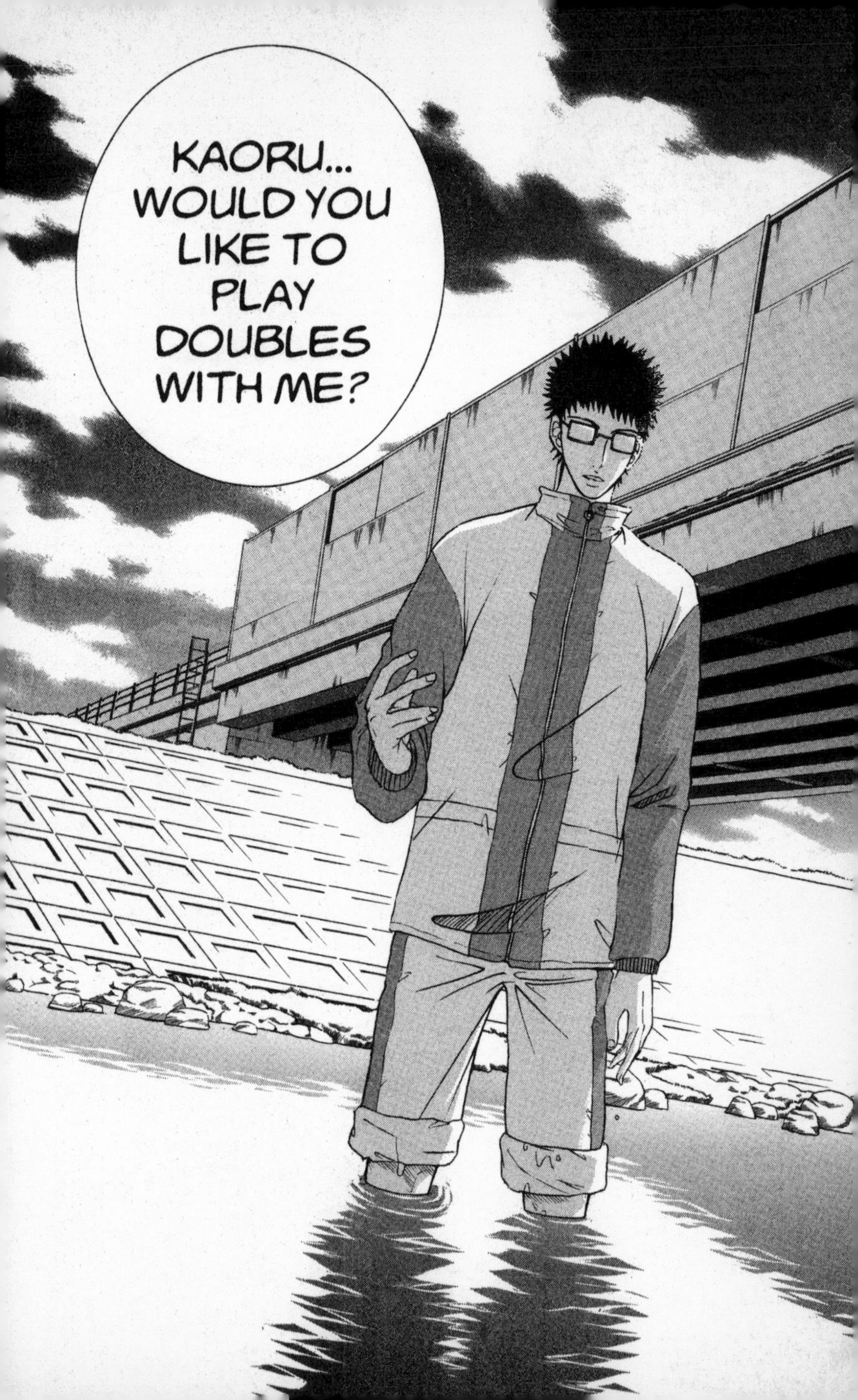
KAORU... WOULD YOU LIKE TO PLAY DOUBLES WITH ME?

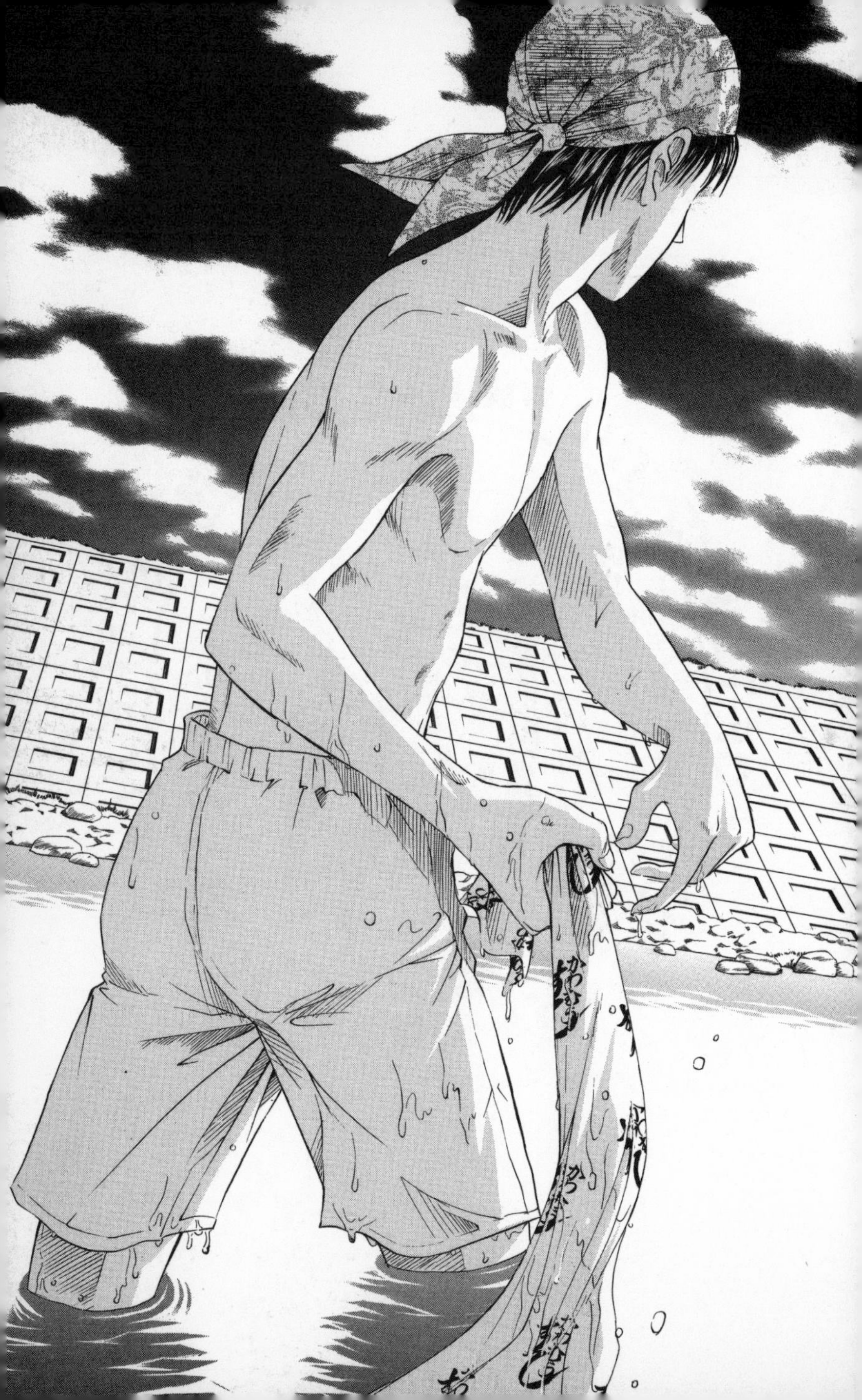

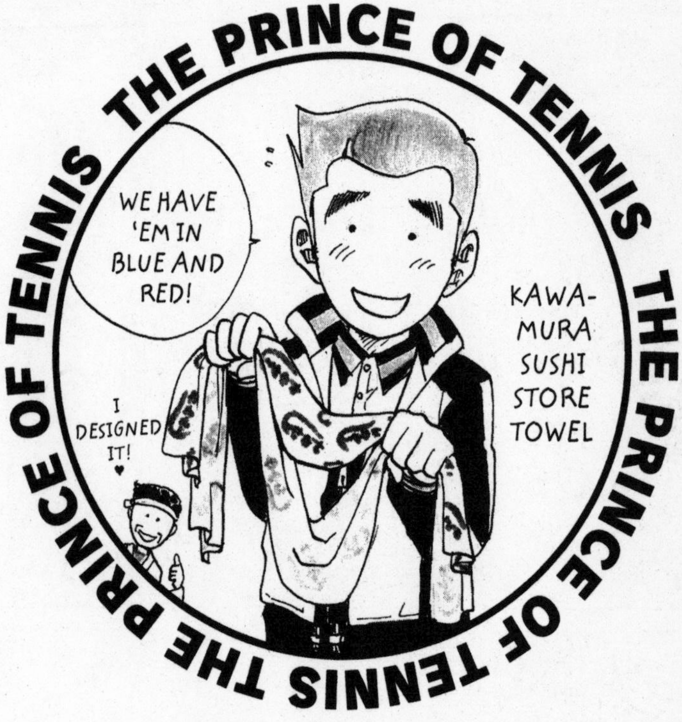
THE PRINCE OF TENNIS THE PRINCE OF TENNIS THE PRINCE OF TENNIS
WE HAVE 'EM IN BLUE AND RED!
KAWA-MURA SUSHI STORE TOWEL
I DESIGNED IT! ♥

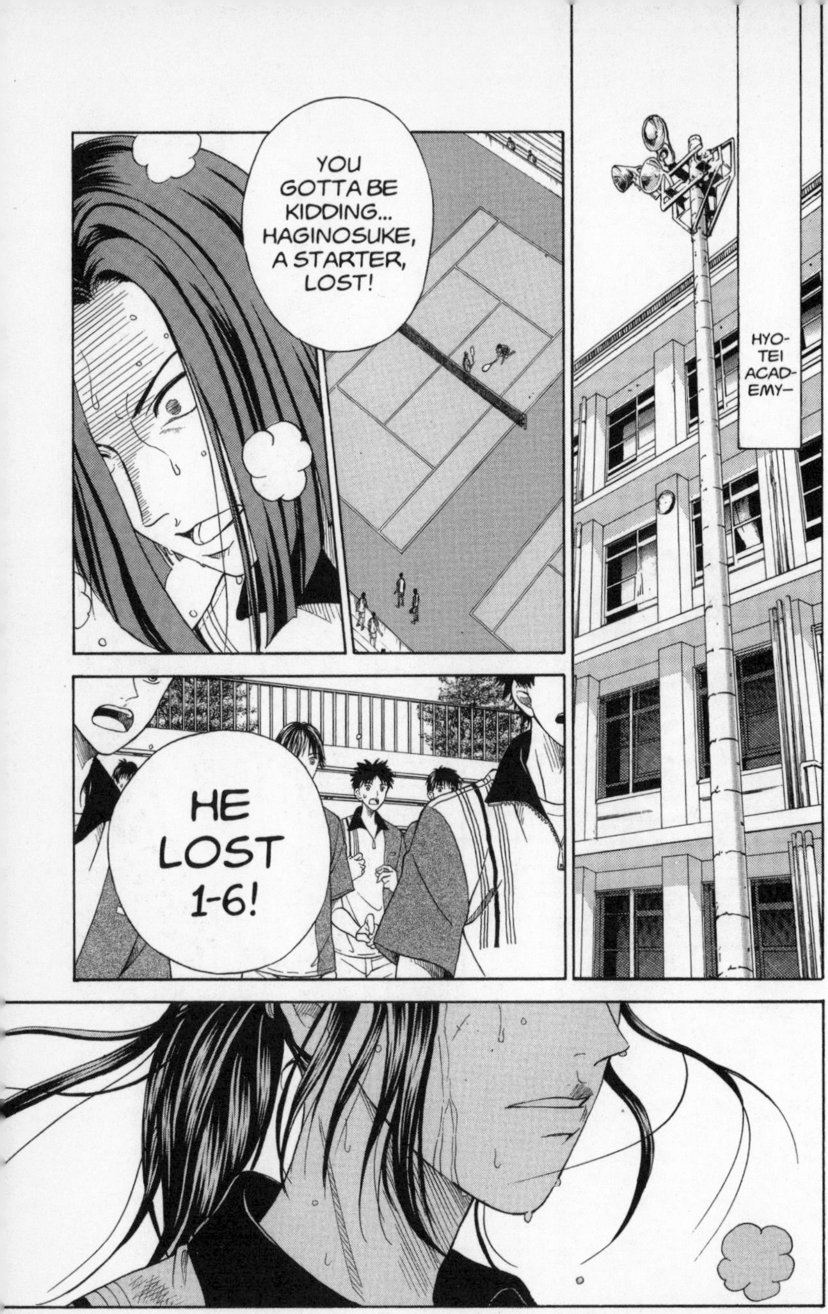
HYO-TEI ACAD-EMY—
YOU GOTTA BE KIDDING... HAGINOSUKE, A STARTER, LOST!
HE LOST 1-6!

GENIUS 121: RYO ONCE AGAIN

GENIUS 121: RYO ONCE AGAIN

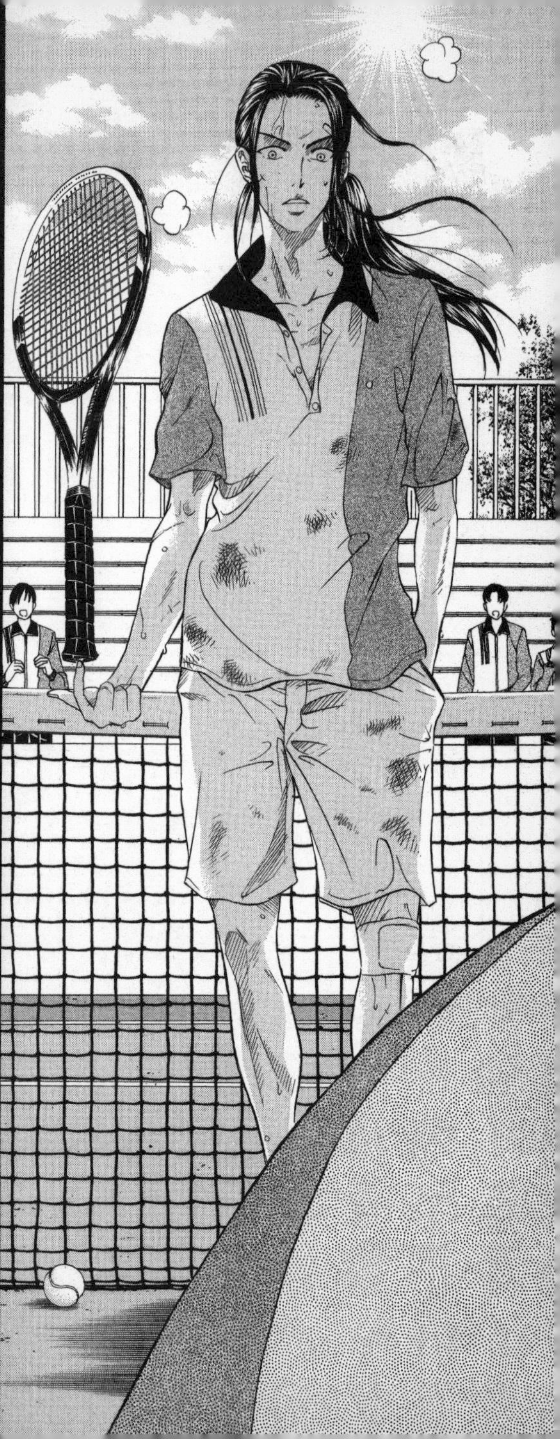

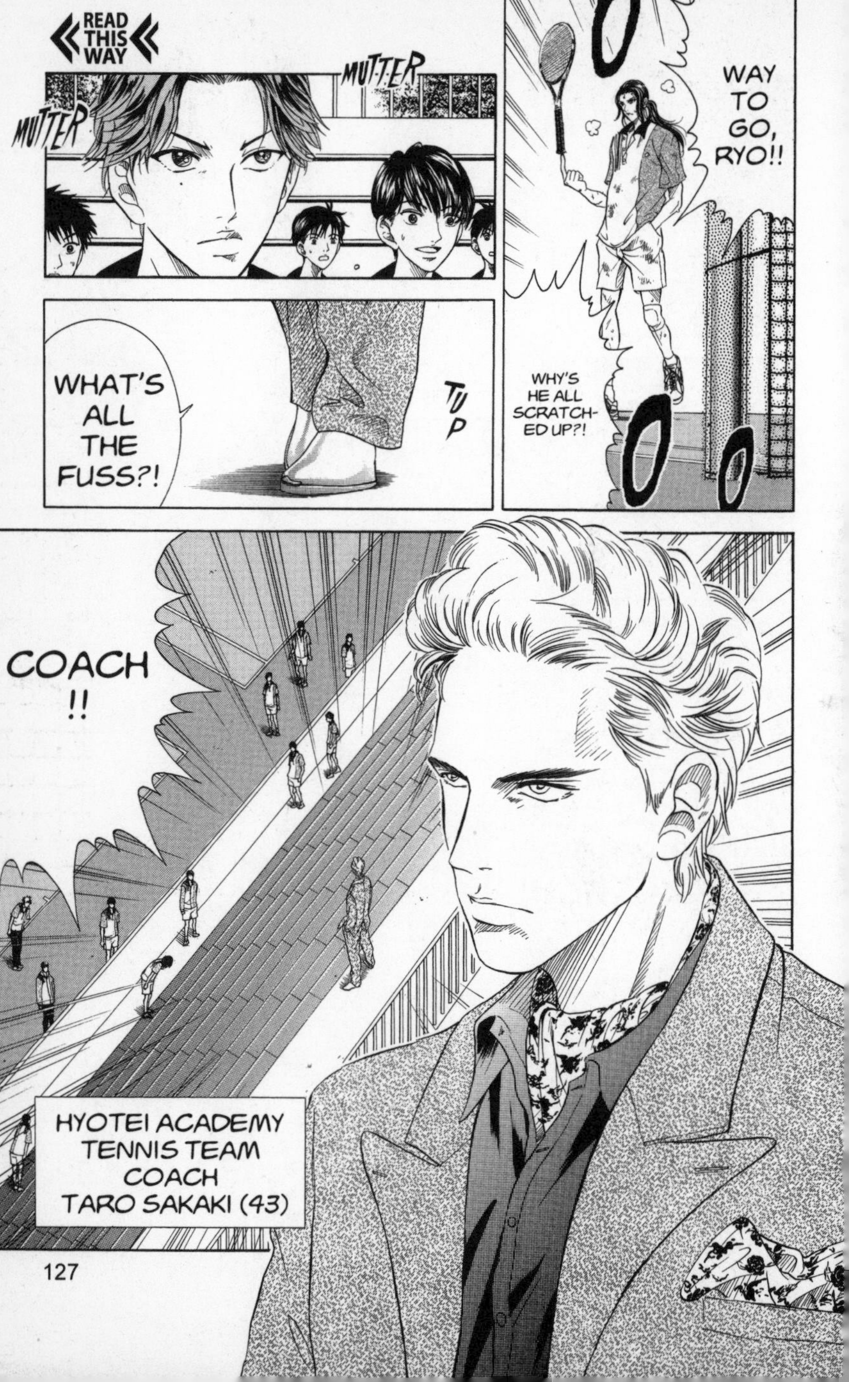
READ THIS WAY
WAY TO GO, RYO!!
WHY'S HE ALL SCRATCHED UP?!
MUTTER
MUTTER
WHAT'S ALL THE FUSS?!
TUP
COACH !!
HYOTEI ACADEMY TENNIS TEAM COACH TARO SAKAKI (43)

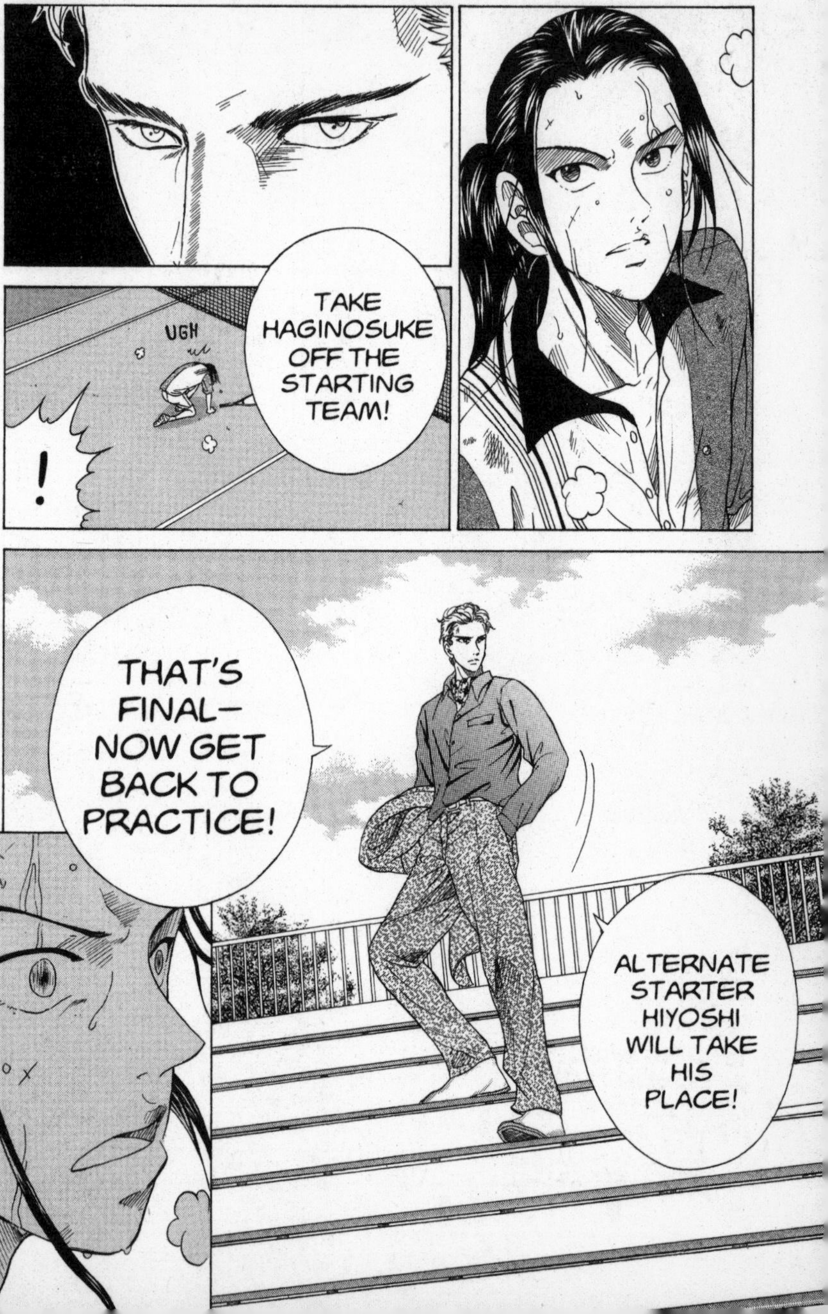
TAKE HAGINOSUKE OFF THE STARTING TEAM!
UGH
!
ALTERNATE STARTER HIYOSHI WILL TAKE HIS PLACE!
THAT'S FINAL— NOW GET BACK TO PRACTICE!

READ THIS WAY

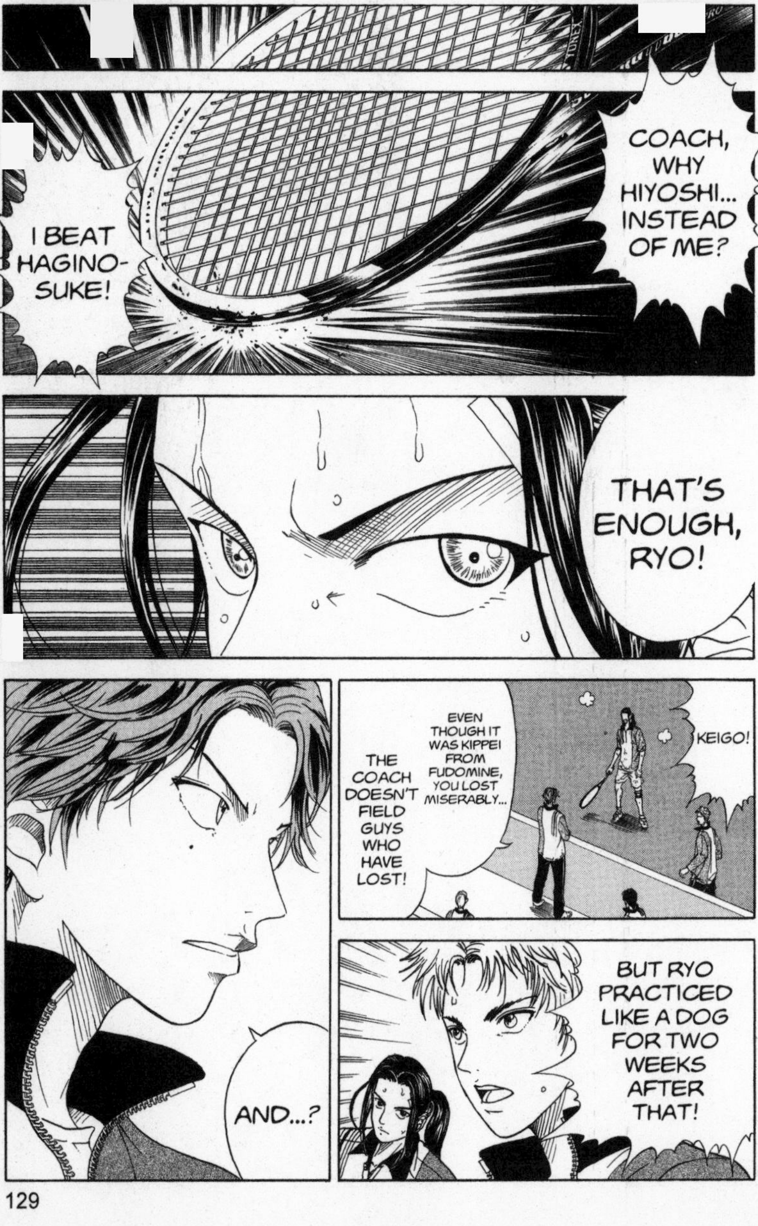
COACH, WHY HIYOSHI... INSTEAD OF ME?
I BEAT HAGINO-SUKE!
THAT'S ENOUGH, RYO!
KEIGO!
EVEN THOUGH IT WAS KIPPEI FROM FUDOMINE, YOU LOST MISERABLY...
THE COACH DOESN'T FIELD GUYS WHO HAVE LOST!
BUT RYO PRACTICED LIKE A DOG FOR TWO WEEKS AFTER THAT!
AND...?

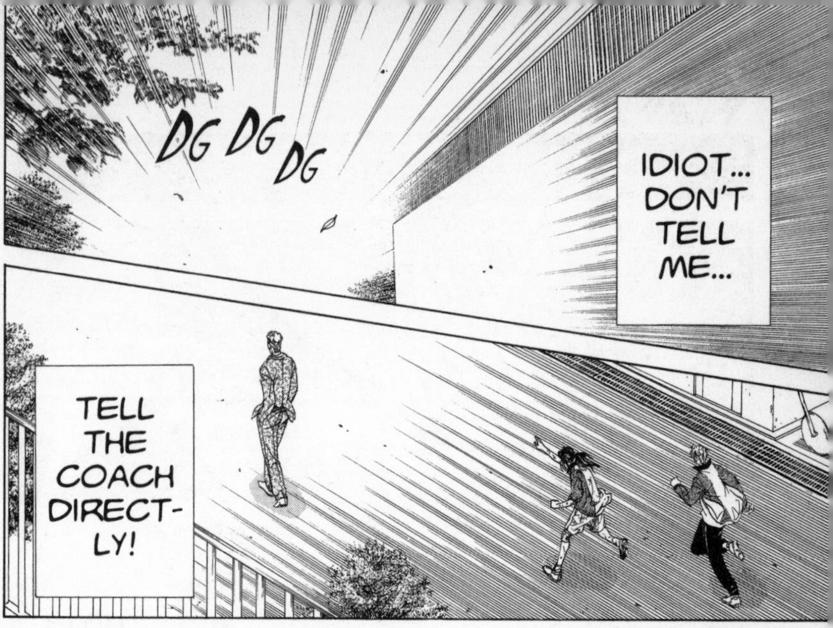
DG DG DG
IDIOT... DON'T TELL ME...
TELL THE COACH DIRECT-LY!

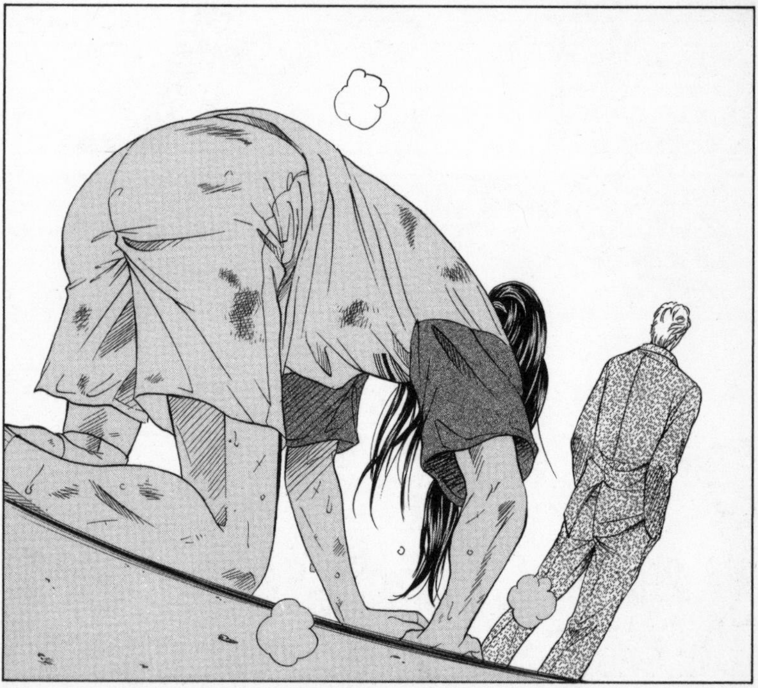

READ THIS WAY

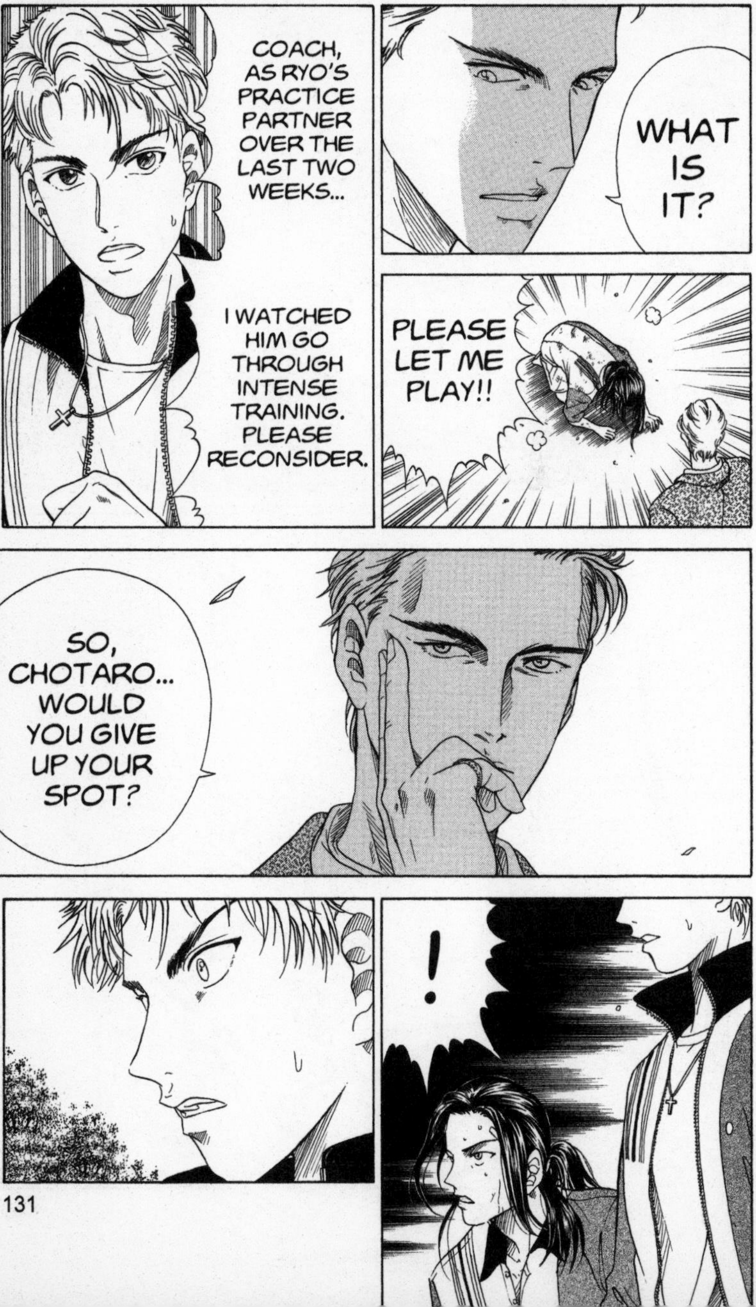
WHAT IS IT?
PLEASE LET ME PLAY!!
COACH, AS RYO'S PRACTICE PARTNER OVER THE LAST TWO WEEKS...
I WATCHED HIM GO THROUGH INTENSE TRAINING. PLEASE RECONSIDER.
SO, CHOTARO... WOULD YOU GIVE UP YOUR SPOT?
!

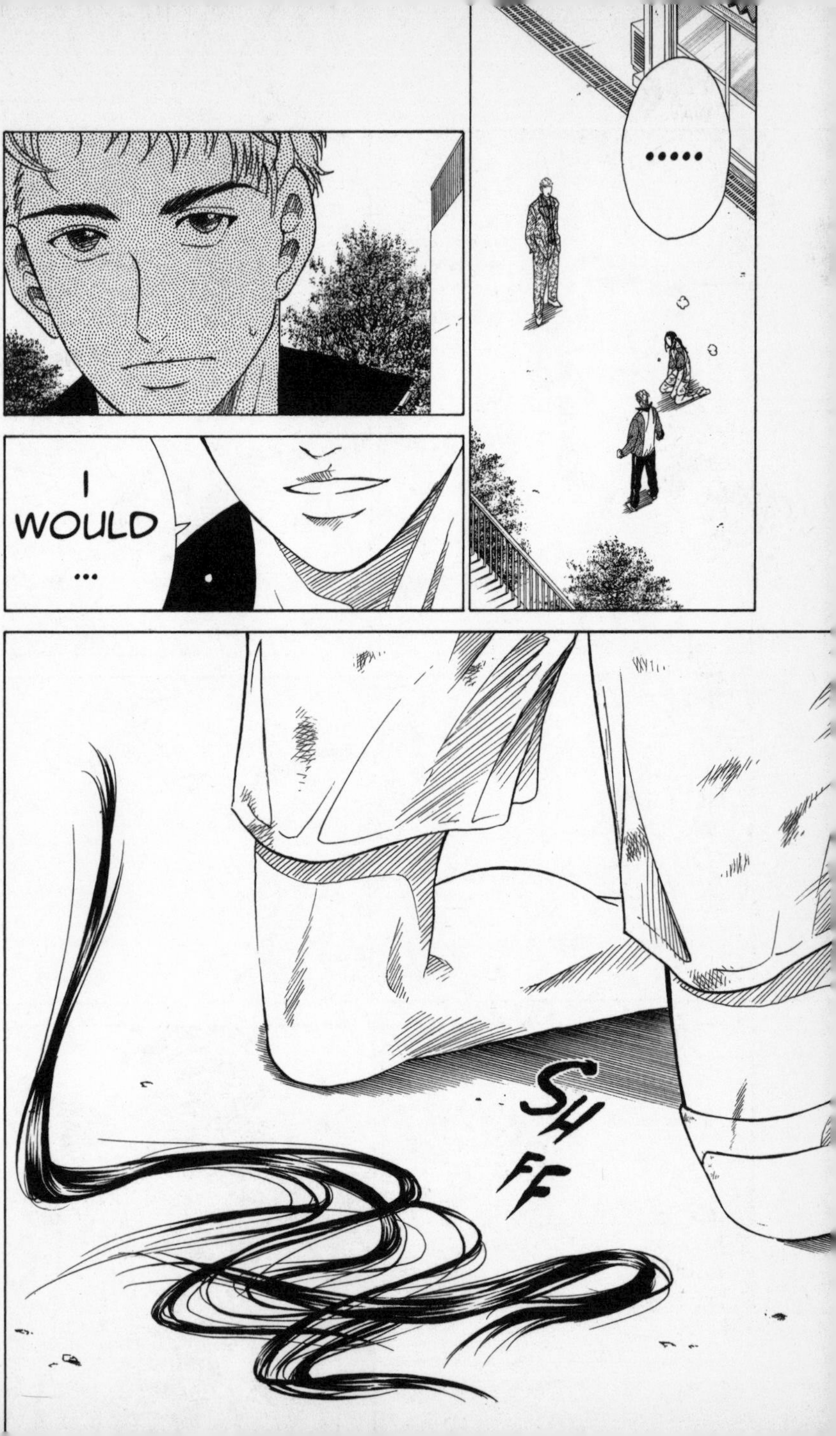
.....
I WOULD ...
SHFF

READ THIS WAY

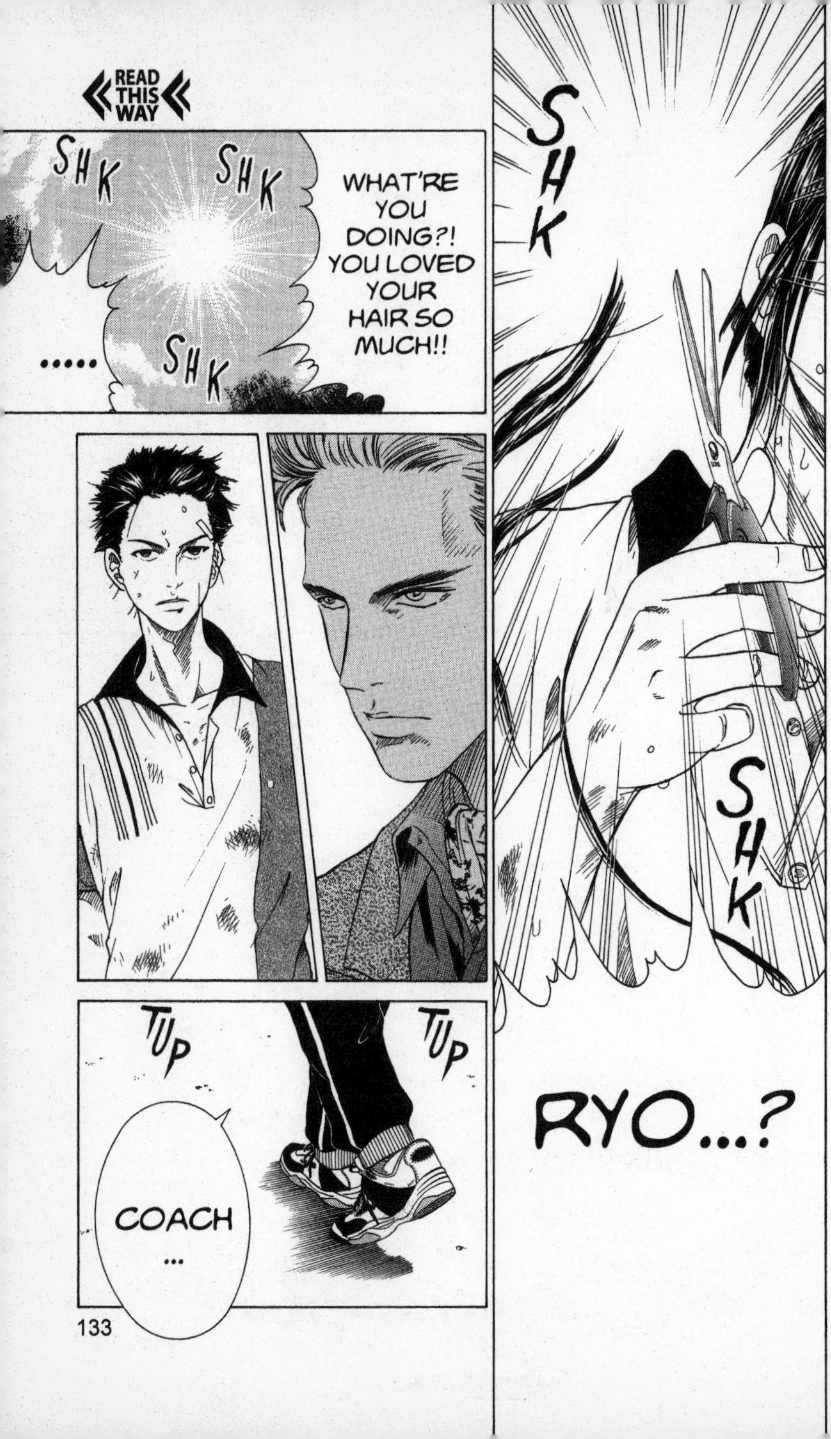
SHK
RYO...?
SHK
SHK
SHK
SHK
WHAT'RE YOU DOING?! YOU LOVED YOUR HAIR SO MUCH!!
.....
TUP
TUP
COACH ...

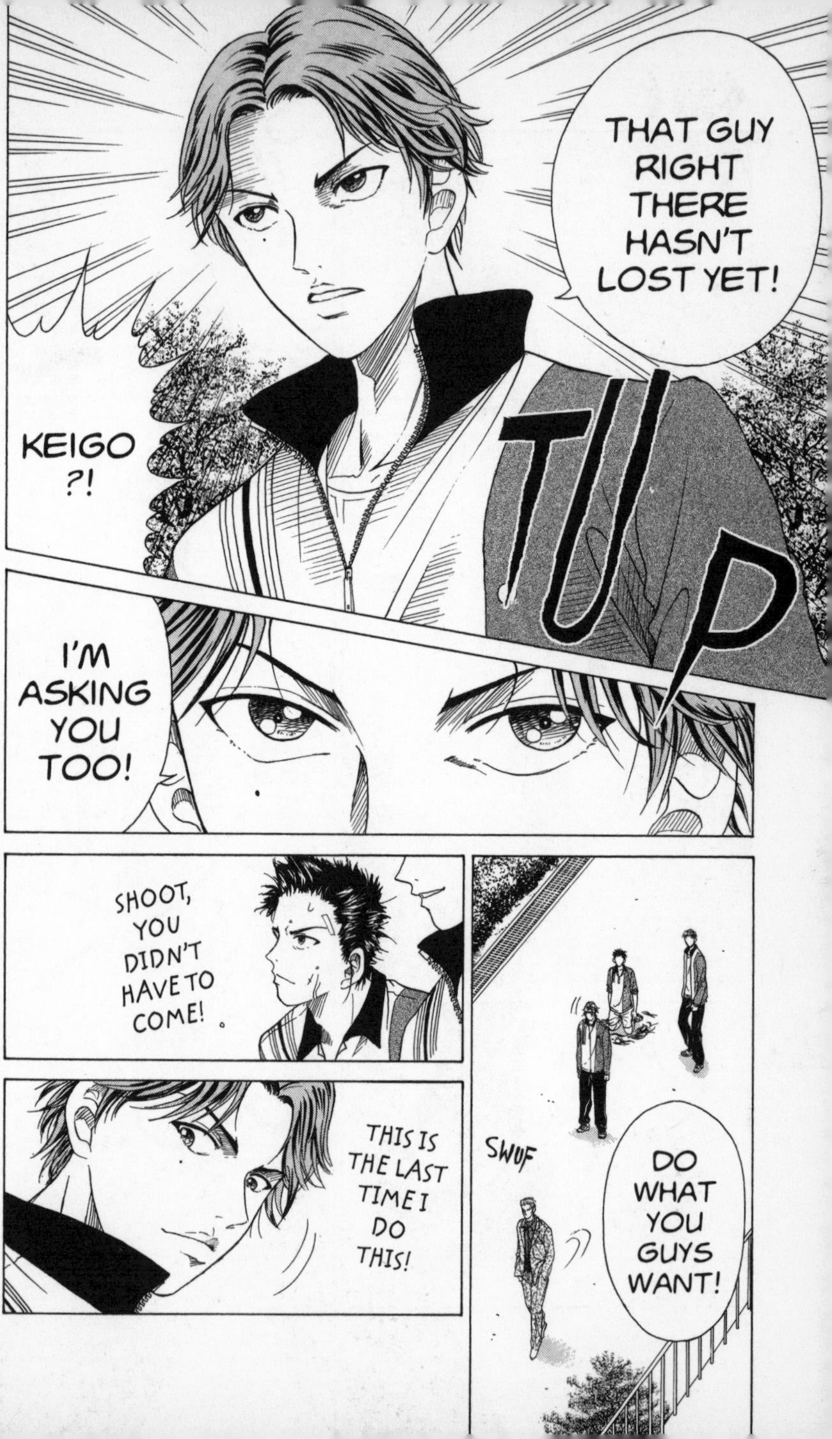
THAT GUY RIGHT THERE HASN'T LOST YET!
TUP
KEIGO ?!
I'M ASKING YOU TOO!
SWUF
DO WHAT YOU GUYS WANT!
SHOOT, YOU DIDN'T HAVE TO COME!
THIS IS THE LAST TIME I DO THIS!

READ THIS WAY

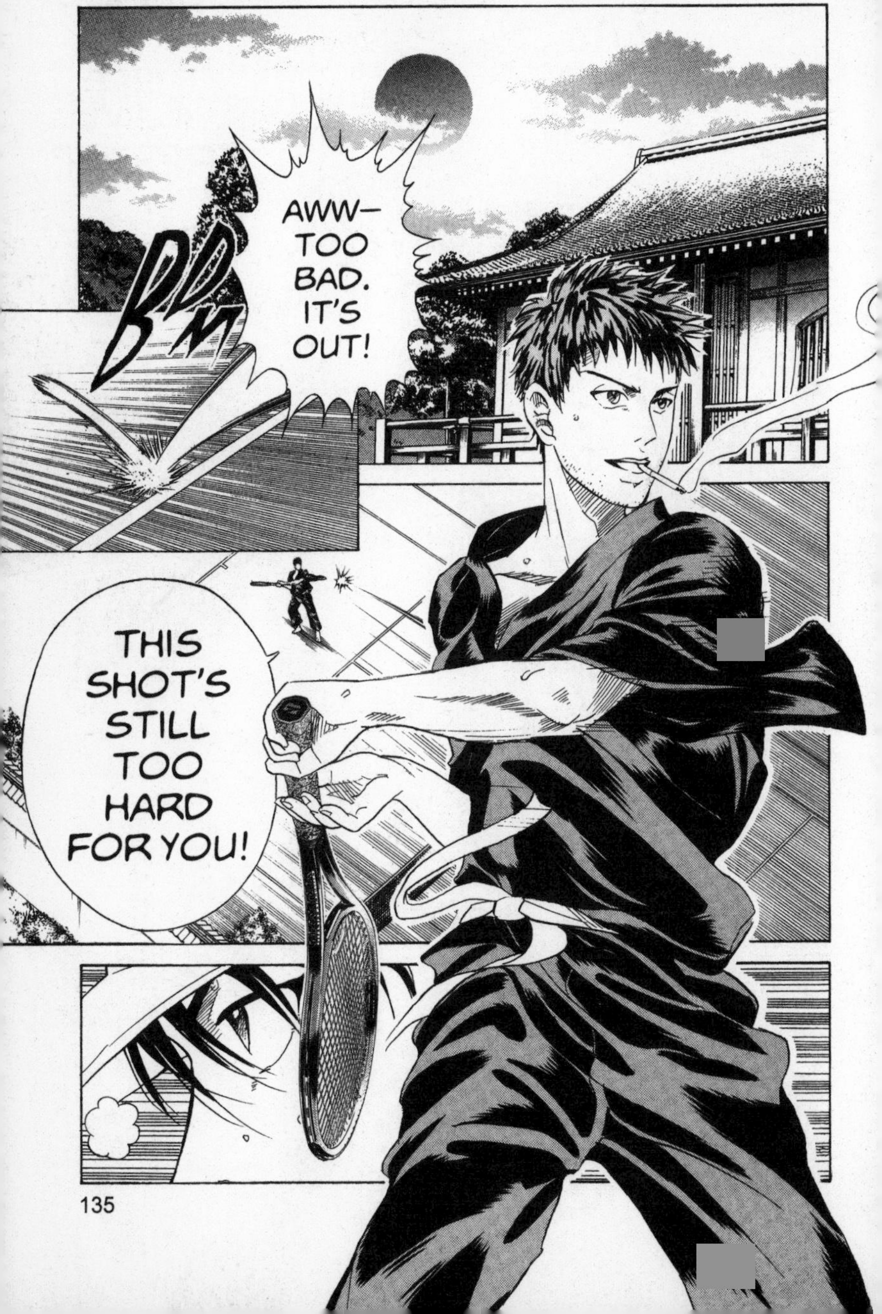
BOOM
AWW— TOO BAD. IT'S OUT!
THIS SHOT'S STILL TOO HARD FOR YOU!

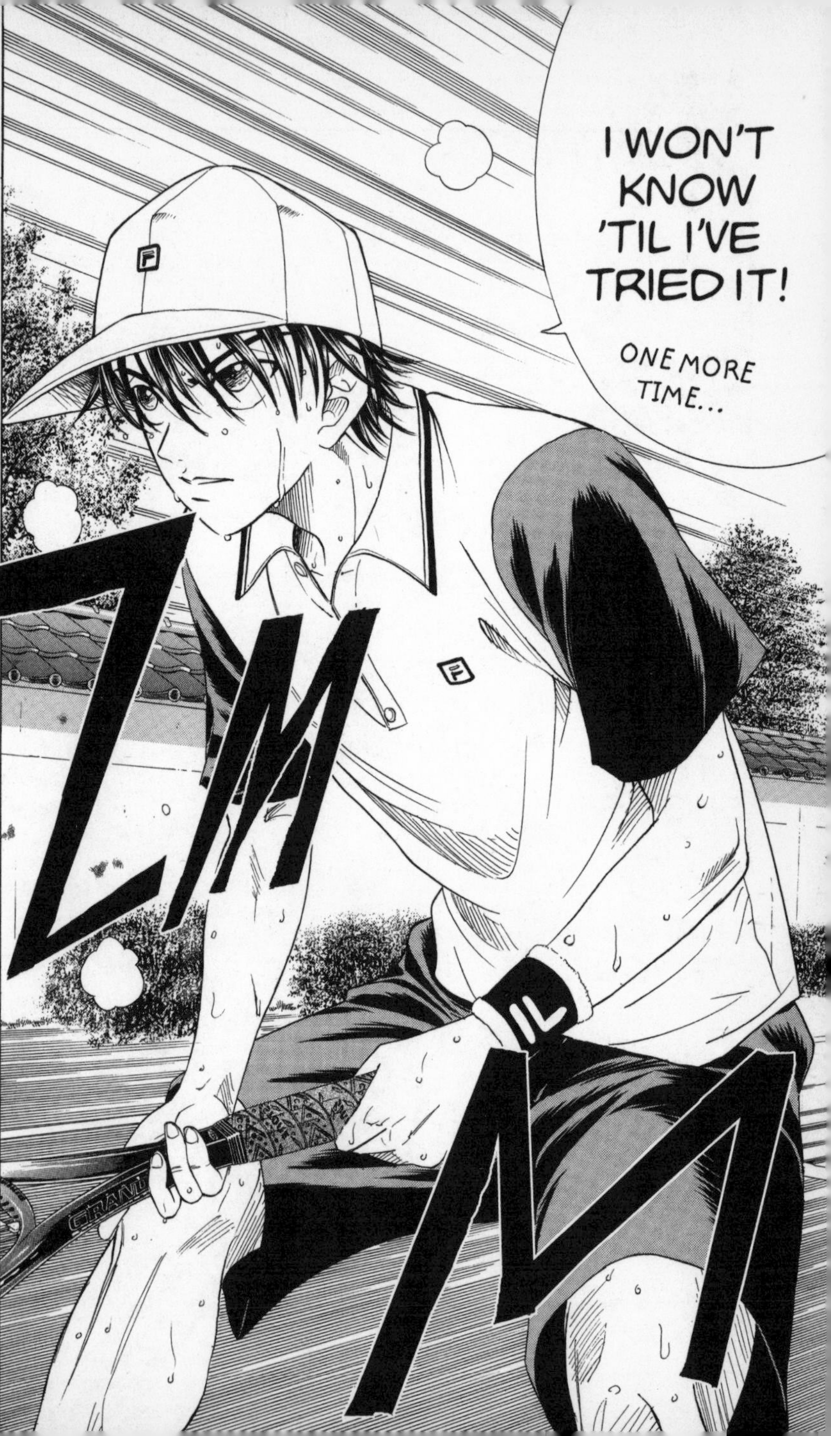
I WON'T KNOW 'TIL I'VE TRIED IT!
ONE MORE TIME...
ZM
M

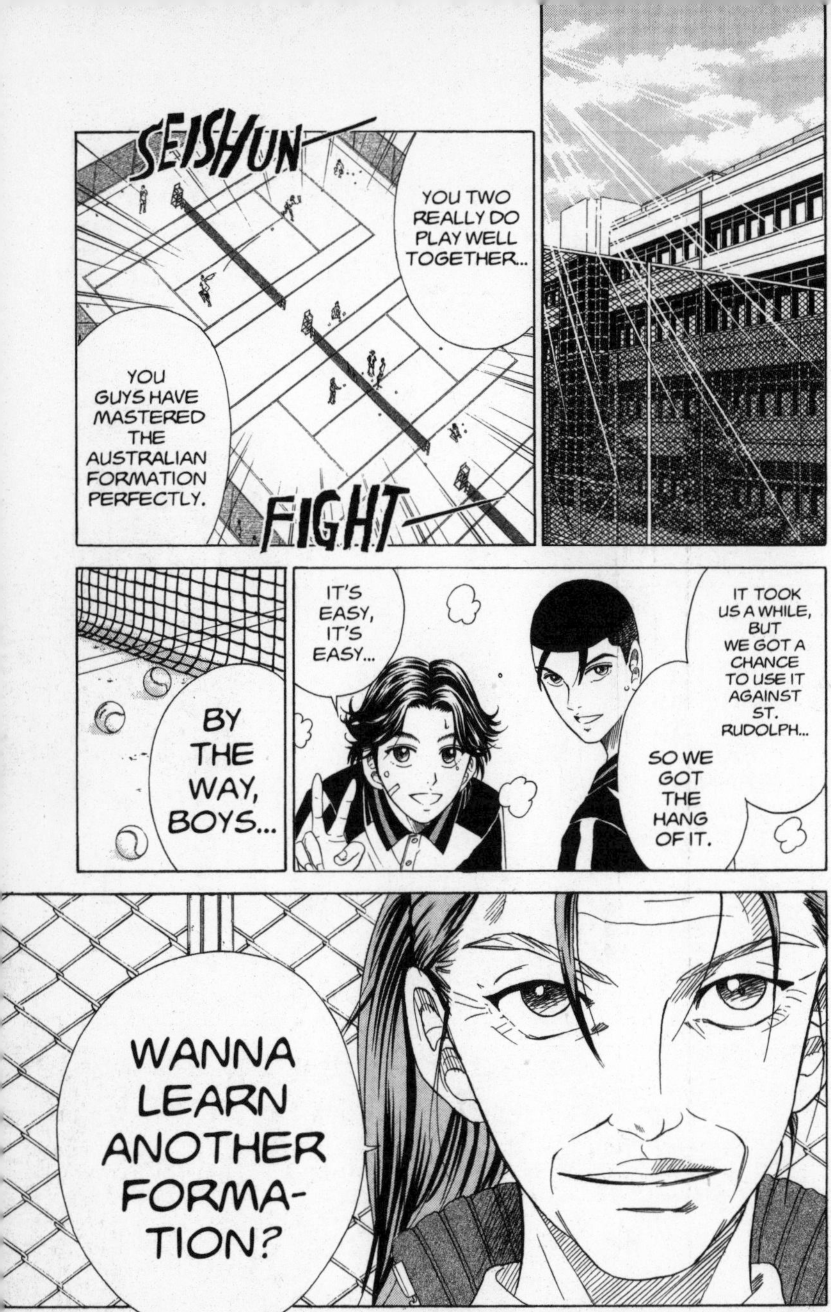
SEISHUN—
YOU TWO REALLY DO PLAY WELL TOGETHER...
YOU GUYS HAVE MASTERED THE AUSTRALIAN FORMATION PERFECTLY.
FIGHT—
IT TOOK US A WHILE, BUT WE GOT A CHANCE TO USE IT AGAINST ST. RUDOLPH...
SO WE GOT THE HANG OF IT.
IT'S EASY, IT'S EASY...
BY THE WAY, BOYS...
WANNA LEARN ANOTHER FORMA-TION?

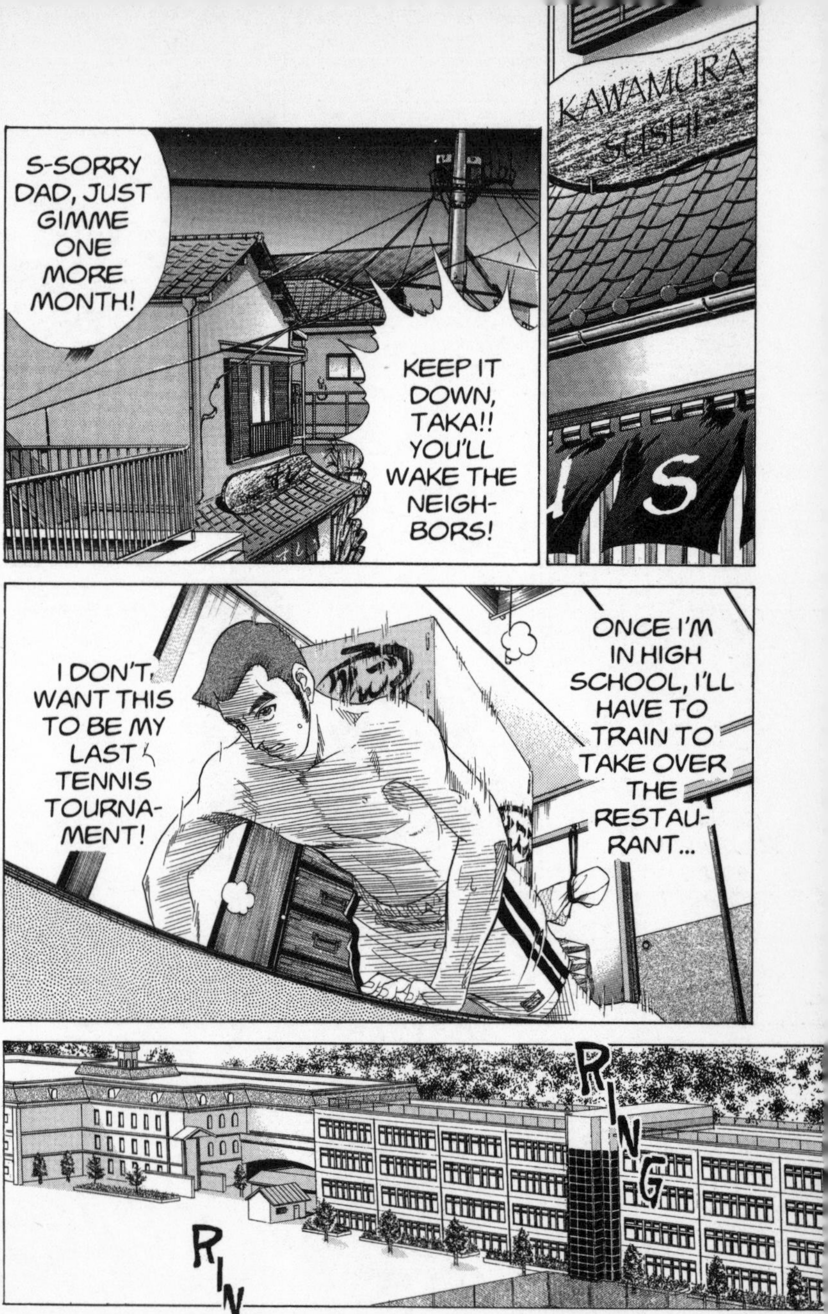
KAWAMURA SUSHI
S
KEEP IT DOWN, TAKA!! YOU'LL WAKE THE NEIGHBORS!
S-SORRY DAD, JUST GIMME ONE MORE MONTH!
ONCE I'M IN HIGH SCHOOL, I'LL HAVE TO TRAIN TO TAKE OVER THE RESTAURANT...
I DON'T WANT THIS TO BE MY LAST TENNIS TOURNAMENT!
RING
RING

READ THIS WAY

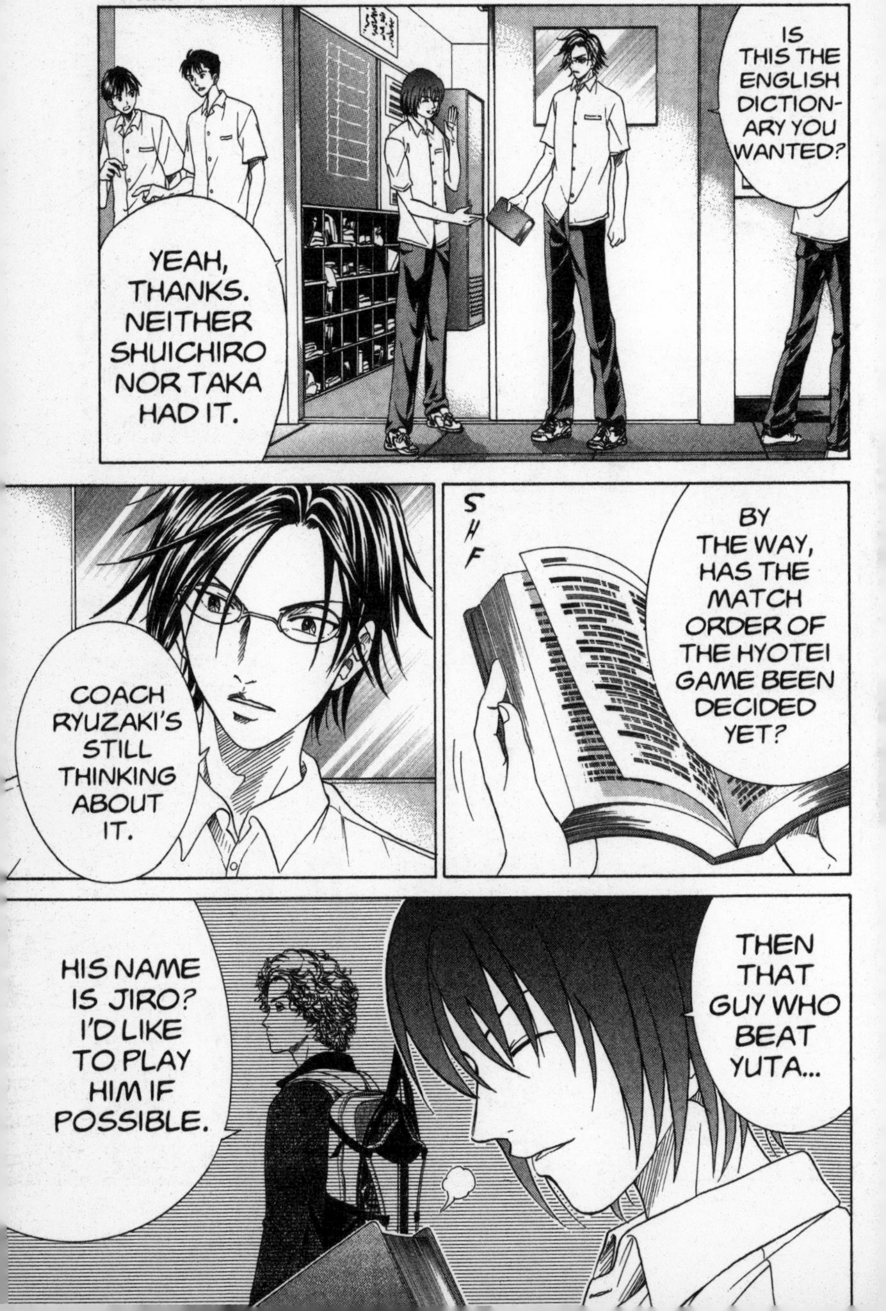
IS THIS THE ENGLISH DICTION-ARY YOU WANTED?
YEAH, THANKS. NEITHER SHUICHIRO NOR TAKA HAD IT.
SHF
BY THE WAY, HAS THE MATCH ORDER OF THE HYOTEI GAME BEEN DECIDED YET?
COACH RYUZAKI'S STILL THINKING ABOUT IT.
THEN THAT GUY WHO BEAT YUTA...
HIS NAME IS JIRO? I'D LIKE TO PLAY HIM IF POSSIBLE.

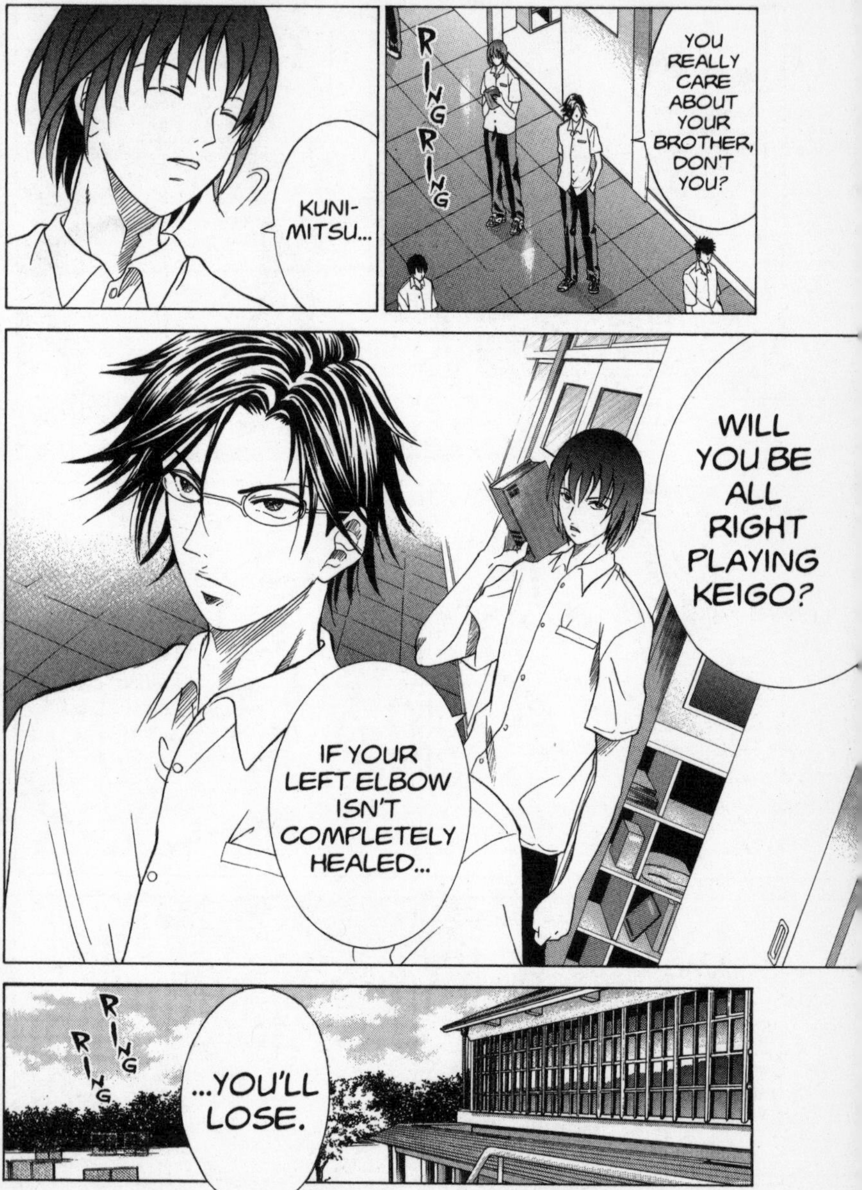
RING RING
YOU REALLY CARE ABOUT YOUR BROTHER, DON'T YOU?
KUNI-MITSU...
WILL YOU BE ALL RIGHT PLAYING KEIGO?
IF YOUR LEFT ELBOW ISN'T COMPLETELY HEALED...
RING RING
...YOU'LL LOSE.

READ THIS WAY

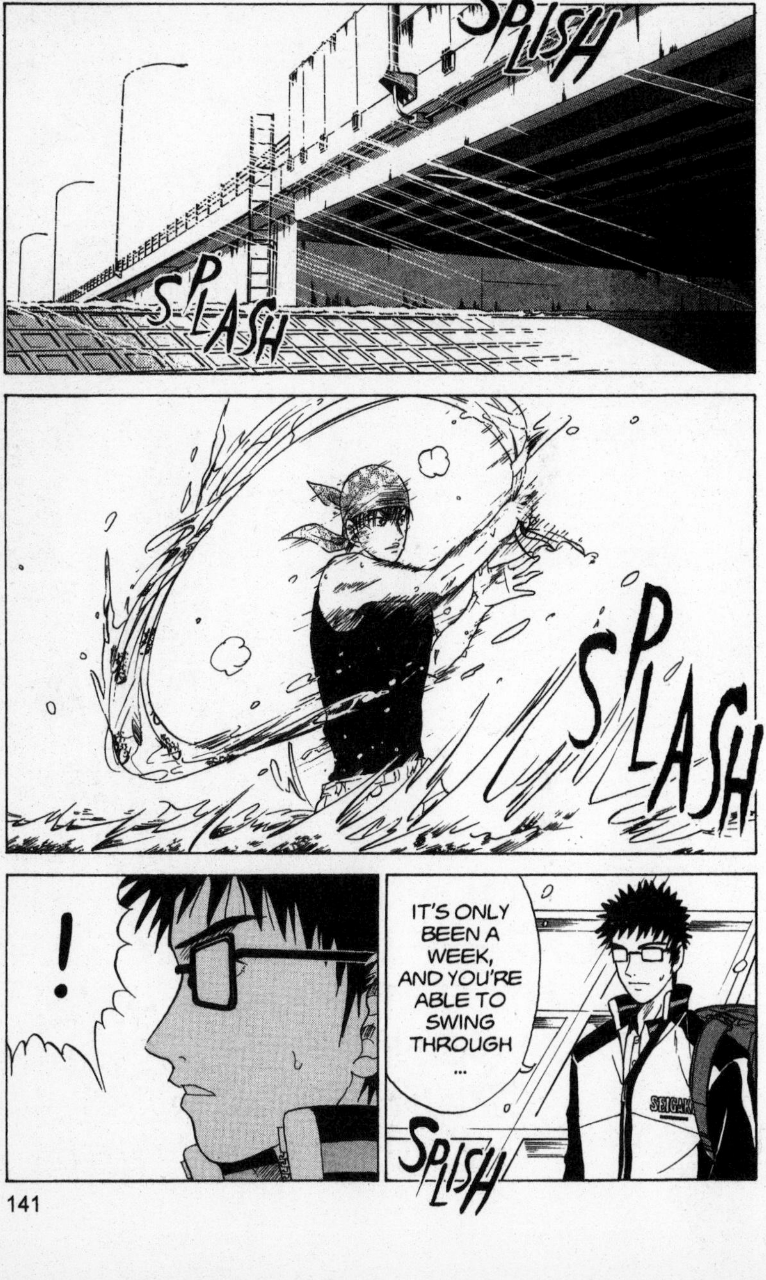
SPLISH
SPLASH
SPLASH
IT'S ONLY BEEN A WEEK, AND YOU'RE ABLE TO SWING THROUGH ...
SPLISH
!
SEIGAKU

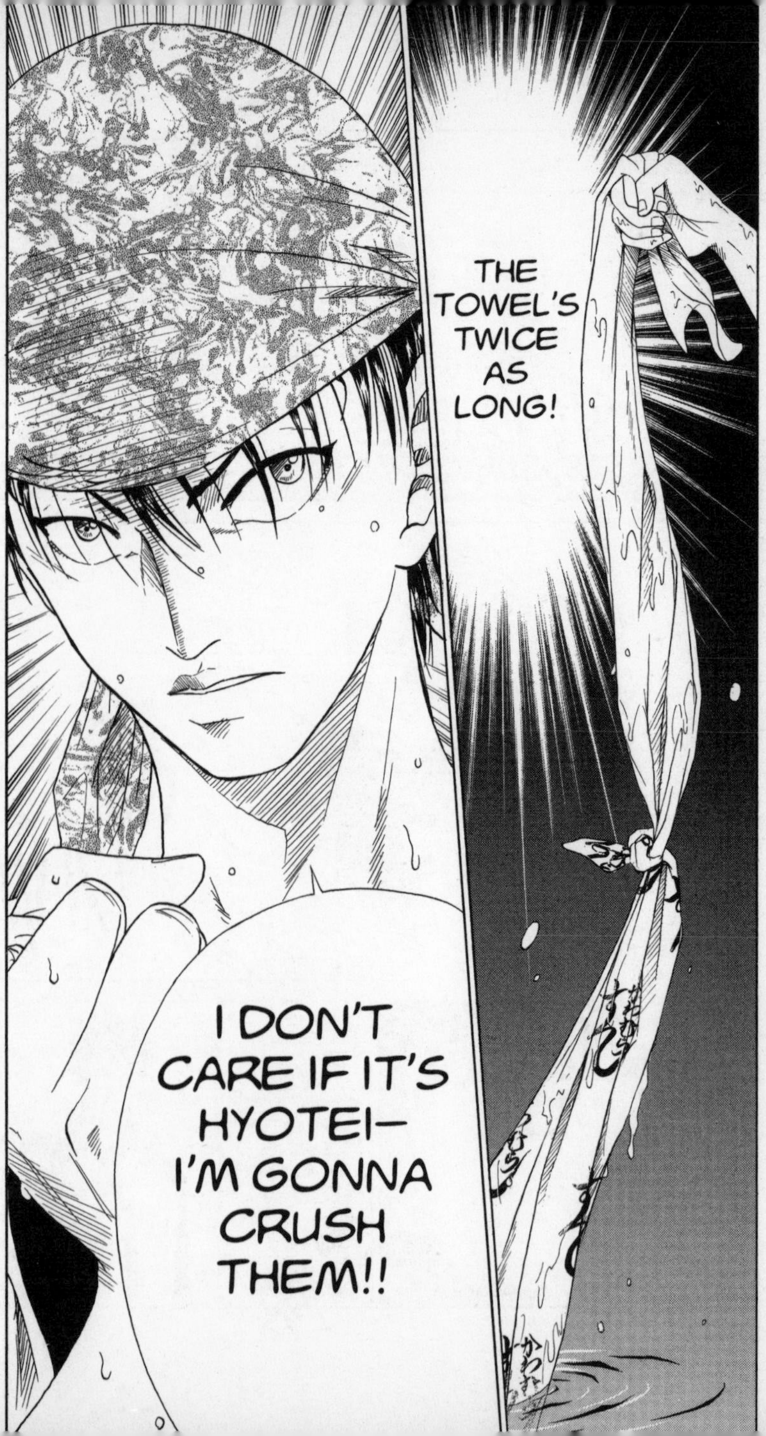
THE TOWEL'S TWICE AS LONG!
I DON'T CARE IF IT'S HYOTEI— I'M GONNA CRUSH THEM!!

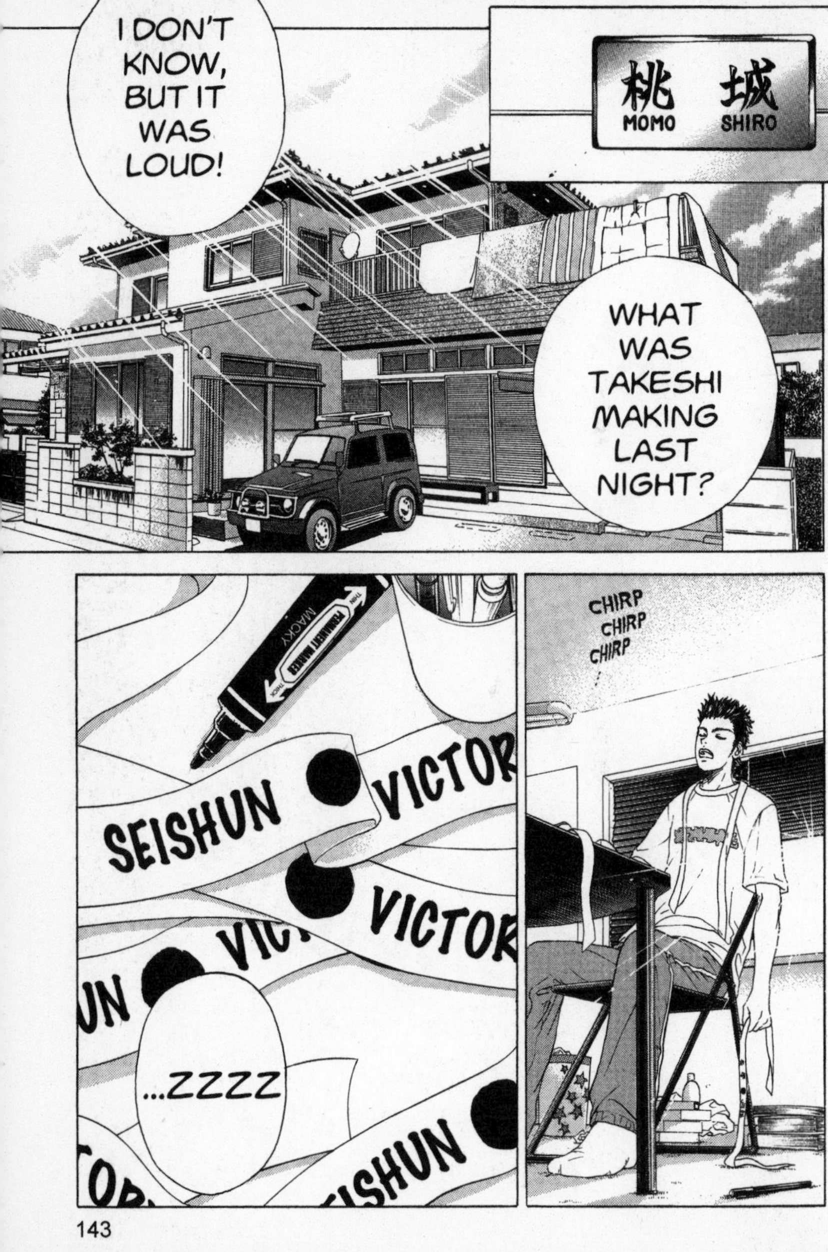
桃 城
MOMO SHIRO
WHAT WAS TAKESHI MAKING LAST NIGHT?
I DON'T KNOW, BUT IT WAS LOUD!
CHIRP CHIRP CHIRP
THIN
PERMANENT MARKER
MACKY
THICK
SEISHUN
VICTOR
VICTOR
...ZZZZ

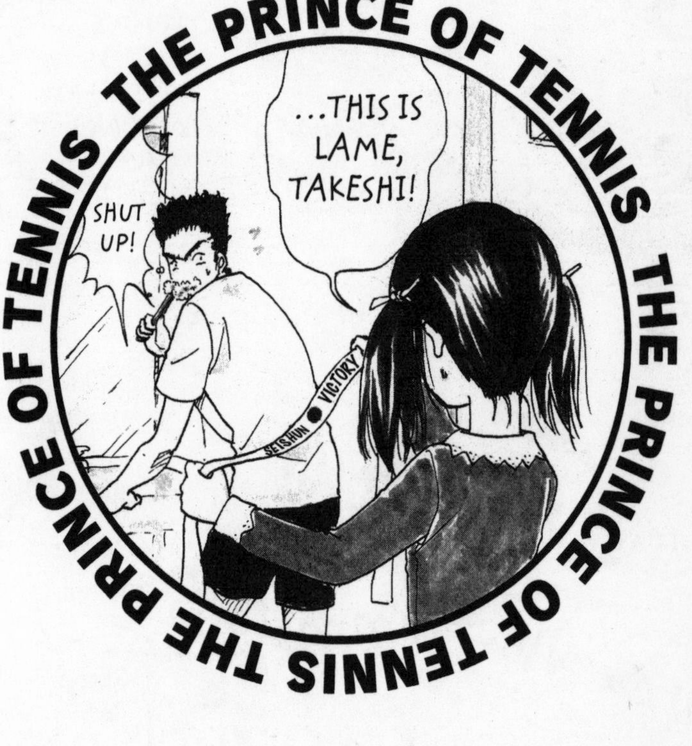
THE PRINCE OF TENNIS THE PRINCE OF TENNIS THE PRINCE OF TENNIS
...THIS IS LAME, TAKESHI!
SHUT UP!
SEISHUN VICTORY

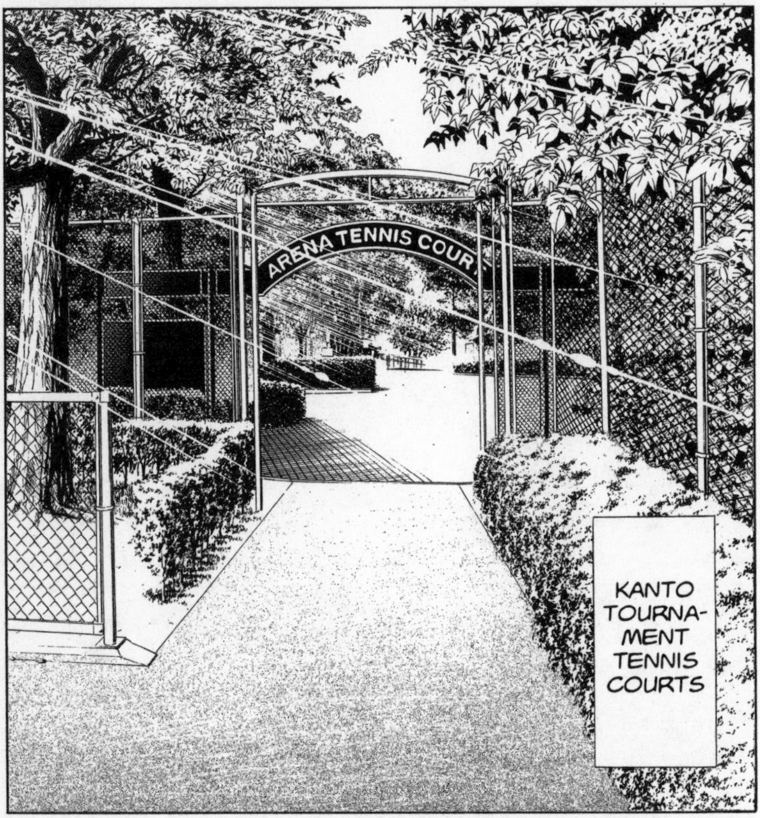
ARENA TENNIS COURT
KANTO TOURNAMENT TENNIS COURTS

GENIUS 122:

CLASH! HYOTEI VS. SEISHUN

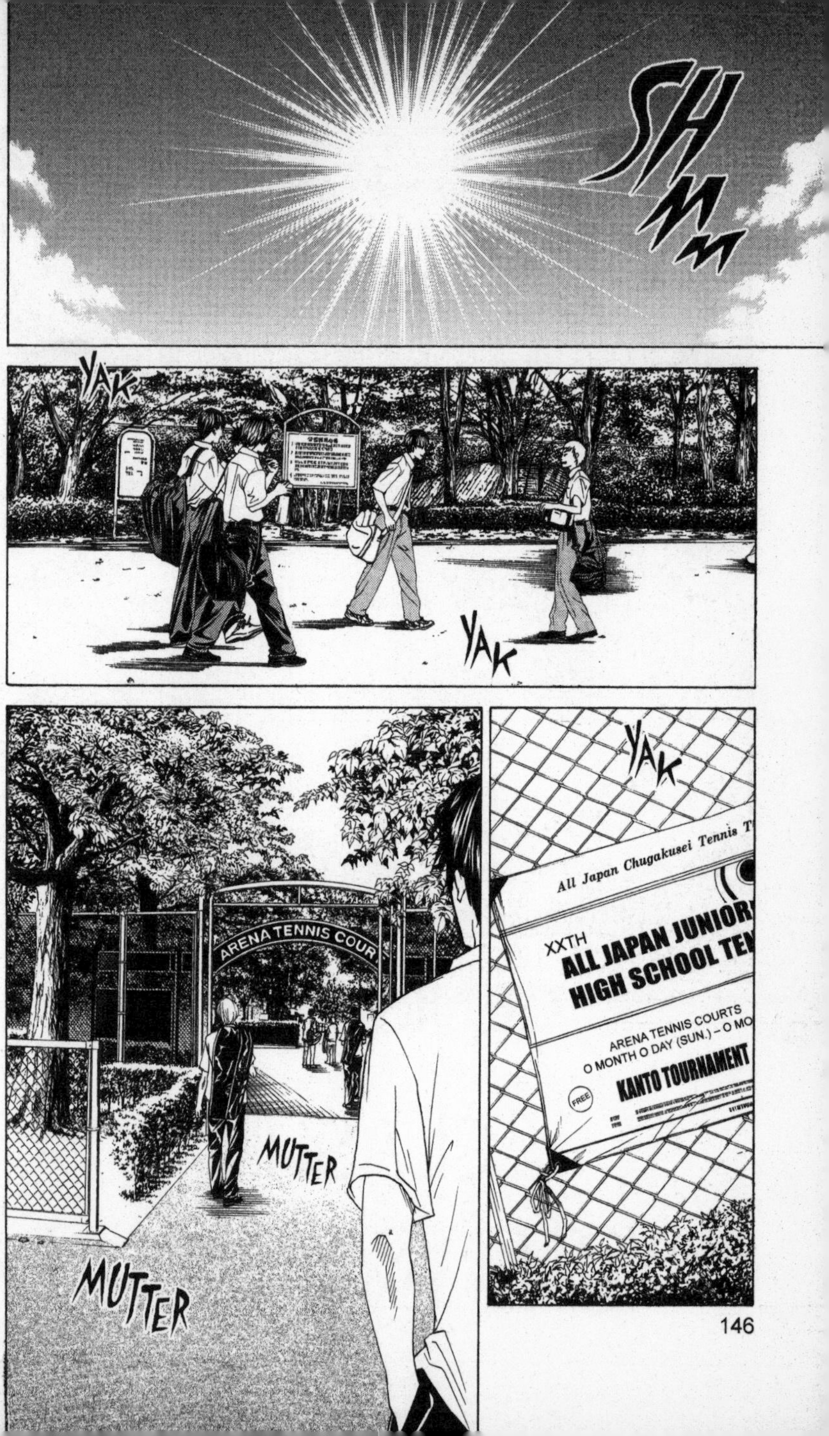
SHMM
YAK
YAK
YAK
All Japan Chugakusei Tennis
XXTH
ALL JAPAN JUNIOR
HIGH SCHOOL TE
ARENA TENNIS COURTS
O MONTH O DAY (SUN.) – O MO
KANTO TOURNAMENT
FREE
ARENA TENNIS COUR
MUTTER
MUTTER

READ THIS WAY

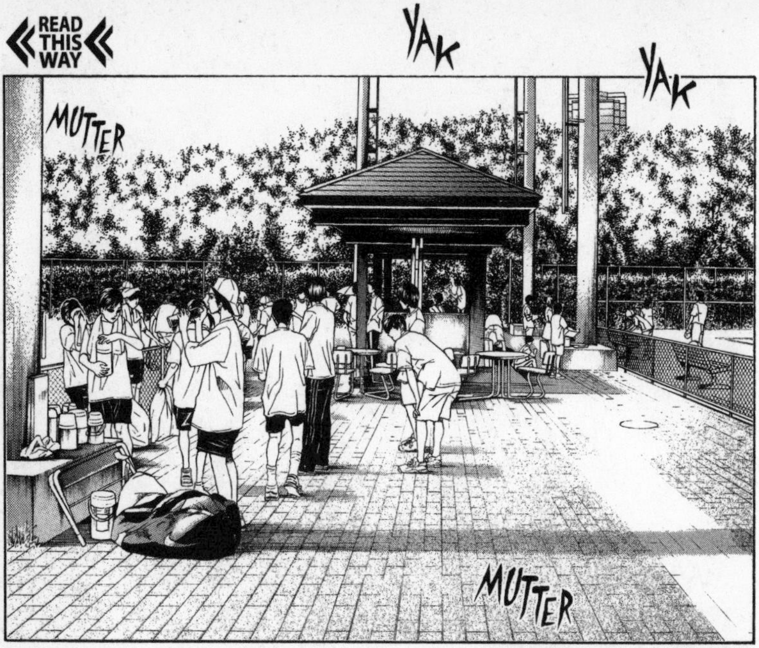
YAK
YAK
MUTTER
MUTTER

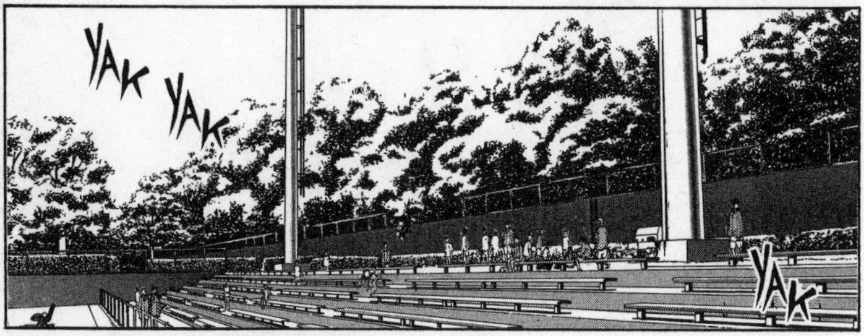
YAK YAK
YAK

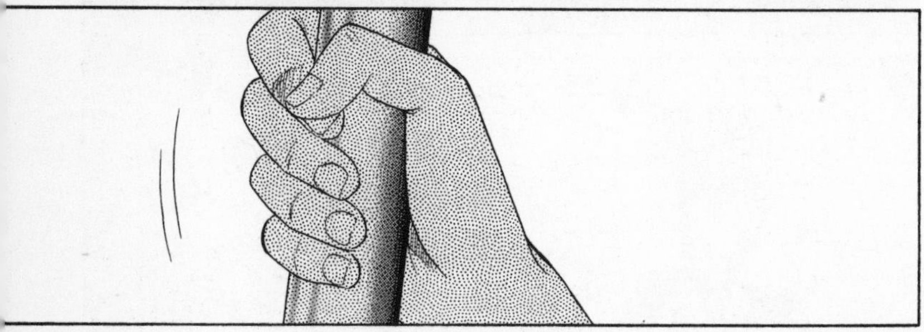

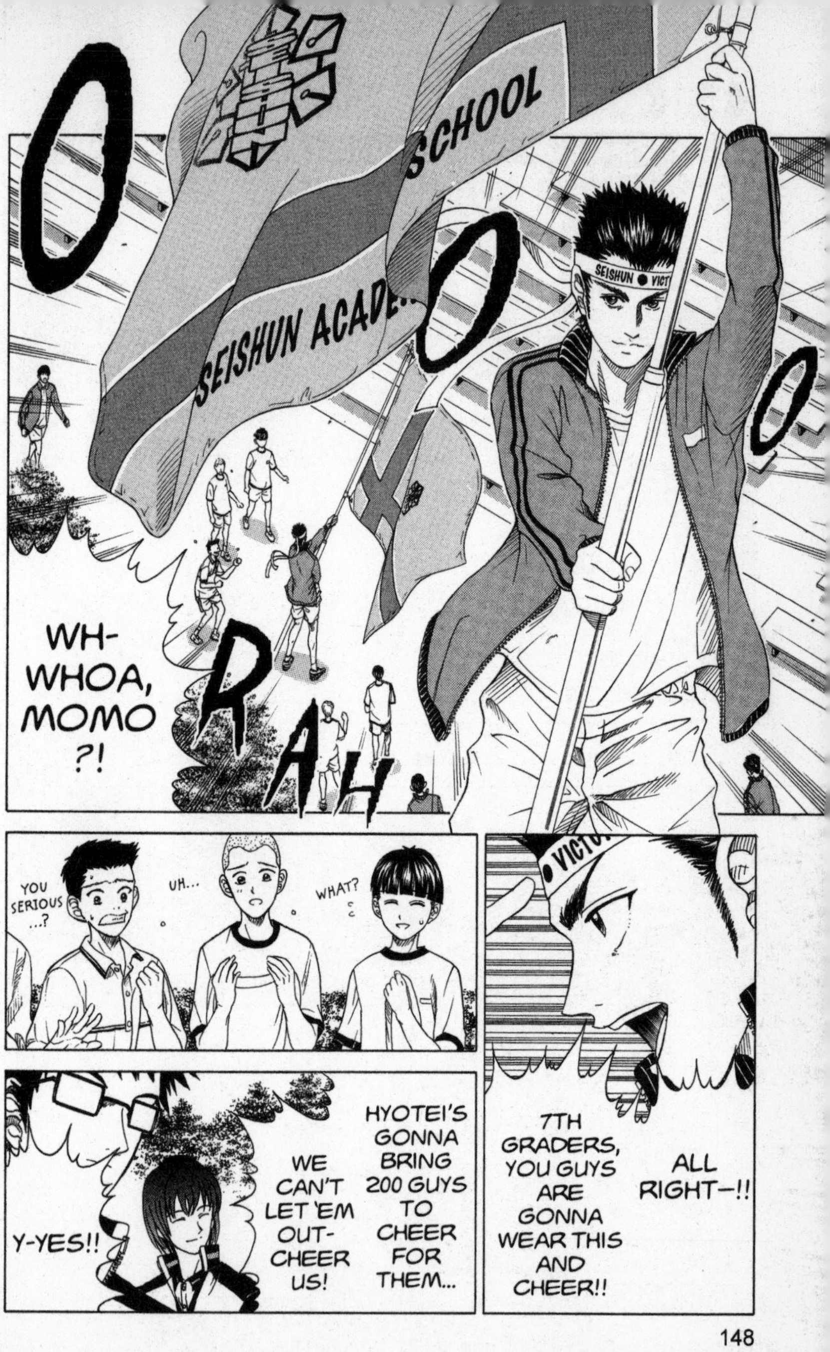
O
O
O
SCHOOL
WH-WHOA, MOMO?!
RAH
WHAT?
UH...
YOU SERIOUS...?
ALL RIGHT—!!
7TH GRADERS, YOU GUYS ARE GONNA WEAR THIS AND CHEER!!
HYOTEI'S GONNA BRING 200 GUYS TO CHEER FOR THEM...
WE CAN'T LET 'EM OUT-CHEER US!
Y-YES!!

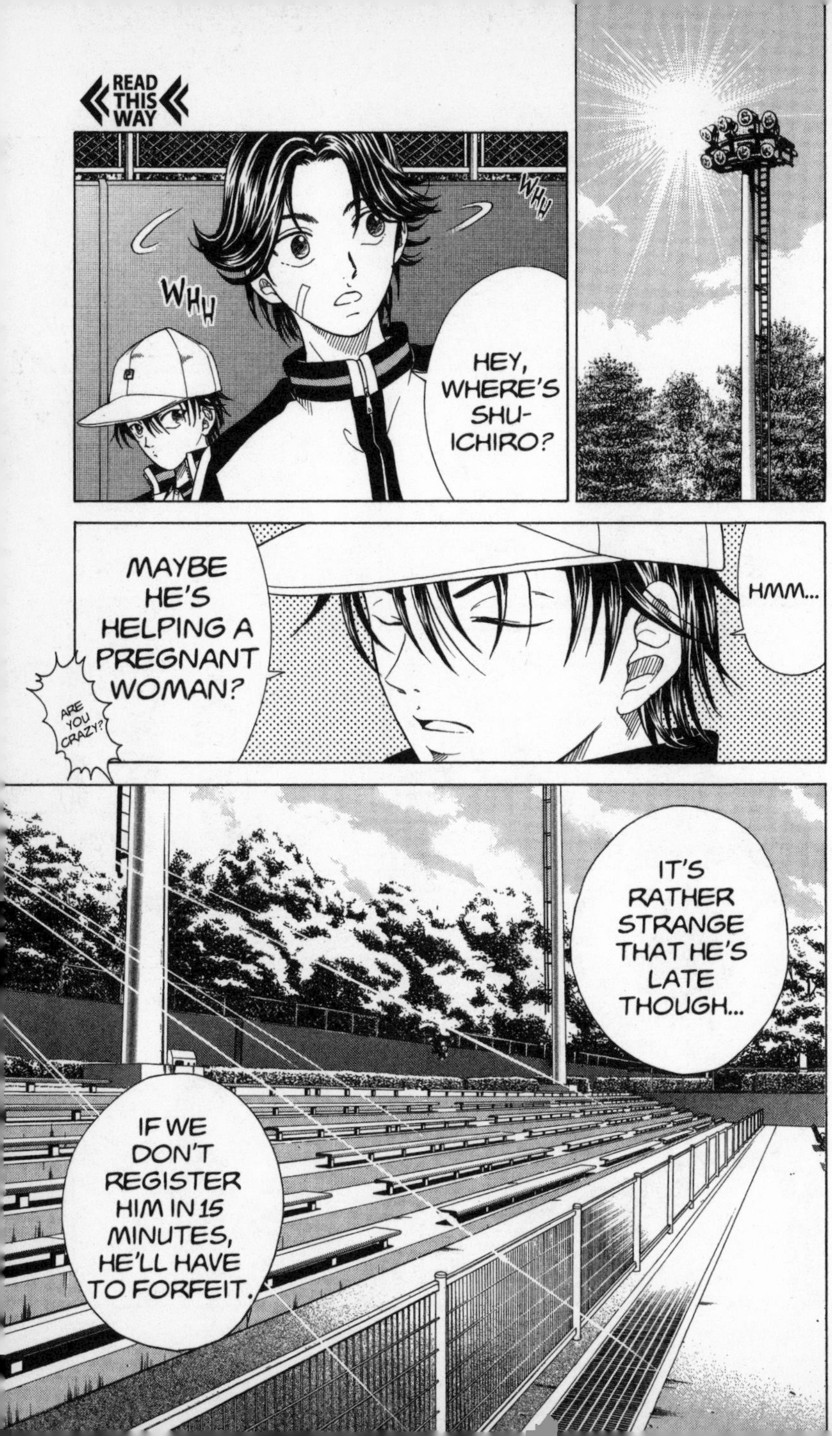
READ THIS WAY
WHH
WHH
HEY, WHERE'S SHU-ICHIRO?
HMM...
MAYBE HE'S HELPING A PREGNANT WOMAN?
ARE YOU CRAZY?
IT'S RATHER STRANGE THAT HE'S LATE THOUGH...
IF WE DON'T REGISTER HIM IN 15 MINUTES, HE'LL HAVE TO FORFEIT.

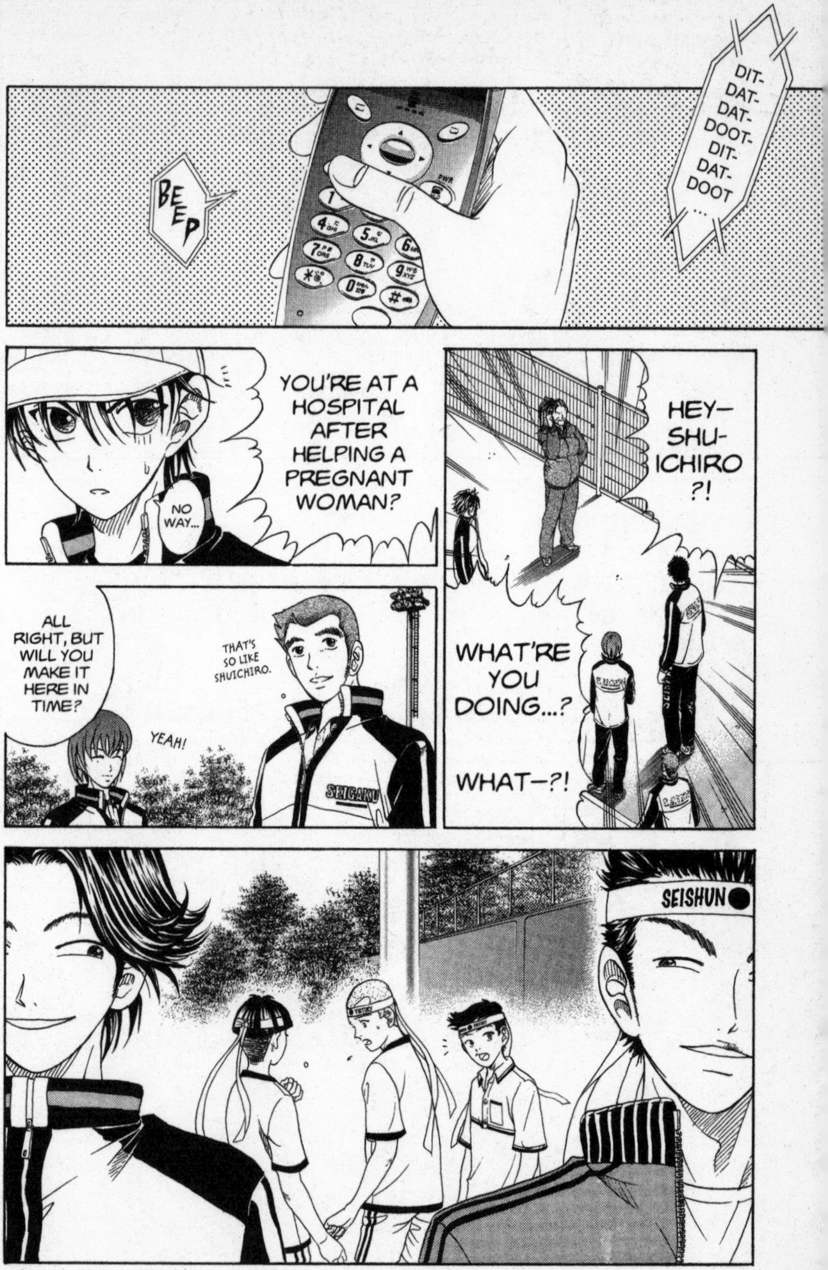
DIT-DAT-DAT-DOOT-DIT-DAT-DOOT...
BEEP
HEY—SHUICHIRO?!
WHAT'RE YOU DOING...?
WHAT—?!
YOU'RE AT A HOSPITAL AFTER HELPING A PREGNANT WOMAN?
NO WAY...
ALL RIGHT, BUT WILL YOU MAKE IT HERE IN TIME?
THAT'S SO LIKE SHUICHIRO.
YEAH!
SEIGAKU
SEISHUN

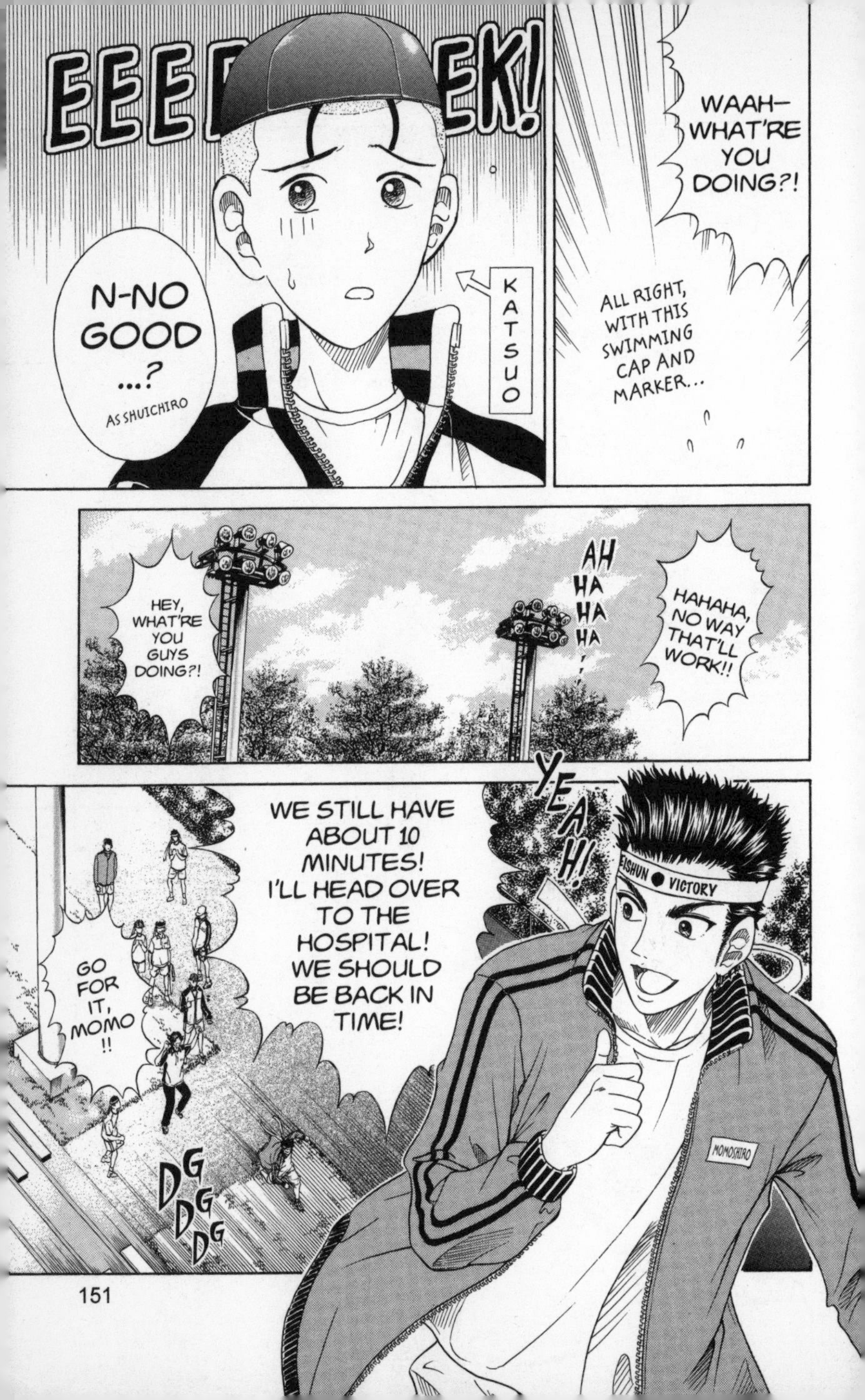
WAAH— WHAT'RE YOU DOING?!
ALL RIGHT, WITH THIS SWIMMING CAP AND MARKER...
EEE EK!
KATSUO
N-NO GOOD ...?
AS SHUICHIRO
HAHAHA, NO WAY THAT'LL WORK!!
AH HA HA HA...
HEY, WHAT'RE YOU GUYS DOING?!
YEAH!
SEISHUN VICTORY
MOMOSHIRO
WE STILL HAVE ABOUT 10 MINUTES! I'LL HEAD OVER TO THE HOSPITAL! WE SHOULD BE BACK IN TIME!
GO FOR IT, MOMO!!
DG DG DG

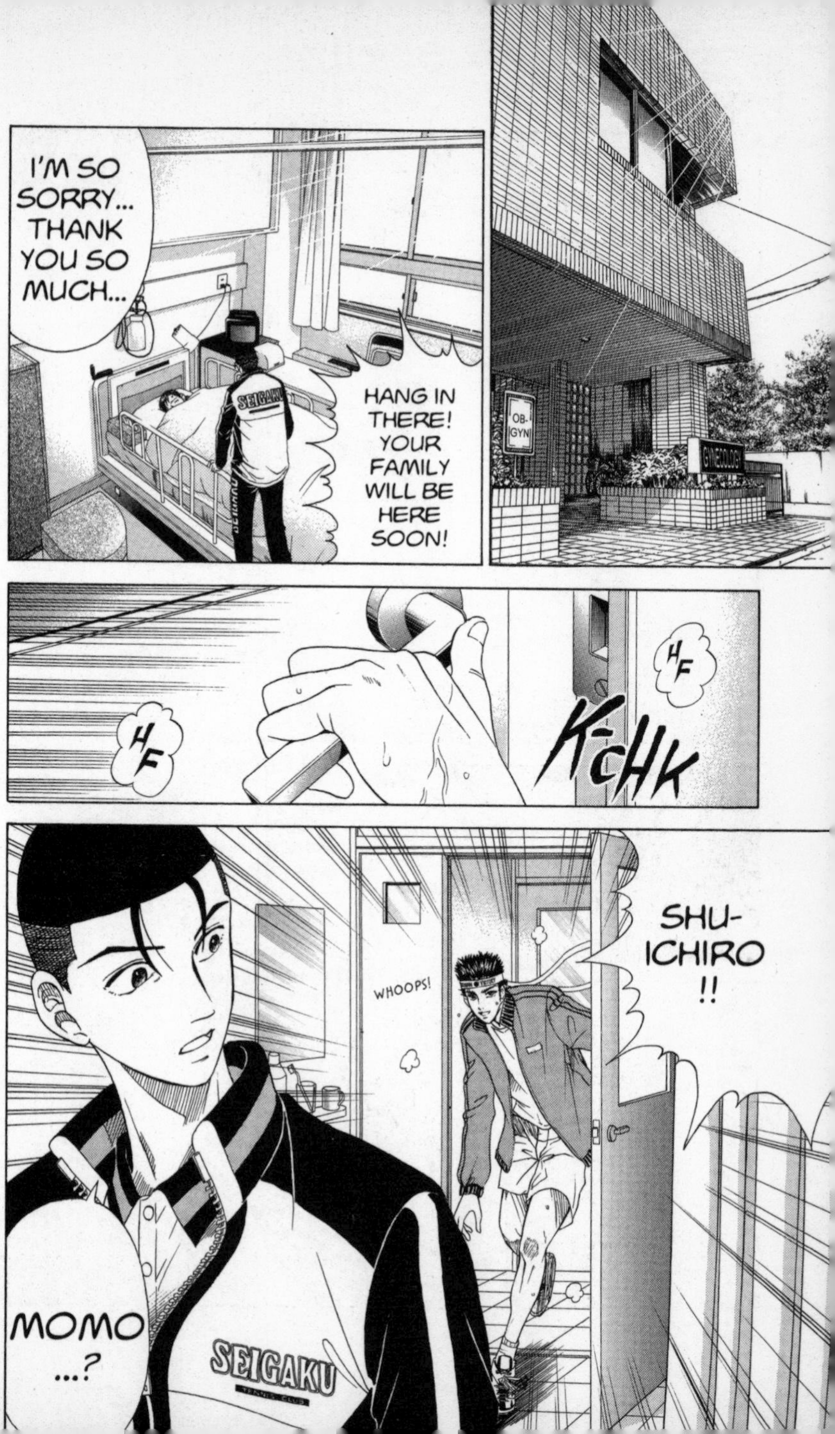
OB-GYN
HANG IN THERE! YOUR FAMILY WILL BE HERE SOON!
I'M SO SORRY... THANK YOU SO MUCH...
HF
K-CHK
HF
SHU-ICHIRO !!
WHOOPS!
MOMO ...?

READ THIS WAY

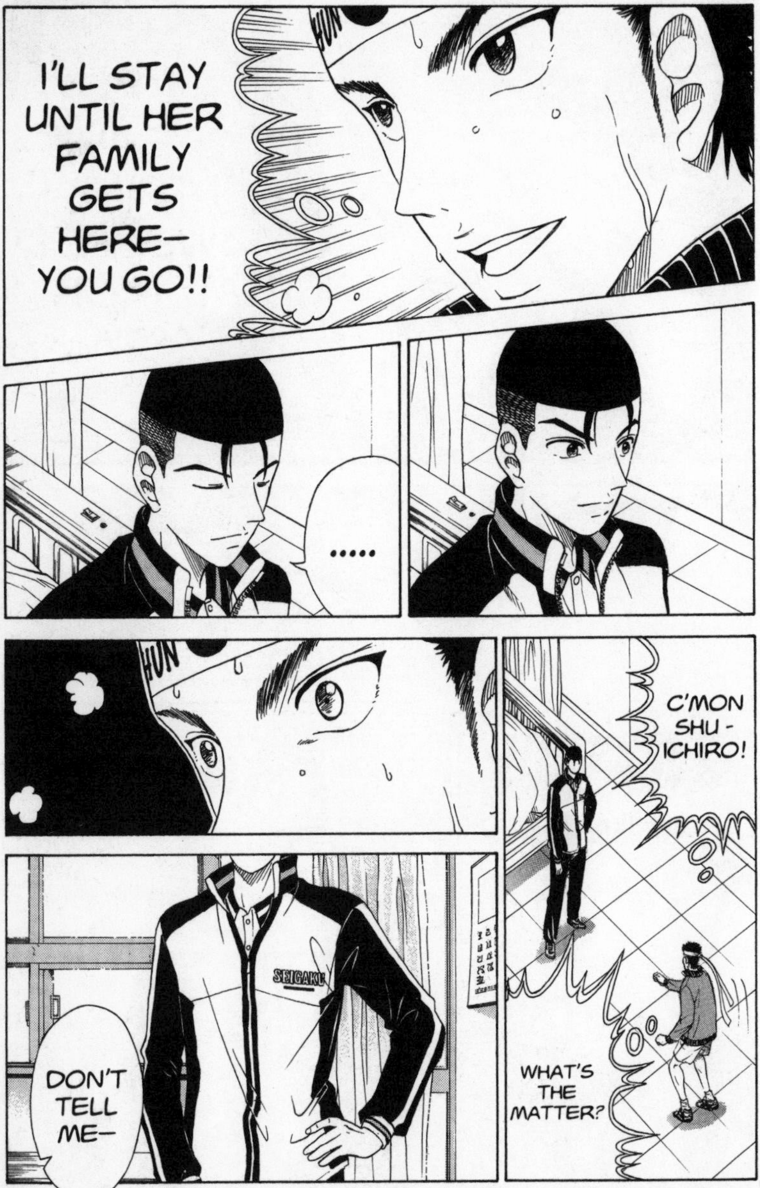
I'LL STAY UNTIL HER FAMILY GETS HERE— YOU GO!!
.....
C'MON SHU-ICHIRO!
WHAT'S THE MATTER?
DON'T TELL ME—

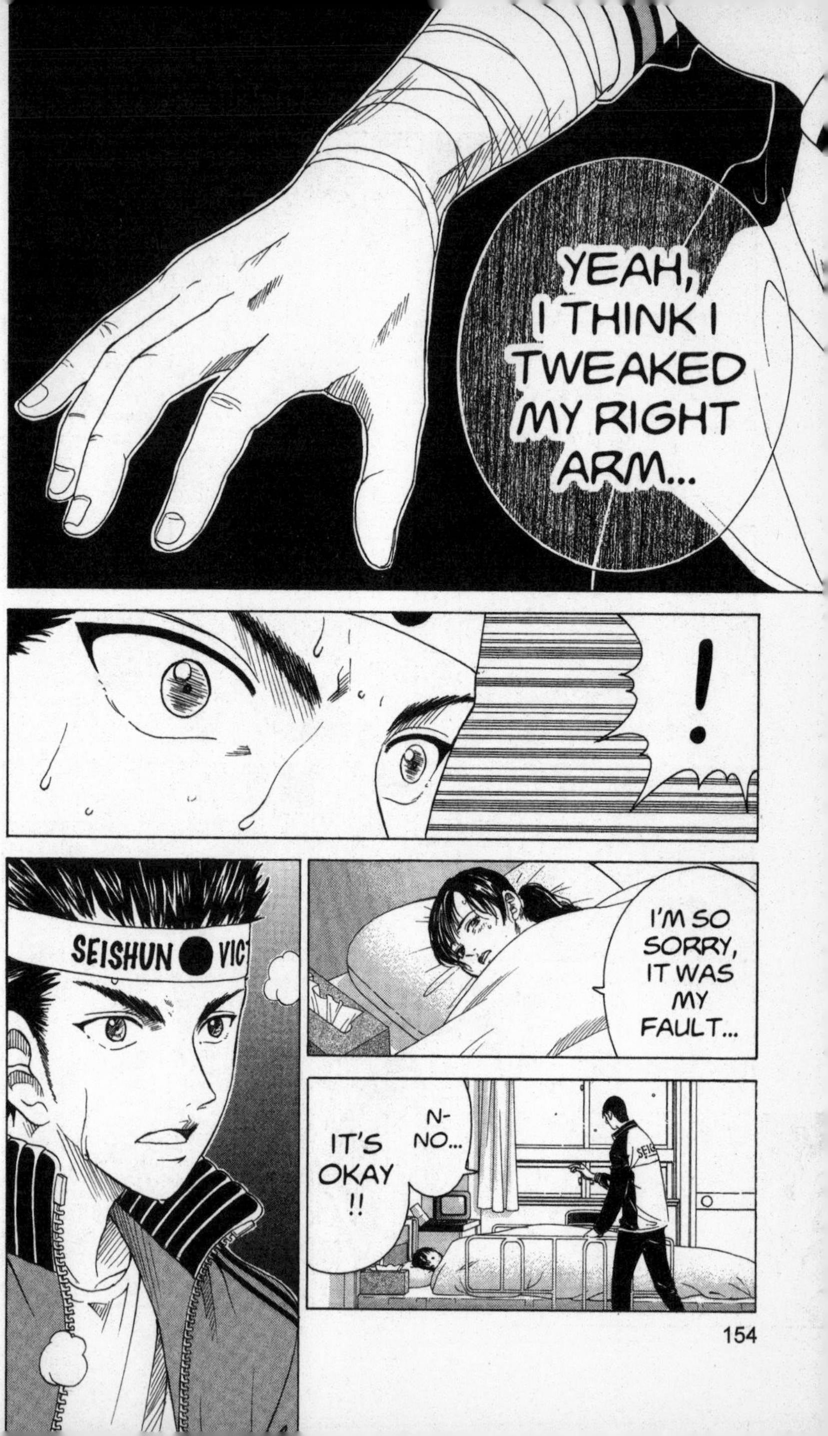
YEAH, I THINK I TWEAKED MY RIGHT ARM...
!
I'M SO SORRY, IT WAS MY FAULT...
N-NO...
IT'S OKAY !!
SEISHUN VICT

READ THIS WAY

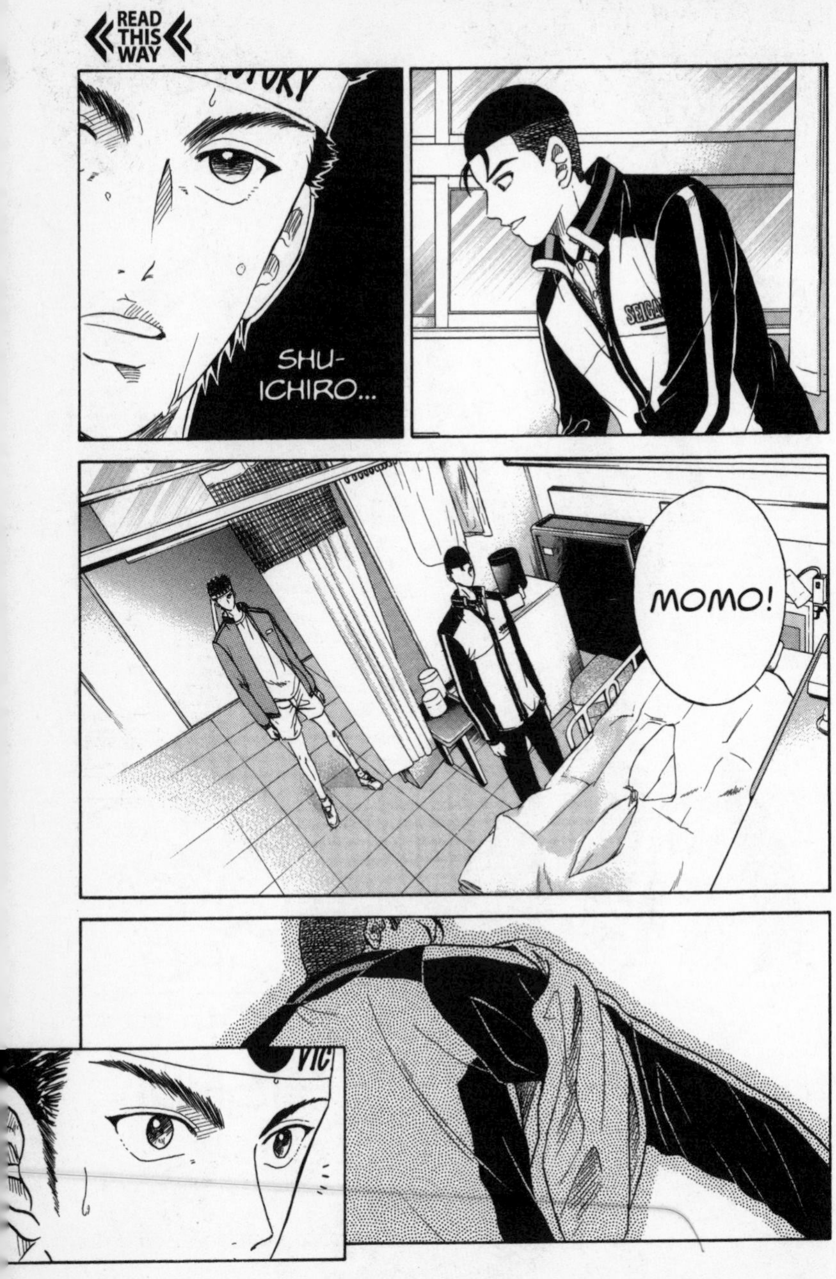
SHU-ICHIRO...
MOMO!

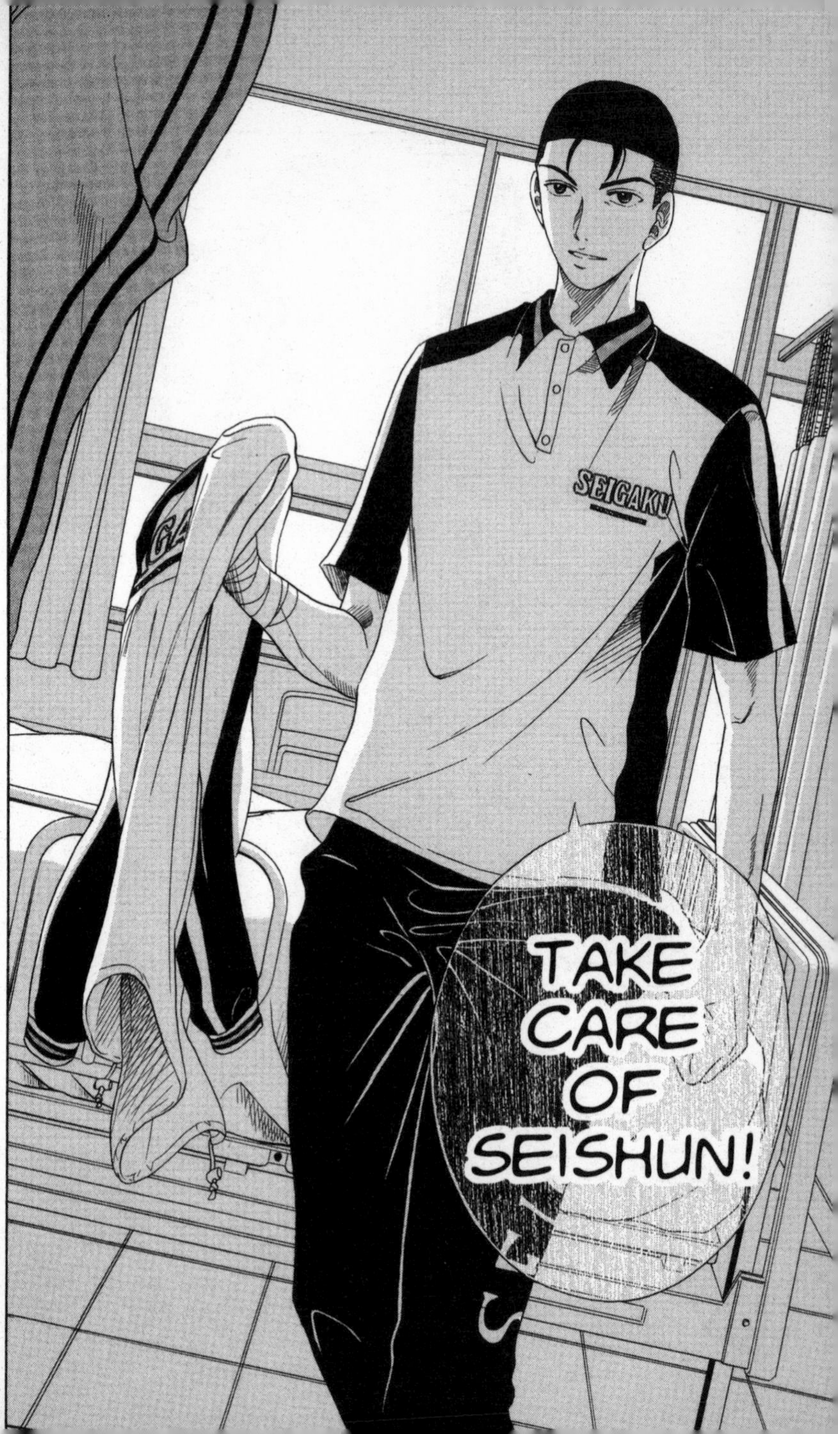
SEIGAKU
TAKE CARE OF SEISHUN!

READ THIS WAY

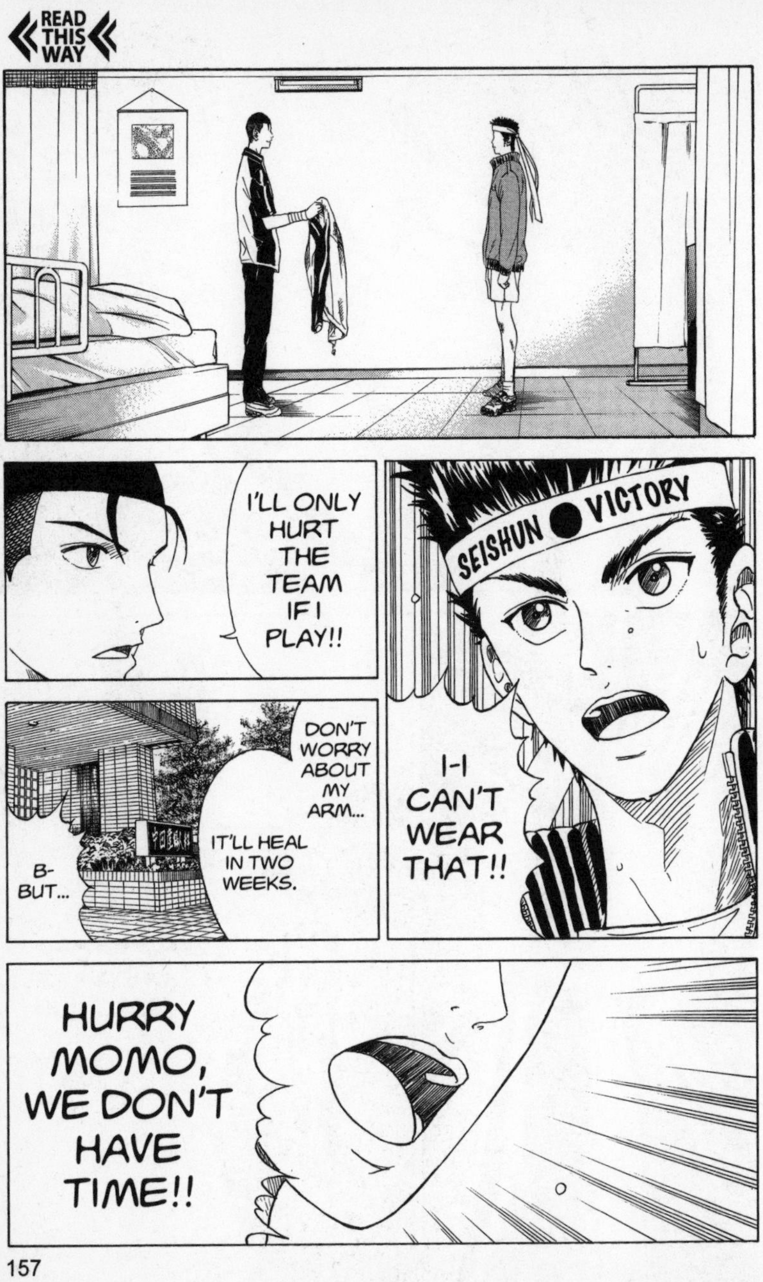
SEISHUN VICTORY
I-I CAN'T WEAR THAT!!
I'LL ONLY HURT THE TEAM IF I PLAY!!
DON'T WORRY ABOUT MY ARM...
IT'LL HEAL IN TWO WEEKS.
B-BUT...
HURRY MOMO, WE DON'T HAVE TIME!!

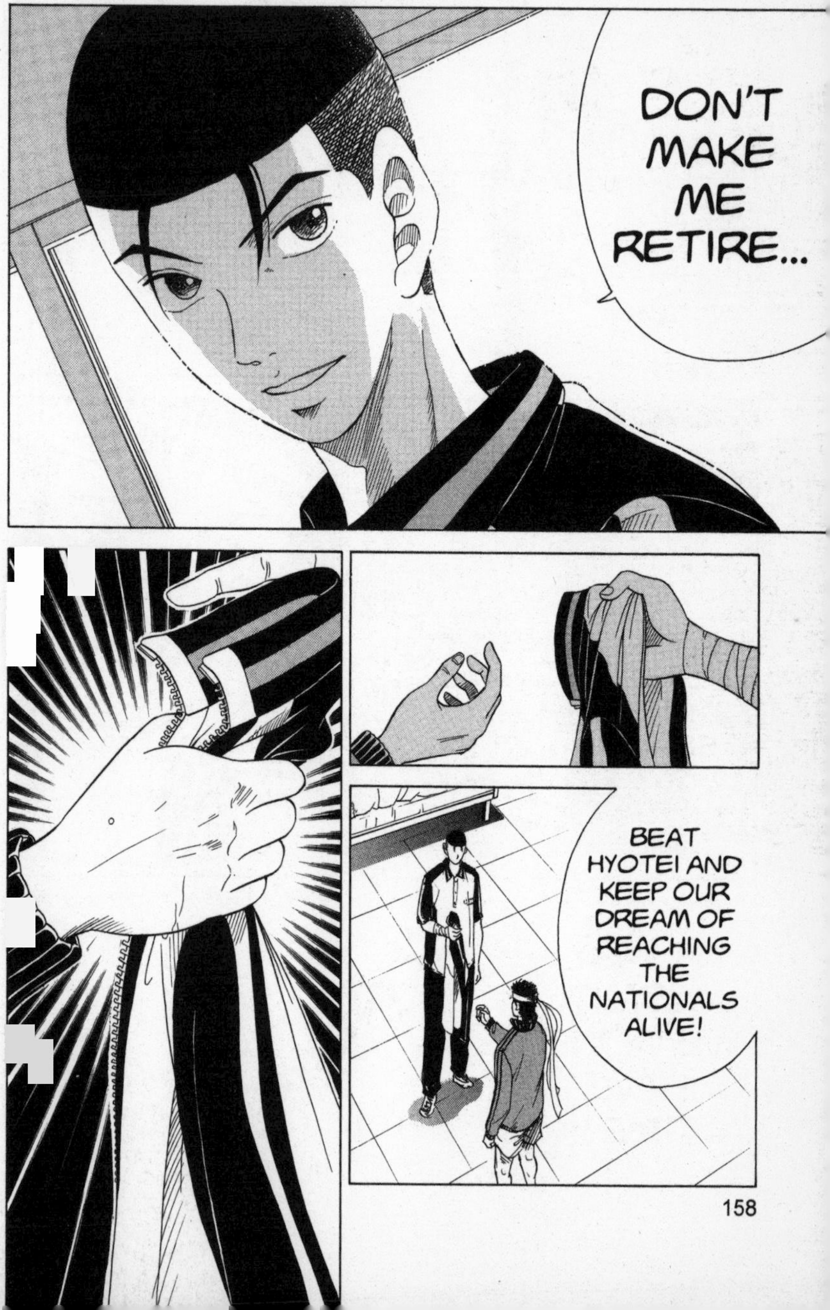
DON'T MAKE ME RETIRE...
BEAT HYOTEI AND KEEP OUR DREAM OF REACHING THE NATIONALS ALIVE!

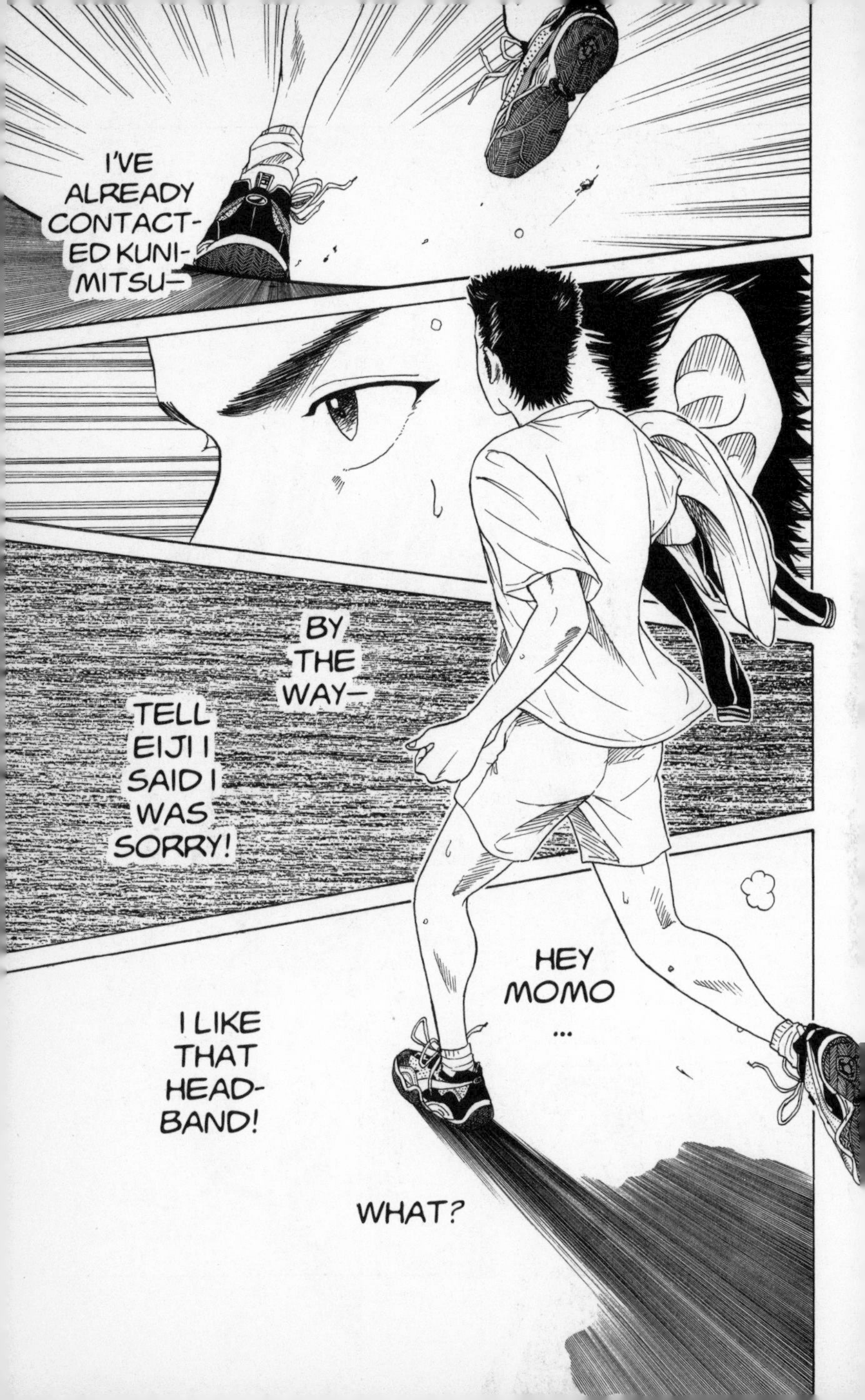
I'VE ALREADY CONTACT-ED KUNI-MITSU—
BY THE WAY—
TELL EIJI I SAID I WAS SORRY!
HEY MOMO ...
I LIKE THAT HEAD-BAND!
WHAT?

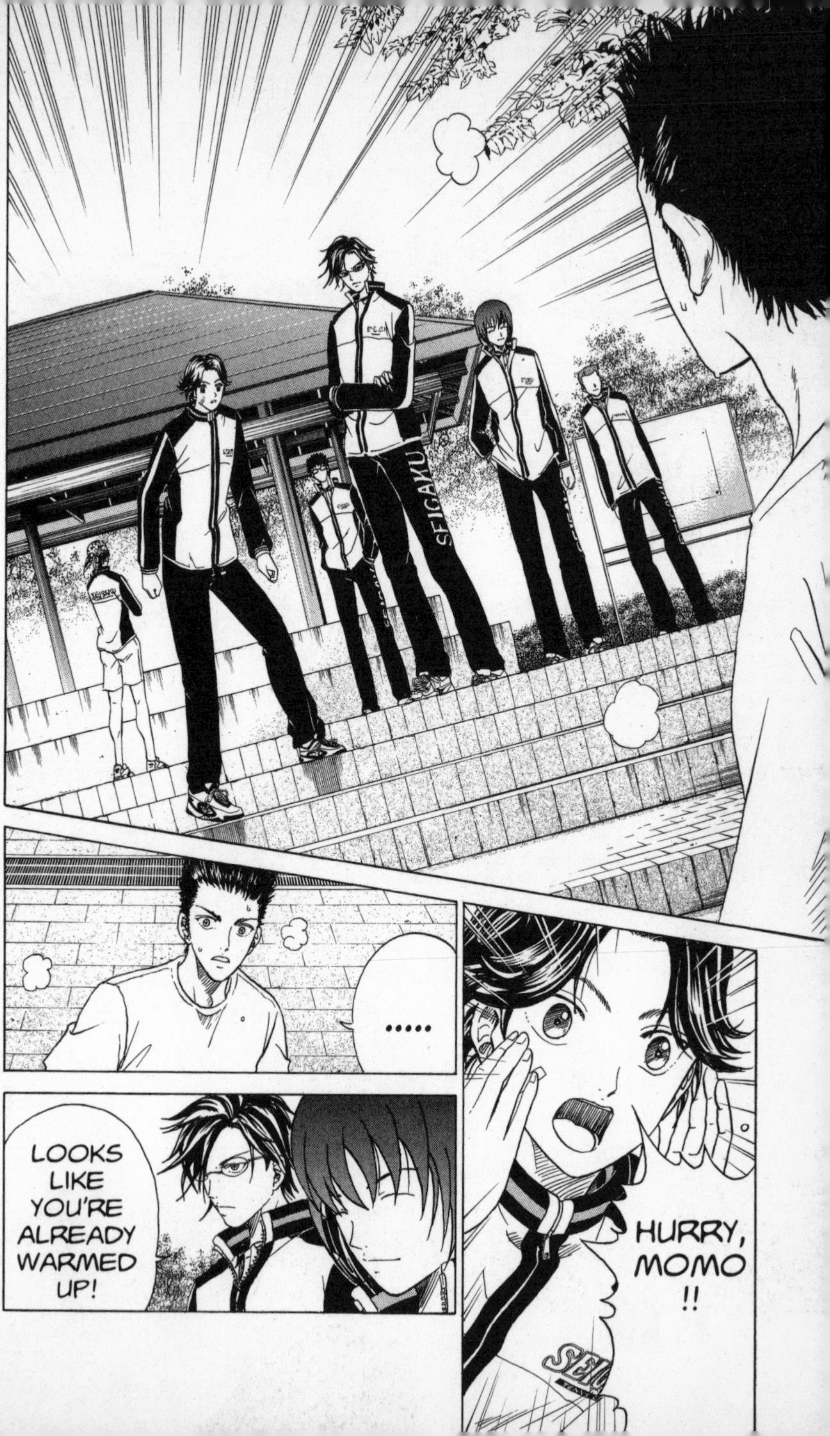
SEIGAKU
HURRY, MOMO!!
.....
LOOKS LIKE YOU'RE ALREADY WARMED UP!

READ THIS WAY

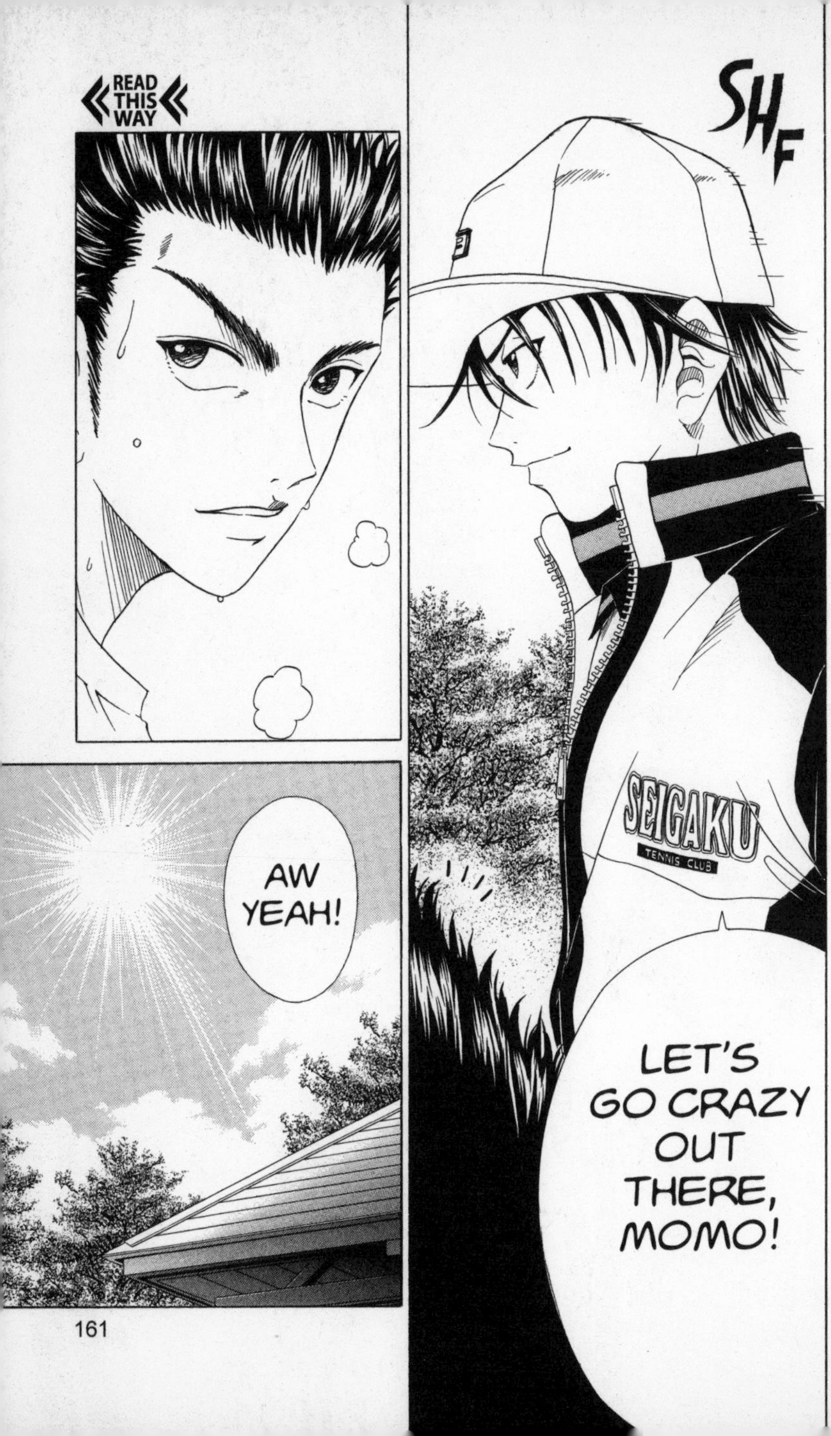
SHF
SEIGAKU
TENNIS CLUB
LET'S GO CRAZY OUT THERE, MOMO!
AW YEAH!

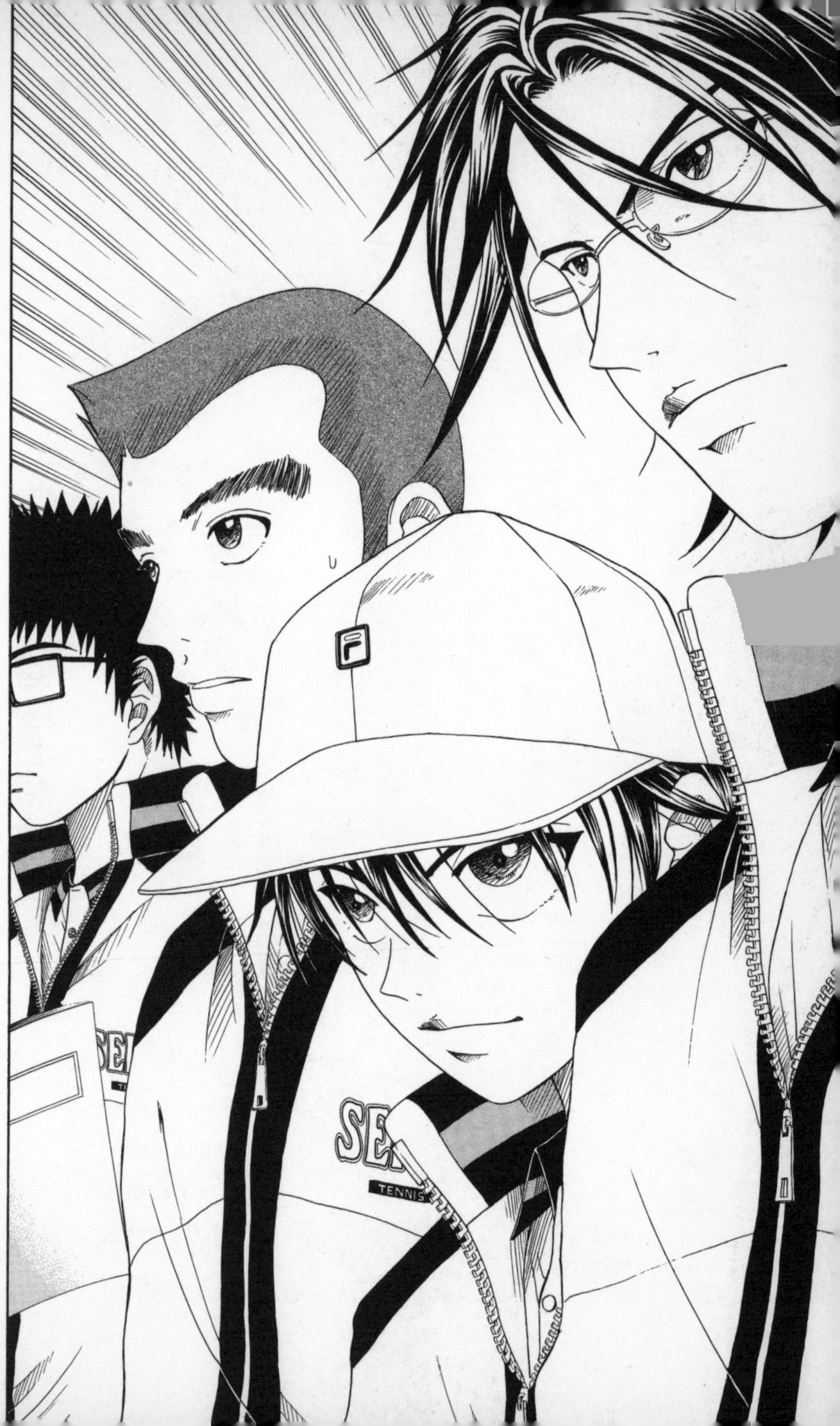
TENNIS

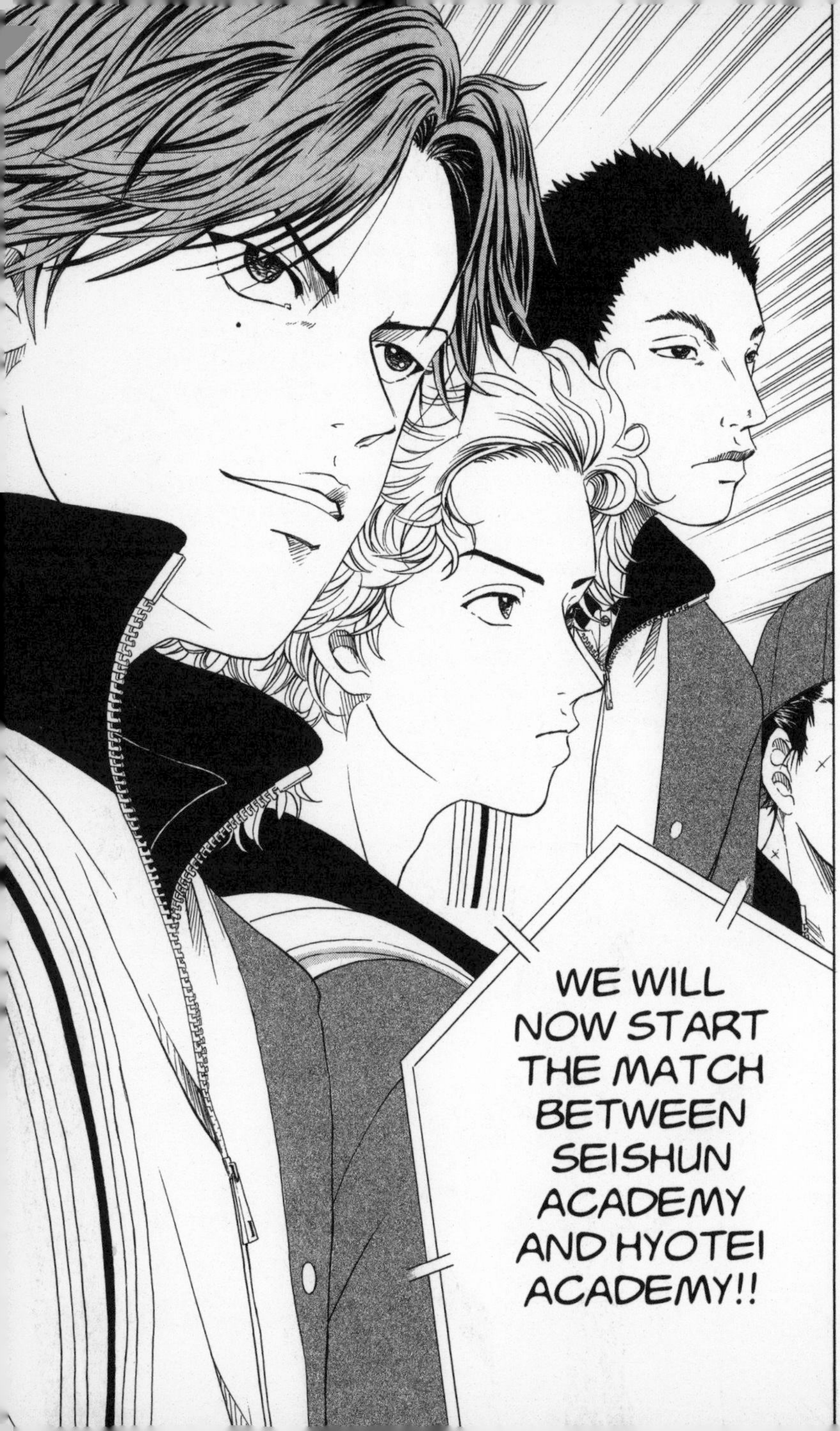
WE WILL NOW START THE MATCH BETWEEN SEISHUN ACADEMY AND HYOTEI ACADEMY!!

Thank you for reading *The Prince of Tennis* Vol. 14.

For the first time since *The Prince of Tennis* started three years ago, I got to take a real "vacation." During 2002's Golden Week, I spent a full day of fun with the "Sushi Tennis Team" pictured on page one. It's been so long since I had a whole day off... Just like the team's name, we spent the day playing tennis and the night eating sushi at (the restaurant I like and used as a model) Kawamura Sushi.
The Price of Tennis voice actors were all great!! On a later date, I heard the actors playing Shuichiro and the umpire (who also plays Masaya) were actually planning on playing tennis. It kinda makes me feel good. For readers who don't know the joy of tennis, check it out! It's fun, but be courteous!

By the time Vol. 14 comes out, I think the second character popularity poll should be starting in *Shonen Jump* Issue 31's third-year anniversary lead-off all-color episode. (Scheduled for sale on 7/2/2002.) Please send in your votes! (This poll was held only in Japan. -Ed.)

Well then, keep supporting *The Price of Tennis* and Ryoma!! See you in the next volume.

Konomi

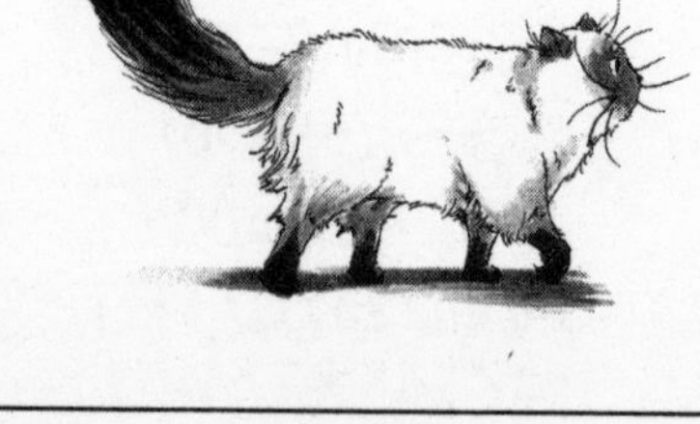

テニスの王子様
T. Konomi
2002.6.3

Send fan letters to: VIZ Media, LLC P.O. Box 77010 San Francisco, CA 94107, Attention: Takeshi Konomi

5TH MATCH— NO. 1 SINGLES	4TH MATCH— NO. 2 SINGLES	3RD MATCH— NO. 3 SINGLES	2ND MATCH— NO. 1 DOUBLES		1ST MATCH— NO. 2 DOUBLES	
KEIGO ATOBE (9TH GRADE) BLOOD TYPE:A	JIRO AKUTAGAWA (9TH GRADE) BLOOD TYPE:AB	MUNEHIRO KABAJI (8TH GRADE) BLOOD TYPE:O	RYO SHISHIDO (9TH GRADE) BLOOD TYPE:B	CHOTARO OTORI (8TH GRADE) BLOOD TYPE:O	GAKUTO MUKAHI (9TH GRADE) BLOOD TYPE:B	YUSHI OSHITARI (9TH GRADE) BLOOD TYPE:A

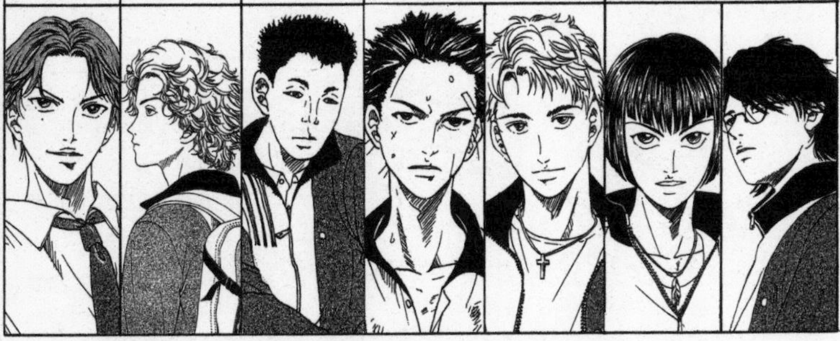

GENIUS 123: WHERE IS RYOMA??!

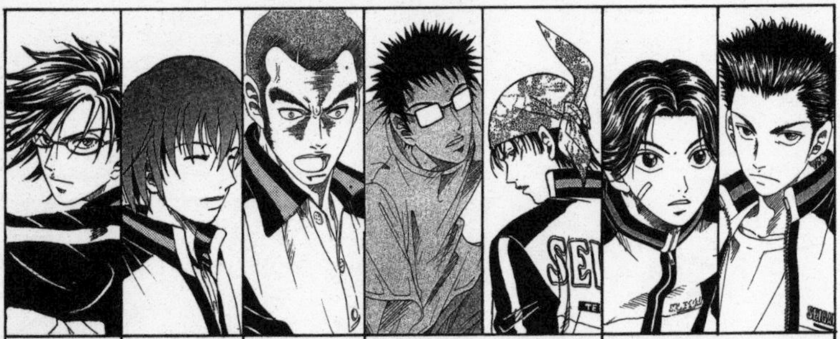
SEI

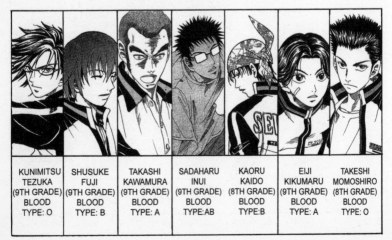

KUNIMITSU TEZUKA (9TH GRADE) BLOOD TYPE: O	SHUSUKE FUJI (9TH GRADE) BLOOD TYPE: B	TAKASHI KAWAMURA (9TH GRADE) BLOOD TYPE: A	SADAHARU INUI (9TH GRADE) BLOOD TYPE:AB	KAORU KAIDO (8TH GRADE) BLOOD TYPE:B	EIJI KIKUMARU (9TH GRADE) BLOOD TYPE: A	TAKESHI MOMOSHIRO (8TH GRADE) BLOOD TYPE: O

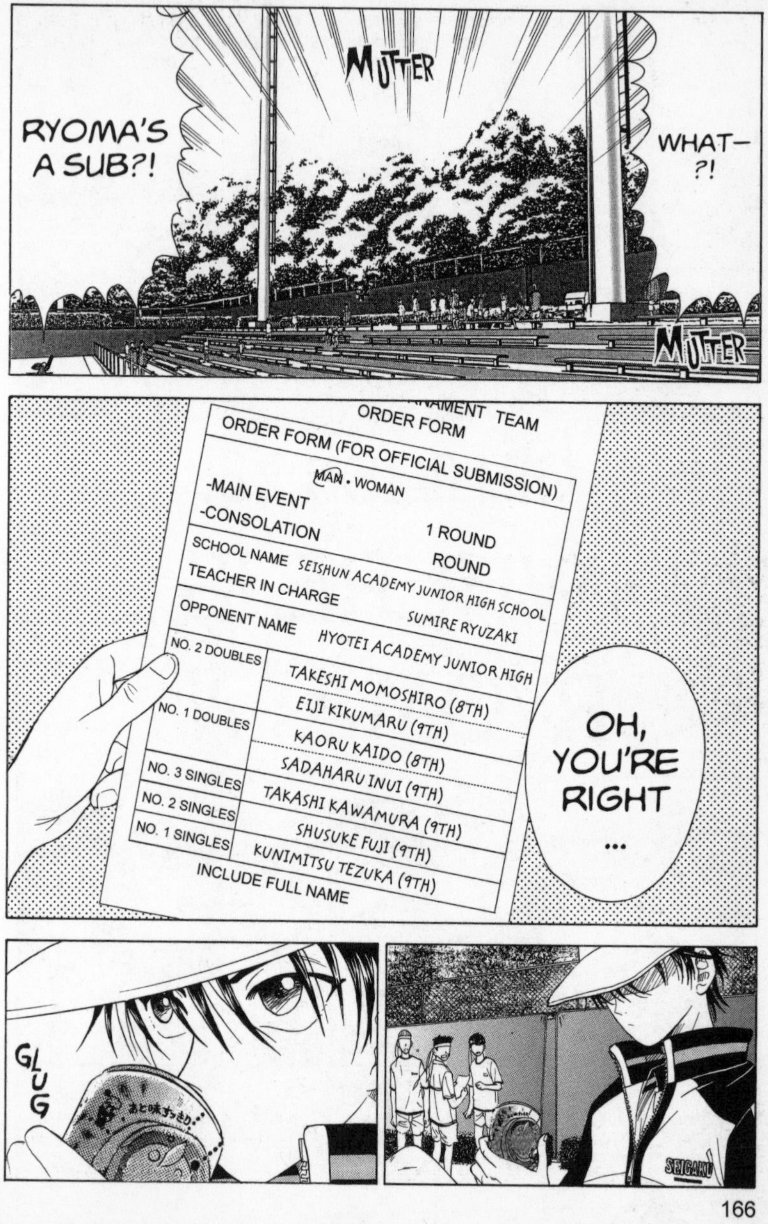
WHAT—?!
MUTTER
RYOMA'S A SUB?!
MUTTER
OH, YOU'RE RIGHT...
NAMENT TEAM ORDER FORM
ORDER FORM (FOR OFFICIAL SUBMISSION)
MAN • WOMAN
-MAIN EVENT
-CONSOLATION
1 ROUND
ROUND
SCHOOL NAME SEISHUN ACADEMY JUNIOR HIGH SCHOOL
TEACHER IN CHARGE SUMIRE RYUZAKI
OPPONENT NAME HYOTEI ACADEMY JUNIOR HIGH
NO. 2 DOUBLES TAKESHI MOMOSHIRO (8TH)
EIJI KIKUMARU (9TH)
NO. 1 DOUBLES KAORU KAIDO (8TH)
SADAHARU INUI (9TH)
NO. 3 SINGLES TAKASHI KAWAMURA (9TH)
NO. 2 SINGLES SHUSUKE FUJI (9TH)
NO. 1 SINGLES KUNIMITSU TEZUKA (9TH)
INCLUDE FULL NAME
SEIGAKU
GLUG
あと味すっきり

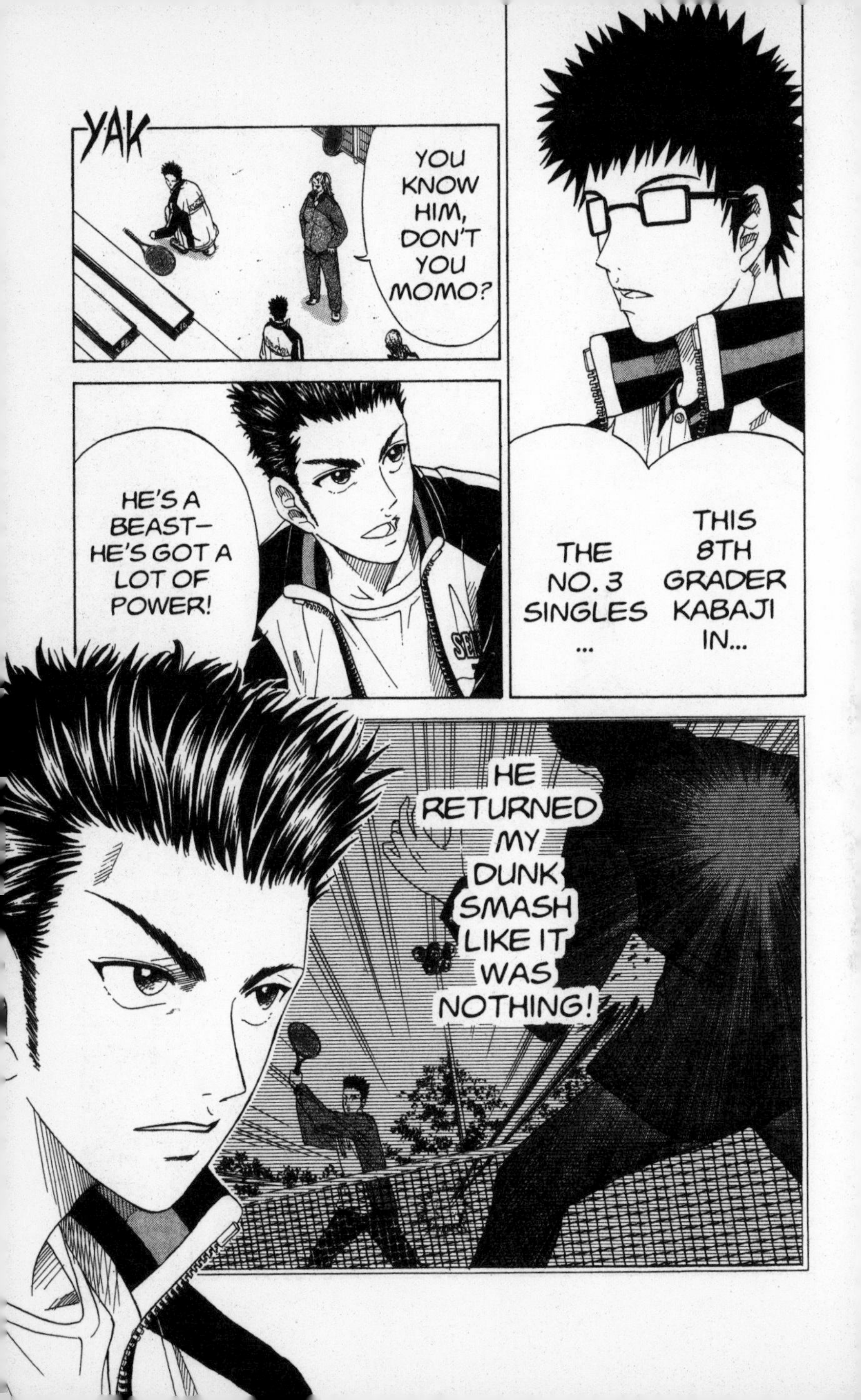
THIS 8TH GRADER KABAJI IN... THE NO. 3 SINGLES ...
YAK
YOU KNOW HIM, DON'T YOU MOMO?
HE'S A BEAST—HE'S GOT A LOT OF POWER!
HE RETURNED MY DUNK SMASH LIKE IT WAS NOTHING!

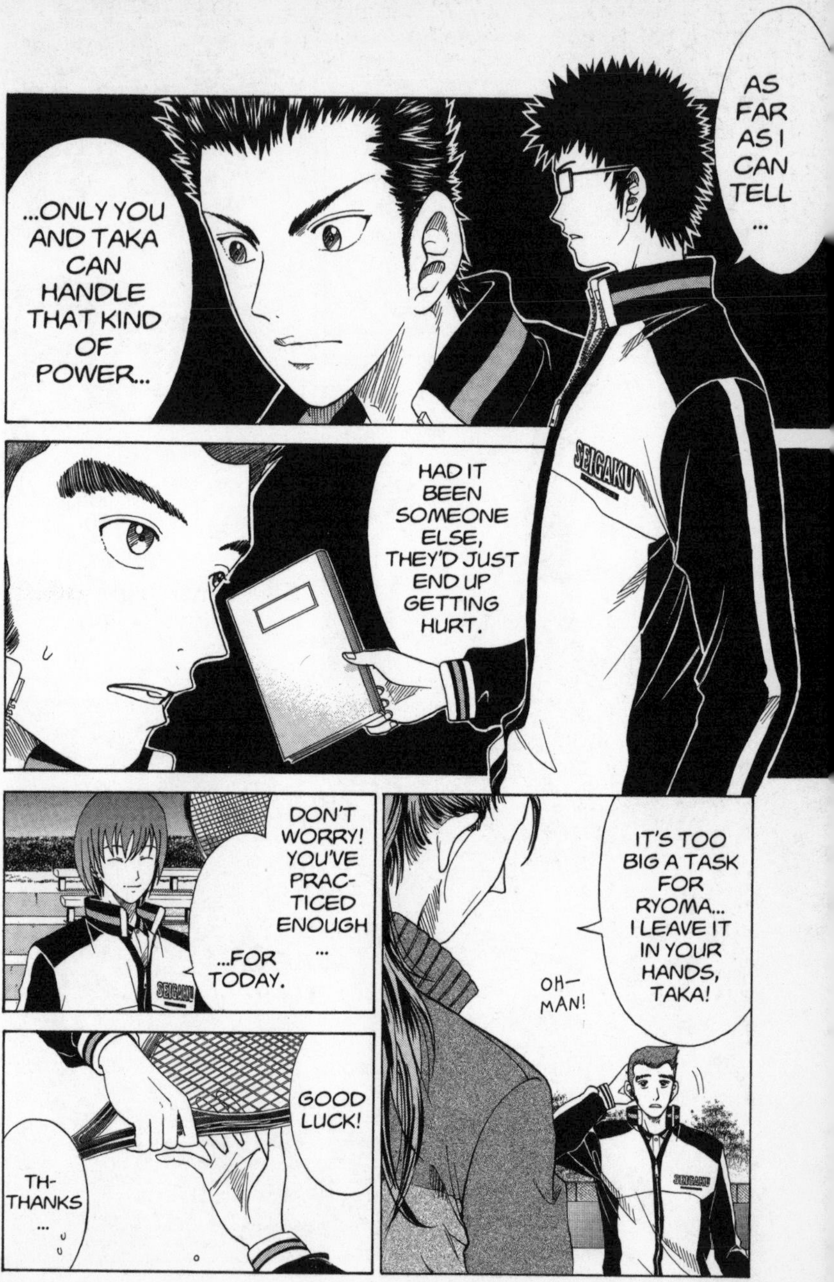
AS FAR AS I CAN TELL...
...ONLY YOU AND TAKA CAN HANDLE THAT KIND OF POWER...
HAD IT BEEN SOMEONE ELSE, THEY'D JUST END UP GETTING HURT.
IT'S TOO BIG A TASK FOR RYOMA... I LEAVE IT IN YOUR HANDS, TAKA!
OH—MAN!
DON'T WORRY! YOU'VE PRACTICED ENOUGH...
...FOR TODAY.
GOOD LUCK!
TH-THANKS...

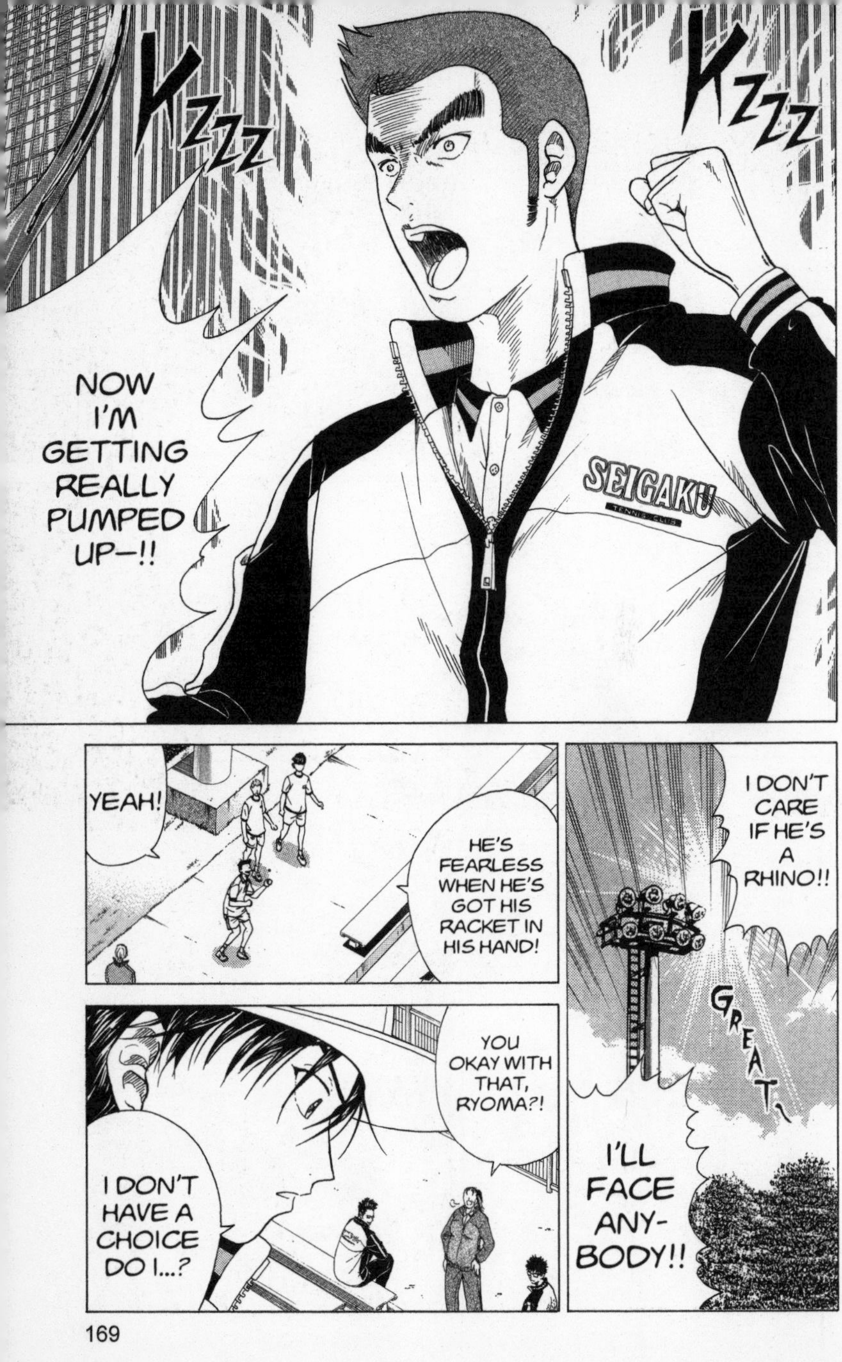
KZZZ
KZZZ
NOW I'M GETTING REALLY PUMPED UP—!!
SEIGAKU
I DON'T CARE IF HE'S A RHINO!!
GREAT,
I'LL FACE ANY-BODY!!
HE'S FEARLESS WHEN HE'S GOT HIS RACKET IN HIS HAND!
YEAH!
YOU OKAY WITH THAT, RYOMA?!
I DON'T HAVE A CHOICE DO I...?

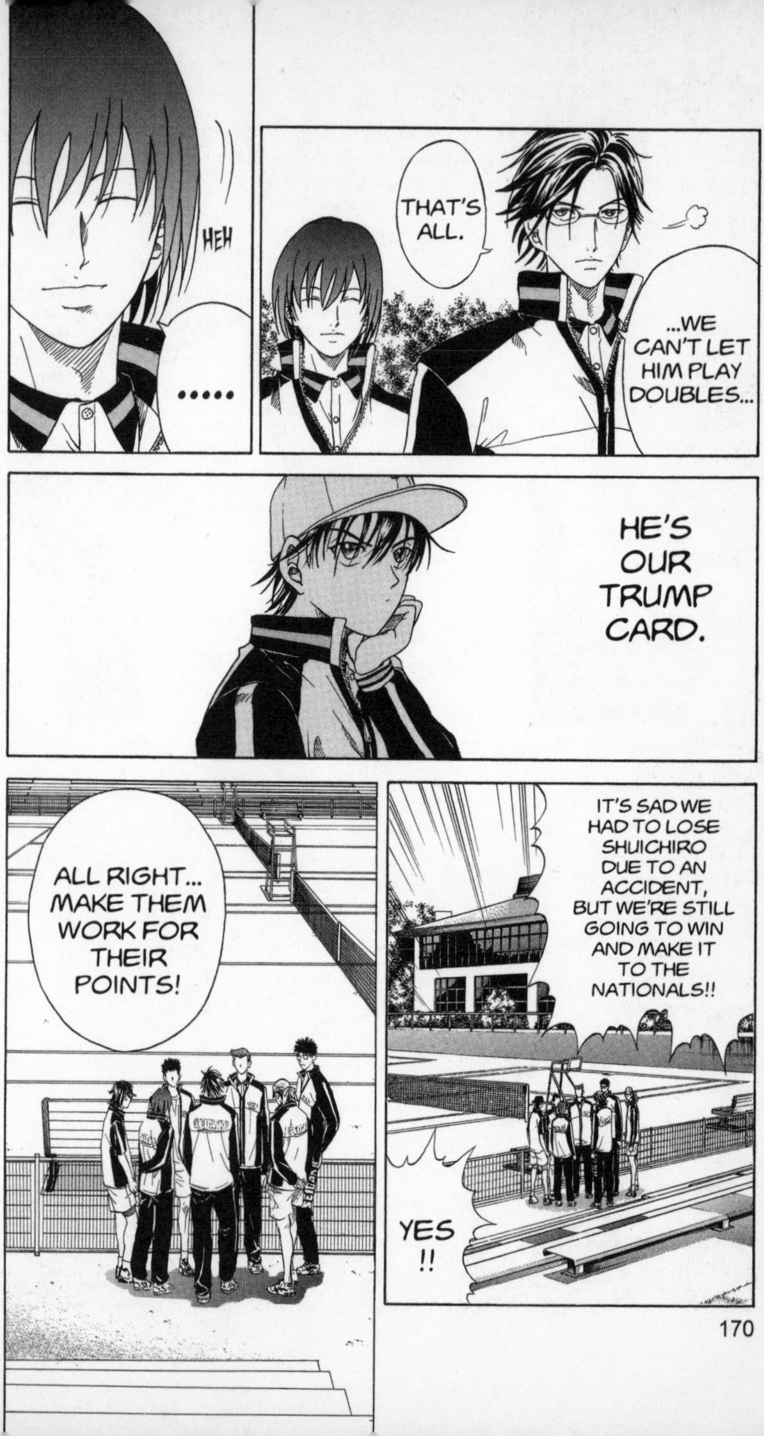
...WE CAN'T LET HIM PLAY DOUBLES...
THAT'S ALL.
HEH
......
HE'S OUR TRUMP CARD.
IT'S SAD WE HAD TO LOSE SHUICHIRO DUE TO AN ACCIDENT, BUT WE'RE STILL GOING TO WIN AND MAKE IT TO THE NATIONALS!!
YES !!
ALL RIGHT... MAKE THEM WORK FOR THEIR POINTS!

READ THIS WAY

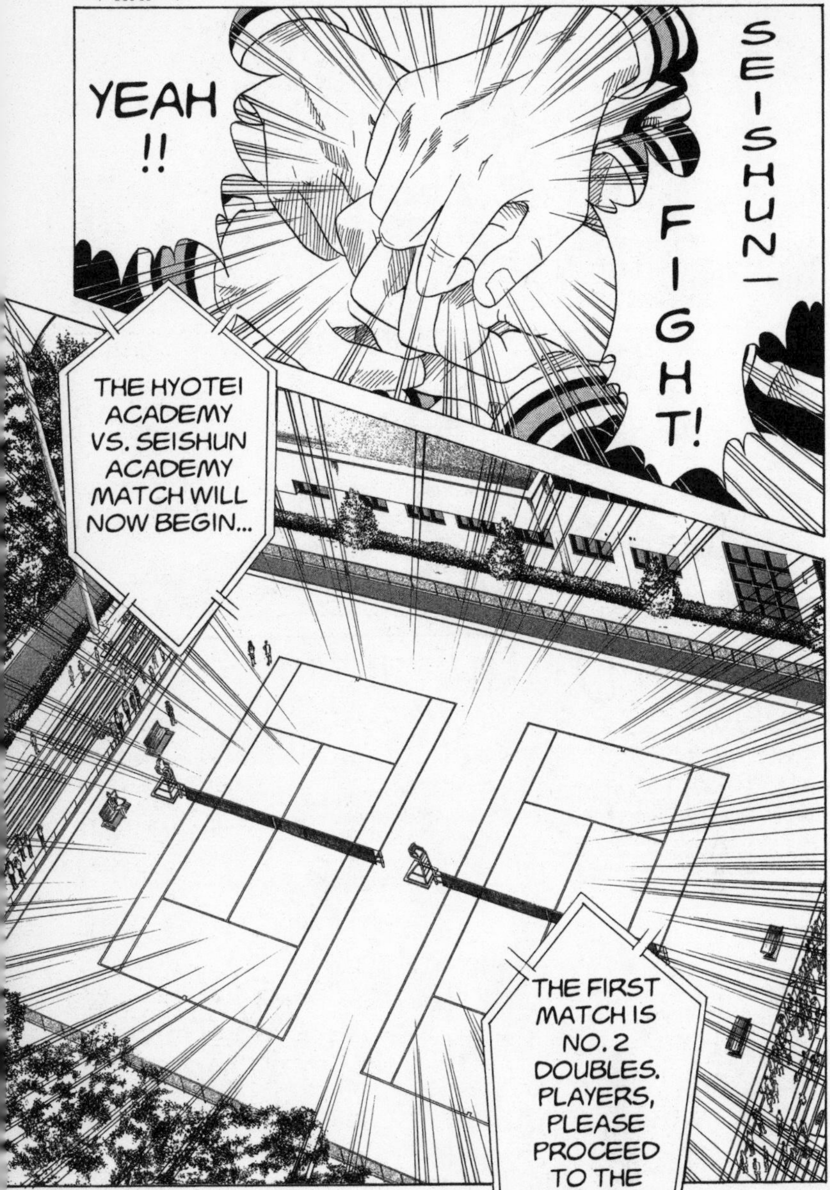
SEISHUN— FIGHT!
YEAH !!
THE HYOTEI ACADEMY VS. SEISHUN ACADEMY MATCH WILL NOW BEGIN...
THE FIRST MATCH IS NO. 2 DOUBLES. PLAYERS, PLEASE PROCEED TO THE COURT.

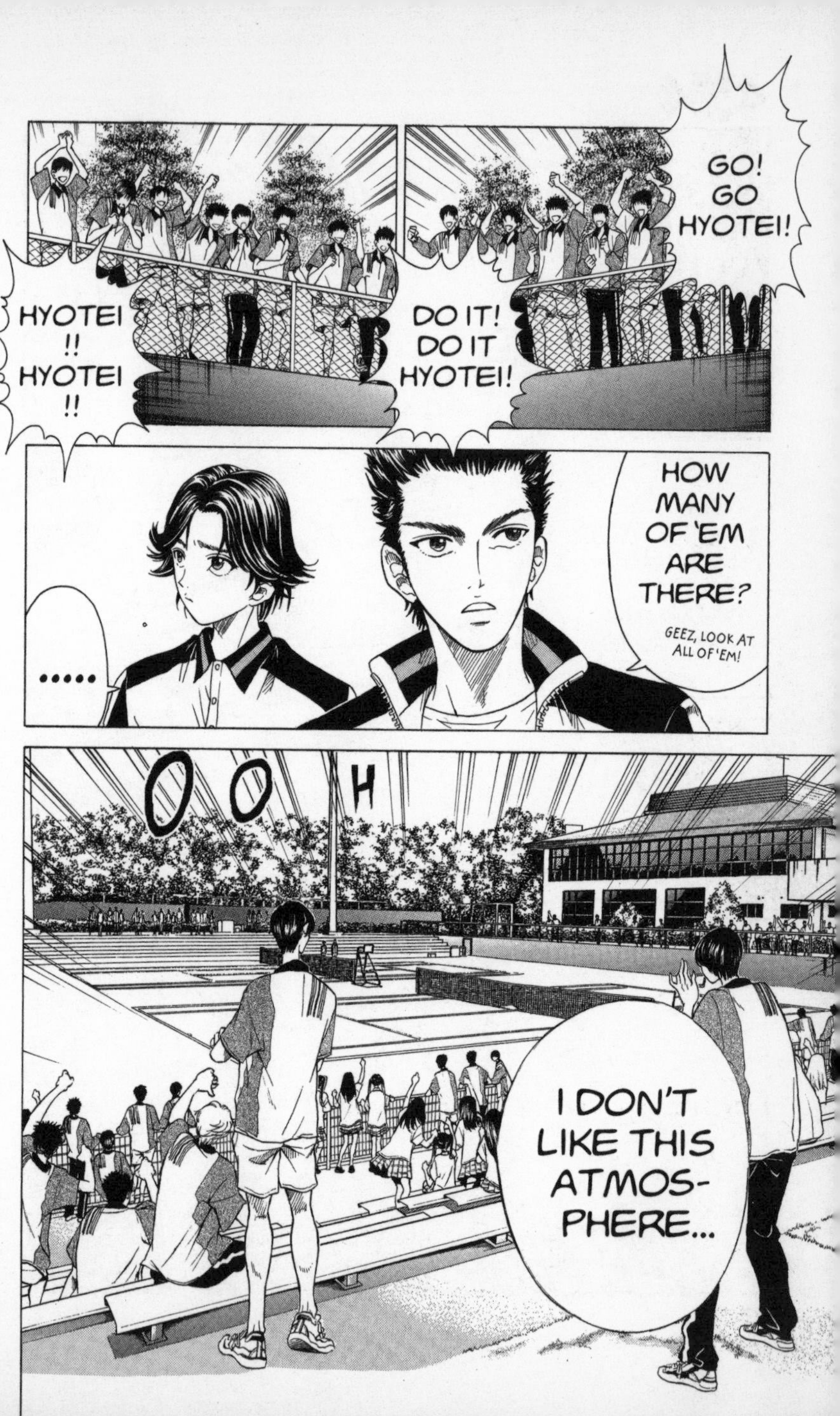
GO! GO HYOTEI!
DO IT! DO IT HYOTEI!
HYOTEI!! HYOTEI!!
HOW MANY OF 'EM ARE THERE?
GEEZ, LOOK AT ALL OF 'EM!
.....
OOH
I DON'T LIKE THIS ATMOSPHERE...

READ THIS WAY

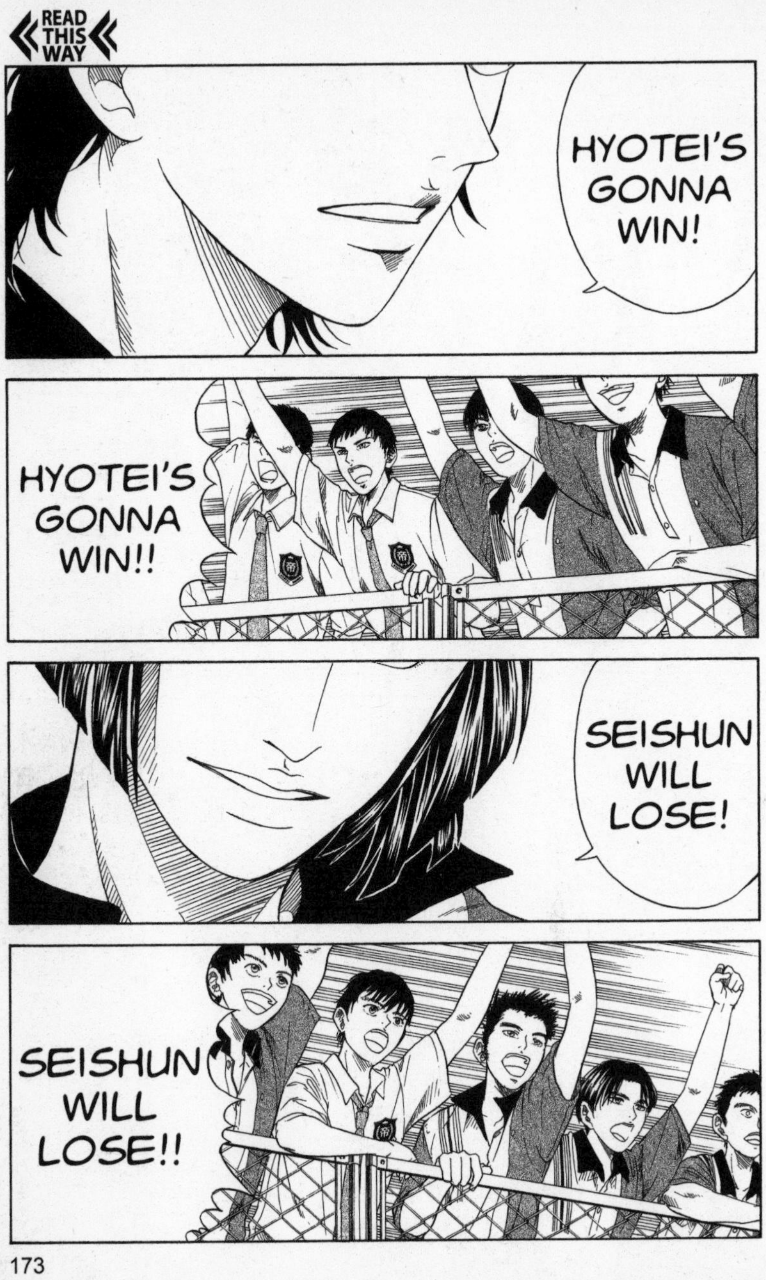
HYOTEI'S GONNA WIN!
HYOTEI'S GONNA WIN!!
SEISHUN WILL LOSE!
SEISHUN WILL LOSE!!

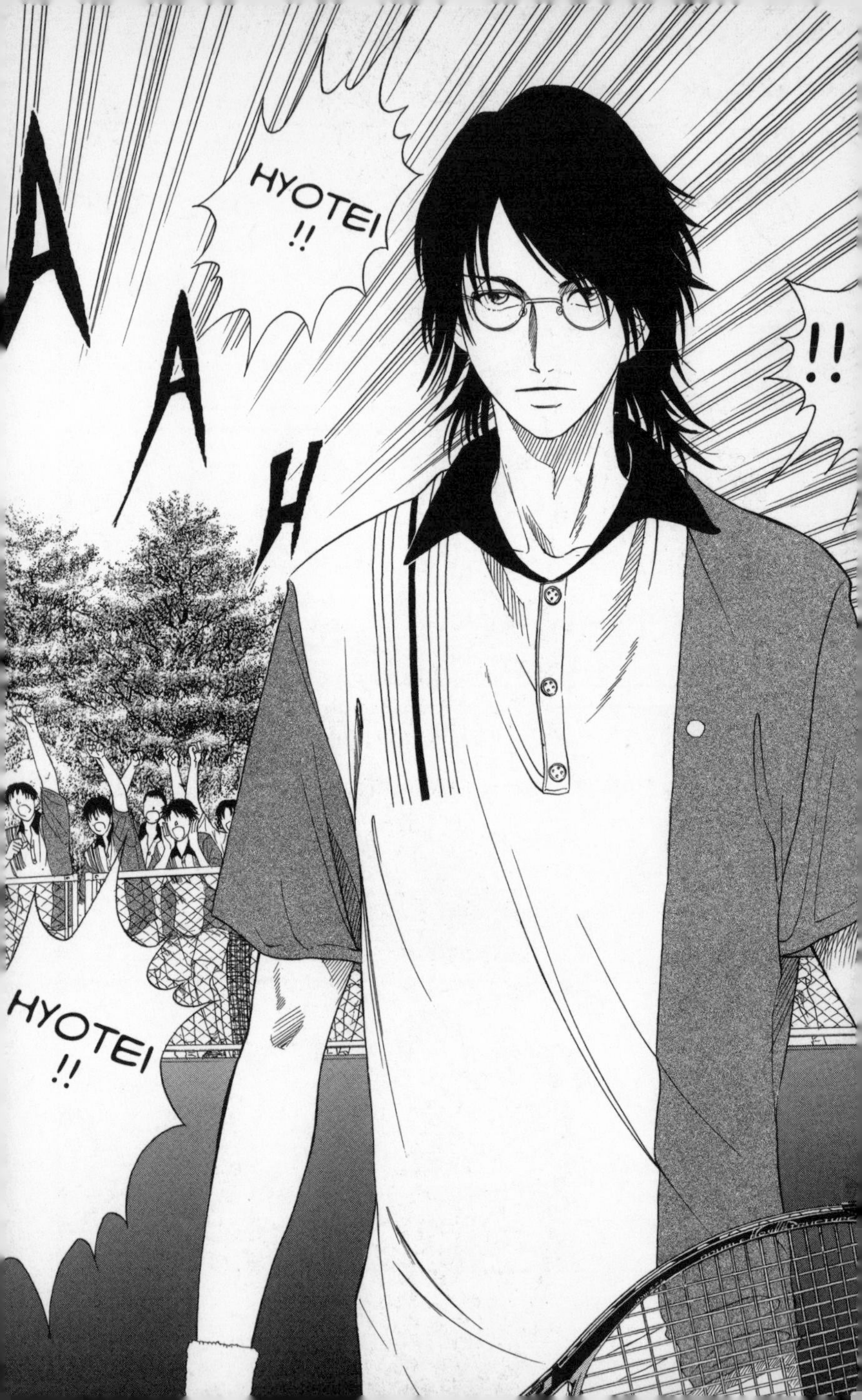
!!
HYOTEI !!
AAH
HYOTEI !!

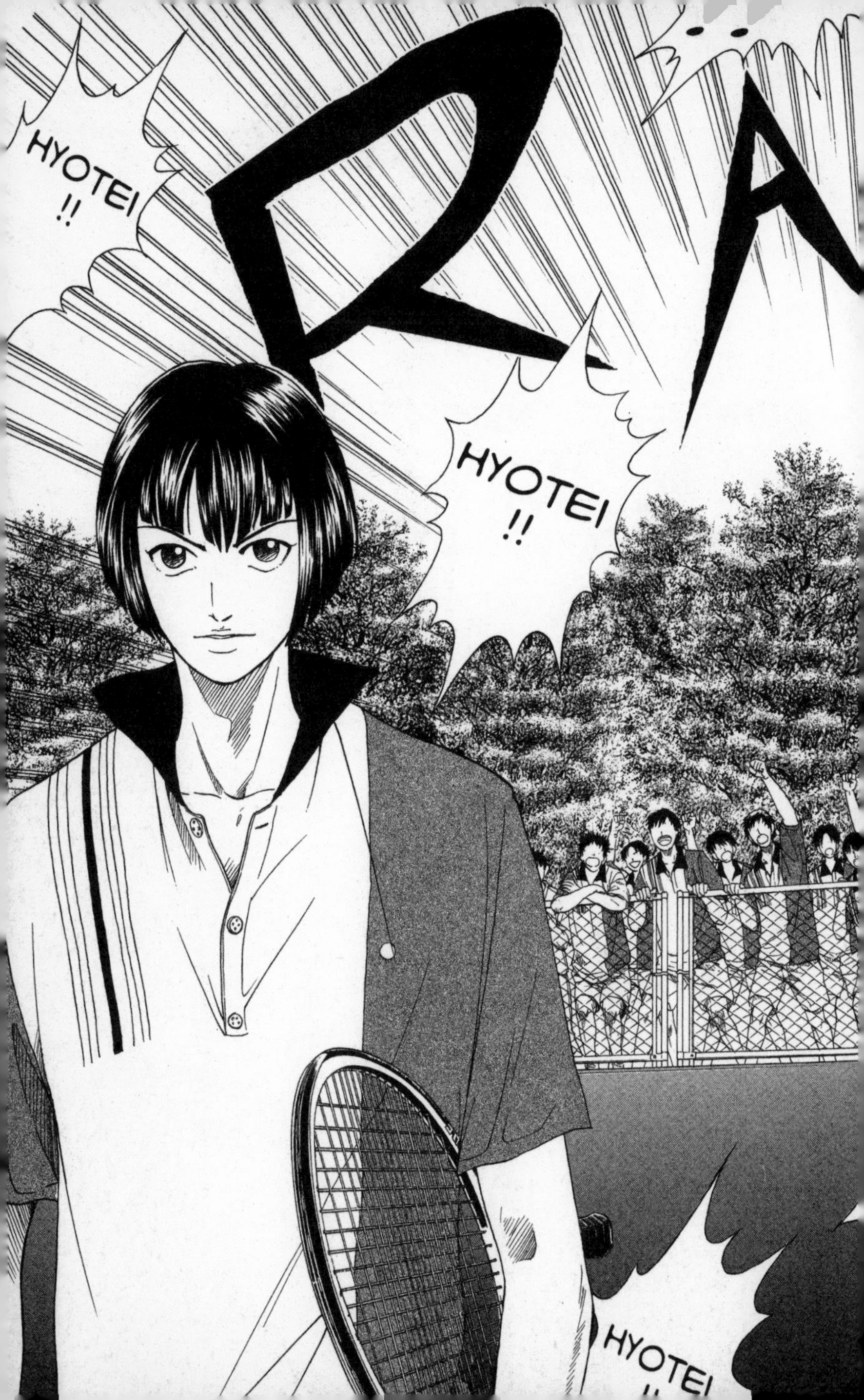
HYOTEI !!
HYOTEI !!
HYOTEI

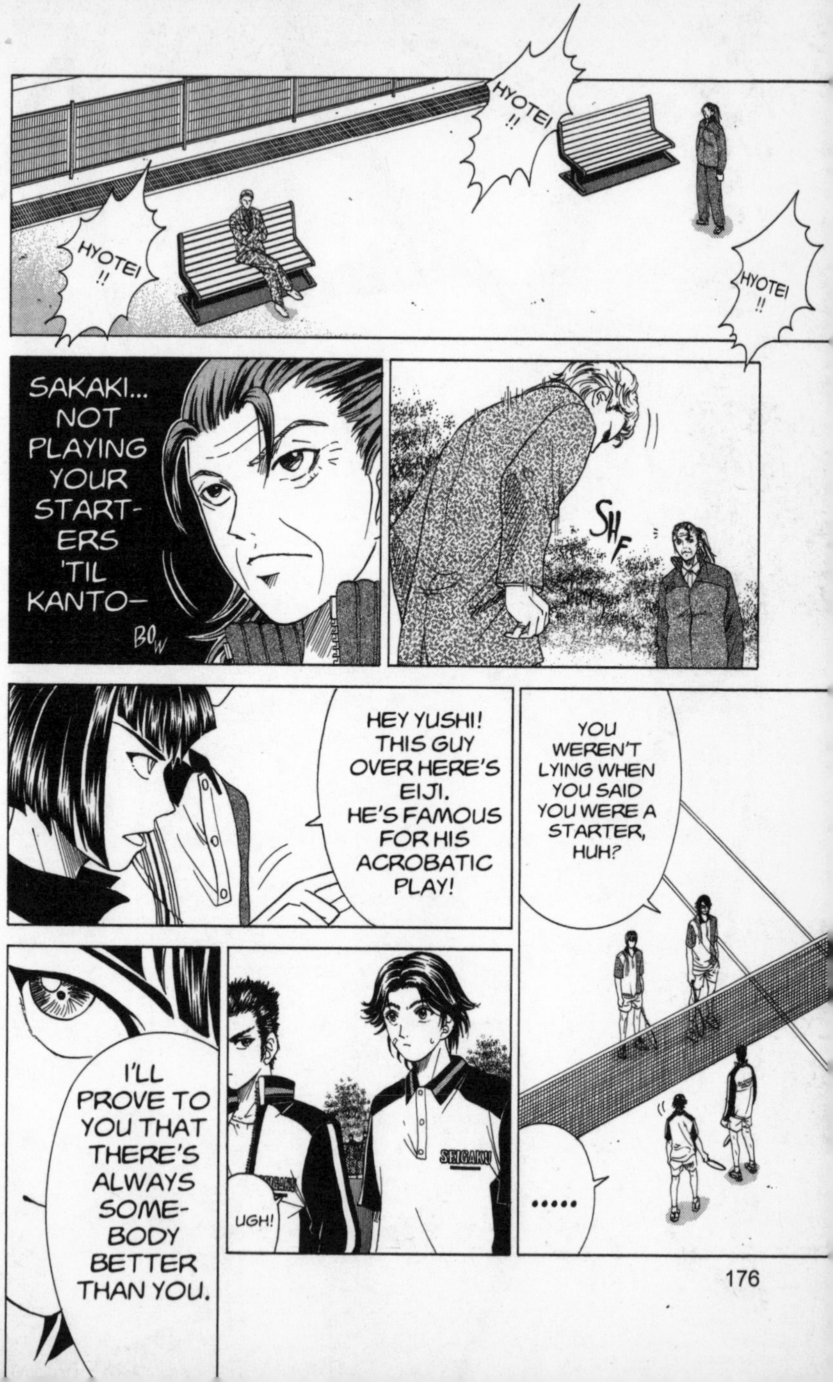
HYOTEI !!
HYOTEI !!
HYOTEI !!
SHF
BOW
SAKAKI... NOT PLAYING YOUR STARTERS 'TIL KANTO—
HEY YUSHI! THIS GUY OVER HERE'S EIJI. HE'S FAMOUS FOR HIS ACROBATIC PLAY!
YOU WEREN'T LYING WHEN YOU SAID YOU WERE A STARTER, HUH?
.....
SEIGAKU
UGH!
I'LL PROVE TO YOU THAT THERE'S ALWAYS SOMEBODY BETTER THAN YOU.

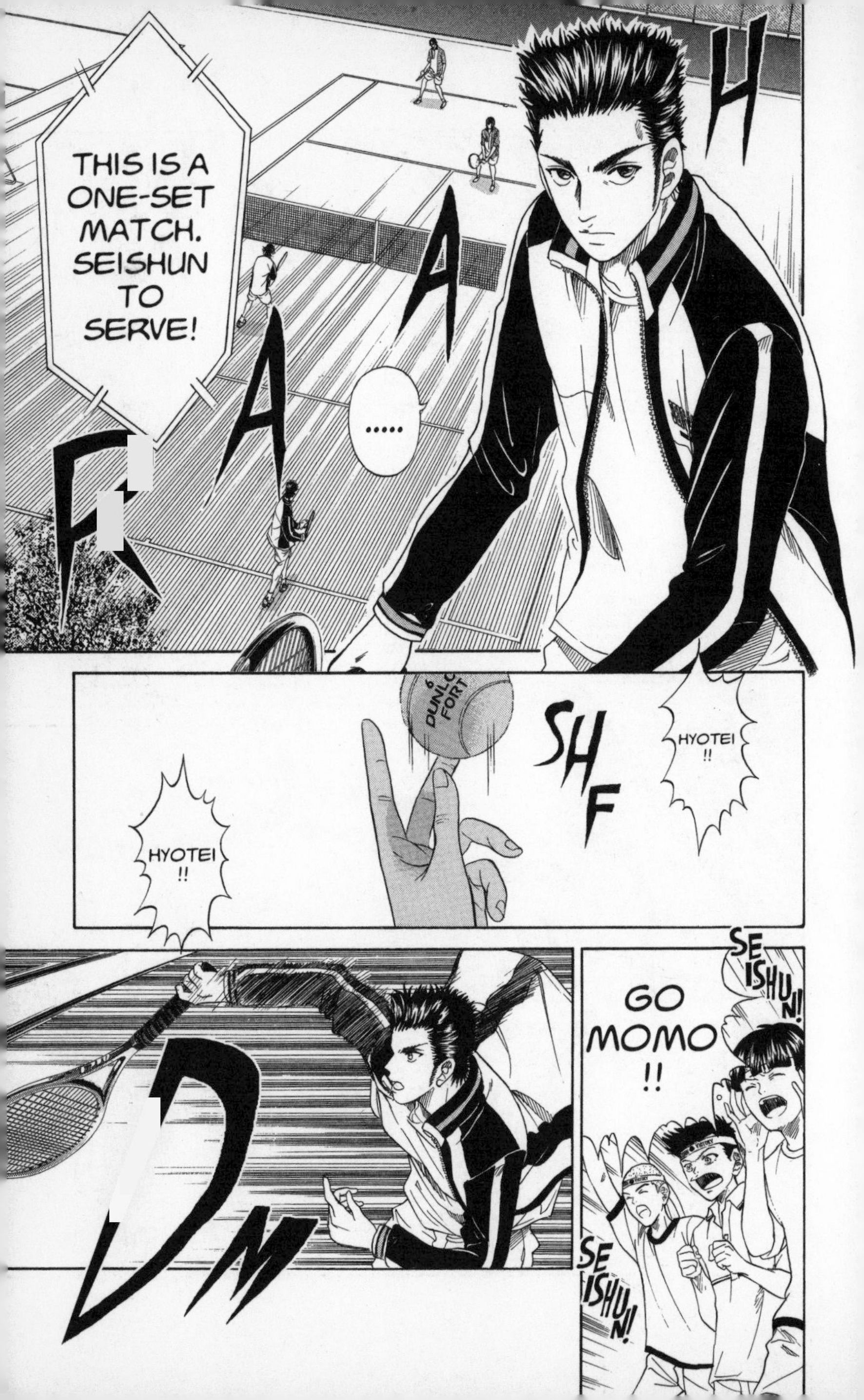
THIS IS A ONE-SET MATCH. SEISHUN TO SERVE!
.....
HYOTEI !!
SHF
HYOTEI !!
SEISHUN!
GO MOMO !!
SEISHUN!

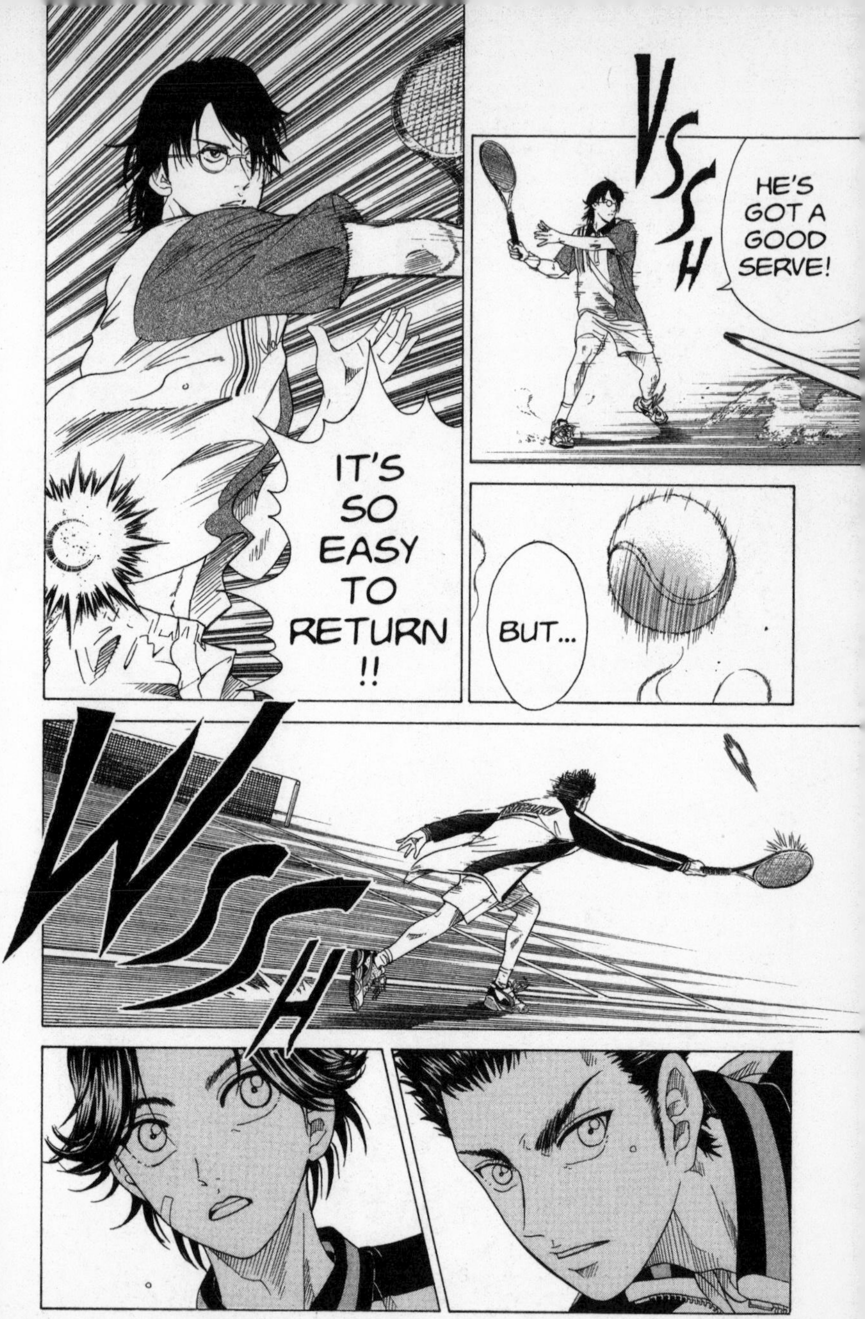
VSSH
HE'S GOT A GOOD SERVE!
IT'S SO EASY TO RETURN !!
BUT...
WSSH

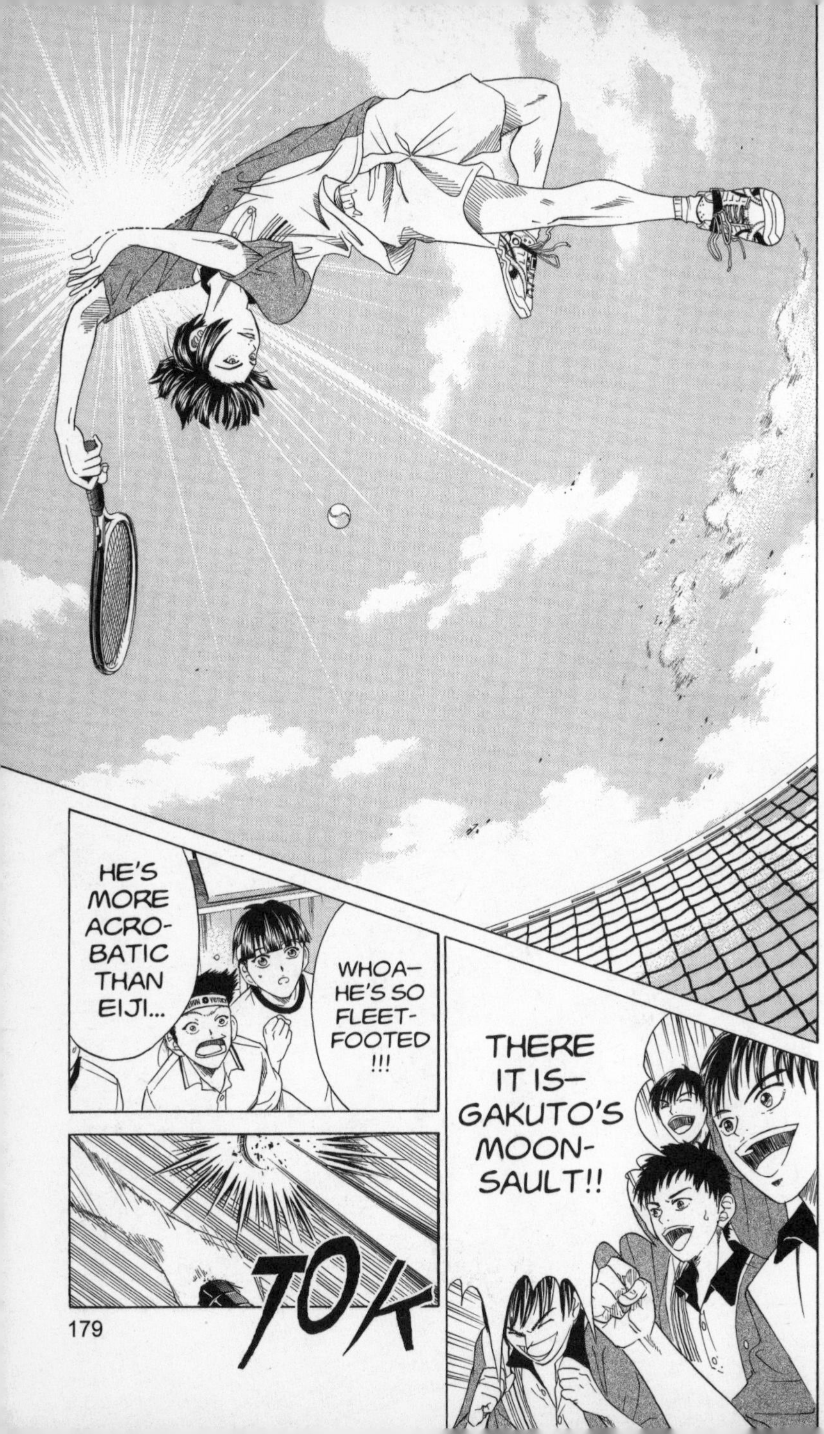
THERE IT IS—GAKUTO'S MOON-SAULT!!
HE'S MORE ACRO-BATIC THAN EIJI...
WHOA—HE'S SO FLEET-FOOTED!!!
TOK

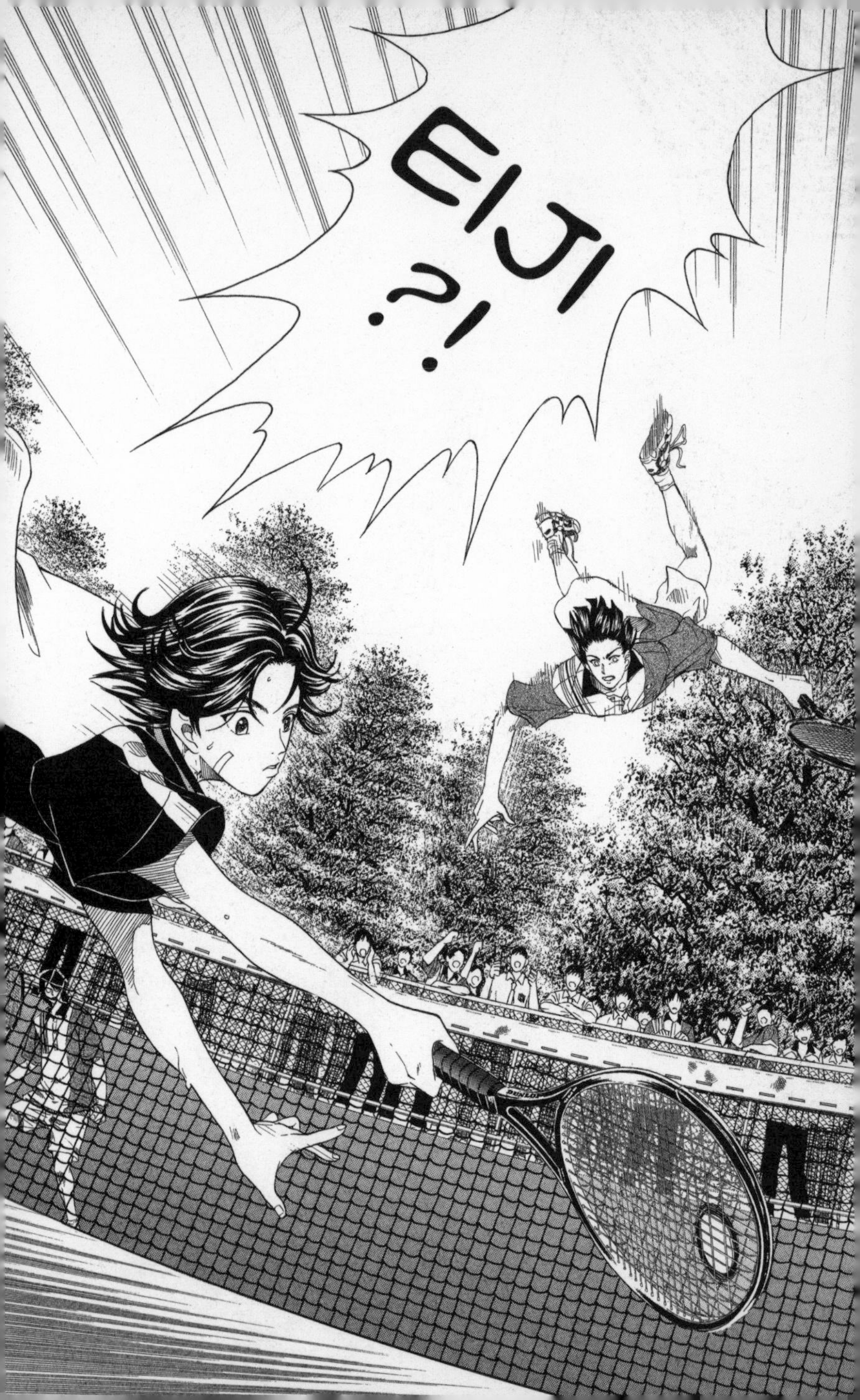
EIJI?!

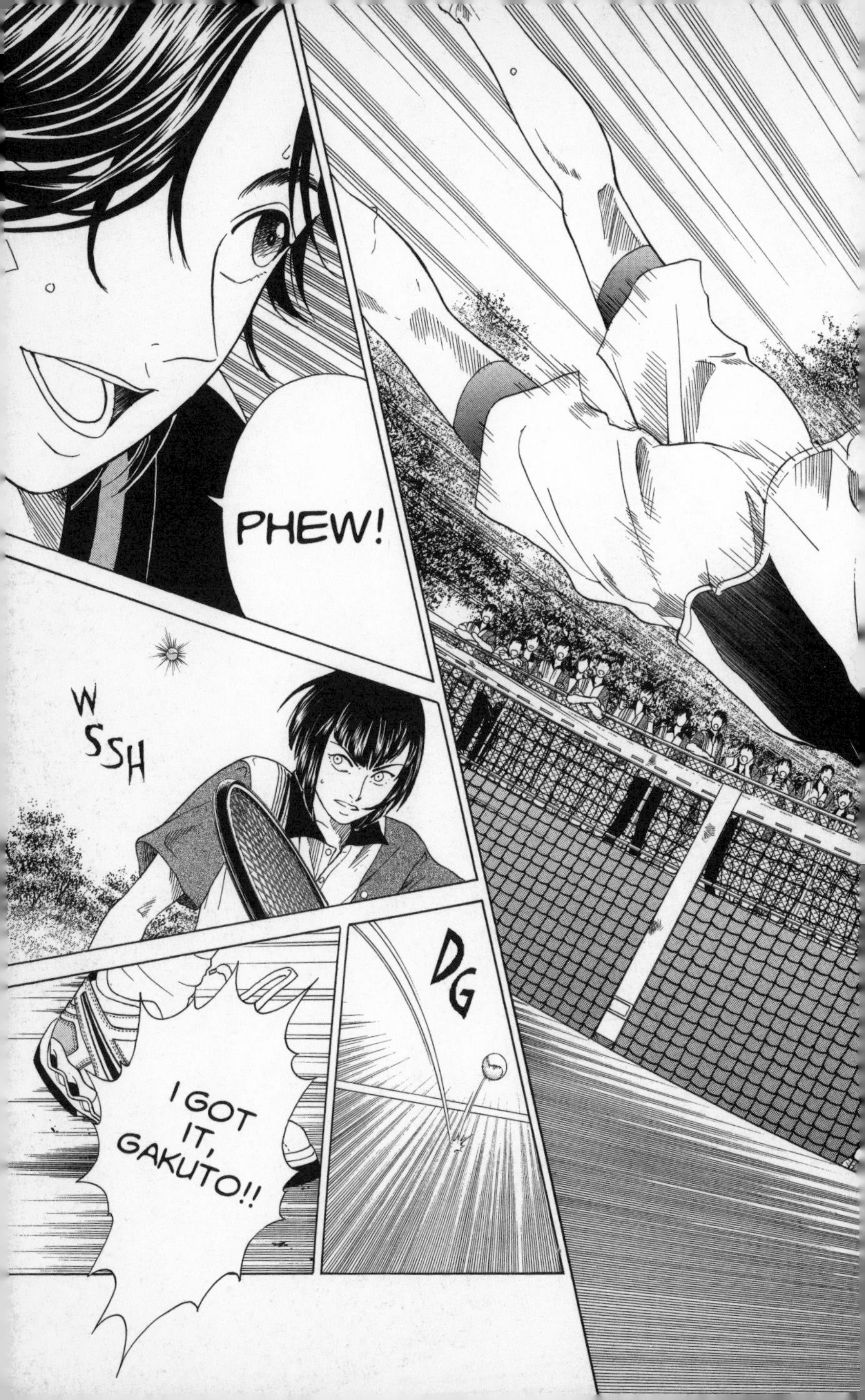
PHEW!
WSSH
DG
I GOT IT, GAKUTO!!

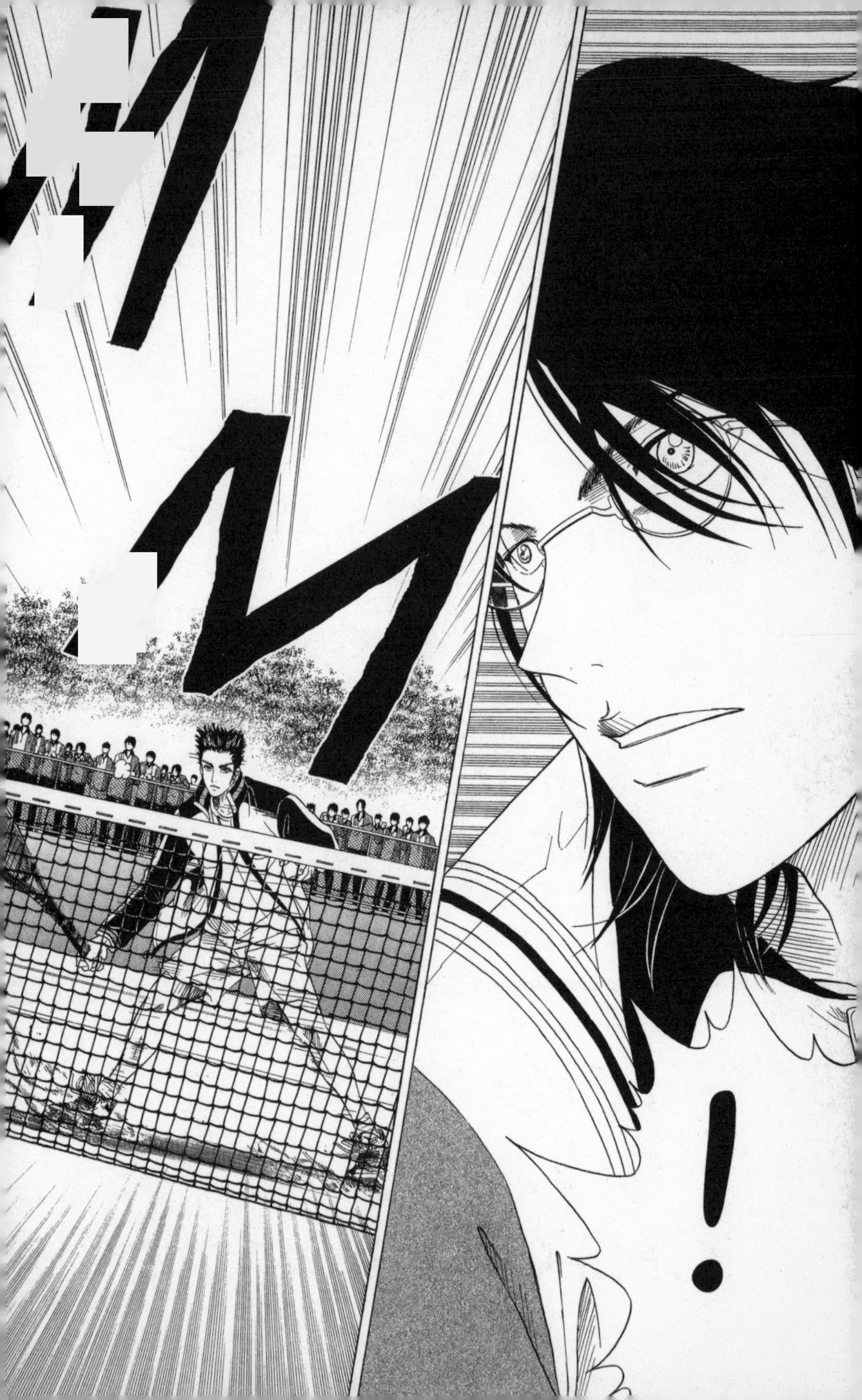

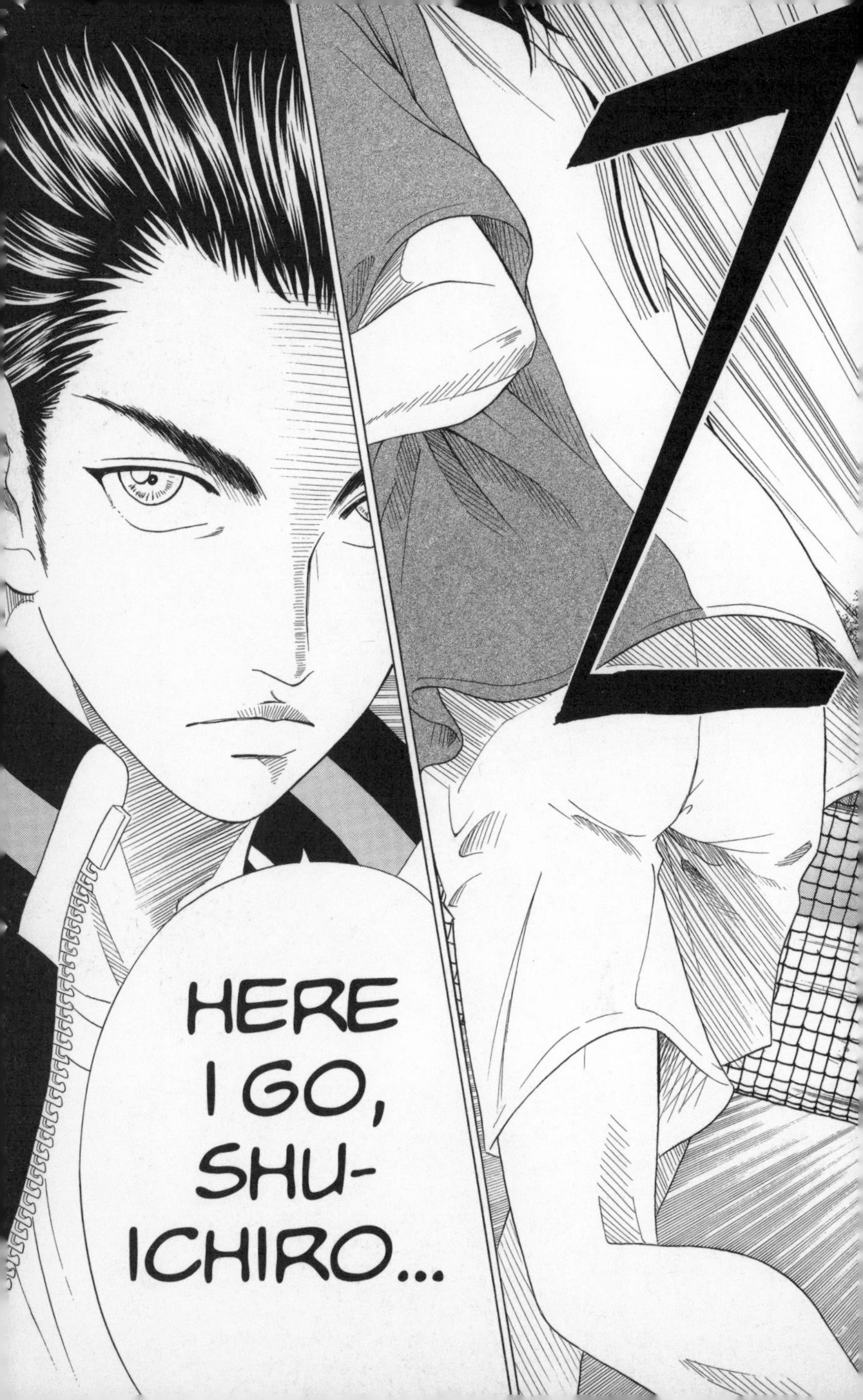
HERE I GO, SHU-ICHIRO...

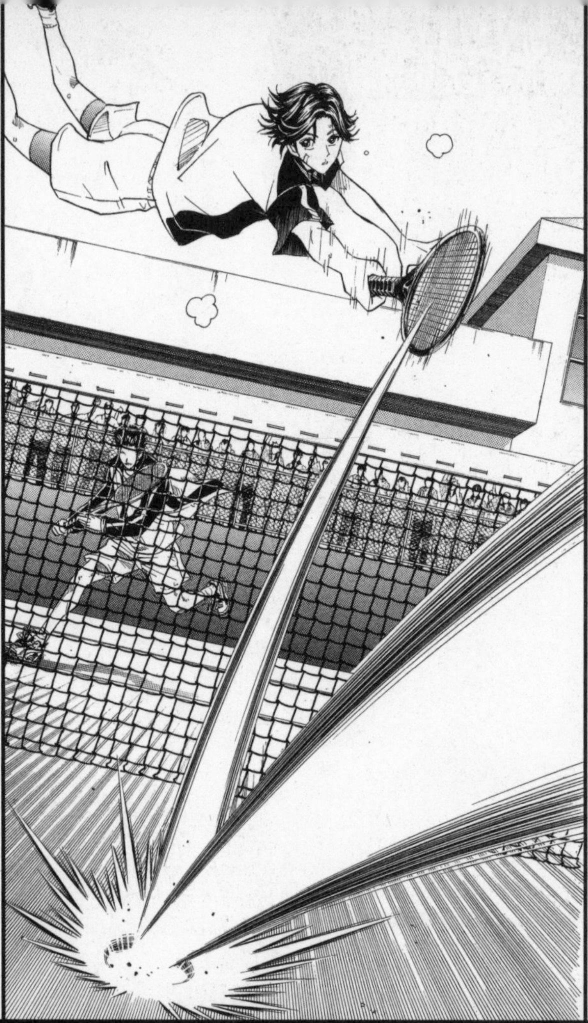

Seishun's boys are at the Kanto Tournament, and doubles action takes center stage. Will Eiji's gravity-defying stunts be good enough to beat Hyotei Academy's star doubles tandem? And check out Shuichiro's "36 Ways to Win at Doubles," which [redacted]

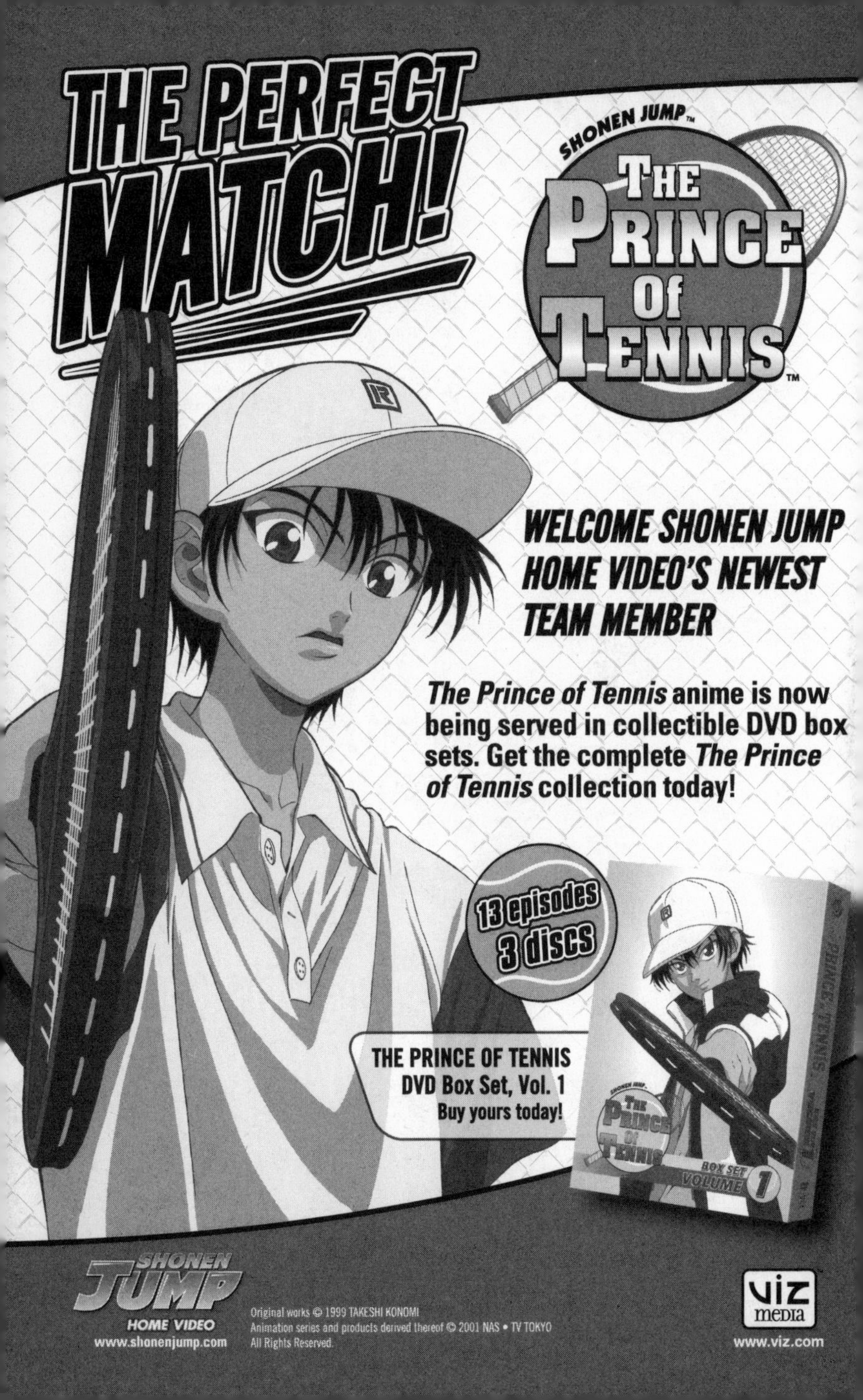
THE PERFECT MATCH!
SHONEN JUMP™
THE PRINCE OF TENNIS™
WELCOME SHONEN JUMP HOME VIDEO'S NEWEST TEAM MEMBER
The Prince of Tennis anime is now being served in collectible DVD box sets. Get the complete The Prince of Tennis collection today!
13 episodes
3 discs
THE PRINCE OF TENNIS
DVD Box Set, Vol. 1
Buy yours today!
BOX SET
VOLUME 1
SHONEN JUMP
HOME VIDEO
www.shonenjump.com
Original works © 1999 TAKESHI KONOMI
Animation series and products derived thereof © 2001 NAS • TV TOKYO
All Rights Reserved.
viz media
www.viz.com

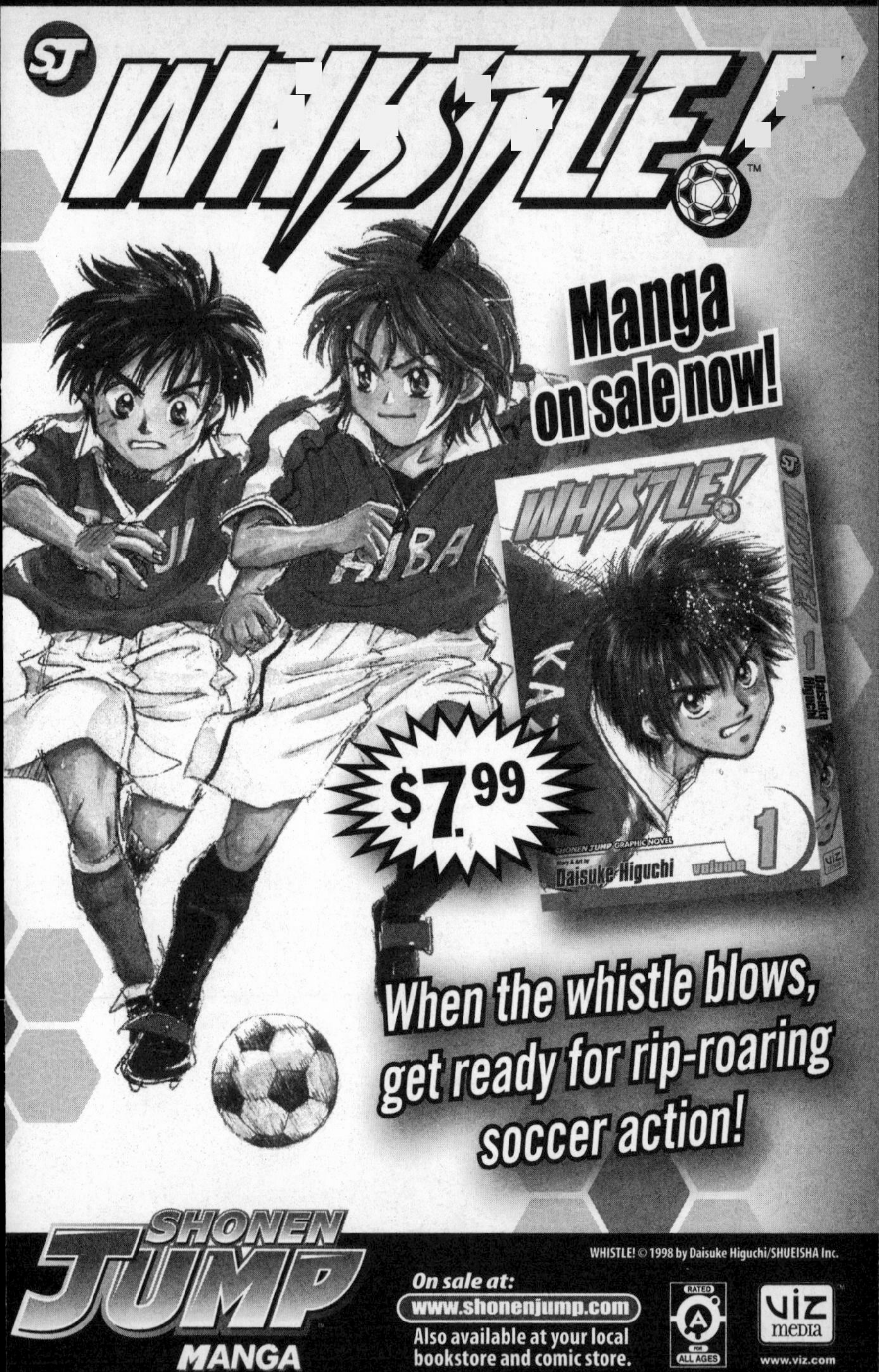
SJ
WHISTLE!™
Manga on sale now!
WHISTLE!
1
Daisuke Higuchi
SHONEN JUMP GRAPHIC NOVEL
Story & Art by Daisuke Higuchi
volume 1
$7.99
When the whistle blows, get ready for rip-roaring soccer action!
SHONEN JUMP MANGA
WHISTLE! © 1998 by Daisuke Higuchi/SHUEISHA Inc.
On sale at:
www.shonenjump.com
Also available at your local bookstore and comic store.
RATED A FOR ALL AGES
VIZ media
www.viz.com

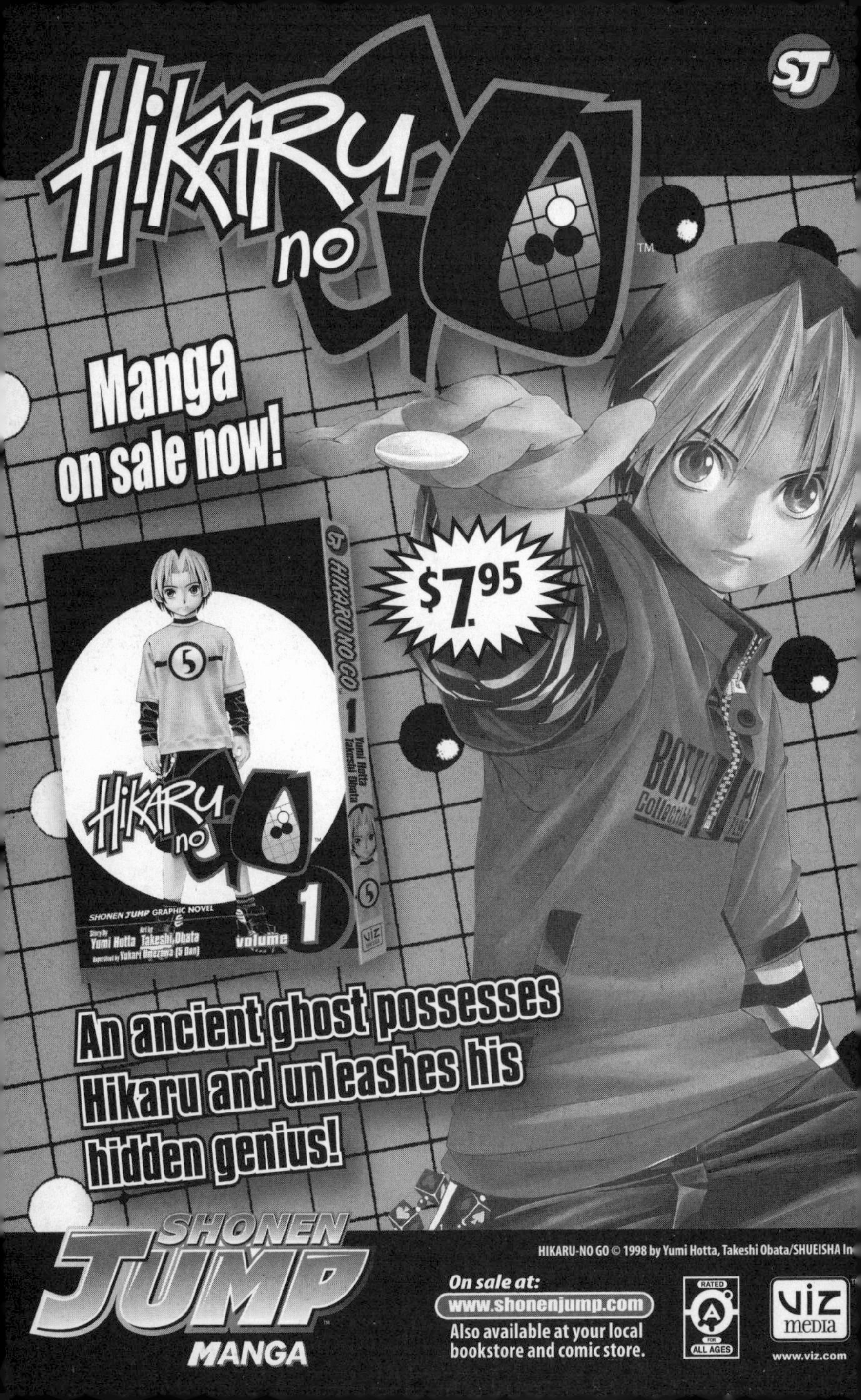
SJ
HIKARU no GO™
Manga on sale now!
$7.95
SJ HIKARU NO GO 1 Yumi Hotta Takeshi Obata
HIKARU no GO
SHONEN JUMP GRAPHIC NOVEL
Yumi Hotta Takeshi Obata
Yukari Umezawa (5 Dan)
volume 1
An ancient ghost possesses Hikaru and unleashes his hidden genius!
SHONEN JUMP MANGA
HIKARU-NO GO © 1998 by Yumi Hotta, Takeshi Obata/SHUEISHA In
On sale at:
www.shonenjump.com
Also available at your local bookstore and comic store.
RATED A FOR ALL AGES
VIZ media
www.viz.com

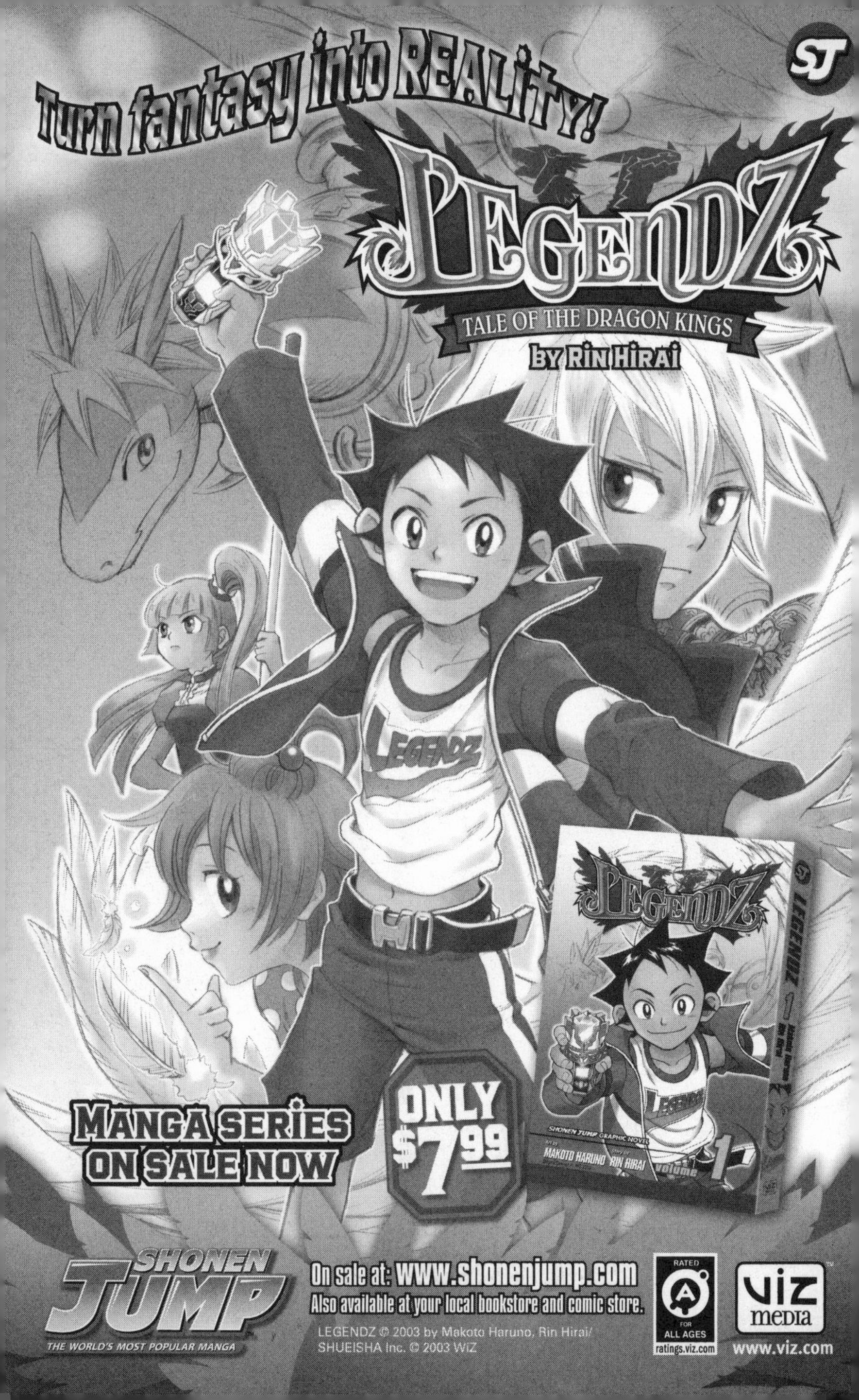

SJ
Turn fantasy into REALity!
LEGENDZ
TALE OF THE DRAGON KINGS
BY RIN HIRAI
LEGENDZ
MANGA SERIES ON SALE NOW
ONLY $7.99
SHONEN JUMP GRAPHIC NOVEL
MAKOTO HARUNO RIN HIRAI
volume 1
SHONEN JUMP
THE WORLD'S MOST POPULAR MANGA
On sale at: www.shonenjump.com
Also available at your local bookstore and comic store.
LEGENDZ © 2003 by Makoto Haruno, Rin Hirai/ SHUEISHA Inc. © 2003 WIZ
RATED A FOR ALL AGES
ratings.viz.com
VIZ media
www.viz.com

Tell us what you think about SHONEN JUMP manga!

Our survey is now available online.
Go to: www.*SHONENJUMP*.com/*mangasurvey*

Help us make our product offering better!

WITHDRAWN

THE REAL ACTION STARTS IN...

SHONEN JUMP
THE WORLD'S MOST POPULAR MANGA
www.shonenjump.com
ADVANCED

3 1901 05000 1165

viz media

Save **50% OFF** the cover price!

SHONEN JUMP
THE WORLD'S MOST POPULAR MANGA

Over **300 pages** per issue!

Each issue of SHONEN JUMP contains the coolest manga available in the U.S., anime news, and info on video & card games, toys AND more!

☑ **YES!** Please enter my one-year subscription (12 HUGE issues) to **SHONEN JUMP** at the LOW SUBSCRIPTION RATE of **$29.95!**

NAME

ADDRESS

CITY   STATE   ZIP

E-MAIL ADDRESS   P7GNC1

☐ MY CHECK IS ENCLOSED (PAYABLE TO SHONEN JUMP)   ☐ BILL ME LATER

CREDIT CARD: ☐ VISA   ☐ MASTERCARD

ACCOUNT #   EXP. DATE

SIGNATURE

CLIP AND MAIL TO ➤

SHONEN JUMP
Subscriptions Service Dept.
P.O. Box 515
Mount Morris, IL 61054-0515

Make checks payable to: **SHONEN JUMP**. Canada price for 12 issues: $41.95 USD, including GST, HST and QST. US/CAN orders only. Allow 6-8 weeks for delivery.

BLEACH © 2001 by Tite Kubo/SHUEISHA Inc. NARUTO © 1999 by Masashi Kishimoto/SHUEISHA Inc.
ONE PIECE © 1997 by Eiichiro Oda/SHUEISHA Inc.

RATED **T** FOR TEEN
ratings.viz.com